GOUVERNEUR MORRIS

Drawn from the life by Du Simitier in Philadelphia. Engraved by B. L. Prevost at Paris.

N.° 7.

Gouverneur Morris as a member of the Continental Congress. Drawing from life by Eugène Du Simitière, 1779. Engraved by Benoit Louis Prevost, 1783.

Gouverneur Morris

AN INDEPENDENT LIFE

WILLIAM HOWARD ADAMS

Yale University Press   New Haven & London

Published with assistance from Furthermore: a program of the J. M. Kaplan Fund.
Publication also published with assistance from the foundation established in memory of
Philip Hamilton McMillan of the class of 1894, Yale College.

Designed by James J. Johnson and set in Adobe Caslon type by Ink, Inc.
Printed in the United States of America by Edwards Brothers, Inc.

Library of Congress Cataloging-in-Publication Data

Adams, William Howard.
Gouverneur Morris : an independent life / William Howard Adams
p. cm.
Includes bibliographical references and index.
ISBN 0-300-09980-0 (alk. paper)

1. Morris, Gouverneur, 1752–1816. 2. Statesman—United States—Biography. 3. United States.
Constitution—Signers—Biography. 4. United States—History—Revolution, 1775–1783—
Biography. 5. New York (State)—History—Revolution, 1775–1783—Biography. 6. United States—
Politics and government—1775–1783. 7. United States—Politics and government—1783–1789.
I. Title
E302.6M7A34 2003
973.4´092—dc21
[B]   2003050050

A catalogue record for this book is available from the British Library.

The paper in this book meets the guidelines for permanence and durability of the Committee on
Production Guidelines for Book Longevity of the Council on Library Resources.

10 9 8 7 6 5 4 3 2 1

To my children

It is the lot of man to be forever the dupe of vain hope or idle apprehension. We are apt to forget the past, neglect the present, and misconceive the future.

GOUVERNEUR MORRIS

Contents

PART V. SETTLING DOWN

Acknowledgments

Virginia Woolf once remarked that contemporary biography was made of facts and the help of friends, meaning the well-acquainted friends of the subject. Dealing with a subject of the distant past, I have found that one's own friends and colleagues are also an essential ingredient adding and correcting fact, giving perspective to, at times, overwhelming detail and most important, acting as benevolent taskmasters. Pauline Maier, Joseph J. Ellis, Andrew Burstein, Herbert Sloan, Leonard L. Richard, and Michael Kammen, having read various parts of the work in progress, have met in full measure the role of supportive colleagues. For their contributions, large and small, I am deeply in their debt.

Because their steady friendship, support, and enthusiastic encouragement extends far beyond the present work, Joan Davidson, Alfred Bush, Adelaide de Menil and Edmund Carpenter, and Eileen and John Harris all occupy a special place that transcends this formal acknowledgment of their contributions. Adelaide also arranged for Rose-Marie Cavazzini to carry out significant research in Paris.

Others who have made material contributions along the way, adding significantly to the outcome include: Robert McDonald, Douglas Wilson, Barbara Oberg, William Reese, Thomas Whitridge, Helen Morris Scorsese, Mary and Jim Holland, Carroll Huxley, Jeffrey S. Harder, William Reider, Jean Ashton, Jeffrey H. Munger, Clare le Corbeiller, Jean-Paul Flahaut, Margaret Cook, Charles Dunkerly, Lloyd Ultan, William Warner, Lois Reamy, Wendell Garrett, Teresa Smith, E. Lee Shepard, Sybil d'Origny, Richard H. Spencer, and Vicki Davis.

A most generous grant from Furthermore, a program of the J. M. Kaplan Fund has made a measurable difference in the results. A fellowship grant from the Gilder Lehman Institute of American History has also been most helpful.

A special thanks goes to my editorial assistant Elizabeth Geist Howard, to my editor Lara Heimert, and to Keith T. Condon. Eliza Childs's unfailing eye improved and polished the final version of the manuscript.

INTRODUCTION

Redeeming Mr. Morris

This book is about one of the most original, engaging, and controversial person-alities among the architects of the early republic. Part of Morris's irresistible appeal is his playful, questioning mind. Of greater consequence is his unsur-passed capacity for confident, rational thinking combined with a passion for jus-tice and order, which he applied to the organization of the American experiment in government. Yet his stature has dwindled to passing references by historians. The last full biography was written by the young Theodore Roosevelt in 1887.

Gouverneur Morris's majestic vision of a national government and his relentless bargaining in the Constitutional Convention at Philadelphia in 1787 helped to put in place the enduring foundation of the American republic. Responsible for the Constitution's final language, he stamped it with his "tal-ents and taste" and emblazoned it with his Preamble and opening words, "We the People of the united States." But the nation remembers him only as a now-irrelevant New York aristocrat. In the course of rescuing him from the aristocratic label, I hope to place him in the top rank of international nation builders struggling through two epochal revolutions on both sides of the Atlantic, leaders who had to choose as best they could between competing, unpredictable alternatives on whether and how to build a new nation.[1]

As to why he has been neglected, one simple answer is that there has been a persistent problem of mistaken identity. Gouverneur Morris has always been confused with the older and unrelated Robert Morris of Philadelphia the "Financier" of the Revolution. Robert spotted his namesake's impressive talents in high finance early. As Gouverneur's mentor—the two worked together to charter the first bank in the United States—Robert invited the twenty-nine-year-old lawyer to help shoulder the critical responsibilities of the Office of Superintendent of Finance, where they carried out daring, outrageous strategies to keep the country afloat to the end of the war. This partnership of genius and brass made a major contribution to the victory of Washington's troops. "'Tis by introducing order into our finances—by restoring public credit," an admiring Alexander Hamilton correctly predicted when the office was turned over to the Morrises, "not by winning battles, that we are finally to gain our object."[2]

In 1776, Gouverneur Morris joined with his older friends John Jay and Robert R. Livingston in drafting New York's first constitution. He boldly and success-fully insisted that religious tolerance be included in that document's framework but failed in his attempt to ban slavery. It would not be his last assault on that institution. When only in his middle twenties, Morris entered the national polit-ical scene and for two years sat in the Continental Congress. Finance, military affairs, and diplomacy grabbed his attention. Concentrating his energy on these crucial areas, he often left his fellow delegates speechless with his brilliance.

One does not have to look far in the pages of the Journal of the Continen-tal Congress to appreciate Morris's articulate and inspiring role in that body, stiffening its backbone at critical junctures. His experience in the Congress confirmed his conclusions on the shortcomings of republican government and his doubts that thirteen separate states loosely called a confederation were up to the task of forming a cohesive union prepared to represent all the people. Nor were the states reliable when it came to individual rights and liberty, a fundamental requirement and test of any government. He had already seen how a popular majority at the state level could ignore the rights of Catholics, Quakers, and slaves.

In summer 1787, Morris reached his full stature as one of the key framers of the Constitution at the convention in Philadelphia. One delegate com-plained that the "glare" of his "charms" made his arguments too easy to swal-low. He did not hesitate to remind his colleagues that they were representa-tives not just of America but "of the whole human race." In the major debates on the central issues of the separation of powers, the role of the president, and the volatile issues of representation, he spoke out more often than any other delegate. Fired with moral disgust, he foresaw more clearly than anyone the catastrophic results of incorporating slavery into the nation's political fabric. When a number of the exhausted delegates, including Hamilton, were pre-pared to give up and abandon the whole experiment of building a nation, Morris was ready to make the gamble that the people were, in the words of his Preamble, prepared "to form a more perfect union." It was a calculated risk he was willing to take. With his ability to translate bold possibilities into reality, his "readiness to aid in making the best of measures in which he had been overruled," as Madison admitted, Morris was the best equipped of all the del-egates, excepting Washington, to be president of the new nation.[3]

I first met Morris through his incomparable, guileless, private diary begin-ning in Paris in the critical year of 1789 and remain puzzled by his neglect in the historical record. The tantalizing remark of Alexander Hamilton, calling him an "exotic genius," has stuck in my mind, hinting at something slightly alien, possibly un-American in his character that managed to separate him not only from his contemporaries, but from us. Hamilton's singular characterization hints at the enigma still hidden at the center of Morris's personality that attracted me to undertake the present work.

History's casual indifference also rests with Morris's personality, which resists the sacred pronouncements we regularly pour on our revolutionary luminaries like Washington, Adams, Jefferson, Madison, or his fellow New Yorker Hamilton. His leery mind uniquely equipped him for the pursuit of truth balanced by an impressive capacity for the pleasures of life. He cared nothing about his image then or how it might be later viewed through the prism of history. It never occurred to him that he should be on anybody's list of "greats." He seemed to be inoculated against illusions, an immunity he shared with both Washington and Adams. There was also a reckless impatience with those whose capacities he considered limited, producing the expected enmity often recorded in his victim's papers. With a fine eye for the absurd, he rarely weighed the political toll his often frank words might cost.

In his personal legacy, there is a uniquely modern, cosmopolitan, urban quality that separates Morris from the nostalgic, pastoral models—Mount Vernon, Monticello, Montpelier, the Adams retreat at Quincy—we associate with most of the founding figures. With his affinity for the city, he seemed to draw his creative energy from the vital, restless urban centers of New York, Philadelphia, Paris, and London when laissez-faire and Adam Smith's "liberal plan of equality, liberty and justice" first stirred the air. His large-scale international business projects have a vastness and a daring sense of an unbounded future that continues to resonate in our own time. His enthusiastic vision of building the Erie Canal and his putting in place the present urban plan of New York City are public projects of a great society that express a rational calculation and imagination in terms that our contemporary sensibilities can readily grasp.

Another incomparable legacy is Morris's papers. His public papers; his stylish, crackling correspondence; and his amazing private diary stand out for their refreshingly honest projection of the whole man, his questioning, independent beliefs about mankind without cant, hypocrisy, or apology. His private letters speak without premeditation, letting us hear his true voice more clearly than that of any other founder in that letter-writing crowd. The diary's deeply penetrating candor, often recording an inner dialogue about his emotional, sensual life in Paris, is itself remarkable in its sensitivity and remains a unique American document. Even in his diary he did not have what one friend called "a conception of the pliancy of truth." The candor that has sometimes made him seem less heroic should now be recognized as a major asset rather than a liability.

His muscular, pragmatic qualities give him a kinship with Adams but without any of the New Englander's gnawing "vanity without bounds," in Hamilton's words. Morris certainly did not suffer from Thomas Jefferson's peculiar ability to hide his true feelings and thoughts, playing a shell game with himself to avoid facing his inner conflicts and contradictions.

In contrast, Morris's politically incorrect style has a particular integrity and forthrightness that is refreshing in our own politically circumspect, cowardly times where dissembling has become a fine art. In one of the great moments of the Constitutional Convention in Philadelphia, you can almost feel the surge of his adrenaline rising even in Madison's cramped, abbreviated notes as he gleefully takes on the powerful slave interests seated all around him in the humid State House, calling slavery a curse that might finally be the republic's downfall. It is not surprising that this audacious quality to say what he meant in plain English both on and off the record in an unambiguous voice did not advance his popularity. It has continued to discourage historians who would prefer to speculate on his more opaque and contradictory colleagues.

Morris's mischievous temperament, his wit and sardonic spirit, more than anything else, set him apart from both his friends and opponents who came from less sophisticated backgrounds. Politicians who are unsure of themselves are always afraid of not being taken seriously by the electorate and avoid these particular qualities like the plague. Only the transatlantic Franklin came close to Morris's sense of humor and passionate love of life. But unlike Franklin, Morris had no taste for popular causes. Nor was he drawn to glorious exploits like Hamilton, the ambitious knight errant, who tragically saw life as a series of personal battles—or duels—to be won or lost in honor and death.

Much of Morris's personal charm was in his vivacious conversation that moved with the ease and a ready bon mot of a born diplomat through any subject that might pop up. Long after his death, acquaintances could still recall his smooth, cultivated voice reflecting "much compass, strength and richness." On public occasions, however, when his rhetoric was in high gear even he admitted that he sometimes went on too long.[4] He was, above all, unapologetically comfortable with himself, at home in any setting from the rural estate of a New York squire to public forums in Philadelphia. He would have been at home in the company of Franklin D. Roosevelt and John F. Kennedy. His confident American-bred assurance, his ease of manners, and his genius for intrigue allowed him to settle into the government and diplomatic circles of Paris, its drawing rooms and boudoirs, making the most of every moment, intellectual and sensual. More than Jefferson, Franklin, and certainly Adams, he was the most effective American in Paris.

Shortly after he arrived in France and before the first signs of serious violence in summer 1789, he and his Paris critics, along with their pro-French American friends, disagreed on the course of events they were witnessing.

Although they had embraced the romantic ideology of a universal revolution in the name of "The Rights of Man" without any practical political machinery to insure its success, Morris believed it was a blueprint for disaster. His skepticism and judgment was focused on the idealistic assumption held by Jefferson and his liberal French confidants, leaders of the Enlightenment, that the American experience and the outcome of its revolution was a template not only for France but for all of the coming democratic revolutions. Along with John Adams, Morris insisted that the French experiment with utopian ideals was headed for calamity.

Unlike his Paris acquaintances, who mostly thought abstractly on paper and without any actual experience, Morris's personal understanding of the background of the American Revolution was deeply ingrained. After all, his family, well established on an estate that embraced the lower half of what we now call the Bronx, had been involved in colonial affairs, holding high office for three generations, a record unequaled by any other member of the upper rank of the vanguard revolutionary leaders. It was this long history of the Morrises and others like them to reshape colonial politics, law, and institutions that would set the American experience apart and underpin its unique results. To Morris, creating state constitutions, negotiating foreign treaties, and setting up an efficient, functioning national government with an army and operating mint were more important priorities at the outset of "nation building," to use that fashionable phrase, than simply declaring that all men were created equal. He foresaw the difficulty of establishing and maintaining an effective authority over any large and volatile territory like America or France. Merely "bawling" liberty, justice, democracy around the countryside would not do it. Political tyranny came under many guises, slogans, and labels not limited to the tyranny of kings but could lurk even in democratic republics and the majority will. Without a carefully crafted constitutional framework, the alternative would be a raw, out-of-control power orchestrated by devious politicians ready to destroy all human rights in the name of liberty.

He instinctively perceived the fundamental differences that separated the American accomplishments from the aspirations fertilized by the pungent rot of the collapsed society and government of France. To Morris, any assumption that France, with a wholly different history, could adopt and install a fully operating American-style government by fiat was pure folly. Time and education were necessary "to bring Slaves to the Enjoyment of Liberty.... The Progress towards Freedom must be slow and can only be compleated in the Course of several Generations."

Because of his consistent criticism and condemnation of the course taken by the erratic French experiment, his American enemies have managed to stick the all-purpose tag of "aristocrat" on Morris. It is a red-herring label, and one that continues to distort his reputation. No doubt his imposing dignity, his height—he was as tall as that other "aristocrat," Washington—and his slightly Gallic hauteur confirmed his central casting role as the arch political villain. (His critics would have felt vindicated if they had known of his love affair with Talleyrand's mistress, the beautiful comtesse de Flahaut.)

To Jeffersonians, his insistence on a strong, national executive in the Constitutional Convention and his contempt for the weak state governments led by "cyphers" was proof of his aristocratic tendencies. His argument that the American system ought to accommodate a senate of what John Adams called "the rich, the well-born and the able," elected for life, was further evidence of the New Yorker's antirepublican prejudice. His famous line uttered in 1774 that the mob—"poor reptiles"—were beginning "to think and to reason" and would soon bite became, for later critics, the smoking gun. Even more incriminating was his extravagant remark near the end of his life that democracy was "the child of squinting envy and self-tormenting spleen!"[5]

The two-hundred-fiftieth anniversary of Morris's birth in 2002 came and went without a single commemorative gesture by the nation he helped to found; by his native state of New York, whose constitution he helped to write; by the city of New York, whose urban plan can be fairly attributed to his bold vision; or by Columbia University, as one of its most distinguished graduates. The recent rehabilitation of John Adams in the public mind by David McCullough and Joseph Ellis suggests that we are capable of cutting through the Jeffersonian fog to see the founding generation in far richer detail. The important work of Stanley Elkins and Eric McKitrick in *The Age of Federalism* has also advanced our ability to see federalism as something more serious than a fleeting aberration. The question is not whether Morris deserves a more permanent place in the American pantheon. The question is whether we are mature enough as a nation to comprehend his greatness.

PART I

Background

CHAPTER 1

The Pedigree

F OR all of his reputation, Gouverneur Morris did not come from an aristocratic family. By the strict code of the English aristocracy, even those on the top rung of colonial society could not make that leap. Although his family was certainly illustrious and its fortune had been established three generations before Morris was born, the Morrises were still parvenu. Families in the American colonies simply lacked the layers of traditions and official props needed to be accepted on anything like an equal footing with the Whig grandees of the home country. Morris understood this fundamental difference very well when he pointed out that established "family, wealth, prejudice or habit to raise a permanent mound of distinction" was not a part of American society. It had already evolved in its unpredictable mixture beyond the ancient aristocracies of Europe, which held little appeal for the endless waves of immigrants who continued to alter the country's inner dynamics.[1]

Yet without the aristocratic underpinnings of feudal privileges, Morris's family, like other prominent colonial families, had managed to create its own native version of an established ruling class. They were, like all good Whigs, opposed to democracy and anarchy, believing in ordered liberty and a say in Parliament's tax policy. In the words of Gouverneur's cousin, the family "relished" public affairs and was quick to defend, if not always successfully, its liberty, property, and above all, its habit of making most of the political decisions that, in its opinion, were important.

Gouverneur Morris inherited an impressive New York name that also reached into the political affairs of New Jersey and Pennsylvania. No other member of the founding generation in the colonies could claim such a long tradition of conspicuous leadership. With the Morris name, he also inherited a matter-of-fact awareness of a deference, a respect taken as a matter of course. Although he spent long stretches of his sixty-four years away from Morrisania, Morris's identification with this large piece of family real estate facing Long Island Sound, some nine miles above the city of New York, gave him a sense of his place in the world. Raised in a vague atmosphere of eighteenth-century rationalism combined with rural common sense, Gouverneur was, like his ancestors, robustly prepared to face life honestly and hold his ground in a tumultuous world.

Morrisania's nineteen hundred acres stretched from the Harlem River on the south and touched the East River at its southeast corner opposite Montresor's, now Randall's, Island. The hospitable front porch of the dignified, solid two-story manor house set in the checkered shade of oaks and elms looked out beyond the edge of the yard to the East River and the mist of the sound in the distance. Its voluptuous meadows were well stocked with cattle, horses, sheep, and hogs. Morris's father, Judge Lewis Morris ran the place with a staff of forty-six Negro slaves. Valuable stands of timber where Gouverneur first learned to hunt were intended for harvesting when the trees were mature, but instead they were cut for firewood by British soldiers who for six cold winters during the Revolution occupied New York City.

The Morris brothers, Lewis and Richard, who first installed the family in the Colony of New York in the 1670s were born near Tintern in Monmouthshire County, Wales. Although imaginative genealogists have tried to link them with the dim world of noble Welsh warriors of the twelfth century, the claim remains a family romance. Like that of most colonial gentry, the Morris rootstock was sturdy but commonplace.

Given their accomplishments, the Morrises hardly need any soaring family trees or noble crests (invented or real). By Gouverneur Morris's generation, they had acquired the attributes of what Thomas Jefferson called "the Patrician order"—the trappings of property, taste, gentility—qualities the ambitious young Jefferson so coveted and yet found difficult to accommodate in his own democratic ideology or his bank account. Morris's legacy included the impressive family makeup of natural abilities, self-confidence, and bursts of energy spiked with what might be called eccentric habits, time-honored ingredients of any aristocracy. If he shared the family indifference to conventions, he also expressed its instinctive mastery of the social arts as if he had been bred to be a citizen of the world.[2]

Ignoring the opinion of others, the Morrises had a way of assuming a certain style, prompting the historian and lawyer William Smith Jr. to call Gouverneur's rich and powerful grandfather—the first of a long line of native-born Morrises called "Lewis"—who loved and played the music of Arcangelo Corelli, "whimsical in his temper... grave in his manners and of penetrating parts." Gouverneur's father, a dignified judge of the New York Court of Vice-Admiralty, is remembered for going around in a hat made from the skin and feathers of a loon. There is a touch of family bravura in Gouverneur's impulsive purchase of some of Marie Antoinette's furniture at the Versailles auctions in 1793 to use in his drawing room while serving as the American minister in Paris. These trademark attitudes, some genuine, some probably feigned, were adequate to allow the first native-born Morris, Gouverneur's grandfather (known as "the Governor") to flaunt his freshly minted title of Lord of the Manor of Morrisania, a title he had secured in 1697 at the age of twenty-six. The same recurring characteristics of provincial pride and a strong family will to play a part in government seemed to set the Morrises apart in their bailiwick. Laced with a normal amount of human greed, their artless abilities survived through three generations of influence to the founding of the American republic and the writing of the Constitution.[3]

This family background endowed Morris with cosmopolitan sensibilities even before he set foot in Europe. The marquis de Chastellux, a sophisticated Parisian, found the New Yorker, who was eighteen years younger, already "refined in the dark history of political intrigue" when the two first met in Philadelphia during the Revolution. The prince de Broglie who also knew Morris in Philadelphia thought he had more "spirit and nerve" than anyone else he had met in America. He added, however, that "his superiority, which he has taken no pains to conceal, will prevent his ever occupying an important place."[4]

Morris also inherited a family political tradition bred in New York's turbulent colonial politics and defined by the debate over the question of who should rule at home. It is never hard to find one or two of his ancestors somewhere in the fray, by turns defending their rights against the royal governors or courting and manipulating their favor according to their own political judgment and shifting interests. Daily political maneuvers, public harangues, printed attacks on the opposition, partisan caucuses, and raucous elections combined with a native, common-sense support of the separation of governmental powers were the political grist of the earlier Morrises and their New York neighbors. Seemingly minor rows over who should pay judicial salaries or who could vote in a county election "skidded off their tracks," in Bernard Bailyn's memorable words, "onto elevated planes of disputation and ended deadlocked in the realm of principle."[5]

The Morrises acted mostly in defense of what Madison called in the first *Federalist* paper their "distinctive interests," meaning their property and their extended mercantile connections. High-flown ideology did not get in the way of their main objectives, nor was it a part of Morris's temperament. Politics for the Morrises, who opposed the De Lancey clan and supported the powerful Livingstons, first of all meant extended families. Matters of principle, which they expressed rather than thought about, were secondary considerations in the tough world of New York politics. All this would be an important political legacy, "a common idiom" for Morris. It would carry him beyond his provincial roots, beyond class, beyond religion, and beyond partisan politics into the age of Revolution.[6]

The Morris family fortune in the American colonies was founded in the last part of the seventeenth century by Richard and Lewis Morris, two immigrant soldiers-of-fortune from Barbados. In a contract dated 1670, Richard Morris is styled as a merchant in New York and his older brother Lewis as a merchant and planter in Barbados. Behind the two Morrises stretched mixed, tenacious careers, marked by another family characteristic—to follow their often erratic impulses.

Because many of the details are missing, the opening of the family saga unfolds at a brisk pace, from misty accounts of captivity on the Spanish Main, a turn at privateering, then building a tidy fortune in the West Indies before successfully fishing in the troubled waters of colonial New York not long after the British defeated the Dutch in 1664. As with many accounts of adventure in the seventeenth century, there are large gaps in the narrative that follows the two brothers from an obscure early life in Wales to finally settling in the colony of New York. Richard would produce the family's only heir, but his older brother Lewis seems to have provided much of the initial wherewithal. For the Morrises, as in the tribute Gouverneur Morris admiringly paid to the Mohawk Indians, perhaps the "most strongly marked...of their moral features, was a high sense of personal independence."[7]

In 1630 at the age of twenty-nine, Lewis Morris, the first Morris in the New World, signed on as a "servant" or indentured apprentice with the Providence Island Company of English Puritans, a colonizing venture that combined good works with an eye for potential profit. The company's first efforts to plant settlements in Massachusetts had been discouraging. During a hunt for a new, warmer climate in which to settle and through a series of unlikely adventures, Lewis Morris became for a time a member of William Jackson's band of "English pirates," preying on Spanish ships in the Caribbean. In command of one of Jackson's ships in 1643, Morris and his cohorts in a single raid captured the island of Jamaica and then ransomed it for a princely sum.[8]

The trail of the first Lewis Morris—a common name in seventeenth-century Anglo-American records—is faint, the evidence skeletal. It appears, however, that the Lewis Morris of the Jamaican adventure was in Barbados in the late 1640s, taking up the cause of the island Roundheads against the royalist supporters among the island's plantocracy. Returning to England, Morris then signed onto an expedition of Parliamentary forces but was wounded while leading a landing party against the Barbadian government in the fall and winter of 1651–52.[9]

After a successful blockade by the Roundhead fleet, the proceeds from seventeen Dutch merchant ships captured by the Parliamentary expedition was divided up among its leaders. Instead of returning to England, Morris decided to settle on the island, investing successfully in a Barbados sugar plantation. Sometime after becoming a Barbados planter and ignoring his new status as a slave owner in a colony that discriminated against all nonconformist Protestants, Lewis Morris converted to the Quaker faith, a faith that may have been latent in his Welsh past. The former privateer's strict new religious convictions predictably stirred up trouble with the island's Anglican establishment when Morris refused to pay his annual tithe to the Church or provide men and horses for the island's militia, which was necessary to keep the huge slave population under control. The heavy fines repeatedly levied against Morris failed to teach him discretion.[10]

Growing increasingly militant, the restless Morris was more than ready to abandon Barbados when word of New York's more tolerant atmosphere of "Ecclesiastical liberties" drifted down to the island. But the commercial interests first developed by his brother Richard were as important to the family's move as was any question of religious doctrine. Richard Morris had joined Lewis in Barbados after the English Civil War, sometime in the 1650s, and had married Sarah Pole, the daughter of a local planter. Acting as a factor for Lewis, Richard, who was fifteen years younger, soon began scouting out the newly won British colony of New York, making a number of business trips there in the 1660s to establish a trading business. In 1670 Richard and his wife decided to move permanently to the colony after Richard bought in partnership with Lewis a 520-acre tract "upon the main over against the Town of Haerlem, commonly called Bronk's Land's." This purchase formed the core of the future Manor of Morrisania in what is now the southwest portion of the Borough of the Bronx. The population of the town of New York at the time was something like three thousand souls.[11]

The family saga took an abrupt turn in 1672 when Richard Morris and his wife suddenly died, leaving in New York the Bronx land, a townhouse on Bridge Street, and "one poor blossom," a son and heir less than a year old. The orphan, the first native-born Morris in Gouverneur's line was immediately placed by the authorities "entirely in the hands of strangers." It was not an auspicious beginning. When word of Richard and Sarah Morris's death reached Lewis, already a man of seventy-two, he and his wife lost no time moving from the West Indies in September 1673 to rescue his Creole nephew and namesake and take charge of the family property.

Once in New York, the Barbadian émigré, invigorated with new challenge, quickly asserted another family characteristic: Morris managed to increase his land holdings nearly eightfold when between 1675 and 1683 he acquired "Tintern and Monmouth," a large estate and a profitable ironwork and sawmill operation in East Jersey, amounting to 3,900 acres. Not content with the modest 520-acre tract in Westchester County, Morris added another 1,400 acres to it by a grant from Governor Edmund Andros in 1676. With his growing wealth, political doors were opened. As a staunch supporter of the duke of York's regime in New York, in 1683 he was appointed to both the New York Council and the East Jersey Council, paving the way for his family's later, more spectacular political rise.

The elder Morris's connections with the West Indies coincided with the boom of New York trade with the islands in the last quarter of the seventeenth century. By the time of Lewis Morris's death, the West Indian market was becoming a cornerstone of the city's economy. Gouverneur Morris's grandfather would build on this island trade. Because of the high risks involved, merchant traders like the Morrises also developed a network of correspondents whom they used for credit, the sale of cargoes, and the collections of debt and intelligence on events that might affect their extended markets. This grammar of international commerce and financial experience was a familiar language to Gouverneur growing up in New York's voracious trading climate.

In addition to raising the family estate to grand proportions, the elderly Lewis Morris and his wife were also forced to take on the thankless job of rearing their orphaned nephew who turned out to be by Quaker standards thoroughly delinquent. In his will, the senior Morris attempted to reduce his nephew's inheritance because of his "Great Miscarriages and Disobedience," claiming he had "adhered to and advized" with "those of bad life and conversation contrary to my directions and example unto him."[12]

The rebellious young Morris, who later became the first royal governor of New Jersey, successfully resisted all efforts to civilize him according to the unbending gospel of George Fox. After a fiery Quaker zealot was hired as tutor, matters worsened. Finally, in open revolt at the age of sixteen, Morris made his escape, running off first to Virginia then to Jamaica, returning two years later, a few days before his uncle died on February 14, 1691. Morris's allergic reaction to the suffocating Quaker precepts no doubt inspired him to introduce a libertarian atmosphere at his own family dinner table that shocked even his friend Benjamin Franklin. In old age, Franklin still remembered how Morris had baited his children into raucous arguments during family meals for his own amusement.[13]

With the death of his Quaker uncle, the second Lewis Morris claimed the inheritance of an impressive estate of 9,120 acres, including the profitable East Jersey estate and ironworks now elevated to the status of Tintern Manor. He also inherited some one hundred slaves and a sizable house in the Bronx. When the former truant suspected that his detested aunt had attempted to disinherit him of the Bronx land by tampering with his uncle's will just before she died intestate, he lost no time in having it thrown out by the court. It was an audacious move that sent his stock up with his neighbors of approving landed gentry. Morris's inheritance amounted to more than sixteen thousand pounds.[14]

More than half the value of the uncle's fortune was in personal property, including slaves. The sixty-four slaves used to operate the ironworks made Morris the largest slave owner in New Jersey. At Tintern Manor (near the present-day Shewsbury), the Barbadian immigrant not only brought his West Indian slaves to operate the works, he also brought the management experience of the sugar plantation, a combination of early industrial production and technical know-how manned by the ancient system of slave labor.

At the age of twenty, "young, sprightly and wild" and with striking good looks that would carry into Gouvernour's generation, the second Lewis Morris suddenly became one of the richest men in the colonies. Having escaped the Quaker classroom, Morris pursued his own self-education with a passion, and his broad literary interests impressed his contemporaries. William Smith recalled that he was "excessively fond of the society of men of sense and reading." During his lifetime he amassed a library of some three thousand works, including volumes of Greek, Arabic, and Latin. He particularly admired the eloquence of Tacitus. "I want my Tacitus," he wrote to one of his sons, "but no hassard in Sending of it nor do not lend it on Any Account to any body whatever for I know that country [New Jersey] too well to lend books in. That is not a book fit to come into a country fellows hand to daub and dirty."[15]

In 1691, Morris elevated himself into the upper rank of Jersey society by marrying an heiress, Isabella Graham. Not content with only a manor in Jersey, in 1697, Morris had no trouble persuading Governor Benjamin Fletcher of New York to raise Morrisania to the grandeur of manor status. Although he was by no means the largest landowner, he had the enviable distinction of now owning manorial estates in both New Jersey and New York.

In 1710, with the help of Robert Hunter, the new governor of New York, Morris shifted his political focus to the New York colony as a zealous supporter of the crown. Hunter and Morris not only shared political ambitions, their literary tastes inspired the two men to collaborate on the first play written and published in the British colonies. In 1715, Hunter appointed him chief justice of New York, a post second only to the governorship. With the colony's revived commercial growth, politics had inevitably become entangled with the colony's affairs. It was in this setting that Gouverneur's grandfather began to build a family political machine, organizing a populist coalition of Hudson River farmers and New York City artisans as a constituency. When Robert Hunter returned to England, he turned the New Jersey government over to Morris as royal governor.[16]

In that predemocratic age, Lewis Morris had no qualms about voicing pop-

View of Morrisania, October 10, 1777, by Archibald Robertson.
Spencer Collection. The New York Public Library. Astor, Lenox and Tilden Foundations.

ular sentiments or manipulating the people if it helped to advance his personal ambitions. A politician to the core, Morris was a formidable adversary wherever he decided to take his stand, whether it was against the royal governor or the colony's representative Assembly. He would have one of the most remarkable political careers in colonial America, spanning more than half a century. Morris did not hesitate to encourage his children to follow his headstrong example. The family's raucous style in politics is captured in his son Robert Hunter Morris's reply to Franklin's advice that he avoid disputes with the Assembly after he was named governor of Pennsylvania; "What w[ould] you have me," he told Franklin, "deprive myself of one of my greatest pleasures[?]"[17]

William Cosby followed Hunter as governor of New York and, like most colonial governors, he had come to "repair his fortunes." Cosby's fight with Lewis Morris is one of the more celebrated political brawls of the early years of the colony. It started out as a relatively minor dispute over Morris's salary as chief justice and quickly escalated to charges of rigged elections, censorship, and freedom of the press; it would move further when Morris carried the battle to London where he raised radical questions of fundamental constitutional principles governing the colonies and the rights of colonists within the empire. He believed, as did his grandson Gouverneur, that "both the letter and the spirit of the British constitution" justified an all-out attack on the crown's representative when contending for their rights as freemen. "I believe the Seeds are sown," Morris wrote prophetically in 1736, "which will one day rise of maturity either in the destruction of the Constitution or fixing of it on so firme a foundation as not to be Shaken."[18]

Gouverneur Morris's grandfather made history in his fight with Governor Cosby, ending in the famous Zenger trial over freedom of the press. Peter Zenger, the émigré printer of the newly founded opposition newspaper *Weekly Journal,* had published Morris's unbridled attack on the governor and was promptly indicted. The Governor's Council sent a message to the Assembly noting that "the scurrilous papers" had alienated "the affections of the people of this Province from his Majesty's government," raising "sedition and tumults among the people, filling their minds with a contempt of his Majesty's government." It was the governor's claim to the "sacred rights of Majesty," as if he were the king, that stuck in the craw of irate New Yorkers.[19]

The arguments of the case, upholding the right to publish the truth no matter what damage it might inflict on government, were printed and widely circulated in the colonies throughout the eighteenth century. During the growing political debate in America, Gouverneur Morris spoke for his generation when he declared: "The trial of Zenger in 1735 was the germ of American freedom—the morning star of that liberty which subsequently revolutionized America." Not long before he died in 1816, Morris impressed a young admirer with the mystique of the case telling him that Lewis Morris's "strictures on the administration of Governor Cosby and his Council in the Weekly Journal of New York, by John Peter Zenger roused the energy of a whole people." The impressive liberty of the public debates in the press on the proposed federal Constitution in 1787 is due in no small part to the precedents set in the Zenger test on the limits of governmental power.[20]

For all their power, inherited standing, and imported Whiggish tastes, the colonial nabobs of New York—the Morrises, Livingstons, Schuylers, Van Cortlands, and Philipses—enjoyed no patrimonial, fixed social position in the eyes of the law. Nor were there any firm rules establishing membership in this oligarchy. As William Livingston put it: "Our Births are our Ancestors, but our Merit is our own." Although the ownership of land in New York had more feudal restrictions than in any other colony, there was no ironclad statute of primogeniture insuring the passing of landed estates intact to successive generations—the basis of all modern aristocracies. In his will, unencumbered by laws and tradition, Gouverneur's grandfather simply divided his manors as he saw fit, Morrisania going to Morris's father Lewis, the New Jersey property passing to his uncle, Robert Hunter Morris.

By far the most splendid possession at Morrisania was the great library begun by Morris's grandfather. The patriarch who was self-educated by "his own pliability" had assembled during his lifetime one of the largest libraries in the colonies. Ezra Stiles estimated it to be second only to the library of Harvard College. The combined family libraries of all the Founding Fathers, most of whom were first generation college graduates, would not begin to approach the baronial holdings at Morrisania. A more introverted, bookish boy than Morris faced with the temptations of such a library—say a Jefferson or Madison—might well have given up the idea of public service altogether and succumbed to the dreamy temptations of Augustan "retirement."

Gouverneur Morris, the only son of his father's second marriage, was born at Morrisania on the morning of January 31, 1752, following two older sisters. Two more sisters arrived during the next five years, leaving Morris the pampered brother in the middle. The very name of the estate and the title of lord that went with it still reverberates with the mystique of feudal rights and grandeur. Yet it conferred few tangible privileges on its owners beyond its substantial value as property. As the last-born son, Morris would inherit no part of the real estate.

Morris's father was forty-eight when he inherited Morrisania in 1746 on the death of his father. Later that year he married for the second time, Sarah Gouverneur, cousin of his first wife, Tryntje Staats Morris, mother of his three sons and a daughter. Morris had waited fifteen years before he married Sarah. To no one's surprise the marriage—a threat to their inheritance—did not set well with his older children. Suspecting that his oldest son might not allow Sarah to be buried in the family vault, Morris begged that he be buried beside her wherever she might be placed. He was fifty-four when Gouverneur was born. Gouverneur's nearest half-brother, Richard, was thirty-two years older than he was.

Judge Morris, like his father, believed that his landed position required him to assume public leadership as a matter of right, duty, and, one might add, necessity, although there was no legal entitlement to any office. He apprenticed with his father in all his various public roles, becoming an outspoken member of the New York Council and serving sixteen years as assemblyman from Westchester County before his appointment as judge of the important Court of Vice-Admiralty.

As Lord of the Manor, Judge Morris was entitled, according to the archaic language of the royal charter, to hold court leet, to make ordinances for his tenants, and to erect a court baron to try cases involving his tenants or disputes about manorial lands. This was mainly an ornamental recital of words that had little force in New York. There is no evidence that Morris ever attempted to exercise any of these obsolete rights except one: he could keep the Westchester County tax assessors and collectors outside his gates. For his own convenience, and with only a hint of seignorial privilege, he would sometimes preside over the Vice-Admiralty Court in his parlor.

Gouverneur Morris's mother remains shadowy in the family annals. She is conspicuous by her absence in her son's surviving letters. Confirmed Huguenots, the Gouverneurs had fled from their small village near Dunkirk to Leyden in 1594, long before the Edict of Nantes was revoked by Louis XIV in 1685, setting off the mass diaspora of French Protestants. The family had been in Holland three-quarters of a century when Nicholas Gouverneur, described as a Dutch merchant, arrived in New Amsterdam in 1663. In portraits from his well-padded, mature years Gouverneur looks very much like a prosperous, well-fed Amsterdam merchant prince.[21]

The Huguenots who settled in New York were mild enough in their faith to fit quietly into a society that already swarmed with dissenting congregations. The chief Huguenot enclaves were New York City, New Paltz, and New Rochelle. By the time the Huguenots arrived, according to Governor Dongan in 1687, New York was already a spiritual grab-bag of "Singing Quakers, ranting Sabbatarians, Antisabbatarians, some Anabaptist, some Independents, some Jews." By the time Morris was born most of the immigrants' religious and ethnic distinctiveness had been smoothly assimilated into the established colonial society. Morris's christening by a divine from New York's Anglican Trinity Church is entered ecumenically in an old illustrated Dutch family Bible.

Sarah Gouverneur harbored a more unlikely ancestry in her pedigree than the nonconforming faith of the Huguenots. She brought to the tribal establishment of the Morrisania Morrises a strain of righteous sedition. Through her mother she was doubly descended from Jacob Leisler, the notorious leader of "Leisler's Rebellion," who briefly ousted the colonial government of New York in 1689. Leisler was hung on May 16, 1691, for "traitorsly levying war against our Sovereign Lord and Lady, the King & Queene in their realme and province of New York." Gouverneur Morris's gloss on the Leisler affair was that Leisler simply "took this city for King William," turning his rebellious ancestor into a respectable Whig defending liberty in the name of the Glorious Revolution. Leisler's personal "revolution" placing individual liberty above the monarchy was, of course, central to Gouverneur's and his family's political philosophy.[22]

Aside from an early immersion in the French language at a country academy in New Rochelle, the common thread of Gouverneur Morris's education was its urban setting. Although country-bred at Morrisania, he was introduced to city life at an early age. Beginning in Philadelphia, the largest city in the colonies, until he finished reading law ten years later in the restless city of New York in 1771, already alive with possibilities, his experience was by colonial standards, distinctly metropolitan. He recognized at an early stage the importance of the mixture of people and cultures in cities. New Yorkers in particular were as he put it, "born cosmopolite," endowed with a rich, polyglot background others could only "acquire by much travel and great expense." This vital background had spared the country "the taint of national prejudice" during the formative years.[23]

Morris's first school in the rustic village of New Rochelle gave him a fortuitous introduction to a foreign language and culture at a formative age. It was a good beginning for his career in foreign affairs. His other two schools, the Philadelphia Academy and King's College (later Columbia) in New York, both recently founded, reflected in their divisive beginnings the larger cultural and political strains and changes taking place within the colonies as they groped and stumbled toward a distinctive American identity.

Morris followed an expected path of education, polishing as he went, without much effort, his "easy and pleasing" disposition. Making the most of every advantage that came his way, he readily admitted—it became a ritual protest—that he had "naturally a taste for pleasure." His impeccable manners did not, as in the case of John Jay, make him remote and guarded. Throughout his life, Morris seemed to captivate the company of distinguished and fascinating people who were charmed by his broad, unpedantic knowledge and racy conversation. As a friend observed, "He is fond of his ease, does his best to procure it, and enjoys it as much as possible." According to one classmate, there had been more than one encounter with the "demons of liberty and idleness." Morris completed his law studies before turning twenty, and in a comment at that time he complained that he had been too "hurried through the different scenes of childhood and youth." But introspective psychological crises of identity and self-esteem, or vague insecurities and moral dilemmas, do not appear to be a part of Morris's unaffected makeup.[24]

As far as thoughts about public duty were concerned (he was sixteen when he addressed the graduating class of 1768 at St. Paul's Chapel), Morris was all for the high-sounding, progressive Whig ideals of honor, liberty, and virtue, knowing full well the limits of rhetoric: "A Briton's Love of Country is firmly fixed on the solid base of Freedom.... O Liberty! Nurse of Heroes! Parent of Worth! best blessing of society! Long—Long—continue to smile upon this happy Soil." The revived classical tradition of the desire for fame or honor in the eighteenth century was another lofty passion that would spur Morris and his generation into action in 1776 and again in 1787 when the horizon "of a wide extended empire," as he called it, opened up to his heroic era. His early capacity for achievement and a precocious knowledge of life may well hint at fame's unspoken role in shaping his character. But in Morris's scale of values at this stage of experience, politics were at the bottom. "Politics I dislike," he declared to a friend not long after he had graduated, "and only look on with pity, while the madness of so many is made the gain of so few."[25]

Morris's lifelong friend and mentor John Jay, also from a Huguenot family, preceded him by six years as a student at the transplanted French community some twelve miles from Morrisania. It was claimed that the bad food served at the rustic academy to the future chief justice of the United States made the first contribution to Jay's "formidable dyspepsia." As for Morris, the future gourmet at Parisian dinner tables and a confessed connoisseur of fine wines, New Rochelle may have had just the opposite effect.

French, once the dominant language in the village, was in steady decline by the time that Morris entered his first class there. Yet this early introduction to French in Reverend Tetard's school, no doubt encouraged at home by his mother, laid a solid foundation for his later fluency. French officers during the Revolution were impressed with his command of the French language. At this impressionable age, Morris also seems to have discovered a subtle identity with and sympathy for French culture and character. He would always prefer it to the English, which he found cold and stiff.

Getting back to the freedom of the open fields, woods, and streams of Morrisania was a relief from the supervisions of Reverend Tetard. The Morrises were a sporting family in the English tradition, and Gouverneur naturally took to hunting, fishing, swimming, and sailing, activities that appealed to his animal nature. It also insured him an impressive physique as a young man.

With the East River at his doorstep, sailing back and forth to the city on the tip of Manhattan Island became second nature. In a letter to a friend he could give precise directions for the two-hour trip, pointing out the great eddy and how to clear the Narrows: "You will see on your starboard bow a round rock…leave it twenty yards on your right. Then the tide will shoot you through Hell Gate.… Discover my house on your right."[26]

In late summer 1761, when Morris was nine and already tall for his age, he left Morrisania to travel to Philadelphia. On August 17, Thomas Lawrence Jr., husband and first cousin of Morris's older half-sister Mary and a prominent leader of the city, enrolled him along with the Lawrences' own son in the Philadelphia Academy. Those three years in Philadelphia while outwardly unremarkable were, in retrospect, oddly predestined, giving Morris firm roots in a city where he would later play out some of his most important public roles during the Revolution and in the Constitutional Convention.

One of the impressive characteristics of the late colonial gentry was its extended yet cohesive network of social and political ties spreading out from the urban centers, crossing provincial lines. Families like the Morrises took their own attenuated connections for granted. Thomas Lawrence, who had twice been mayor of Philadelphia, had played an important role in the establishment of the academy. Morris's uncle (his father's brother) Robert Hunter Morris, as governor of Pennsylvania, issued the charter allowing the school to create a college as part of its educational mission.

This secure and pleasant yet narrow world no doubt contributed to what Jared Sparks called Morris's "almost daring self-possession." Within his limited world of family, friends, and classmates, all were nominal egalitarians. His strikingly handsome, well-cut features were set off by a full, sensual mouth and brilliantly animated blue eyes. His offhand poise complementing his large yet graceful frame gave him a distinctive presence that was probably apparent by the time he entered the Philadelphia Academy. Although the Tory Judge

Morrisania, from a painting in the collection of Livingston Rutherford,
published in Livingston Rutherford, *Family Records and Events,*
Compiled Principally from the Original Manuscripts
in the Rutherford Collection (New York, 1894).
Princeton University Library.

Thomas Jones thought the young student "polite, sensible, judicious," Morris
instinctively erred, in his first biographer's words, more "on the side of boldness and presumption, than on that of timidity and reserve." He could also be
impulsive, as when he tried to jump over a scalding kettle of boiling water in
the yard at Morrisania and badly burned his arm.[27]

When the newly formed academy opened its doors in 1751, it had received
a major boost from the pen of Benjamin Franklin who in 1749 had published
his *Proposals Relating to the Education of Youth in Pennsylvania.* On the academy's tenth anniversary, the year Gouverneur began, the provost reported an
enrollment of eighty students, making it the foremost preparatory school in
the Middle Colonies. It now served its own newly founded college, chartered
in 1755, as well as King's College in New York, then also struggling to its feet in
spite of sectarian wrangling between the Episcopalians and Presbyterians.[28]

In a melancholy will drawn up at Morrisania little more than a year before
Morris left for Philadelphia, his depressed and gloomy father had confessed
his vague disappointments with his own sixty-four years of life. "My Actions
have been so inconsiderable in the World," he wrote, "that the most durable
Monument will but perpetuate my folly," ordering that "not so much as a line
in a News Paper" announce to the world that he was dead. After declaring his

desire that his youngest son "have the best Education in Europe or America," Morris went on to make sure that it would not be at Yale or anywhere else in the benighted colony of Connecticut, the most Puritan of all the New England settlements. By "Express Will and Direction," he underlined his firm patrician resolve that under no circumstances was Gouverneur to be sent to the neighboring colony and exposed to New England provincialism for any part of his education "least he should imbibe in his youth that low Craft and cunning so Incident to the People of that Country, which is so interwoven in their constitutions that all their art cannot disguise it from the World tho' many of them under the sanctified Garb of Religion have Endeavored to impose themselves on the World of honest Men." Both of Morris's much older half-brothers had studied at Yale, and the results somehow distressed their father. Shortly before he died early on the morning of July 3, 1762, the judge asked that his silver shaving box, his gold seal ring, and his favorite gold cuff buttons be given to Gouverneur, now finishing his first year at the academy. It was a sign of his special affection.[29]

When Gouverneur Morris arrived in Philadelphia in 1761, the city of nearly twenty-five thousand was already twice as large as New York and was a center of commerce, politics, finance, science, education, art, architecture, and good living. For all of the rancorous rivalry between the Anglicans, Presbyterians, and Quakers who dominated both the city's religious and mercantile life, Philadelphia had achieved a level of toleration surpassing that of any other colony. In the words of the academy's founders, students were to be admitted without regard to "sect or party." Alexander Graydon, a fellow student of Morris's, recalled later, "the puritanical spirit was unknown among us." Certainly, Puritanism or any dark sense of Calvinist guilt so ingrained at an early stage in the American character, and notably among many of the Founding Fathers, was never part of Morris's worldly, uninhibited makeup.[30]

Throughout the Middle Colonies, it was a critical period of educational ferment. Educational reformers, including Franklin, believed strongly that the emphasis should be on the mastery of English rather than the classics. Morris's brother-in-law Thomas Lawrence, a leader of the establishment and the the chief financial supporter of the academy would have none of this revolt against tradition and insisted that the classics have their own department. When the school was established, it had two departments: the English School, favored by Franklin, and the Latin School, strongly backed by the Anglican-dominated board of trustees. By the time Morris was enrolled ten years later, three-quarters of the trustees were Anglican while the rest were, in Franklin's words "of moderate principles."[31]

The English School was headed by Ebenezer Kinnersley, a provincial Baptist clergyman from England "of no great, general erudition." Kinnersley pioneered in the teaching of public speaking and required weekly practice in oratory by the reciting of poetry and prose. Morris's own natural forensic talents, which he later used to such effect, "conspicuous and flourishing in public debate," were no doubt stimulated by what was then considered experimental training.

The traditional part of the curriculum covered Latin and Greek grammar and the classic literature of Virgil, Caesar, Sallust, the Greek Testament, Horace, Terence, Livy, Lucian, Xenophon, and Homer. From the beginning, Morris was headed for college and after three years and in spite of "the demons of liberty and idleness" was able to pass the entrance examination based on the classics laid down by King's College. The test required "a rational account of the Latin and Greek grammars" and the translation of Sallust, Caesar's *Commentaries on the Gallic War*, or a portion of the Gospels from Greek into Latin.

In fall 1764, Gouverneur Morris was prepared to enter King's College. At the age of twelve, he was three years younger than most first year students. John Jay, who had graduated from the college the preceding May, was fifteen when he was admitted in 1760. The imposing new college building stood at the northwest edge of New York City bounded by Church, Greenwich, Barclay, and Murray Streets and overlooking the broad waters of the Hudson River.

The much-admired college building impressed a Scottish traveler who wrote: "[it made] a fine appearance, of the finest situations perhaps of any college in the world. Here are taught divinity, mathematics, the theory of medicine, chymistry, surgery, and meteria medica." There was only one jarring note: "the entrance of this college is thro' one of the streets where most of the prostitutes live. This is certainly a temptation to the youth that have to pass often this way." He also noted, with what must be presumed to be Presbyterian exaggeration, that "above 500 ladies of pleasure keep lodgings contiguous within the consecrated liberties of St. Pauls." Besides these temptations, there were also a number of drinking houses nearby where Morris was introduced to rambunctious New York discourse that regularly shocked visitors. On the eve of the Revolution, the straight-laced John Adams did not find "one real Gentleman, one well bred Man" in the city, and "no Conversation that is agreeable. There is no modesty—No attention to one another. They talk very loud, very fast and altogether. If they ask you a Question, before you can utter 3 words of your Answer, they will break out upon you again—and talk away."[32]

The chartering of King's College in 1754 and its shaky beginnings reflected some of the same religious tensions and debates that had surrounded the Philadelphia Academy. Thomas Jones said the town was divided between "republicans and Episcopalians." William Livingston called the proposed college, to be established by the crown, a "contracted Receptacle of Bigotry." In the end, the college received, as did Trinity Church, a royal charter.[33]

The first president of the King's College, Myles Cooper, believed that the Church of England and the British nation were one. But the college was a public institution in a very mixed, competitive society, its students drawn from most of the colony's religious groups. The student body was required to attend daily morning and evening prayers taken from the liturgy of the *Book of Common Prayer.* As for Sunday worship, and in a gesture of realistic compromise, students were allowed to attend, according to college statutes, "such places as his respective parents or guardians shall appoint."

Morris's four years at King's followed a classical curriculum founded on the Greek and Roman classics and in line with the teaching at Oxford. Logic, rhetoric, metaphysics, English verse, and "moral philosophy" were generously piled on, as were Latin and mathematics, Morris's two favorite subjects. It was at this time that he discovered Shakespeare. While he found the plays badly organized, he no doubt saw mirrored in Shakespeare's characters his own opinion that feelings and "passion," rather than the dictates of cold reason, were the basic forces in human history. In his commencement address on "Wit and Beauty," Morris expressed the growing belief that "reason had become something of a handmaiden to passion." Reason alone, the young orator argued, could not have convinced mankind to chose an ordered society over barbarism. "Passions...must have had too great an Influence upon their Understandings to commence this arduous task."[34]

President Cooper, a High Church divine, did not include the philosophy of John Locke and his radical arguments in support of a binding social compact between the government and the people. Not fourteen when Parliament passed the Stamp Act and only sixteen when he graduated from King's, Morris likely had more pressing private concerns on his mind than John Locke or the tense public crisis that erupted when word of the Stamp Act reached New Yorkers in fall 1765 with the arrival of bundles of the inflammatory stamps.

Between 1764, the year of the Sugar Act when tax revenues were first earmarked to support British troops stationed in the colonies, and the eve of war in 1775 there were more than fifty civil disturbances recorded in New York City and throughout the colony. During the winter of 1766–67, following the Stamp Act disorders, tenant farmers in Westchester, Duchess, and Albany Counties took the law of land titles into their own hands in disputes over ownership, and troops were brought in to restore order. Morris later believed that Parliament's assessment of additional taxes in 1767, which were to be used to pay for these troops stationed in the colony, was "a bolder experiment on the patience of America" than any of the earlier attempts to crack down. When New Yorkers refused to support the military as demanded in the Billeting Act, Whitehall tightened the screws by passing the Mutiny Act, requiring the governor to veto all legislation of the Assembly until it complied with the earlier order. But none of these alarums carried much political significance for Morris, nor could it have been more than passing interest to a young man with all the advantages of a prominent family and a fine talent for living.

At every step, compromises had to be invented to keep the simmering agitation that marked Morris's youth from becoming more disruptive. It seemed that every public spat might turn into a grappling match over constitutional liberties, especially when demagogic politicians, in Morris's dismissive words, "roared out liberty and property and religion" to agitate the multitude. The year before Morris finished law studies in 1771, public quarrels led by men like Isaac Sears and Alexander McDougall became increasingly political and economic, linked to constitutional issues that cropped up at every turn. In the winter of economic discontent, 1769–70, there had been more than a roar when the streets and taverns erupted into an open clash over the quartering of British troops. The radical cause was advanced further on January 17, 1770, when soldiers cut down the town's Liberty Pole only to have a taller one put in place by the defiant Liberty Boys.

Morris was certainly not distracted from an active social life by all the commotion and howls in Broad Street, the sound of Liberty Poles being felled, or by a too strenuous load of studies at King's College. "While at college," Jared Sparks concluded, Morris was far "more distinguished for quickness of parts and facility of acquisition, than for industry, a passion for learning, or general scholarship." If "quickness of parts" included high spirits, Sparks's assessment was probably understated. In his sophomore year and already prepared to assess character by infallible instinct, Morris along with three other students circulated a "scandalous report...virulently attacking the Moral Character" of Robert Harpur, professor of mathematics. The trustees were forced to take action and after a hearing absolving Harpur of any misconduct. Morris and another instigator were personally admonished by the president in front of a student assembly.

Morris was well aware of his natural high voltage, later telling his cousin Robert Morris, "My Spirits Bob, they're the Rock I shall split on." But verve, dash, whatever you want to call it was a instinctive part of Morris's personality, and he was not prepared to renounce it or to conceal it under a veneer of hypocrisy. Barely suppressed, mocking energy combined with nimble intelligence marked Morris's developing character during his King's College years and on into the study of law.[35]

CHAPTER 2

A Profession

ORRIS was only sixteen when, in 1768, he became a clerk in the
office of William Smith Jr., New York's leading lawyer. His education had been rushed, giving him the disposition of someone who
had come of age early in life. Judge Thomas Jones, who knew the family well,
thought he had "more knowledge (though still a youth) than all his brothers
put together." It was not just that he was brighter than his much older half-
brothers, now settled with families and in unremarkable careers, his intelligence seemed to operate on totally different lines—imaginative, skeptical, disinterested.

With his self-confident manner, Morris slipped easily into the numbing
routines of his three-year apprenticeship in Smith's office. He was much
younger than most King's College graduates beginning the study of law. The
"hard reading" John Jay, burdened with probity at an early age, was twenty
when he became a clerk to Benjamin Kissam in 1765. Another older friend,
Robert R. ("Chancellor") Livingston Jr., a Clermont Livingston who, like Jay
and Morris, was a graduate of King's, began his practice in Smith's law office,
where he had clerked, the same year that Gouverneur began his apprenticeship.

Law ran in the Morris family, and for good reason. Lawyers wielded enormous power. Without a nobility, literary class, or an all-powerful clergy as in
New England, lawyers occupied the highest position in New York society,
dominating the political life. In those predemocratic days, members of influential families could claim the chief prizes of the profession, insuring their
powerful leverage in the informal establishment. Even before Morris's genera-

A Southeast View of the City of New York,
engraving after drawing by Thomas Howdell, ca. 1764.
Museum of the City of New York, J. Clarence Davies Collection.

tion, the prestige of his family had guaranteed both his grandfather and father a seat on the provincial bench. When a group of the city's lawyers decided to organize themselves into a bar association in 1756, a wary Cadwallader Colden, the lieutenant governor, laid out his concerns in a letter to Lord Halifax: "In a Country like this, where few men, except in the profession of the Law, have any kind of literature, where the most opulent families, in our own memory, have risen from the lowest rank of the people, such an association must have more influence than can be imagined. By means of their profession . . . every man who knows their influence in the Courts of Justice is desirous of their favor & affrayed of their resentment."[1]

Realistically, Morris had little choice but to prepare for a profession. His inheritance, postponed until his mother's death, was not large, but even at this early age he seemed to have the ability to make a calculated, appraisal of his circumstances. His father's Westchester estate had been divided between his half-brothers Lewis and Staats Long Morris, now an officer in the British army. Lewis, the last lord of the manor, was given his own estate in the western portion of the original Morrisania tract. Gouverneur and Richard Morris were each to receive 2,000 pounds upon Staats Morris's deferred inheritance of his part of the land. Sarah Morris, deeply distrusted by her stepsons, particularly Lewis and Richard, was given a life interest in Staats Morris's portion of the land. Left with five children to raise, she was not much financial help to her only son. The management of Morrisania was a full-time, difficult job for a widow. Family tensions were aggravated by Richard Morris's resentment over his deferred inheritance. "You have," Richard coldly wrote his step-mother, "served your Children, but they never can Create in us either an affec-tion for you or a desire to serve the second children."²

Put in the hands of William Smith Jr., scholar, historian, a man of property, and member of the Governor's Council, Morris was assured of impeccable pro-fessional credentials by Smith's elevated position in the colony. Smith's father had also been a leader of the bar and both men believed in the old, hands-off style of uninstructed legal apprenticeship. Standard legal forms had not yet appeared, so a major part of a clerk's drudgery was drafting endless stacks of paper that cluttered Smith's office. Peter Van Schaack, who clerked alongside Gouverneur, bitterly complained of the grind: "For my part, how many hours have I hunted, how many books turned up for what three minutes of explana-tion from any tolerable lawyer would have been made evident to me."³

Billy Smith's law office—Morris and the other clerks ate with him at his table every day—was the ideal introduction to the rowdy, high-pitched poli-tics of New York City in the years leading up to Revolution. Although his law practice and teaching took much of his time, Smith was a master of partisan infighting and his "tenacious memory" provided a unique perspective to the growing turbulence in the British-American conflict in the colony. Not only had Smith written a major work, *The History of the Province of New-York*, but he and his friends were deeply involved in many of the political controversies over colonial rights and independence. Smith and William Livingston Jr., had led the Livingston party to victory in 1758. His strong but prudent opposition to the Stamp Act had earned him the title "Patriotic Billy."

These same festering issues would be central of the debates that Morris's generation would wrestle with on the eve of the final break. Smith's deep skepticism of mankind's common sense and innate goodness—solid Presby-terian doctrine—extended democratically to royal governors and the unwashed in the taverns. Like the Calvinist clergy of Yale, he was grounded in the conviction of human depravity and drew his political inspiration from the earlier republican ideals of the English Puritans. Replacing bad rulers and upholding good ones was a part of Puritan theology. To Smith, the lawyer and historian, constitutional legitimacy guided by reasoned precedent was the only guarantee of liberty in a civilized, well-run society. Morris would echo Smith's reservations concerning popular government forty years later when he wrote, "a democracy will ever be in the hands of weak and wicked men unless when distress or danger shall compell a reluctant people to choose a wise and virtu-ous administration."

Morris was eleven when his father died. During the crucial teenage years of his clerkship, Smith no doubt played a significant role in his life. The epitome of cultivated rectitude, Smith was a prolific writer and his feeling for language and literary style left its mark on Morris's sensitive ear. Having known three generations of Morrises—Gouverneur's grandfather, father, and two of his stepbrothers are mentioned in his *History* of the colony—Smith was an expert on their personalities, temperament, and quirks. When Gouverneur proposed to go abroad after finishing his studies, the seasoned lawyer's practical advice was informed by family history: "Rather imitate your grandfather [Governor Lewis Morris], than your uncle [Robert Hunter Morris]. The first sought preferment *here*, and built upon his American stock. The other *there* and died the moment before shipwreck."[4]

Like all loyalists, Smith revered the British constitution, the very essence of the liberties it insured. He would damn both sides for not resolving their differences and refusing to find a reasonable resolution to the escalating constitutional dispute. If the Americans were stubborn and hardheaded, he found the British often arrogant and myopic. He claimed that to his "old Whigg Friends of Rank" he was seen as a Tory, "but to the Lower Sort as favoring the popular Measures."[5]

Smith's unyielding notions of individual liberty and the idealism of his early law partner, William Livingston, provide an important backdrop to Morris's education, projecting politically sophisticated themes at odds with the more conventional attitudes of the times. If Smith was, in Michael Kammen's words, "a disgruntled dissenter—uncomfortable with the Establishment even while a part of it," Livingston was the ultimate Whig iconoclast often disagreeing with Smith. The intellectual independence and grit of the two older men no doubt impressed and reinforced Morris's instinctive individuality.[6]

While upholding law and order under the crown, Smith and Livingston were of a reforming, liberal disposition when it came to civil and religious liberty. Their commitment to tolerance in a secular society, which they regularly advanced in the press was reflected in Morris's own ecumenical political philosophy. This perspective, shaped by the tangled politics of a commercial port city already swarming with immigrants, was in sharp contrast to the far more traditional, conservative sentiments of Morris's extended family of landed gentry and the Tory harangues of the arch-high churchmen he had listened to in chapel at King's College and Trinity Church. When he entered Smith's office, the imperial issues and ideology that provoked his elders in the 1750s and 1760s were only faint stirrings well outside Morris's narrow provincial world of Morrisania's sporting life and the pleasures of New York City. But by the time he became an ambitious member of the New York bar, these prickly contentions had grown into a full-blown political crisis.

Unlike the Anglican Morrises, both Smith and Livingston were "Free-Thinking," anticlerical Presbyterians. Both had attended Yale and then studied law in the office of the senior Smith. William Livingston, who was the younger brother of the third lord of Livingston Manor and later the revolutionary governor of New Jersey, was, like Smith, a visionary with down-to-earth political instincts. Both men, like everyone else, called themselves Whigs, but they were much more of the progressive, reforming stripe. During the years leading up to the Revolution in the small, elite society of New York City, Smith, Livingston, and their more boisterous collaborator, John Morin Scott, collectively known as the Triumvirate, were familiar figures to the young law clerk. No doubt impressed by their contrarian independence, Morris's own independent streak insured that he did not always follow their political lead.

In his history of the Revolution, Judge Jones divined that 1752, the year Gouverneur Morris was born, precisely marked the end of New York's golden era as a part of the empire. That year Smith, Livingston, and John Morin Scott founded the Whig Club, which was dedicated, in Jones's word, to pulling down "Church and State, to raise their own government and religion upon its ruins or to throw the whole province into anarchy and confusion." Jones knew that the end was nigh when he heard that the club members were drinking toasts to Oliver Cromwell, John Hampden, "and other distinguished actors in the grand English rebellion at their meetings in the King's Arms tavern."[7]

The Triumvirate also found time to launch a provocative weekly called the *Independent Reflector*, aimed at the power of the Church of England and the Tory leadership it represented. The trio were masters of literary war. "The Press to them," Cadwallader Colden sourly complained, "what the Pulpit was in the times of Popery." A noisy partisan fight with deeper implications soon broke out in the *Reflector* over who would control the administration of the proposed new King's College. At the heart of the dispute were the chartering powers of the crown and the threat they posed to the powers and autonomy of the colonial Assembly.[8]

The *Reflector* argued that a charter issued by fiat from London would unbalance the vaunted English constitution of mixed powers in favor of the executive. It is important to remember that these "popular," divisive arguments challenging the crown were not commonplace in English eighteenth-century political debate, yet they dramatically foreshadow the future political issues over home rule that Morris and his rebelling generation would eventually resolve by arms.

The paper war of the Triumvirate over King's College in the 1750s had been, from its beginning, predictably political, exposing the fragile relation between church and state. The quarrel would gradually become an argument for religious freedom and the complete separation of the Church from government, throwing the colony, in Judge Jones's words, into "uproar and disorder." The *Reflector*'s first issue in 1752 left no doubt who the villain was in matters of pedagogy and theology when it proclaimed "the cause of truth and liberty" in opposition to "superstition, bigotry, priest craft, tyranny, servitude, public mis-management and dishonesty in office" in all its forms. Years later, the secular sentiments of the *Reflector* (as well as his Huguenot heritage) surfaced in Morris's reaction to a church school he visited in Flanders: "I suppose Religion comes in for Something in this Business, and certainly those [who] desire that their Children should imbibe the most blind and obstinate Prejudices which Superstition ever engendered upon Ignorance, cannot do better than send them to Flanders for Education."[9]

In the late 1760s the Church stirred up yet more dissension by pushing for an American bishop, setting off another public exchange between the Angli-cans and Dissenters. In the dispute, the opposing clerics mounted a popular campaign that was at once nationalistic and revolutionary. William Livingston saw this as an opportunity to launch a new radical publication called the *American Whig* with "a few Friends of Liberty," adding provocatively, "'Tis Noise and clamour that is our best Policy."[10]

A few months before Morris became a law clerk in 1768, Livingston now a seasoned controversialist, predicted in the pages of the new journal what amounted to a remarkable anticipation of Morris's destiny and that of his generation.

> The day dawns in which the foundation of this mighty empire is to be laid, by the establishment of a *regular American Constitution*. All that has hitherto been done, seems to be little besides the collection of materials for the construction of this glori-ous fabrick. 'Tis time to put them together. The transfer of the European part of the great family is so swift, and our growth is so vast, that before seven years the first stone must be laid. Peace or war; famine or plenty; poverty or affluence; in a word, no circumstance, whether prosperous or adverse, can happen to our parent; no, nay no conduct of hers, whether wise or imprudent, no possible temper on her part, whether kind or cross-grained, will put a stop to this building.... What an aera is this to America! and how loud the call to vigilance and activity! As we conduct, so will it fare with us and our children.[11]

By the time King's College awarded Morris a master of arts degree in 1771, he already had a promising reputation, a firm grounding in the practice of law, and at least an inkling of how the world worked beyond the narrow streets and noisy coffee houses lining the harbor of New York City. Smith's broad curricu-lum became a solid foundation for the future statesman: "The sciences neces-sary for a lawyer are 1. The English, Latin and French Tongues. 2. Writing, Arithmetic, Geometry, Surveying, Merchant's Accounts or Bookkeeping. 3. Geography, Cronology, History. Logick and Rhetorick. 5. Divinity. Law of Nature and Nations. 7. Law of England."[12]

During his legal apprenticeship, Morris was able to absorb the all-impor-tant manners and the art of cultivated, original conversation, that sociability so central to the ideals of the age. He had read Lord Chesterfield's instructions on a gentleman's education and the Englishman's definition of *les bienséances*, "a most necessary part of the knowledge of the world...the relations of persons, things, time and place; good sense points them out, good company perfects them (supposing always an attention and a desire to please), and good policy recommends them." Later Morris admonished a young relative in his characteristic style: "Tell Ned to read Chesterfield, and for God's sake cure him of sensibility. It is certainly as dangerous to be under the control of the soft as the rough emotion."[13]

Morris demonstrated again his canny ability to stand aside and appraise his experience when he told William Smith after finishing his legal clerkship that he had "been so hurried through the different scenes of childhood and youth," he felt he had missed an important part of his education. Morris's cool self-possession sometimes bordering on the egotistical did not always extend to the compromising art of politics. He agreed with his cousin Robert Hunter Morris that he had "too much Honesty ever to mend [his] fortunes by 'government office' or to make a good politician." His dedication to truth in all matters did not mean that he would give up the Morris passion—some might say the family failing—for the intrigues and power of government.[14]

On May 21, 1771, King's College awarded Morris his advanced degree at commencement in Trinity Church. In contrast to his commencement address entitled "Oration on Love," underlining the love of liberty under a constitution, the valedictory given by a candidate for the Anglican cloth was on "the fatal Effects of misguided ambition." Six years earlier Morris's close friend Robert Livingston had also been au courant when he spoke "in praise of *Liberty*." His Majesty's governor, Lord Dunmore, responded to the speech with diplomatic silence as a member of the audience at Trinity. Before he departed for Virginia in a drunken haze, Dunmore signed Morris's license to practice law. On October 26 Morris appeared before the Supreme Court of Judicature, presided over by Judge R. R. Livingston, Robert's father, and took the attorney's oath before adjourning to Fraunces Tavern to celebrate. He had not yet turned twenty.

At this point in his career, as Jared Sparks accurately observed, "his views reached no further than to the limited distinction of a colonial lawyer." Morris was well aware that his education and experience had been parochial and certainly peripheral to the distant worlds of London and Paris. In 1769, his older half-brother Staats Morris, now an officer in the British army had returned for a visit from England with his newly wed, eccentric Scottish wife, the former Dowager Duchess of Gordon "richly deckt with Diamonds and other Jewels and dressed most splendidly in Silver Silks." American newspapers reported on the social swath the couple cut in the provinces, from Philadelphia to New York. Impressed by the transcontinental glamour of his flamboyant relatives, Morris was made aware of the gap in his limited social experience. The confines of a city of little more than twenty thousand compressed within an area roughly one mile in length and a mile and a half wide now suddenly seemed claustrophobic.[15]

On February 20, 1772, shortly after he turned twenty and already urbane in his ambitions, Morris wrote Smith, outlining his plans to explore the mysteries of European society. He thought that his deportment revealed "those many barbarisms, which characterize a provincial education" and confessed that he needed to find more sophisticated models of "manners and address by the example of the truly polite, . . . by conversing with our superiors in understanding." New York's small-town bickering, obscure political cabals, and the sharp elbowing of ambitious lawyers and merchants offered very little in the way of what could be called a polished model. Unconcerned with the perils of misguided ambitions, he intended to "cut a figure" in the law, he told Smith, and a little travel would help rub off the telltale signs of what he now considered to be a backwater upbringing.

The world-weary old lawyer immediately saw the perils of Morris's travel plans. There was, first of all, the cost, which neither Morris nor his mother could afford. But Smith also hinted at more expensive temptations that might lead to ruin. There was still plenty of time for him to end up nothing more than a charming, burned-out man of fashion. Playing the paterfamilias, Smith reminded Gouverneur of his notorious uncle, Robert Hunter Morris, the chief justice of New Jersey, who after three extravagant trips to England dropped dead at a country dance just before financial disaster struck. Smith's sober financial advice—where money was involved, Gouverneur could be sober as well—struck home. Throughout his life Morris was punctilious about his finances, and while open-handed to needy friends, he kept detailed personal accounts with a discipline that might have suggested the impoverished background of a country bookkeeper.

Morris's travel plans were postponed if not altogether abandoned because of what he claimed was the hard, grinding work of a young lawyer. His early practice involved mostly commercial and real estate transactions. The entries in his law journal record run-of-the mill but profitable legal work, making money and spending money with a forthright dedication to the domestic claims of taste and comfort.

He did find time, however, for the pleasures of the Social Club and the dancing assemblies that dominated New York's social life. In November 1771, Morris met and was smitten by a "Soft Disturber of the Mind," Catherine Livingston, the daughter of William Livingston. He discovered just how susceptible he was to feminine beauty and feminine company. The following May he pleaded in verse "Sweet Tormenter now be kind" and asked for a lock of Catherine's hair. But by August he had been politely rejected by Miss Livingston. Resigned and philosophical but not at all depressed, he moved on in his thoughts and with his plans, telling Catherine "how uncomfortable a hopeless Passion of this kind is." Seemingly unscarred by gnawing emotions of rejection, Morris also told her quite frankly that he was "constitutionally one of the happiest of men," a shameless inner balance of feelings that did not often suffer from bruising frustrations and disappointments.

To put it more accurately, Morris was a born hedonist, indifferent to the possibility that natural sensual pleasure might be a vice. He would casually flaunt this disposition throughout his life without the slightest twinge of Puritanical guilt or romantic angst. In his unapologetic taste for natural pleasure, he expressed the French strain and spirit in his makeup that set him apart from many of his contemporaries. Probably no other Founding Father with the exception of Benjamin Franklin and Robert Livingston Jr. could claim such a worldly, sophisticated disposition. It should be added that all three men understood and enjoyed the intimate company of intelligent women.

There are strong hints of the rakish in Morris's early years as a young lawyer-about-town. In his indifference to temptation he was much closer to Robert Livingston, also a man of pleasure, than to the staid, shy Jay who considered himself above the unprincipled ways of the ordinary world. By the time Morris lost his leg in a carriage accident in 1780, the reputation would be well established. According to his cousin Robert Morris, living in New Jersey, Gouverneur's life included plenty of good wine, admiring companions, and attractive young women. In May 1772, when Gouverneur admitted to Robert that he was suffering from a passing bout of "melancholy," for him a rare, pensive mood, his surprised cousin replied, "I did not suspect of it while there was Youth Beauty C[laret] Wine and Company to be had in New York." In a letter to a friend, Robert prudishly condemned his city cousin's dissipation, his "folly in prostituting his abilities to the trifling purpose of an Evening's Gollity with a set of beings whose Merits are that they have discernment enough to admire him." All this may well be nothing more than the speculations of an envious relative. In fact, whatever his extracurricular distractions were, the young lawyer was successfully establishing a solid professional reputation during this period and his annual earnings were steadily growing.

In fall 1773, at age twenty-one, Morris made his first venture into real estate speculation. Land would later underpin his substantial wealth. Using as security a promissory bond of 475 pounds that was actually owned by his mother, he bought at a New York auction a tract of wilderness on the edge of the frontier in what is now Saratoga County. Visiting his much-expanded stake many years later in the winter of 1800 to oversee land sales to settlers, he could hardly believe the transformation and his good fortune. One measure of incipient civilization, Morris the gourmet noted, was the availability and quality of fresh oysters he ate in the rustic inn where he stayed. "In this short space of fifteen years," since the end of the war, he wrote in his diary, "a whole region is converted from a wilderness into a settled country. Already in this neighborhood fuel is beginning to grow scarce, and already industry ministers to luxury by bringing oysters near two hundred miles from the sea. This is indeed wonderful. Had imagination pictured anything like it twenty years ago, he who would have ventured to express an idea so fanciful, would have been deemed a madman."[16]

In January 1774, some months after investing in the future of the country's wilderness, Morris wrote to his friend Thomas Penn in Philadelphia, describing the dramatic change that had come over him. "Business—it has so transformed, and transmigrated, and almost transubstantiated me, as hardly to leave the memory of what I was." But in a note to his friend's wife appended to the same letter, the exuberant other Morris—"happiest of men"—surfaces from the familiar image of an overworked young lawyer, crushed with briefs, arguments, and endless legal references. "Pity it is that you are not here," he seductively writes to Mrs. Penn, "balls, concerts, assemblies—all of us mad in the pursuit of pleasure. Not a pause. Grave phizes are grinned out of countenance, prudence kicked out of doors, and your sober, solid, sedate friend (myself meaning) has become the butt of unfledged witlings."[17]

Onward and upward, in March 1774, the imminently clubable lawyer was elected to the Moot, the most important association of lawyers in New York City. Unique in the colonies, it served as an ongoing professional seminar in legal education. William Livingston was president. Gouverneur's youngest half-brother, Judge Richard Morris; John Morin Scott; and William Smith Jr. were pillars of the exclusive society. John Jay, Robert R. Livingston Jr., and James Duane were his good friends and mentors among the twenty-seven conspicuously talented members out of a bar of more than seventy. Based on the Moot of London's famed Gray's Inn, it was a congenial, competitive atmosphere of ambitious lawyers setting professional standards for the bar. The political factions of both the Livingstons and the De Lanceys were well represented, but it was piously agreed that no discussion of "the Party Politics of this Province," be permitted. Such matters were for the Council, the Assembly, newspapers and family gatherings.[18]

On April 22, 1774, a month after Morris and his friends celebrated his election to the Moot at Fraunces Tavern, quite another kind of crowd gathered at the popular tavern. A nervous ship's captain, whose ship the *London* had just arrived in the New York harbor, was forced to confess to an intimidating committee of inspection, that, contrary to his bill of lading, he did in fact have eighteen cases of tea on board, subject to the hated imperial tax. He was told that he could either leave without unloading his cargo or it would be destroyed. The trouble in the New York tavern, of course, had its origins in Parliament's Tea Act, passed in 1773, which imposed a customs tax on imported tea. There had been a running political skirmish throughout the spring about whether New York should follow Boston and Philadelphia in blocking the admission of the tea into the colony.

Weeks before Captain Chambers's explosive admission in the tavern hit the streets, New York had become "a town filled with politics," John Jay told a friend. Heated arguments erupted on street corners and coffee houses over the infamous tax on tea and whether Parliament had the right to impose it or any tax on the colonies without their consent. The fundamental issue, as Morris's friend Peter Van Schaack and others saw it, was "the determination to establish a supremacy of Parliament over these colonies." If the colonies' exemption from the Parliamentary tax was not absolute, Van Schaack wrote his brother-in-law in London, then "they did not enjoy the privilege of British subjects." If Parliament could tax the colonists at its pleasure, the act itself reduced the colony to second-class citizens. The tax revenues in turn would be used to undermine colonial self-government with royal restrictions. The very bitterness of New York's reaction to the tax was all the more intense because it struck at its commercial prosperity and international trade.[19]

When news of Boston's Tea Party on December 21, 1773, reached New York, the town's rowdy and popular Sons of Liberty loudly announced their intentions to follow Boston's example and take direct and summary action at the first opportunity, not waiting for a nod from the more cautious merchants. An alarmed Governor William Tryon reported to the secretary of state that tea could be unloaded in New York's harbor only at "point of a bayonet, and muzzle of the cannon." Captain Chambers's confession in Fraunces Tavern the following April was all that was needed to set things off. That evening eighteen cases of English tea were dumped overboard without waiting for "the Mohawks" who were prepared "to perform their duty properly costumed and at the proper hour."[20]

The affair in the harbor acted as a catalyst in the city's charged political air. The impromptu tea party on the *London* had drawn a large number of spectators, alerting "the principle inhabitants" (code words for the better sort) that more "violent proceedings of the pretended patriots" were likely to follow. The next morning church bells were rung and a large flag of defiance hoisted on the Liberty Pole. The same day, Captain Chambers was shipped off as a passenger on a boat returning to London. A committee of the town made sure that he was on board and triumphantly reported back: "Thus to the mortification of secret and open enemies of America and to the joy of all friends of liberty and human nature, the union of this colony is maintained."[21]

On May 12, two weeks after all the excitement, news arrived from London of the passage by Parliament of the Boston Port Act to close and blockade the Boston port to commercial trade. The act prohibiting all loading and unloading in Boston harbor would take effect on June 1 if the city did not pay for tea destroyed in the "tea party." Lord North understood the high stakes. "They deny our legislative authority," North told Parliament. "If they deny authority in one instance it goes to all. We must control them or submit to them." The Massachusetts government accepted the challenge and immediately annulled the colony's charter and gave the governor control over public rallies.[22]

Word soon spread in New York's taverns that the now rejuvenated Sons of Liberty, acting without any official authority, had called a public rally on May 16 to name a committee to protest Parliament's closing of Boston's harbor. The Sons of Liberty's agenda to impose an immediate embargo on all imports was a dangerous step and one opposed by the city's more conservative merchants who would have had the most to lose in an all-out trade war. William Smith was deeply disturbed by the abrupt turn of events to radical action: "a general consternation and disgust works among the people....I fear we shall lose all that Attachmt. we once had in so great a Degree for the Parent Country."[23]

Foreseeing a crowd of "flaming patriots without property, or anything else but impudence"—Morris dubbed them the "mobility"—the city's alarmed leaders turned out in force on the sixteenth, forcing the meeting to adjourn from Fraunces Tavern to the Merchants Exchange. There must be no more rioting in the streets, no violence, and no dictatorship by popular troublemakers like Isaac Spears and Alexander McDonald. Without rejecting the slate of twenty-five committee members proposed by the Sons of Liberty, the moderates and conservatives, to casually use those misleading, threadbare labels, successfully countered with a proposal to enlarge the committee with the nomination of an additional twenty-five members. Francis Lewis, an old family friend of the Morrises, was added later, transforming it into the famous Committee of Fifty-one.

On May 19, when "a great concourse" poured into Fraunces Tavern to confirm the nominations, Morris, who had just turned twenty-two and was already a fledgling "connoisseur of the games people play with each other," watched closely from one side. He put down his observations in a letter to Thomas Penn the next day: "We have appointed a committee, or rather we have nominated one." It appeared that the wary, moderating Whigs had taken control of the committee by a narrow margin.

The Social Club was represented on the committee by Morris's friends John Jay, James Duane, and Peter Van Schaack. For Morris, it was the first of the many gatherings rhetorically called in the name of the "people" that he would witness throughout his life, as "they fairly contended about the future forms of government, whether it should be founded upon Aristocratic or Democratic principles." It should be recalled that these tricky words "aristocratic" and "democratic," while common to political thinkers, had not yet entered popular speech. As Robert R. Palmer has reminded us, "No 'democrats' fought in the American revolution."

The scene at Fraunces Tavern was an instructive experience in Morris's political education. His often-quoted letter, dated May 20, 1774, is laced with unguarded Morris irony regularly cited by historians as a reactionary sound bite opposing the popular, patriotic cause. "I was present at a great division of the city," he wrote, "and there I beheld my fellow citizens very accurately counting all their chickens not only before any of them were hatched, but before above one half of the eggs were laid.... I stood in the balcony, and on my right hand was ranged all the people of property, with some dependents, and on the other all the tradesmen, &c. who thought it worth their while to leave daily labor for the good of the country."[24]

To Morris's eye, the coalition of "tradesmen, &c.," mechanics, small merchants, and working people arranged on his left had suddenly emerged as an independent force in New York politics eager to participate in the debate on the rights of the colony. "The mob begins to think and reason," Morris astutely observed. "Poor reptiles! it is with them a vernal morning, they are casting off their winter's slough, they bask in the sunshine, and ere noon they will bite, depend on it." But not all is on the side of the "patricians"—Morris's label—standing on the right in this somewhat exaggerated tableau. "Their committee [the patricians] will be appointed, they will deceive the people, and again forfeit a share of their confidence."

The pervasive division between classes in colonial society had always been fluid and vaguely defined. And as the Morrises had known for generations, the political power of the gentry was only maintained by careful cultivation of popular support. Morris's grandfather knew very well how to reach out to tradesmen and small farmers when he needed their help in his fight to remove William Cosby, the royal governor. Gouverneur's father would deliberately insult the governor sitting in session with the Assembly by ostentatiously seeing that no bills introduced in the chamber were handed to the indignant royal elect seated at the end of the table.

The neat symmetry of Morris's picture of the right and left—not yet political labels—lined up in the street ready to do battle may be misleading. In fact, although the men of property, into whose "hands was to be committed the majesty of the people," calling for "the dictates of calm reason" had won the day, they were learning to accommodate to popular forces they could not stop or control. Robert Livingston Jr. perceptively summed it up when he spoke of "swimming with a stream it is impossible to stem," yielding "to the torent," in order to "direct its course." It was the same pragmatic conclusion that would shape Morris's course.

"I see, and I see it with fear and trembling," Morris warned somewhat melodramatically in his letter to Penn, "that if the disputes with Britain continue, we shall be under the worst of all possible dominations. We shall be under the domination of a riotous mob." Morris and others of his class worried that these rowdy street meetings where the enfranchised and everyone else freely mixed but without any legal or constitutional restraints could in a flash transform themselves into "representative" bodies prepared to take over, by fiat, the reins of government. The lax and generous suffrage requirements of New York had long encouraged a diverse and shifting, if nebulous, sense of participation among ordinary people. Their own leaders, themselves skeptical of too much popular intervention from below, understood the importance of exercising strong leadership to impress the deeply ingrained habits of deference held by their followers.[25]

To the "tradesmen, &c." working on the wharves or drinking ale in the alehouses, Morris and his well-dressed friends seemed to live and move in a world apart. For their part, these demigods were unlikely or unable to imagine the hardships and daily concerns of the "leather aprons." In fact, it was one of the peculiarities of New York politics that the ordinary people of the city showed little interest in taking an active role in government so long as they were heard by their betters on issues that directly affected them. But when things got too disruptive and loud, the ruling order might collectively feel a nervous stab. To Morris's mind, any threat to tranquillity and stability was a threat to liberty itself.

Without a safety net of even a rudimentary government in place to enforce order, Morris realistically saw how even the threat of chaos could easily provoke harsh retaliation by the crown, wiping out all the political gains the colonies had extracted from Parliament over the years. This was one of the deepest fears of most in Morris's circle. Putting aside all those "fair or foul words such as Liberty, Patriotism, Virtue, Treason, Aristocracy" carelessly thrown around by all sides, if orderly constitutional government was to be maintained, members of the establishment like Morris, Jay, and Livingston must not be put off by the rough game of revolutionary politics or its misleading slogans and words.[26]

The extralegal Committee of Fifty-one that transfixed the young lawyer as it took form in New York City in spring 1774 set the stage to carefully address and advance illegal opposition to Parliament using the language of English common law and tradition. Morris was aware that during the rebellion led by his ancestor Jacob Leisler, Leisler had also received his authority to take over the function of government from a similar extralegal "Committee for the Safety of the People" as an unacknowledged precedent for these new committees prepared to channel public discontent into a functional form without falling into anarchy. From May 1774 until spring 1776, New York had two governments operating side by side. The official royal government within the assembly struggled to uphold the crown's authority in the face of mounting opposition. The opposition ad hoc government, emerging first in the streets, evolved into the unwieldy committees and eventually into the provincial congresses of a new government.[27]

At this point, the only resolution of the conflict that Morris could see was a reconciliation "with the parent state," even if it meant conceding to the regulation of trade by the mother country, the seat of Empire, "where alone is found the power to protect it." Britain admittedly was in the position to take destructive advantage of colonial commerce. But if she grabbed all the profit, she would kill it, he argued, and both sides would lose. Away from the pressures of the "mobility," sensible leadership somehow had to repair the widening gap of disunion short of war.

Watching the same ominous turn of events, Morris's dejected friend Peter Van Schaack predicted that the hardening on both sides in the New York streets, taverns, and committee meetings would lead to bloodshed. "An appeal to the sword I am afraid is inevitable, but palliating measures might have kept it off for a long time. The mutual interests of both should have restrained either from hastening the crisis, but I am afraid the die is cast. *Divis permittitur, coetera!*"[28]

In little more than a year, Morris and most of his friends would be preparing to use military force to defend their rights against the mother country. The Moot and the Social Club would disappear. Shorn of its royal charter, King's College saw its buildings turned into military barracks and its president, Myles Cooper, run out of town. Morris's own family would be badly split, with his mother and two of his sisters' families remaining loyal while their husbands escaped in exile. His mentor, William Smith, would also be banished. The gentle, agonizing Peter Van Schaack, declaring himself neutral in the conflict, retreated for the duration to his farm at Kinderhook. He would later remind John Jay of those simpler, legendary days of old New York before the break: "A recollection, of those happy scenes, of our clubs, our moots, and our Broadway evenings, fill me with pleasing, melancholy reflections,—*fuimus Troes, fuit Ilium.*"[29]

On May 23, 1774, the Committee of Fifty-one set things in motion in a letter to their beleaguered colleagues in Boston: "we conclude that a congress of deputies from the Colonies in general is of the utmost moment; that it ought to be summoned without delay." Even some New York loyalists saw this continental parley as a positive move. It would at least, a relieved Myles Cooper declared, take the debate "out of the hands of the herd." In mid-June the decision was made to hold a general congress in Philadelphia, and on September 5, the opening meeting of the First Continental Congress to prepare for a common defense, got under way in Philadelphia's Carpenters Hall. New York's delegates to the Congress, selected without the help of the Sons of Liberty, included Morris's friends, the lawyers John Jay and James Duane, and the merchant Philip Livingston. Like most delegates they were instructed to work for reconciliation while preparing for war.

One question loomed over the proceedings: how far were the delegates willing to go in weakening the bonds with the mother country while placating the radical elements in the streets. Patrick Henry speaking for the extremists of Virginia declared that "Government is dissolved.... I am not a Virginian but an American." But John Jay might well have been using Morris's words when he objected: "I cant yet think that all Government is at an End. The Measure of arbitrary Power is not full, and I think it must run over, before We undertake to frame a new Constitution."[30]

John Adams complained that the first Congress suffered from "The Fidgets, the Whims, the Caprices, the Vanity, the Superstition, the irritability" of the delegates of the national Congress. Nevertheless declarations of principles appealing to both American and British opinion were published, including a petition to the king signed by all of the members.

When James Galloway's proposed plan for reconciliation by negotiation failed by one vote, the Congress adopted on October 20, 1774, the fateful, defining Continental Association binding all of the colonies to nonimportation, nonexportation, and nonconsumption of British goods. The terms of the oath of allegiance demanded by the association effectively separated the patriots from the loyalists, cutting across all political, social, and economic lines. The Congress recommended that any citizen who ignored the boycott of British goods be publicly declared an enemy of "American freedom" and outlawed by the community. New York published only the names of those who refused to take the oath.

In November, New York City chose a Committee of Sixty, later expanded to one hundred, to enforce the regulations of the association cutting off trade, the lifeline of the port. Throughout the fall, however, Morris and many of his friends, not as depressed and immobilized as Peter Van Schaack, still held on to the possibility of a negotiated truce short of civil war, but the outlines of such a solution were difficult to see as sides were taken and positions hardened.

Jay had supported Galloway's plan but his "Address to the People of Great Britain," written to justify the association was stronger stuff: "a Nation led to greatness by the hand of Liberty" was now becoming an "advocate for Slavery and Oppression." Jay's constitutional theories laid out in his address articulated a marked shift away from the moderate position identified with both Jay and Morris and most of the New York leadership that had looked for some kind of a negotiated reunification. Avoiding the ultimate question of independence, the usually reserved Jay displayed unexpected passion, leaving no doubt where the colonies stood at the end of 1774; "if you are determined that your Ministers shall wantonly sport with the rights of Mankind," the future chief justice of the Supreme Court declared, "if neither the voice of justice, the dictates of the law, the principles of the constitution, or the suggestions of humanity can restrain your hands from shedding human blood in such an impious cause, we must tell you, that we will never submit to be hewers of wood or drawers of water for any ministry or nation in the world."[31]

The old family, social, and professional ties of New York could not hold the Moot together in the face of the mounting gale. On January 6, 1775, the club met for the last time in Fraunces Tavern. The divisions within this little society bound by training, manners, and custom, like the widening breach throughout the disjointed province, dictated its end. Of the twenty-two members, nine remained loyal to the crown, and ten joined the rebellion. Three desperately tried to straddle the fence.

PART II

Revolution

CHAPTER 3

Things Fall Apart

A FTER the final meeting of the Moot in early January 1775, events in
New York moved inexorably to a climax. Only rhetoric and pious illusions now held the colonies and empire together. But given the peculiar
mixture of New York politics, where the establishment had usually managed to
accommodate the exuberance of the radicals—visionaries and troublemakers
alike—Morris still could not believe that a complete break with Britain was
inevitable. The dilemma he and his well-connected friends—"sensible and disinterested men"—wrestled with was how to remain a part of the empire on
terms that would pacify Parliament yet not alienate those pushing "the extravagant notion of independence." Throughout 1775, as he regularly repeated, his
effort was an attempt to "seek for reunion with the parent state" while heading
off militant confrontation. Armed resistance would prove fatal to both sides.[1]

No romantic dreamer and believing that "government should be founded
on stationary not revolutionary principle," Morris, the cautious loyalist, finally
emerged as an unflinching patriot in the republican cause. If there was a single
emotion driving him and defining his transformation into a supporter of independence, it was his rising contempt for what he considered the tyranny of the
British ministry and its representatives. This feeling, shared by many New
York patricians, had surfaced more than once in his family's restive history
under the crown. As he wrote in his account of the origins of the war, a free
people simply could not tolerate "arbitrary edicts of the prince." Even more
humiliating and intolerable was to "be bound by the more arbitrary edicts of
our fellow subjects" living in Britain.[2]

When, on April 23, 1775, the news reached New York that the king's troops had opened fire on the citizens of Lexington and Concord on April 19, "tales of all Kinds invented, believed, denied, discredited," swept through a tense city. Six days later "the most active Citizens," led by Isaac Sears and John Lamb, cleaned out the town's arsenal and took over the Custom House, leaving, in William Smith's words, "consternation in the faces of the Principal Inhabitants."

Morris remained slightly to one side when a public rally of an estimated eight thousand authorized the city's Committee of Sixty to act "with full & unlimited Power to consult upon and determine & direct the means" to protect the city and to enforce "*whatever measures* may be recommended by the Continental Association." A revolutionary government of the city was suddenly created by acclamation. An oath of the Association of Defense was adopted to be sworn to by every citizen "that we will, in all things, follow the advice of our General Committee respecting the...preservation of peace and good order, and the safety of individuals and private property." The militant tone of the oath, resolving "never to become slaves," seemed to assure that there would be no compromise as some of the radical leadership had charged. Three days after the rally, the committee took another crucial step and called for the election of a provincial congress. The new congress would, in turn, elect delegates to Philadelphia to join representatives from the other colonies at the second Continental Congress.[3]

For several weeks following the news from Boston, Morris continued to monitor the growing signs of anarchy in the city, the self-appointed patriots roaming the town's streets looking for Tory victims. In the middle of this uproar, the Committee of Sixty, enlarged to a committee of one hundred, including men of "weight and consequence," shrewdly strengthened its moderate position when it forced some suspected Tories to take an oath supporting the patriotic cause.

Both the president of King's College, Dr. Cooper, and the printer James Rivington, a Tory sympathizer, were appealing targets of the popular crowds in the streets and taverns. Not only was Rivington the publisher of a conservative newspaper, he was also in the pay of the government with an annual salary as king's printer. Cooper also received a ministerial honorarium for his loyal "merits and services" to the crown. With the help of a student, Cooper, the "obnoxious Tory," managed to flee the mob. The student, a pale, thin sixteen-year-old Creole immigrant named Alexander Hamilton had arrived in New York from the West Indies the year before nearly penniless. Standing on the stoop of the college, he lectured the throng on "the disgrace it would bring on the cause of liberty," buying just enough time for Cooper to escape. Morris had first heard of Hamilton in winter 1774–75 when he defended the work of the Continental Congress in an open letter called "A Full Vindication of the

Pleasures of Congress, &c.," published in Rivington's *Gazetteer*. Buried in Hamilton's avalanche of words was the kernel of the imperial dispute. "It is this," the new man in town declared, "whether we shall preserve that security to our lives, which the law of nature, the genius of the British constitution, and our charters afford us, or whether we shall resign them into the hands of the British House of Commons, which is no more privileged to dispose of them than the Grand Mogul?"[4]

After routing President Cooper, the mob then turned to Rivington who had notoriously carried on a press war with the Sons of Liberty in his paper. While claiming to keep a free and open press, as he had demonstrated by publishing Hamilton's reply to a Tory pamphlet, his often intemperate attacks on the "Modern Whigs"—supporters of "licentiousness, insurrection and rebellion,"—had grown throughout the agitated spring of 1775. Warming to his attack, Rivington declared the sacred Liberty Pole on the commons where the Sons of Liberty held their rallies to be the very emblem of immorality.[5]

Morris was no friend of Rivington, dismissing him as "indifferently wise," but he was indignant on principle that he had been driven from his house and been threatened and intimidated when he tried to operate his press. Even though Rivington had signed an oath pledging his "sacred honor . . . in defense of the rights and liberties of America" and had published a broadside promising to avoid irritating the people of the city, to Morris the continuing attacks on the editor were public "madness" that posed a threat to the community and could trigger greater violence.

Whatever the provocation for these reckless acts of "popular vengeance," Morris held to his conviction that liberty could only be achieved through an established order of things. He believed that the efforts of the individual colonies must be united and that an "implicit obedience ought to be paid to every recommendation of the Continental Congress." By tying independence to the balancing act of the Congress in Philadelphia, attempting to work out a compromise short of open war, the strategy could be undone by the impulsive crowds enforcing their own notions of law and justice. Besides, a free press— even a prejudiced one like Rivington's—as the price of liberty; the festering issue recalled Morris's grandfather's defense of the printer John Paul Zenger.[6]

Convinced that Rivington was "a sincere penitent," Morris discreetly wrote General Charles Lee, a soldier of fortune now in Philadelphia and aligned with the revolutionary element, urging him to use his influence to head off any further retribution by the Continental Congress, which might be persuaded to pass "mischievous Resolutions against this unfortunate Printer." New York City's request to the Continental Congress that it censure Rivington made Morris uncomfortable on another ground: allowing Congress to exercise judicial power along with its legislative authority would set a dangerous precedent. "It is the giving a new Power to the Congress our Association hath given them the legislative," he told Richard Henry Lee, the revolutionary Virginia delegate in the Congress, "and this now tenders them the judicial Supremacy." Rivington should be let off: "A mild and favorable Sentence will conciliate the Opinions of Mankind."[7]

To Morris, it was not simply a constitutional ideal to be ignored in times of crisis but a dangerous precedent for later and more serious abuses. "The power of government, as of man," he argued in defense of the printer, "is to be collected from small instances; great affairs are more the object of reflection and policy. Here both join." This was the solid liberal Whig philosophy he had learned from William Smith. William Livingston had underlined it in the *Independent Reflector*, arguing that government must be "divided into separate Branches, for a check on each other.... Such is the restless and aspiring Nature of the human Mind, that a Man entrusted with Power, seldom contents himself with his due Proportion" and must be restrained.[8]

Morris's private efforts saved Rivington, and he was allowed "to return to his house and family" with the assurance (no doubt drafted by Morris) "not to molest him in his person or property." When a New Haven mob later invaded New York, demolished Rivington's press, and carried off his type, the words of protest that the New York Congress fired off to the Connecticut governor has the unmistakable ring of Morris: "We are fully sensible of his [Rivington's] demerits; but we earnestly wish that the glory of the present contest for liberty may not be sullied by an attempt to restrain the Freedom of the Press."[9]

So far, Morris believed that any sign of overt opposition might throw the city into the hands of firebrands calling for complete independence. There were also sinister pockets of Toryism capable of causing serious mischief. Robert Livingston confessed to John Jay that he dreaded "division among ourselves infinitely more than the power of Great Britain." Faced with open rebellion, Morris shared with Livingston and Jay "the necessity of a serious regard to the affairs of our province." He agreed with Jay's favorite maxim that in such a crisis, "those who own the country ought to govern it." The crowd might "roar out" words like liberty, property, and religion, but the gentry "controlled the dictionary of the day, and like the mysteries of ancient mythology, it was not for profane eyes and ears."[10]

On May 8, 1775, fifteen days after the city's arsenal had been raided, alarmed freeholders of Westchester met in White Plains to elect delegates to the proposed Provincial Congress. Morris's middle-aged half-brother Lewis pulled himself out of his congenial role of lord of the manor and assumed the leadership of the Westchester Patriots. Some thought he was finally roused from his prosaic, foreordained existence because he had not been properly rewarded with public office by the crown.

The county leaned to the loyalist side led by Isaac Wilkins, an obstinate Tory and brother-in-law of the Morrises. Denouncing the patriot leadership as "void of common sense," Wilkins loudly proclaimed his hostility to these "illegal and disorderly…Committees, Associations and Congresses" in which the Morris brothers were now conspicuous. When Wilkins was out maneuvered and routed, Gouverneur, Lewis, and their followers celebrated their victory as they pranced their horses around the village green. Gouverneur was elected a delegate to New York's first Provincial Congress, and Lewis, the last lord of the Manor of Morrisania, was elected a delegate to the crucial Second Continental Congress where he would sign the Declaration of Independence.

Whatever their motives leading to the political skirmish in White Plains, both Lewis and Gouverneur harbored a strong emotional scorn for any threat of autocratic despotism coming from the mob in the street or from a remote government in London. Like their contentious grandfather, they wanted to govern themselves with the help of those of their neighbors who agreed with them. In retrospect, their slow evolution into revolutionaries reveals few signs of any emotion susceptible of analysis and was well under way before the encounters at Concord and Lexington or the White Plains elections. There is no single pronouncement suggesting that in their pragmatic act they realized they had stepped over the line into possibly fatal armed resistance.[11]

While insisting it was not in open rebellion, in fact, the new congress Morris joined assumed the full governing power and authority of New York's old Provincial Assembly. From Morris's perspective and understanding, he and the delegates were not acting outside the law in defense of it; rather, they believed their actions to be their God-given rights as Englishmen. These rights were no different, as John Jay declared in the First Continental Congress, whether a subject "live three thousand miles from the royal palace" or three hundred. It was the king who was the outlaw and the outrageous policies of Parliament that abused the law and the constitution, not the colonists. A provision strongly supported by Morris placed the political destiny of the colony in the hands of the Congress in Philadelphia with a declaration of intent to take up arms "to adopt and endeavor to carry into execution whatever measures may be recommended by the Continental Congress, or resolved upon our Provincial Convention, opposing the execution of the several arbitrary and oppressive Acts."[12]

No family expressed more painfully than the Morrises the bitter divisiveness of political warfare on the eve of the Revolution. By every outward sign of privilege, position, and family tradition, Morris's family appeared to represent the quintessential colonial clan of property with far more to lose than to gain by opposing the constituted authority of the crown. The awkward display of family tensions at the White Plains Court House election brought the feud to the surface when Wilkins tried to block Lewis Morris's selection as delegate to Philadelphia. Gouverneur's mother remained a disconsolate Tory, staying behind the British lines in occupied New York City. After Wilkins fled to

England, Sarah Morris rescued her daughter Isabella Wilkins and her children who had been driven from their home. Throughout the war, the loyalty of Gouverneur's mother to the crown was used by his political enemies to challenge his loyalty to the Revolution.

Five days after Morris joined, the upstart Provincial Congress of New York met on May 22 in the Royal Assembly's handsome chamber in city hall, with the British man-of-war *Asia*, bristling with sixty-four guns, anchored in the East River near Nutten (now Governor's) Island. The battleship was carrying orders to evacuate the Royal Irish regiment, the last contingent of troops stationed in Manhattan. More incendiary was the rumor that the token garrison numbering 107 soldiers would be shipped north to join General Thomas Gage's army at Boston, which was attempting to put down the insurrection in that city. This handful of troop kept to barrack for their own protection and was no threat to the colony, but it did pose a tempting excuse for troublemakers to provoke a confrontation.

Morris had an intuitive sense of the delicate strategy of the Continental Congress even if he might not have had all the details. Just as he had seen the dangers of mob action against loyalists, he immediately saw the threat of open clashes in the streets when the garrison was moved in rank to the waiting ship on June 6. If there was even a remote possibility that negotiations in the Continental Congress might prevent civil war, the Irish contingent must be gotten out of town without incident. At Morris's urging, the Provincial Congress took preemptive action to head off any street trouble, publishing orders that the people were "not to obstruct the embarkation of said troops, but permit them to depart this City peaceably."

An impatient John Adams called the tense days of June "a strange Oscillation between love and hatred, between War and Peace." Pushed by Philadelphia, New York was already taking steps to strengthen its defenses, removing the cannon and stores from the British forts at Crown Point and Ticonderoga, which had fallen that spring to Ethan Allen's Green Mountain Boys. The newly assembled Second Continental Congress rushed more warnings to the city to step up defense preparations. Fortifications and gun batteries around the approaches to Manhattan Island were quickly put in place. Consistent with Morris's cautious stance, Jay warned that in removing "Military Stores" in these defensive preparations, care was to be taken not to touch crown property. He also ordered an inventory to be made of any captured armament so they could be "safely returned when the restoration of the former harmony between great Britain and these colonies so ardently wished for by the latter shall render it prudent and consistent with the overwhelming law of self preservation."

On the same day that Morris and the New York Congress were warning citizens not to interfere with the departing British troops, the Continental

Congress reluctantly expressed its readiness to make one last attempt to negotiate with Parliament. While John Adams grumbled that such "Puerilities
become not a great assembly like this the Representative of a great People,"
John Jay was appointed to the committee he had promoted to draft a last-
ditch plea to the king, mostly the work of John Dickinson. Later known as the
Olive Branch Petition, it expressed the colonies' willingness to find a way to
resolve the issues in dispute. Morris, like Jay, still believed that reconciliation
was possible. To British eyes, however, the insurgent capture of Ticonderoga
and the defensive activities in and around New York undercut any professions
of peaceful reconciliation coming from Philadelphia.[13]

On the morning of June 6, Morris knew that the crown's troops, with their
arms and equipment, were ready to leave their barrack and move to the man-
of-war waiting in the harbor. He was at the corner of Broad Street and Beaver
when Marinus Willett, a zealous partisan decided to challenge the crown's
military authority single-handedly by grabbing the reins of the lead horse and
bringing the train to an abrupt halt. In the confusion, a crowd gathered, forcing all the loaded carts out of the line. Just as Willett started to address the
commanding officer, "Mr. Gouverneur Morris suddenly made his appearance," interrupting Willett's patriotic harangue and insisting on the authority
of the Provincial Congress, to allow the baggage carts to proceed. "To be
opposed by Mr. Morris stagard me," Willett recalled. A deferential man of the
people and member of the Sons of Liberty, Willett was clearly intimidated by
the imposing, fastidiously dressed young lawyer speaking with the authority of
the Provincial Congress. "He was a Whig of very respectable Connections," an
awed Willett remembered, "and tho young of Brilliant talents.... I doubt
whether all my Zeal and Enthusiasm would have supported me had it not
been for the arrival at that Critical moment by John Morin Scott."

Silenced by Morris's unexpected appearance, Willett was ready to cave in
to the tall patrician when he heard Scott's loud voice in the crowd exclaim,
"You are right Willett, the committee have not given them permission to carry
off spare arms." Speaking as a member of the committee, which had assumed
the powers of government in the city, Scott had become a ready leader of the
popular, antigovernment faction in the Provincial Congress. On Scott's cue,
Willett suddenly turned the head of the lead horse out of the line, ordering
the others to follow while the Irish recruits began to move toward the harbor
where they "embarked under the Hiffes of the citizens." Willett jumped on to
one of the stalled carts and urged the bewildered soldiers to give up their
"unnatural work of sheding the blood of their Countrymen." A few defected,
to the cheers of the crowd. Morris saw that it was hopeless to attempt to settle
the matter by himself, but four days later after tensions cooled he lost no time
in reversing the crowd's action by moving "that the Arms and military Accou-
terments taken from His Majesty's Troop on Tuesday last, be restored." The

Provincial Congress upheld Morris's resolution and its own untested authority by a vote of nineteen to four.[14]

To Morris, the protocol of friendly relations with both the civil and military agents of the English government had to be maintained at all cost, buying time while defensive plans were thrown together to "repel force with force," if pushed to it. Confronting Willett and the crowd in the street, his hopes of reconciliation were seriously challenged. Looking back with hindsight four years later, Morris decided that his and the Congress's defensive posture had been wrong and more aggressive action should have been taken after the battle at Bunker Hill. "Congress," he concluded in 1779, "at this time wore very much the appearance of pusillanimity."[15]

Morris's careful style in summer 1775 reflected that of the majority of the members of the Provincial Congress, an unsure body of hastily chosen, nervous delegates. Although lawyers and city merchants, whose combative rhetoric with Parliament had shifted from trade reforms to political rights were conspicuous, for the most part it was a colorless lot with little experience in the rudiments of statecraft. Of the 119 members, 19 would later move over to the loyalist side. Yet within the first few days, this irregular body without legal authority and representing every factional shade had somehow managed to convince the crown's representative, Lieutenant Governor Colden, to warn London that "the legal authority of Government is now superseded in this Place." Congress was "acting with all the confidence and authority of a legal government," ready to defend itself. Colden understood the message sent by the Provincial Congress when it adopted the Continental Congress's Declaration of Association with Morris's strong support, binding those who signed it to the decisions made in Philadelphia. It also proclaimed that any armed loyalist would be held as "an enemy of the Country." But to make sure that all bridges to conciliation were not burned—or was it just buying time to prepare for war?—a committee of the Provincial Congress was quickly named to draw up a plan for the Continental Congress to somehow close the breach with Parliament. Morris was made a member. Even before the Continental Congress had moved on the Olive Branch Petition, Morris had been working with his brother Lewis on a peace plan and as a diplomatic gesture had asked William Smith to send him his thoughts "on the Great Subject."[16]

From the first day of the Provincial Congress, Morris had matter-of-factly joined in the perilous, even treasonable, act of replacing the royal authority with an unprecedented experiment in self-government. It would build on the practical experience of self-government that had grown steadily in the colony over the past two decades. Any claim to being representative did not bear close scrutiny, given the emotional, irregular selection of delegates in the badly divided colony. Yet to its members, the atmosphere in this admittedly illegal laboratory was familiar, self-reliant, and temperamentally republican. Although much was confusing, unpredictable, and faintly bizarre at the time, it is clear that Morris, like many of his friends, was being subtly transformed from a British subject into a citizen of a new country that had not yet defined itself or the precise terms of its loyalty. In Morris's case, the lack of a single declaration or defining act makes it impossible to identify a moment of epiphany.

Unlike the introspective Peter Van Schaack, moaning that his mind was "distressed with the gloomy prospects" of his country, Morris's spirit seemed to soar when confronting the puzzling new obstacles. Personal reservations and family considerations were pushed into the background. For Morris, the prospects of revolutionary change offered an opportunity that was hard to resist by someone who thrived on the ingenious idealism of the inexperienced. At the time, John Jay grumbled that he had a "volatile" political streak in his character.

As the Provincial Congress struggled to build the machinery of government during its opening weeks, Morris's instinctive talent for public debate became evident: he spoke clearly and confidently on his feet. He had little competition from the other delegates who lacked his natural ability. "Gouv Morris cuts a figure... a very fine young fellow," an impressed Richard Montgomery, a dashing, fearless delegate from Dutchess County reported. Morris's steady gaze was focused on the immediate problems facing the unprecedented venture. Without fully realizing it, he was moving toward a turning point in his life, toward the beckoning, audacious career of a committed revolutionary patriot with an unknown future. Although he carefully avoided any appearance of equivocation as his optimism for conciliation slowly faded, the abrupt, unexpected changes of course in the roiling current carried him deeper and deeper into the patriotic cause.

The need for funds to operate the government was the first serious order of business of the Provincial Congress. On May 26, Morris was named to the committee to determine whether or how the Continental Congress should issue paper currency. He already had a reputation for a grasp of arcane financial problems. While he was clerking in William Smith's office, his persuasive argument against the colony's proposed financing by issuing bills of credit to pay for the French and Indian War debt revealed a precocious understanding of the colony's economic state.

Morris's bravado performance in the finance committee was carried out with an impeccable sense of urgency and drama. Leaving the question of how to pay for defense and war up to the vagaries of each state assembly would lead to disaster. At the crux of Morris's argument was a visionary comprehension of the need for a unifying political authority prepared to finance the fledgling state governments in revolt. Morris painted a tempting picture of a money tree, which the Continental Congress would establish and the former colonies could pluck at will. He recommended that the Continental Congress simply issue the entire fund and then apportion its obligation among the former colonies. The

Congress would print paper money and each province would be accountable for its share. Congress would pay any defaulting debt. This would insure a wide credit and circulation of the currency by guaranteeing the redemption of the currency issued. It would also strengthen the bond between the twelve—Georgia had not yet made it thirteen—struggling provincial assemblies beyond the unpredictable patriotic fervor fueled by the prospects of war.

The idea of a North American union, however tentative, seemed to fascinate Morris from the beginning of his political life. When the question of continental-provincial (or federal and state) relations came up on the first day of the New York Congress, he quickly endorsed Isaac Low's motion: "Resolved, as the opinion of this Congress, that explicit obedience ought to be paid to every recommendation of the Continental Congress, for the general regulation of associated colonies; but that this Congress is competent to and ought freely to deliberate and determine on all matters relative to the internal policies of this colony." The motion was defeated as both premature as well as an affront to state pride by conceding to the authority of the Continental Congress, but Morris continued to work for support of Philadelphia's paramount role in the escalating crisis. In his peace plan of accommodation, the provision for a permanent national assembly hinted at the direction of Morris's thinking. It would continue to grow in his imagination. The seed of his thinking may well have been in place as early as his graduation address at King's College when he declared that he was one of those "who can boast the glorious Title of free born American."[17]

Morris asked to postpone the debate on his financial plan for three days in order to invite the leading merchants to attend his presentation. His closing speech resulted in a unanimous approval. The merchant Egret Benson later recalled the impression the young lawyer had made: "Mr. Morris appeared to have comprehended it [paper currency] throughout, and as it were by intuition. He advanced and maintained opinions new to all. There was none who did not ultimately perceive and acknowledge them to be just."[18]

Morris's report was then sent to Philadelphia where it was adopted by an impressed Continental Congress. While Congress struggled with the mechanics of printing, numbering, and signing the new bills, the New York government lost no time in letting its delegates in Philadelphia know just how desperate things were getting. All the work on defenses was outrunning any means to pay for it. "For God's sake," they demanded, "send us money, send us arms, send us ammunition."

Membership on the committee drafting a "Plan of Accommodation" for consideration by the Continental Congress gave Morris his last opportunity to advance his hope for a solution short of war. To New York, it was also an important gesture calculated to hold the weak, divided coalition of the de facto provincial government together. By offering a plan for negotiations to "prevent the horrors of civil war," the Provincial Congress and its fractured members would not be seen as a rogue body in open rebellion. The range of conflicting opinions on such a delicate subject, however, made it far more difficult to draft a coherent report than it had been to set out a formula to fix financial problems, where Morris was the sole recognized expert.

Little more than three weeks after the committee went to work on its recommendations, Morris drafted a letter to the colony's delegates in Philadelphia for the signature of Peter Van Brugh Livingston, the president of the Provincial Congress. It opened with a polished statement of the volatile issues.

> The Breach hath been widened since our first Dispute on the Subject of Taxation; and as this was the Source of all our Grievances, so we have the hope that the Temptation being taken away, our Civil and religious and political Rights, will be easily adjusted and confirmed.... We must now repeat to You, the common and just Observation that contests for Liberty, fostered in their Infancy by the virtuous and wise, become Sources of Power to wicked and designing Men. From whence it follows that such Controversies as we are now engaged in, frequently end in the Demolition of those Rights and Privileges, which they were instituted to defend. We pray you therefore to use every Effort for the compromising of this unnatural Quarrel between the Parent and Child.[19]

In Morris's judgment, the final recommendations from the New York Congress were badly flawed with irrelevant issues. He was impatient with the committee's slow progress, so he had prepared a long draft of a proposed report, "to which," he rather arrogantly told John Jay, "the members could make no Objections excepting that none of them could understand it." In a shorter version, he kept to what he believed to be the key issues: the colonial right to levy taxes and to conduct its internal affairs without interference. Morris conceded Parliament's imperial right to regulate trade and for colonial contributions to the defense of the empire. But that was not all. The New York plan called for "a Continental Congress deputed from the several Colonies, to meet with a President appointed by the Crown." In other words, the tentative union of the colonies expressed by their Philadelphia Congress and Association would become, according to Morris's plan, a virtually autonomous institution of national government of the colonies within the framework of the empire.

The New York committee accepted Morris's abbreviated draft but insisted on two additional articles, which he thought were completely irrelevant. One article with a strong anti-Catholic bias of intolerance condemned "the indulgence and establishment of Popery all along the interior confines of the old Protestant colonies" from the old Quebec boundaries running to the Ohio River. The other article called for the repeal of all acts objected to in its initial association drawn up by the first Continental Congress.

Before the approved plan was forwarded to Philadelphia, Morris fired off a private letter to his friend Jay: "The foolish Religious business. I opposed until I was weary." It was "arrant Nonsense and would do as well in a high Dutch Bible as the Place it now stands in." Although he voted against the final text, he managed to insert a warning "that neither the Parliament of Great Britain, or any other earthly legislature or tribunal, ought or can interfere or interpose in any wise howsoever, in the religious and ecclesiastical concerns of the Colonies." At the last minute, Morris also shrewdly managed to add that no part of the report was binding on the New York delegates in the Continental Congress.[20]

When the New York plan reached Philadelphia, Jay's committee took Morris's hint that it could ignore the recommendations "provided our essential Rights be secured on solid Foundations we may safely permit the British parliament to use big sounding Words." Jay, the staunch Protestant, nevertheless agreed with his friend that it was no time to stir up religious rows, "disputes on ecclesiastical Points, which have for ages had no other Tendency than that of banishing Peace and Charity from the world."[21]

By summer 1775, all the former colonies except for Maryland and Pennsylvania were now under the extralegal direction of the Continental Congress working through the independent provincial conventions and congresses. (Georgia signed up on July 6.) With money being printed and an army raised by its orders, Philadelphia had established, in spite of itself, the beginnings of a confederation. On June 21, a discouraged William Smith noted in his diary that the Congress had "appointed Genl Washington Generalisimo of the Boston army." More accurately, Washington had been named "General and commander-in-chief of the United Colonies," invested with "full power and authority... for the welfare of the service."[22]

It was poor timing when on Sunday morning, June 25, the *Juliana,* carrying the royal governor of New York, William Tryon, arrived at Sandy Hook from England where he had been on leave for more than a year. Around noon the same day "the rebel Generals" Washington, Philip Schuyler, and Charles Lee with his pack of hounds, arrived from Philadelphia on the Jersey shore opposite the city. Washington and Lee were on their way to Boston. Schuyler, a frail but tough Albany squire, had been named to command the military expedition against Canada. There had been little warning of a likely collision between the crown's representative and Congress's military leader.

A warm Sunday afternoon had filled the tree-lined streets with people, disguising the divided, tense city. Morris was named to the greeting committee to work out the delicate choreography designed to avoid any embarrassing confrontations. After the committee settled the timing and staging and notified the Washington party of the risky contingencies, Morris along with Richard Montgomery crossed the Hudson and briefed the Philadelphia visitors waiting on the Jersey side, alerting them to an official reception around 4 P.M., when they

stepped ashore in Manhattan. To avoid a diplomatic collision of comic proportions, Governor Tryon remained fuming on the *Juliana* until later in the evening.

Judge Jones's Tory bias placed the stirring Washington tableau "amidst the
repeated shouts and huzzas of the seditious and rebellious multitude." With
eight militia companies lined up in rank on the city's commons, the enthusiastic crowd appeared to give the lie to the rumors that New York was lukewarm
to the American cause. Wearing an impressive new purple sash over his blue
uniform and with a waving plume in his hat, the general stood as tall as young
Morris in the greeting party. It was the largest ceremonial welcome the Virginian had ever faced.

Earlier that morning, the Provincial Congress had stopped an express
rider headed for Philadelphia carrying a sealed letter from the Massachusetts
Congress addressed to John Hancock, president of the Continental Congress.
The letter confirmed that there had been a bloody battle in Boston.
Charlestown Neck was lost along with Breed's Hill and Bunker Hill, but the
British had paid a high price. The Massachusetts authorities warned Philadelphia that they were running out of gunpowder. Holding up the official parade
to the commons, Washington wrote Hancock, to apologize for opening his
mail and assure him he would do whatever he could about the gunpowder crisis although New York was also in bad shape, having shipped every pound it
could spare to Boston three days earlier.

At eight o'clock on the evening of Washington's arrival, a hastily orches-
trated body of his Majesty's Council, the judges of the Supreme Court, and
the governors of King's College along with Morris and the committee of the
Provincial Congress repeated their greetings to the tired, sullen royal governor.
"What a farce!" Jones raged later in his *History*. "What cursed! A scheme was
at this very time laid by these people to subvert the British Government in the
Colonies, in Church and State, and to erect one of their own upon its ruins."
William Smith managed to whisper in the ear of the irritated governor "that
there was a great & strange Reverse since he left us in the State of our Public
Affairs." The governor could only answer with a "distracted sigh."[23]

The next morning Morris was up early and in the assembly when Washington met with the delegates, described by Billy Smith as being in "pompous
attendance." Their diplomatic address ended with prudent advice to the general "that whenever this important contest will be decided, by the fondest wish
of each American soul, an accommodation with our Mother Country, you will
cheerfully resign the important deposit committed into your hands and reas-
sume the character of our worthiest citizen." At that moment, New York's
patriots were not quite ready to give up all hope of an accommodation. The
ceremonies of tribute by the Provincial Congress managed to delay the party's
departure until late afternoon. Before the Congress reluctantly brought the
eulogies to a conclusion, its members managed to include all shades of opinion

in their address, steering a masterful middle course: while deploring the "calamities of this divided Empire," they went on to "rejoice in the appointment of a gentleman from whose abilities we are taught to expect both security and peace."[24]

Throughout June and July, Morris attended the meetings of the Provincial Congress almost every day at city hall, rushing through business, often putting in sixteen hour days, and working late into the evening to execute the legislative decisions. Without precedent and with only the vaguest notion of what was expected of him, he and the members had to test their authority and strategies at every step. They had no way to gauge the extent of their public support beyond their private measure of the town's erratic temperature in the streets and alehouses. On July 8, Morris was appointed to the first Committee of Safety, a device allowing it to act on behalf of the Congress for two weeks in July when no quorum could be assembled, cleverly hiding this dispiriting fact from the enemy. By August, with Congress back in session, Morris was anxious to return to his neglected law practice while carefully watching developments as the climate changed.

On the night of August 23, a shattering boom from the *Asia*, anchored off the Battery, woke the sleeping city. It was a signal of an abrupt rise of temperature and tension that could lead to a disastrous showdown. One of the warship's sloops, carrying a load of armed sailors, had been spotted by the town's guards with muskets loaded, primed, and cocked. When one of the sailors in the sloop fired his musket, the Americans were ready and opened fire. Panic spread in the dark streets when the city's residents first heard the exchange, followed by the *Asia*'s thirty-two-gun broadside, blasting away with an unmistakable warning.

The trouble had been precipitated by the provocateur Isaac Sears, who had maneuvered the Congress into agreeing to secure canon and military stores to defend the Highlands, a narrow stretch of the Hudson between Peekskill and West Point. What he did not reveal until it was too late was his plan to appropriate the British canon on the Battery below Fort George and haul them up to the Highland forts. To cover the men removing the guns during the night of the twenty-third, a company of enthusiastic ringleaders and soldiers formed a semicircle of musketmen facing the harbor. The British sloop coming close to the shore to see what the Americans were up to triggered the exchange.

Governor Tryon was also surprised and shaken and quickly called a conference the next morning with members of the Provincial Congress and town leaders in the council room at city hall. Outmanned and outgunned, Morris realized the serious implications of the unexpected ruckus the night before. An atmosphere of conciliation swept through the room of the "peace talks" as both sides scrambled to calm the dangerous situation. Papering over the embarrassing events after a family quarrel, everyone reached for accommodating gestures but left a field of confusion and nervous guesses of what might follow. In the next few days, a flurry of advertisements for houses to rent on Long Island and New Jersey appeared in the newspapers. In increasing numbers, those who could afford it, fled to the country as the town took on an abandoned, disconsolate look. Morris's moderate policy of accommodation had failed while the militants had exposed the limits to which the British could be pushed. But it did not take long for the town's shock to turn into apathy.

As the fall wore on, the policy of nonimportation enforced by the Provincial Congress took a serious toll on the city's faltering economy. Armed neutrality had its price. Without English imports, business came to a standstill. The hope of reconciliation grew dimmer by the day. In October, Washington warned Congress he saw no hope for conciliation and that the British were preparing to vigorously prosecute the war. When Governor Tryon received word that there were patriotic plans afoot to make him prisoner, he took refuge on HMS *Duchess of Gordon* parked in the harbor. To give his retreat a respectable spin, a wily William Smith advised the governor to say that it would enable him to "Check upon the Ships of War who might insult the Town." All official business was then conducted on the secure decks of the British man-of-war.

By November, so many representatives were absent that the first Provincial Congress was forced to close down without formal adjournment and new elections were announced. Friends of Morris like Philip Livingston and James Duane, both delegates in Philadelphia, had moved their families out of the city to safety in the countryside. The derelict streets and empty shuttered houses gave the town an ominous look of a collapsing society.

The election for a new congress was set for November 7, and it would turn out that the Second Provincial Congress was just as timid as the first. When, with difficulty, a bare quorum of twenty-three members out of the seventy-four that were chosen finally met on December 1, Morris was not among the elected. The hopeless irresolution of the Second Congress during its brief life of six weeks was a failure hiding the hardening opposition of public opinion well beyond Morris's immediate circle. In the last issues of the patriotic journal *The Monitor*, published just before the year was out, the vacillating politicians of the Congress were pilloried: "nothing wise, provident, manly or decisive is to be expected; a scandalous remissness, imbecility and inaction, characterize the general current of affairs."[25]

On January 10, 1776, a pamphlet entitled *Common Sense* was published in Philadelphia and, in William Smith's words, was "industriously distributed by the emissaries of Congress throughout the continent." One hundred thousand copies in twenty-seven editions would quickly flood the colonies. Shortly after it appeared on the streets of New York, Hugh Hughes wrote Samuel Adams: "The people are determined to read and think as they please. It is certain...that there never was any thing published here within these thirty years, or so since I have been in this place, that has been more universally approved and admired." When New York loyalists published a sharp rebuttal to Tom Paine's explosive tract, a body of "warm, inveterate republicans" led by Isaac Sears, after first preparing itself in Drakes Tavern, broke into the printer's house in the middle of the night, "pulled him out of bed, and forcibly seized upon and destroyed the whole impression with the original manuscript." The next morning, every printer in town received a warning from "the committee of tarring and feathering" that "destruction, ruin and perdition" would be their fate if they printed "anything against the rights and liberties of America." These were the same people, Judge Jones wrote in disgust, who were themselves "contending for *liberty*."[26]

To Morris as well as to his friends Robert Livingston, John Jay, and other members of his elite coterie, it was apparent that if the empire was abandoned, some kind of "good and well ordered" constitutional government led by "free born Americans" was the only alternative to "that Anarchy which already too much prevails." Wavering loyalty to a remote monarch three thousand miles away was no longer a solution. Livingston told Duane that "another year of war and devastation" would turn him into a republican.

Early in January, the king's October speech to Parliament reached New York papers. In it he declared his intention to end the rebellion "by the most decisive terms," offering no compromise to "the authors and promoters of this desperate conspiracy." In a quick response to the king's message, General Charles Lee prepared to bring his troops into the city on the orders of Congress to fortify it against an expected British attack. New York was reduced to a ghost town, a Connecticut patriot recorded; "you would scarce see any person or but few in the street, carts and wagons all employed in carrying out goods and furniture, the men-o-war lying broadside against the town and near the wharfs sails bent and prepared at a moments warning. Their present consternation in New York arises from the near approach of Gen'l Lee."[27]

On January 6, 1776, William Smith glumly conceded that the news "greatly inflamed the multitude upon the certain prospect of a new [military] campaign.... The Clouds are indeed Dark, from the Obstinacy and Pride of both Countries." General Lee, wiry, weak-chinned, and as offhand in his dress as Washington was punctilious, lost no time in taking charge when he arrived from Cambridge. The brilliant, eccentric, British-trained soldier of fortune who had fought for the king of Poland knew what he was doing as he proceeded to prepare the town for battle, giving no quarter to the conflicted and weak-kneed.[28]

Sometime in that dark January as the city was turned into a battlefield, it appeared to Morris's realistic mind that further "appeals to reason" were useless. The king's angry words calling leaders like the Morrises "dangerous and ill-designing Men" made any more "Olive Branch" gestures useless. To Morris, the fundamental principles of government by consent and no taxation without representation, very old, very simple, and very important arguments, were reason and doctrine enough. His formal commonplace words written two years later to Peter Van Schaack, that when the appeal was to the sword, he felt it his duty "to join in the great cause," gives no hint of any inner reservations. For Morris, there was no looking back or agonizing over his decision once the line was crossed. Here he was totally unlike his friend who, rightly and nostalgically, feared that the colony and its way of life would never return "to the old channels and that affection which is the bond of our common union with the mother country."[29]

On February 27, 1776, New Yorkers finally learned that two months earlier, in December, Parliament had placed the thirteen colonies beyond the pale of British law by interdicting all trade with them. Any American who did not immediately make unconditional submission to the crown's authority was declared a rebel. Delivered in slow motion underlining the psychological as well as the physical distance that separated the parties, the Prohibitory Bill put an official end to Morris's failed hope for a negotiated peace. As Morris told Charles Lee, the slightest sign of wavering to join the patriots was "branded with Infamy." Any wobblings now were out of the question. He admitted that he and everyone else suddenly went out of their way to express "the excess of his Zeal by the Madness of his Actions."[30]

Somehow, "old channels" and the provincial sentiments of a "bond" with the empire no longer held any appeal to Morris. He had moved well beyond the so-called turning point in the country's history. Three generations of American Morrises, beginning with his orphaned, independent, successful grandfather, had established for Morris a far greater sense of being an unfettered American rather than a second-class, bullied subject living on the edge of the imperial system in which he had little political or social stake.

When Morris learned that a battalion in defense of New York was being organized, he decided to apply for a commission on little more than the class conceit that it was his duty and privilege. Like many of his friends, he suffered from the assumption that the Revolution ought to be a gentleman's war, at least in its direction, and the rank and file ought to be grateful. In making this enthusiastic, patriotic, even arrogant gesture, he never stopped to consider the fact that he had not had a single day of military experience in his life. When the gentry insisted on appointing their own officers, the Provincial Congress rejected their plan, proposing as colonel John Lasher, a cobbler by trade but a man who had solid militia experience. Morris's nomination as lieutenant colonel would have made him subordinate to a shoemaker. He hotly complained to his brother that he was very sorry to find that "a herd of Mechanics are preferred before the best Families in the Colony." Later when the Continental Congress, asserting its control over military affairs, rejected all New York nominations, including Morris's, he wrote his brother that he had offered his services "merely for the Benefit of the general Cause," adding with a remarkable insight that his abilities "were more adapted to the deliberations of the Cabinet than the glorious Labours of the Field."[31]

In the military mobilization of the people, Morris first confronted, head on, the politics of the rising new democracy as a force to be reckoned with, deciding that he was not yet prepared to fully accommodate this social and political alteration. The new political climate was changing the rules, cutting across the established social lines that defined a vanishing world. No one was less equipped to lead independent farmers and mechanics into battle. To the troops, his very name would have been suspect. He was shocked, he wrote Robert Livingston in late fall 1775, that the new military organizations were "officered by the vulgar" drawn from the ranks of ordinary people.[32]

After he was elected to the Third Provincial Congress of New York in spring 1776, Morris returned to the "the deliberations of the Cabinet," his natural habitat. His new acquaintance, the precocious Alexander Hamilton, consumed with dreams of military glory, was appointed captain in command of a provincial company of artillery. Morris's position in the New York Congress put him in regular contact with Hamilton who was coordinating the state's troops with Washington's Continental Army.

The decisive battle between the old order and the new, threatened for most of Morris's twenty-four years, was about to be joined. Only a few like Peter Van Schaack, and not without great personal cost, held to their tormented, riven consciences and attempted to avoid taking sides. Morris now took his place in the forefront of the Patriotic cause.

CHAPTER 4

"The Great Question of Independency"

WHEN Gouverneur Morris learned that the Continental Congress had, on April 6, 1776, declared American ports open to the entire world—except Great Britain—he knew that the breach had suddenly widened. The colonies had cut themselves adrift under the banner of a new government in all but name. Morris had always considered the regulation of trade one of the essential elements of a government's sovereignty. His failed peace plan of a year earlier had, in fact, conceded the ordering of colonial trade to Parliament in a futile attempt to find a compromise to the quarrel. Simply put, the congressional resolution, in response to Parliament's effort to close American ports, had broken the British colonial economic system by severing all trading ties with the mother country. Even though one New York Whig whistling in the dark on the same day declared that Philadelphians "have never lisped the least desire for independence," political independence was now inevitable.[1]

A little past noon a week later, on April 13, General Washington, his adjutant general Horatio Gates, and their staff lumbered into an almost empty town of shuttered and boarded-up houses. They brought with them from Boston an army of fewer than ten thousand, a force far too small to defend the city. Without ceremony, Washington went straight to William Smith's house at 5 Broadway, which had been temporarily commandeered for his headquarters. Like many of his neighbors who had abandoned the city, the old lawyer rusticated at Haverstraw, his country estate thirty miles north of the city, still hoping the storm would somehow blow itself out.[2]

The defense of New York and the capture of Quebec were uppermost on the generalissimo's mind, and he was anxious to get to work. Charles Lee had spelled out New York's dangerous predicament: "the uncertainties of the enemy's designs and motion, who can fly in an instant to any spot where they chose with their canvass wings, throw me or Julius Caesar into this inevitable dilemma.... I can only act with surmise and have a very good chance of surmising wrong." In a matter of days, Washington's strategy, following on Lee's advance work, turned the city into a temporary rebel stronghold according to Thomas Jones, further isolating the Tories and their uncertain followers: "The rebel army took possession of the city, converted it into a garrison, pulled down houses, dug up streets, built fortifications, and threatened, robbed, confined, imprisoned, and banished his majesty' loyal subjects without mercy."[3]

Morris, the congressional delegate, enthusiastically backed the depredations of the rebel military authority described by Jones. Before Washington moved his headquarters to New York, General Lee, had taken matters into his own hands when he arrived in the city, cheerfully rounding up suspected loyalists and confining or banishing them right and left. His brusque strategy shocked many of the fence-sitters out of their lethargy. There was no room for vacillation. He personally administered his own, quite original oath of allegiance to suspects, contrary to orders of the Continental Congress that this was strictly a matter for civil authorities. Those who refused summary redemption at the hands of the ferocious Lee were clapped in jail or deported under military order. Although he could not prevent the city's capture by tearing up streets, cutting trees, and throwing up earth works, it would cost the enemy, like at Bunker Hill, a very high price. On February 19, Lee had reported his plans for the city's defense to Washington in Boston: "Tomorrow I shall begin to dismantle that part of the fort next to the town, to prevent it being converted into a citadel. I shall barrier the principle streets, and at least if I cannot make it a continental garrison, it shall be a disputable field of battle."[4]

Morris found himself in the middle of all the tension and confusion fed by rumors of Tory plots. In March, Philadelphia declared open season on anyone "inimical to the grand cause," which included Morris's two brothers-in-law. John Adams told Washington that the "dangerous banditti of tories" in New York were no better than British troops, to be dealt with as he saw fit. An agitated Continental Congress recommended the disarming of "all who have not associated, and refuse to associate, to defend by arms these united colonies." After some debate, the New York Congress had passed the resolution on to local committees but cautioned them to "use all possible prudence and moderation."[5]

During the spring days following the April decree that opened American ports to the world, agitation for independence picked up in Philadelphia. New York warned its Philadelphia delegation, however, not to go too fast. On April 12, the delegates received instructions "to concert and determine upon such measures as shall be judged most effectual for the preservation and re-establishment of American rights and privileges," with the added flickering hope "for the restoration of harmony between great Britain and the Colonies." New York's delegates were not released from these waffling instructions until July 9, after independence had been approved and the Declaration of Independence published.

On May 10, Morris learned, the Continental Congress had advised New York and the other colonies to immediately "adopt such government as shall, in the opinion of the Representatives of the People best conduce to the happiness and safety of their constituents." A few days later, Philadelphia made clear that the next step—Adams called it the last—would be independence by adding to its earlier resolution the following preamble: "it is necessary that the exercise of every kind of authority under the said crown should be totally suppressed, and all the powers of government exerted, under the authority of the people of the colonies...for the defence of their lives, liberties and properties, against the hostile invasions and cruel depredations of their enemies."[6]

When Morris stood for reelection from Westchester County, the props were in place for the curtain to rise on the brief first act of New York's version of the revolutionary drama, the opening of the Third Provincial Congress. The election was speedy when Morris along with other patriots—John Jay, James Duane, Francis Lewis, and Philip Livingston—was reelected from the old congress. Jay, Lewis, and Duane also remained as delegates to the Continental Congress in Philadelphia. With the loyalists effectively defeated in the election, the big issues would no longer be fought out at the polls.[7]

When Morris did not turn up for the first day's session of the Congress in city hall, the embarrassing political fracture of the Morris family was again exposed in yet another display of divided loyalties. On May 14, his brother-in-law Vincent Ashfield had been arrested and summarily jailed for refusing to sign the association's oath of allegiance. Morris's terrified and expectant sister Sarah Ashfield had no one but him to turn to for help, thus delaying his joining the new Congress.[8]

Morris was in his seat on May 24, however, when Congress confronted head-on three critical revolutionary questions: the silencing of the Tory opposition, independence, and the creation of a permanent governmental structure for the colony. On all three issues, Morris was eager to weigh in with ready arguments. While he agreed with the "boldly cautious" Jay in Philadelphia, who dismissed the extremists on both sides of the issue as either "all Flame or all Frost," Morris's sense of urgency, like that of the fire-eating Charles Lee, was greater, carried along particularly by the frantic military preparations being carried out around the city under the tough leadership of Lee.[9]

The small assembly room was packed when Morris with his decisive high-bridged profile calmly "opened the business by a long argument showing the necessity of the measure [to form a new government], and that this is the crisis in which it should be done." This was one of the few things on which he agreed with Thomas Paine who urged in *Common Sense,* "The present time...is that peculiar time which never happens to a nation but once...to form the noblest, purest constitution on the face of the earth. We have it in our power to begin the world all over again."[10]

For Morris, the linking of imminent independence with the imperative need to form a regular government was clear. In his judgment, a new government should come first. In the confusion of war, extralegal committees were unable to provide the stability and legitimacy offered by a permanent constitution. Without a formal structure of authority, private property and individual freedoms were threatened by anarchy. As John Jay had written to Alexander McDougall earlier in April, framing a new government was the first order of business: "The first Thing therefore in my Opinion to be done is to erect good and well ordered Governments in all the Colonies, and thereby exclude that Anarchy which already too much prevails."[11]

Morris was well aware that the tensions he outlined in his famous letter to Thomas Penn in 1774 were building between those—the "unfranchised masses"—who advocated democratic ideals and those, like himself, who would put some limit on popular participation. Even the populist Paine admitted that it was dangerous if "The Mind of the multitude is left at random," free to "pursue such as fancy presents." To Morris, if the ordinary people would follow the reasonable Whig gentlemen like himself, the dangers of both tyranny and anarchy could be avoided. Here again the use of threadbare labels like "conservative" or "aristocratic" are misleading for the times. Panic brought on by "intestine broils," under whatever name, could lead the country into chaos with the dissolution of ties to Parliament and the abandonment of colonial charters.[12]

The issue had been framed in a resolution by John Jay who asked the Provincial Congress to address the question of a new plan of government "with full power to deliberate and determine on every question whatever, that may concern or effect the interest of this colony, and to conclude upon, ordain, and execute every act and measure, which to them shall appear conducive to the happiness, security and welfare of this colony." It was, as Jay put it, "the great question of independency," the question that had been incubating in Morris's mind for weeks. His advance preparation allowed him to take the offensive.

Throughout his oration to the Congress, delivered from notes, Morris's clear, resolute identity as an American is striking. The word "American" like "democrat" was just coming into common use and both words, more often than not, were used in a pejorative, mocking tone by the British. "America" and "American" are proudly invoked nine times in the surviving sixteen-page fragment, a reminder to Morris's audience that they were now distinguished by their new unity brought on by the break with Britain over accountability, the crux of the issue.[13]

After dismissing all hope for a peace treaty, which he called the phantom of reconciliation, Morris starkly declared, "a connection with Great Britain cannot again exist, without enslaving America, *an independence is absolutely necessary.*" Referring to the question of the use of colonial tax revenues, Morris elevated the issue to the general exercise of power. "*Power can not safely be entrusted to Men, who are not accountable to those over whom it is exercised.* On this Rock I build."

Independence was not just the prerequisite to considering a new government. The very act of forming a new government would assume, in fact, an independent state. Some tepid delegates like James Duane questioned Morris's timing. Such a move was "too precipitate." That independence might bring "all the powers of Europe on our back, as by a general consent, to share our country amongst them" was dismissed by Morris as a "hackneyed topic," and he disposed of it in short order with persuasive reasons: "Nations do not make war without some view. Should they be able to conquer America, it would cost them more to maintain such conquest" than the value of the fee simple of the country. As for a protracted war, the logistics of maintaining three-thousand-mile supply lines over "a boisterous ocean" made it unlikely that the British would undertake such a venture. This would certainly be the outcome, he argued, if an American navy was quickly organized to defend the country's shores.[14]

Britain's protection was another illusion that some in the audience clung to. "*Protection,* Sir, is a very good thing," Morris admitted ironically, "yet a man may pay too much for diamonds. There is a common story of a certain juggler, who would undertake to cut off a man's head, and clap it back on again so neatly, as to cure him without a scar. Much such sort of juggling business is this protection we are to receive. Great Britain will not fail to bring us into a war with some of her neighbors, and then protect us as a lawyer defends a suit; the client paying for it." But "a wise man," he concluded, "would rather, I think, get rid of the suit and the lawyer together." The twenty-four-year-old legislator's most impressive argument, however, was in his conclusion, when he echoed John Adams in stating that America had already evolved into an "independent State" in all but name. Both the Continental Congress and the Provincial Congress had assumed at least the basic elements, Morris argued, and had already taken on the "grand lineaments and characteristics which mark out independence."[15]

At times, Morris's argument appears bifurcated, addressing both the Provincial and the Continental Congresses. Not only could the scarcely formed government of New York execute essential functions of legislation and security even without an executive branch, the Continental Congress also had superior and more efficient aspects of sovereignty of "coining money, raising armies, regulating commerce, peace, war." Peace and war, as he and everyone else knew from their history books, signified the ultimate power of sovereignty. The presence of Washington's Continental Army had already announced the sovereignty of the new nation to the world when he took command.[16]

With remarkable vision, Morris also saw the act of independence opening up the possibility of western expansion, with all it implied in growth and national wealth. Parliament had repeatedly been unable to extend law and order over the colonial frontier. "We never yet had a Government in this Country of sufficient Energy to restrain the lawless and the indigent. Whenever a Form of Government is established which deserves the Name, these Insurrections must cease." The western settlements "acknowledge no authority but their own" beyond the reach of both the colonies and London and would pose a serious threat to future peace and security if they were not brought within the new framework. As these settlements grew but were separated from the sea by the original colonies, they might be tempted to "carve out a passage to the ocean." Now was the moment to seize the opportunity and bring that wilderness with its still scattered pioneers within the fold of the new nation. "Those settlements, sensible of their present weakness and our power, will be made under the authority of that body, which is the legislature of the continent. They will constantly look up to it for laws and protection."

No one at that moment was thinking, as Adams recalled, "of consolidating this vast Continent under one national government." But Morris saw something more than a loose confederation of independent states. His words unequivocally predicted the outlines of the distant federal Constitution with its sovereign, national powers extending into new territory. He anticipated not only the constitutional settlement of 1787 but, by thirty years, his support of Jefferson's Louisiana Purchase in 1803. With the unparalleled advantages of a free and flourishing commerce and new wealth, the increase of territory and population would in his prescient words "cause all nations to resort hither as an asylum from oppression." Although it was embryonic in its details, Morris was setting out his core revolutionary principle, a principle that would shape his unwavering political values throughout his life. It represented a sharp alternative vision to the "pure republicanism" later advanced by the Jeffersonians and defenders of states' rights, that the Revolution was, by implication, libertarian in spirit, opposed to all but the most essential intervention or discipline by a central government.

To Morris, even in spring 1776, the ultimate sovereignty should rest with the national state and its ability to discipline and bind its unruly, restless individualistic parts given to "capricious legislation," often at the expense of individual or minority liberties. Without this discipline, Morris argued, a nation with settled habits and customs simply could not be created out of volatile democratic chaos. Or as he put it many years later, it would be "as vain to expect permanency from democracy, as to construct a palace on the surface of the sea." It was a position that Alexander Hamilton would later champion as the leader of the Federalist party. In the words of one historian, it was the only way that these framers—Morris, Washington, Franklin, Jay, and, of course, Hamilton—hammering out the checks and balances in the Constitution of 1787 "got us from the short run to the long run."[17]

As for the "inconveniences," the increase of population would bring about the "regulated" power of a strong Constitution, giving "perfect freedom" by protecting civil liberties and at the same time dampen down if not eliminate "intestine broils." While admitting that some of his patrician friends might lose "a little consequence, and importance by living in a country where all are on an equal footing," it was a small price. On the other hand, "the Indulgence of a few in Luxurious Ease, to the Prejudice of their fellow Creatures, is at best not laudable; but when it tends to thin the Ranks of Mankind, and to encourage a general Profligacy of Manners, it is then," he argued, "criminal in the highest degree." Classical virtue—honor, justice, courage, humanity—the moral authority in such a civil society, however, would always be esteemed, "and that alone should be respected in any country."

When it came to the immediate political question of actually forming a new state government, Morris did not believe New York's Third Congress had the express authority to do so. This was more than a procedural question. It was a profound intellectual issue of governance that Morris cared deeply about. Even with the danger of an invasion by General William Howe's army and the British fleet, there was still time to move with constitutional decorum beyond the mere drafting and passing of bills. A wartime government needed all the popular legitimacy it could muster. Since widespread warfare would make a later popular ratification impossible, Morris urged the participation of the people as essential at the outset. He believed that government rested on the assumption, as he would later draft into the federal Constitution, that it was an act of "the people." The people of New York had not yet given their consent, but Morris's solution was somewhat ambiguous by not actually calling for a convention. Instead, he asked for an express referendum by the people to approve "a recommendation" that the Congress frame a government.

John Morin Scott, an impatient member of the Congress and Morris's ready adversary, wanted independence immediately. He was indifferent to constitutional theory or refinements, arguing that Morris's resolution was too time-consuming, merely a delaying tactic by the conservatives. Scott's friends in the Mechanics Committee, watching the proceedings, saw in Morris's proposal the danger of a designing "oligarchy" consolidating its power while it stalled. To many, the influence of Morris's circle—Jay, Duane, the Livingstons—was dubious. As one suspicious contemporary put it, there were forces who were "for keeping as near the old form of government" as possible. They did not seem to grasp that a later legislature of a de facto government could, with impunity, easily wipe out any civil safeguards adopted earlier: "a Constitution," the citizens of Concord, Massachusetts, warned their provincial congress, "alterable by the Supreme Legislative is no Security at all to the Subject against Encroachment of the Governing part on any or on all their Rights and privileges." Scott quickly moved to derail Morris's motion, arguing that the Provincial Congress did have power to form a government.[18]

Jay and Scott were named to a committee to solve the conundrum. Instead of calling for a special constitutional convention, the committee recommended the immediate election of a Fourth Provincial Congress or Convention, as it would soon call itself, authorized to consider "the necessity and propriety of instituting such new Government as...is described and recommended in the resolves of the Constitutional Congress." If the decision was affirmative, then the Congress or convention could move forward to "establish such government as they shall deem calculated to secure the rights, liberty and happiness of the good people of this colony." Morris's insistence on legitimacy through the fiction of popular sovereignty was upheld when the special committee's resolution was adopted on May 31, calling for the election of a new congress with the power to deal with the question of a constitution. In effect, Morris had given the Mechanics exactly what they wanted, a government constituted by the will of the people.

Two days before, on May 29, the Mechanics Committee had petitioned the New York Congress to instruct the Continental delegates "to use their utmost endeavors...to cause these united colonies to become independent of Great Britain." The Congress suspended business to hear the Mechanics address. With Morris's efforts, the provincial body was determined to keep tight control of the divisive question of independence and the question of a new government. Morris had urged in his oration that "Everything like Independence should form secret Articles." Ambassadors should be sent to European courts and informed by the Articles of Treaty that independence was a fait accompli. "This Measure, will both discourage and preclude, impertinent Enquerry: and when the People of this Country enjoy the solid Advantages which arise from our Measures, they will thank us for the Deception."

The diplomatic but firm reply to the Mechanics sounds very much like Morris, who had earlier declared that he was not proposing "to hire a Number of Men to go and bawl Independence along the Continent." The Third Provincial Congress's message was also reserved and noncommittal on independence because the new elections were still pending. It not only intended to protect its own deliberations, it also recognized the ultimate supremacy of Philadelphia: "We are of the opinion that the Continental Congress alone have that enlarged view of our political circumstances which will enable them to decide upon those measures which are necessary for the general welfare."

The New York Congress was still sharply divided on the "great question" and ignored their Continental delegates' request for instructions on the question. They were far more concerned with military preparations and the covert activities of "intestine enemies." Tory "plots, conspiracies and chimeras dire," in John Jay's words, were reported in every county. On May 18, Morris joined Jay and Philip Livingston as members of a "secret committee" on public safety to work closely with Washington in ferreting out the enemy within as the general prepared his defenses against the arrival of the British armada. It was the beginning of an intimate, confident friendship between the young lawyer and the general that would grow and endure until Washington's death in 1799.

Morris was also named to a committee to raise badly needed troops for Washington's Continental army, a frustrating task he nevertheless addressed in his natural high—some thought "whimsical"—spirits. Putting aside his usual defense of civil liberty, he quickly saw that terror could be a useful political tool. Later, in summer 1777, when Burgoyne's invasion threatened the state, Morris did not hesitate to advocate a reign of terror on the loyalists who might give comfort to the invading enemy. "I think the tories should be as the common Enemies of Mankind to be treated like the Savages. That is to say their Houses &ca. should be burnt and they themselves destroyed," he told Philip Schuyler.

When he heard that the Tory steward at Livingston Manor had been arrested for recruiting tenants for the loyalists, he persuaded the local posse not to shoot him. He had a better idea. "Fit out a sloop," instead, he recommended, "take the man down in it to the manor, call out the tenants and hang him in their presence." The results were salutary. The week following the execution of the hapless steward, Livingston Manor was the only locality to fill its quota of the military draft call.[19]

From the beginning, Morris and his fellow revolutionists did not hesitate in their brusque and exclusive pursuit of liberty. Although expressing personal sympathy and regret when loyalists complained to him of rough, unfair treatment, Morris also became one of the most relentless and unforgiving. As one loyalist victim exclaimed, "These are the people who are contending for liberty; they engross the whole of it to themselves and allow not a tittle to their opponents." With the imminent threat of military attack, civil and legal scruples were put aside when it came to dealing with any sign of "disaffection" to the cause.

Later, when political violence in the name of liberty seemed to have the loyalists on the run, Morris boasted to Hamilton: "If it is not it will soon be so. For they shall have a few more Executions than which nothing can be more efficacious. I speak from Experience but then it is necessary to disperse the Victums of public Justice throughout the different Parts of the several States for nothing but occular Demonstration can convince these incredulous Beings that we really do hang them. I wish the several states would follow our Example."[20]

The mobs hunting down Tories in the streets of New York in early June 1776 anticipated in their violence the ugly Parisian scenes Morris would later witness in the early days of the French Revolution. Unhappy victims hoisted and tied on rails, some tarred and feathered, were paraded beneath the windows of the very building where the Provincial Congress met and where Morris's committee "for hearing and trying disaffected persons and those of equivocal character" was actually in session. Washington, who saw what was going on in the streets, severely reprimanded a compassionate General Israel Putnam for trying to stop the "warm friends of liberty," declaring it would discourage and "injure the cause of freedom."[21]

For Morris, John Jay, and Philip Livingston, members of the special committee, sorting out the allegations—often with only a *soupçonne d'être suspect*—against individuals caught in the net of suspicion proved as difficult as recruiting trustworthy troops. Summonses were drafted and issued for arrests while Washington's Continental troops executed the orders, an interesting collaboration between local government and the Continental military. Among the first to be caught in the roundup and ordered to appear before the committee were Gouverneur's half-brother Richard Morris and William Smith Jr. Richard, who had resigned his judgeship on the Court of Admiralty, was actually hauled in and questioned because he had not become an associator, making him an "equivocal," just one notch below an "inimical" pariah. Later, on oath, he reluctantly threw in his lot with the patriots but Smith would remain a confirmed loyalist.

At its first secret meeting, the committee was confronted with evidence of what appeared to be a dangerous conspiracy. Under Morris's forceful interrogation, a plot by one Thomas Hickey, a member of Washington's guard, was uncovered and immediately arraigned before a court-martial, tried, and convicted. Rumor was that the plotters were preparing to assassinate Washington and his staff. Washington confirmed Hickey's sentence by hanging the next day, and the culprit was quickly dispatched that afternoon before a crowd of twenty thousand.

On the morning of June 29, two days after Hickey's execution, a signal from Staten Island announced the arrival of the first ships of the British fleet off Sandy Hook, looking as if "all London was afloat," and added to the uproar. On June 27, Morris had signed the summons for his old law preceptor, confidant, and mentor "TO SHEW CAUSE, (if any you have) why you shoul'd be considered as a friend to the American cause." By the time Smith received the committee's order on July 1, the Provincial Congress had temporarily adjourned to White Plains at Morris's urging. He had heard that the enemy was at the city's front door preparing to make an assault by overwhelming force, and he knew that his blatant role in the patriotic cause had already insured him a place on the enemy's list of those to be hung if he should fall into the enemy's hand.[22]

Morris's committee continued to meet in city hall well into July and to investigate reports of subversion while he stayed at Morrisania. On the night of July 4, William Smith's servant found the former law clerk at the estate and delivered the jurist's letter addressed to the "Committee of Congress." Smith's defense was neutrality, having earlier announced that he "would list on neither side during the present troubles" as he prepared to retreat, for the duration, to his country seat on the Hudson.

To Morris, Smith's neutrality had long been unconvincing, tainted with a "suspicious light." A year earlier, when he had been confronted with a request to sign the association's oath, Smith had pled that as a member of the Governor's Council, he could better advance the cause of peace without publicly taking sides. Now he was deemed a loyalist if he was unwilling to join those who were ready to "risque their Lives & Fortunes in Defense of the Rights and Liberties of America," those stirring words, with slight variations, repeated throughout the colonies in oaths and declarations, a shared incantation invoked to ward off any lingering doubts and reservations, no matter what the outcome, price, or perils.[23]

Morris replied the next morning "from the Heart of Friendship," not waiting to discuss Smith's letter with other committee members. While the committee might accept his neutrality until negotiations had resolved, as Smith put it, the "unnatural and destructive war," Morris frankly hoped "that it may be put in your Power to cross over into the Road whither you are beckoned by your Countrymen." Smith, like Morris and others in their circle, had to make the hard choice. Conscience and consistency in principles were the moral guidelines, but with the enemy at the gate, to Morris, Smith's neutrality failed to meet his standards. "The Intention of Congress...was to discriminate between the Friends and Foes of America and...give their Friends and Friends of Mankind an opportunity to declaring with a loud Voice their Attachment to the Rights of Humane Nature." Then with an elegantly worded warning Morris added, "that at this Moment when the Ties between Britain & America are haggled away by the Sword of War, the future Consequence of every Gentleman in the Country depends upon the Decision of his present Conduct." Morris, the youth, the former clerk, looked to the future. Smith, the quintessential pillar and successful servant of the "antient Union, according to that Compact, which so eminently advanced the Prosperity of the Empire," could only see his world collapsing.[24]

Smith's study of history and in particular the Scottish philosopher and historian David Hume had made him distrustful of all revolutions. He dismissed his former clerk's revolutionary resolve as nothing more than proof that Morris—"This Youth who has Parts"—had merely "joined the popular Party to obtain emoluments he supposed to be in their Gift." After being paroled to Livingston Manor where he could be watched by various Livingston patriots for refusing the oath of allegiance, the lawyer became increasingly convinced that the rebel cause of independence was lost. In 1778, Smith moved back to New York City within British lines, remaining there until he left for England with the defeated troops in 1783.

Morris's friend Peter Van Schaack also held with great fortitude to the neutral course in spite of the high cost to his family. After first being paroled by the Provincial Congress, he was summarily banished to England in 1778. Before he left, he wrote a farewell letter to Morris who, with deep compassion, replied: "I would to God, that every tear could be wiped away from every eye. But so long as there are men, so long it will and must happen that they will minister to the miseries of each other. It is a delightful object in history to see order, and peace, and happiness result from confusion, and war and distress. It is a pleasing hope of life. It is your misfortune to be one of the many who have suffered. In your philosophy, in yourself, in the consciousness of acting as you think right, you are to seek consolation, while you shape your old course in a country new."[25]

With the arrival of heavy British forces on Staten Island on July 3, Washington's advance guards were ordered to their alarm posts before dawn. Two days later when Morris admonished Smith to declare his allegiance, the enemy had begun throwing up breast works on the island in view of Washington's troops. On July 6, John Hancock, president of the Continental Congress wrote Washington that "for some Time past," the delegates "have had their Attention occupied by one of the most interesting and important Subjects that could possibly come before them or any assembly of Men. Altho it is not possible to foresee the Consequences of Human Actions," he continued, "yet it is nevertheless a Duty we owe ourselves and Posterity, in all our public Counsels, to decide in the best Manner we are able, and leave the Event to that Being who controls both Causes and Events to bring down his own Determination."[26]

Morris heard about the debate on the great "Subject" from his friend Robert Livingston and others when he went briefly to Philadelphia in the second week of June to argue successfully before the Congress that the undermanned New York regiments in the Continental Army should be fairly paid. He had no doubt privately briefed Washington on these developments. On June 8, while he was in Philadelphia, the New York delegates expressed an inquiry to the Provincial Congress requesting instructions on independence.

Rumors that Congress had adopted Independence without New York's vote, was anticipated in New York's taverns the same night. When Washington received official word of the Declaration on July 9, he immediately issued the general order that "the paper adopted on July 4, shewing the grounds and reasons of this measure is to be read in an audible voice" to all the troops, after confirming in the same order that court-martialed deserters would receive thirty-nine lashes. Later in the evening of the ninth, an edgy, rowdy crowd gathered in the Bowling Green and knocked the gilded statue of George III garbed as a Roman emperor off its white marble pedestal. As one observer wrote; "the IMAGE of the BEAST was thrown down and his HEAD severed from his body." The overthrown king produced four thousand pounds of much-needed lead bullets, which it was hoped would "make a deep impression" on the king's redcoats. Conspicuously missing from the printed Declaration Washington ordered read to the troops was the word "unanimous" because New York's delegates had abstained. The later calligraphic version completed on August 2 recorded the words "*The* Unanimous Declaration," New York's tardy endorsement of independence.[27]

That same day, the Fourth Provincial Congress convened in the Court House at White Plains. Westchester County was once again represented by Gouverneur Morris. The Congress had been elected from a large enfranchised group representing every patriot freeholder in New York and Albany and every freeholder in the rest of the state. It was resolved unanimously that New York agreed with the Continental Congress's cogent and conclusive argument: there was no alternative to independence. "We approve the same and will at the Risque of our Lives and fortunes join with the other Colonies in supporting it." The Congress directed the colony's delegates in Philadelphia to take whatever measures they "deemed necessary to the happiness and Welfare of America."

The following day, July 10, the Provincial Congress changed its name to "The Provincial Convention of the Representatives of the State of New York," announcing its plan to draft a constitution. On the eleventh, the Convention notified John Hancock that his request to proclaim the Declaration had been anticipated by two days. It also urged the Continental Congress to edit the *Book of Common Prayer,* eliminating "all such prayers as interfere with the American cause."[28]

The election of the new government had confirmed a mandate for independence, an act that would test its predestined revolutionary mettle. No loyalist from the third congress was reelected. The New York delegates in Philadelphia were finally released from their "singular and delicate" situation when they were told to join the other states in ratifying the Declaration. Gouverneur's brother Lewis was on hand and joined the other delegates in signing the revised document. It would later become the preamble to New York's first constitution. On August 1, "Mr. Morris moved and was seconded by Mr. Duer, that a Committee be appointed to take into consideration and report a plan for instituting and framing a new form of Government." Gouverneur was named to the committee, its youngest member. The other members were Jay, Robert Livingston, William Duer, John Sloss Hobart, Abraham Yates Jr., Robert Yates, Henry Wisner, William Smith (of Suffolk), John Broome, Samuel Townsend, and Charles DeWitt.[29]

For a creative mind like Morris's, these beginnings of a government at White Plains, which would mature in the heat of war at Kingston in spring 1777, were exhilarating, extraordinary in their implications. Like his friends Jay and Livingston, he believed that constitution-making should not be rushed but must be carefully considered and cautiously urged forward. It would be eight months before the first New York constitution was completed.

Even while they were on the run in the critical fall and winter of 1776–77, Morris and his colleagues found time somehow to think about and then begin to build the state from the bottom up, as if it were an uncomplicated, public demonstration in the art of political science, a simple case study in solving the problems of a free, republican government. But the fear of popular government was widespread, and not only among the gentry of New York. Samuel Chase proposed that Maryland postpone indefinitely forming a state government since "a distemper of Governing has seized all Ranks of Men." Charles Carroll was even more depressed, predicting that most states "will be simple Democracies, of all governts the worst and will end as all democracies have, in despotism." Robert Livingston expressed similar conflicted alarms. "We see daily more and more strongly the necessity of forming a new government," he wrote in September 1776, "and yet dare not begin it because of the absurd ideas that some have on that subject. A weak executive, considering the disposition of the people and claims of their neighbors, must end in our ruin; and officers chosen either by the people or Assembly involve us in perpetual faction, or bring the magistrey into contempt."

With all the anxiety and civil disarray, Morris, like Jay and a reluctant Livingston—one can now hear a chorus of nervous whistles in the dark—believed that it was necessary to find in Livingston's words, "a period of more tranquillity, and a fairer prospect of calm reflection and deliberation among members, and when the people likewise would be in a better condition to understand and receive the results of their labor."[30]

CHAPTER 5

Breaking the Fetters

O N August 12, 1776, Morris could see from the Battery the sails of Sir William Howe's fleet, now numbering three hundred warships, hovering off Staten Island. Loaded with troops, mostly hired Hessians, the expeditionary force stood at nearly thirty thousand. Having abandoned the police action in Boston, the British ministry was now ready to reconquer the insurgent colonies, striking first at New York with the largest military force it had ever launched against a foreign enemy. Faced with such an armada, Washington ordered his men to keep their canteens filled and have two days rations on hand. He also thought it prudent to pack his headquarters papers and dispatch them to Philadelphia for safekeeping. The city itself, surrounded by water and protected by the British navy, was a perfect base of operations for the enemy. And the Hudson River, leading almost to Lake George, which in turn led to Lake Champlain and Quebec, was an obvious line to control in the British strategy of cutting New England off from the rest of the colonies, the prime goal in bringing the rebels to heel.

In late August, Washington suffered a sharp defeat in the battle of Long Island. He had managed to successfully extricate his army, but he was now faced with the crisis of what to do about the city of New York. There was no doubt that he had been outmaneuvered and outfought by the British general. What followed were a series of humiliating reversals as Washington's green, ragged troops—mostly "beardless youths"—abandoned the city, the only place to be held continuously by the British throughout the remainder of the war.

As embarrassing as the retreat was to Washington—for twenty-four hours

"View of the Narrows between Long Island and Staten Island with Our Fleet at Anchor and Lord Howe Coming In," July 12, 1776, by Archibald Robertson.
Spencer Collection. The New York Public Library. Astor, Lenox and Tilden Foundations.

after leaving Long Island he was "entirely unfit to take a pen in hand"—he had already settled on movement as the grand strategy of the war. On the question of evacuation and withdrawal, he later explained to the politicians in Philadelphia that ultimate success would be won by avoiding the enemy, not exactly what they wanted to hear: "It has even been called a war of posts: that we should on all occasions avoid a general action or put anything to the risk, unless compelled by necessity, into which we ought never to be drawn."[1]

As Washington's forces gave ground in the last weeks of August and early September, Morris and the fugitive Provincial Convention were also on the run, never knowing where it would meet from one day to the next. Lewis Morris, a member of the Convention, wrote John Jay on September 8, anxiously inquiring how things stood and "at what Place our convention are." Gouverneur's fractured family had also scattered. Morrisania, abandoned to the enemy became a hunting ground for British troops in search of food and wood.[2]

Morris attempted to reach his mother by letter but had only secondhand reports from her. There is no surviving evidence of how she weathered the battle for New York and the fire that immediately followed. One painful report that reached him of the death of his sister described how deeply distressed his mother was over his defection. "Would to God it were in my power to alleviate the pangs of a sorrowing parent," he wrote, apologizing for offering a letter "of an improper complexion to one already afflicted." But in face of what he now believed to be nothing less than a political turning point for mankind, personal feelings had to be put aside for the collective good. "Where the happiness of a considerable part of our fellow creatures is deeply concerned, we soon feel the insignificancy of an individual," he told his isolated and grieving mother in not particularly comforting words. Morris's private emotions were not so much repressed as subordinated to his growing perception of the significance of the Revolution. On his moral scale, there could be no ambivalence. The implications of the Revolution transcended the filial duty to an aged parent now cut off from any comfort he could offer.[3]

When it came to family bonds, Morris's priorities were by no means unique among the rebelling patriots. John Adams declared that he would have hanged his own brother if he had been a loyalist. The universal significance of the outcome was clear to most of the zealous, implacable participants and their international admirers. Colonel Joseph Reed, caught up in Washington's losing struggle to save New York City, urged his wife to "endeavor cheerfully to submit to the dispensations of Providence, whatever they may be. My honor, duty and every other tie held sacred to men," he wrote, "call upon me to proceed with firmness and resolution; and I trust that neither you or the children will have reason to be ashamed of my conduct." Whatever his fate, he told her, "My country will I trust be free."[4]

But by the time the British had captured New York, in September 1776, Morris had suddenly and mysteriously disappeared from the scene of action. On Sunday September 15, three weeks after the decisive battle at Brooklyn delivered Long Island into the hands of the enemy, General Howe dispatched the Royal Army in flat boats across the East River to Manhattan. Thinking that the landing might take place on the plains of Morrisania across the Harlem River, Washington personally reconnoitered the ground and ordered the roads leading from Morrisania to Manhattan blocked. The sound of heavy firing the general heard rolling up the East River, however, came from the cannonade of enemy ships covering the enemy's landing at Kip's Bay.

Without the loss of a single man, the British and Hessian troops quickly took possession of the Heights of Inclenbergh forming a line through the middle of the island. That evening, the British army entered and took possession of the city. Six nights later some "emissaries of rebellion" set fire to the city. A quarter of it was burned before the flames could be brought under control. Washington reported to his brother Lund that "Providence, or some good honest fellow, has done more for us than we were disposed to do for oureselves."[5]

Only gaunt ruins were left of Trinity Church, King's College, and St. Paul's Chapel. The college library, the core of Gouverneur's early studies, deposited in the city hall for safety, was plundered by the occupying army, "the books publically hawked about town for sale by private soldiers, their trulls and doxeys." The same fate was waiting for Morrisania's "most elegant, large, beautiful and well-collected library" two years later when British troops found it in Norwalk, Connecticut, where it had been removed for safety. The Morris books were then carted back to New York, and many of them sold in the streets by "the thieves, the robbers and the plunders...in the same manner" as those of King's College.[6]

After the British forces had driven Washington from New York and White Plains—the general called it "a disgraceful and dastardly" retreat—Westchester County was turned into a no-man's-land, devastated by advancing and retreating armies of both sides. The badly depleted Provincial Convention had already moved to regroup temporarily in the remote village of Fishkill. Confronted with the series of military disasters in early August, the Convention temporarily turned affairs over to the a small Committee of Safety. From October 1776 until March 1777, the entire Convention met only one day.

On October 10, an exasperated Robert Livingston wrote the South Carolinian Edward Rutledge, a member of the Continental Congress, about their missing friend: "Gouverneur thro' what cause God alone knows has deserted in this hour of danger retired to some obscure corner of the Jerseys where he enjoys his jest and his ease while his friends are struggling with every difficulty and danger & blushing while they make apologies for him which they do not themselves believe." Rutledge was even more caustic in his indignation: "I am amazed at Gouverneur! Good God what will mankind come to! Is it not possible to awaken him to a sense of duty? Has he no one Virtue left that can plead in favour of an oppressed & bleeding Country?"[7]

Morris's puzzling motives were not clarified by his lame excuse sent to the Convention. "A series of Accidents too trifling for recital," he nonchalantly explained in the middle of October, "have prevented me the pleasure of attending the Convention according to my intentions for over a Month past." He added that he would come as soon as he could replace his missing horses. The note was sent from Boonton, New Jersey, where Morris had been staying with his sister Euphema Ogden and her family. The truant did not return to the Convention for another six weeks, an aberrant breech in the code of honor that governed both the private and public conduct of gentlemen.

The record is silent on just what happened or the nature of the "trifling" accidents Morris referred to. It may well have been a mishap more serious than Morris let on, or it may have been more complicated. Family problems, a passing love affair, or simply his easily frayed impatience at being forced to work with colleagues he considered "not the best qualified for the job," as he later told Alexander Hamilton. Or it might have been a fit of obscure Morris pique now lost in the record. All remains speculation. What appears clear is the absence of any censorious criticism or hard feelings when Morris finally rejoined the Convention, suggesting the sometimes unconventional Morris foibles were given a certain gentleman's latitude, at least by his peers. Robert

Livingston himself had a similar record of withdrawal, "sick of politics and power," periodically returning to the bucolic life of Clermont, but doing his duty in his long, distinguished career as he saw it and, like Morris, making no excuses or apologies.[8]

By the time Morris was in his seat in the Reformed Dutch Church at Fishkill on December 9, his committee, assigned to recommend the form of a state government, had already been excused to prepare its report. Setting up a revolutionary government and its possible cost to the conspirators was on his mind ten days later when he wrote his mother, who could hardly be comforted by such melodramatic sermons: "Great revolutions of empire are seldom achieved without human calamity; but the worst, which can happen, is to fall on the last bleak mountain of America, and he who dies there, in defense of the injured rights of mankind, is happier than his conqueror, more beloved by mankind, more applauded by his own heart."[9]

Morris's high-flown language was not inspired by the decrepit surroundings in which he and the Convention found themselves huddled: the abandoned church in the winter of 1777, "desperately, and almost convulsively, struggling to break the fetters of trans-Atlantic despotism," as one veteran later put it. Throughout the heroic era of the Revolution, the inspired rhetoric and acts of bravery often masked the actual squalor of the settings where the struggles to break free of the empire took place. In the last bleak days of December, John Jay, for example, managed to frame and issue from the melancholy church in Fishkill a stirring appeal on behalf of the Convention with words fit for a marble tablet, in an attempt to rally the dispirited people of New York, who were not at all sure they or their leaders were on the right track: "You and all men were created free, and authorized to establish civil government, for the preservation of your rights against oppression, and the security of that freedom which God hath given you, against the rapacious hand of tyranny and lawless power."[10]

It would take more than fine words to rally the sagging patriotic spirit in winter 1776–77, when the peace conference called by General Howe failed and there was yet no sign that France was prepared to come to the rescue. Pessimism, bordering on panic, was spreading even among key Congressional leaders like Robert Morris of Pennsylvania and Charles Carroll of Maryland. In December, Morris wrote the American commissioners in Paris that "when death and ruin stare us in the face... many of those who were foremost in noise shrink coward like from the danger and are begging pardon without striking a blow."

When word of the American victories at Trenton and Princeton reached the Hudson Valley a few days after Robert Morris penned his grim letter to Paris, a new confidence was evident even among Gouverneur's harried fellow delegates. On their way to Kingston where the Convention now moved for safety, the would-be constitutional architects, Morris, Robert Livingston, and James Duane paid a call on their aged mentor, William Smith Jr., now living under house arrest at Livingston Manor. The tough old lawyer, still determined he "would list on neither side," was stunned by the militant optimism of his unexpected visitors. "The Enthusiasm of those who lead the People at this Day if not counterfeited is astonishing," Smith confessed to his diary, after listening in silence to their "Vauntings." "These young heroes seem not apprized of any danger.... From the Discords of the Provinces, The unanimity of Great Britain or The improbability that France will plunge into a War or the fatal consequences if she does."[11]

Although Kingston's position on the west side of the Hudson appeared safer, the delegates found little improvement in their accommodations. Well aware of his low tolerance of boredom, Morris had managed to carry a few of Morrisania's books with him into exile to relieve the tedium. He loaned Sally Jay his copy of the memoirs of Madame de Maintenon when he stopped overnight at her house in New Jersey while traveling with her husband on one of their fast trips to Philadelphia to beg for help.

At Kingston, a bedraggled town some thirty miles south of Albany, the Convention now found itself housed above the stinking local jail. In these cramped, pungent chambers the final draft of the state's first constitution was adopted on April 20, 1777. The town's prison hardly conformed to Morris's insistent fastidiousness or Robert Livingston's seignorial style at Clermont where one visitor found "more of the spirit of feudal aristocracy, than might be supposed to be harbored in the breast of one of the *staunchest republicans* in the United States."[12]

The committee appointed at Morris's urging in August 1776 to prepare a plan of government included some of the ablest men in the state: John Jay, John Sloss Hobart, William Duer, Robert Livingston, John Morin Scott, and Abraham Yates, men whose ideological leanings stretched across the political spectrum. But in spite of a democratically leaning majority who elected Yates chairman, the power—the power of persuasion and the pen—was quickly ceded to Jay, Morris, and Livingston. Scott, now in his fifties, a ready speaker with years of experience in political infighting—John Adams judged him "a sensible Man but not very polite"—could have seriously challenged these youthful Turks. With his rough yet genial manners he rarely missed the chance to be the popular spokesman, especially when in the majority. Morris had tried to prevent Scott, whom he had long viewed with serious reservations, as well as a certain social disdain, from being seated in the Convention because the lawyer also held the rank of general in the state militia, contrary to a recent statute preventing officers from serving in the legislature. On August 3, 1776, when the vote on Scott was to come up, it was now John Jay who was evading his duty in attendance. "If you play Truant thus, *Le tout est perdue*," Morris wrote his comrade-in-arms. "How do you expect that your unruly

Horses can be kept in Order by a Whip and a Spur. They want the Reins. On Tuesday next it is to be determined as to the seat of our General." Morris's efforts to block Scott's election were defeated but for some reason, Scott, the aging, bibulous Yale provocateur, was too preoccupied with military matters to challenge the prejudiced King's College members of the Convention. He would leave no mark on the new constitution.[13]

Earlier, when Livingston was pleading for Morris to return from Boonton, it was not just the deteriorating military predicament that alarmed him. In October, he told Edward Rutledge that he and Jay could not return to the Continental Congress at a moment when a new government was to be formed. "Every thing is at stake here—*two thirds of our gentlemen fell off early in this controversy*," and he and the few that were left had to struggle as best they could. Otherwise, New Yorkers would be condemned to spend the rest of their lives under a government "without that influence that is derived from respect to old families, wealth, age etc," a government beholden to people made up of "that mixture of jealousy and cunning into which Genius long occupied in trifles generally degenerate when unimproved by education and unrefined by honor.... Believe me there is a greater mixture of intrigue, artifice and address in the [Convention] of N.Y. than in a conclave of cardinals."[14]

History and the tradition of a two-party system have conditioned Americans to think of politics in terms of two opposing groups, seeing that pattern even in the country's early political order. But New York's Constitutional Convention did not fall into this neat political division. Under various labels—loyalists and patriots, radicals and conservatives, democrats and aristocrats—a misleading dualism over issues has been imposed on a far more complex pattern of events. The vivid tableau Morris painted of the New York political scene in 1774 in his letter to Thomas Penn when Parliament closed the port of Boston emphasized a black-and-white dichotomy between the gentry and the people as he watched from the balcony of the Merchants Exchange. Yet in 1777, Morris, the quintessential patrician would advocate the direct election of governor, the first radically democratic step in any state constitution. And John Jay, who seemed to favor a more liberal qualification for suffrage, opposed religious freedom for Catholics. So it is a mistake, as Cecelia Kenyon has argued, to see the Revolution or the New York Constitutional Convention split along radical and conservative lines, the members grouped in stereotyped, partisan camps. Although there were a number of factors that defined revolutionary society and politics, the total absence of parties as we think of them was certainly the state of things when the unprepared members of the Convention took up the work of forming a government.[15]

Because the American Revolution and the state constitutions it quickly spawned were, in retrospect, political events of epochal importance, a mythical aura has gathered around those present at their creation, exaggerating their accomplishments and originality. In New York State, as in the other former colonies, the framers were, in fact, building on more than one hundred fifty years of experience of fitful, evolving governance under the British colonial system. Out of that history would come from the participants an interplay of competing interests and ideas aired in contentious debate on the nature of the state.

After symbolically incorporating the Declaration of Independence into the constitutional document and designating the day following the battle of Lexington as the state's birthday, the democratically inclined majority, more "energetic than coherent" in the words of one historian, turned the heavy lifting over to the highly educated, sophisticated team of Morris, Jay, and Livingston, the future penman (and more) of the Constitution of the United States, the first chief justice of the Supreme Court of the United States, and the future first chancellor of the state of New York. This deference was not surprising since for much of the colonial period, members of the Morris, Livingston, and Jay clans—"the polished people"—along with their extended connections, had played ringleaders as well as lesser roles in the public theater of government, asserting their rights, first in one guise and then another. As graduates of King's, the three brilliant lawyers were well armed with an array of political tracts familiar to Whig leadership throughout the former colonies. They knew their Montesquieu, Puffendorf, Grotius, their Blackstone, and, we may assume, their Locke. All but Locke had been required reading at King's.

James Duane asked John Adams if he had seen the New York constitution and hoped it was "conformable" to the New Englander's ideas set out in a letter to George Wythe and widely published earlier that spring. Adams modestly took credit for the constitution's wisdom, replying that it was the best plan that had yet been adopted.[16]

The Convention also had to deal with the tedious business of a renegade government in time of war. Exhausted with all the detail and tension, Robert Livingston frankly longed for "more refined pleasures, conversation and friendship...nor would in my present humor," he wrote to Philip Schuyler, "give one scene of Shakespear for a 1000 Harringtons, Lockes, Sidneys and Adams to boot." Morris and Jay agreed with Livingston.[17]

It is hard to say which of the three had the largest store of theoretical and political grounding. As John Adams remarked, "The art of Lawgiving is not so easy as that of Architecture or Painting." No doubt, all three of the well-read constitutional engineers working in Fishkill and Kingston shared an eclectic assortment of useful gleanings on the subject. As did most American lawmakers of the time, they shared the fundamental conviction that the enjoyment of political liberty required a separation of powers. They undoubtedly knew John Adams's "Thoughts on Government." In his old age, Adams boasted that Jay carried in his pocket a copy of Adams's orderly guide when Jay left Philadelphia to work on the New York constitution.[18]

The New York framers accepted the old colonial government pretty much as they found it. There was, however, a diversity of opinion "not whether the government should be of the republican form partaking of monarchy, aristocracy and democracy: but what proportion of ingredients out of each should make up the compound." Quickly eliminating all the royal features of the old order, cutting all state ties to the Anglican Episcopal Church, and editing the *Book of Common Prayer* to make sure no prayers were offered up on behalf of the odious George III, they proceeded to preserve the principle structural elements of government that they had inherited. The finished body of the constitution itself consisted of forty-five compact sections of "unsuspecting simplicity," as Charles Lincoln has written. When it was finished and well laced with compromise, the framers "had a Constitution which gave them the right of self-government and they knew how to use that right judiciously," in spite of many reservations. The old elite with its potent spell to captivate the populace had rid themselves of the oppressive prerogatives of Parliament without abolishing, at least for the time being, their well-honed privileges of governing.[19]

The independent judicial system in all its ancient majesty and the entrenched local governments of the former colony were preserved substantially unaltered. The chief task was to spell out the rights of citizens (former subjects), to construct a new legislature and provide for its election, and to establish a separate executive branch. Under the revolutionary congresses, the legislature, mainly through committees, had carried out the executive duties. Morris opposed framing a bill of rights before framing a government, as some members of the Convention had urged. The motion for a bill of rights that was defeated requested that it declare "the essential rights and privileges of the good people of the state," and that it serve as the "foundation of government." Morris saw this preamble as attempting to go beyond the limited objectives of breaking the bonds with Britain and its despotic tax system. His scruple was not merely structural. The people, as he would famously declare in the United States Senate, must first be protected from "the baneful effects of their own precipitation, their passion, their misguided zeal."[20]

Enumerated rights in the constitution were few and succinctly stated. In the new constitution, all power is derived from "our Sovereign Lords the People," as John Adams put it. Taking the language of the Magna Carta, each citizen was entitled to full protection of his individual rights. Each citizen was also entitled to the enjoyment of complete religious liberty. The right of trial by jury remained inviolate forever. General but not universal suffrage was established, and the legislature was authorized to provide for the use of ballots instead of the established practice of viva voce. In fact, virtually all these liberties were a part of the British constitution by 1689. But Morris, the scion of a slave-owning family, would have added an essential liberty denied to some twenty thousand New Yorkers who were held in bondage as slaves if he had

had his way. His bold first step to explore the issue, however, did set in motion eventual abolition.[21]

At the age of twenty-five, Gouverneur Morris had clearly sorted out his political ideas during the dispute with Great Britain. With independence at hand, the security of human liberty, including property rights, must be guarded by limiting provisions built into the constitutional order. Merely claiming that the object of government was to promote the "public good" was not enough to insure stability, as he had recently written in a brief outline of essays on government. Life, liberty, and property, like the separation of powers in a republic, had to be respected, protected, and balanced. "In the sincere Desire to promote it [the public good] just Men may be proscribed, unjust Wars be declared. Property be invaded & Violence patronized. Alas! How often has the Maxim, Salus populi Lex [esto], been written in blood."[22]

To Morris, as it was to most articulate, thoughtful Americans, liberty and property were one and inseparable. For the revolutionary generation, property was the only foundation for security of life and liberty. A constitution must have its own built-in restraints and limitations, as James Madison would shrewdly write, making "it less probable that a majority of the whole will have a common motive to invade the rights of other citizens." The rise of democratic appetites for a greater role in government posed critical questions producing contradictory and ambiguous answers for the civil rights and liberties of each individual, rights that might otherwise be compromised by the demagoguery of the majority. All this had been anticipated by Morris in his letter to Penn in 1774 when New Yorkers "fairly contended about the future forms of our government, whether it should be founded upon Aristocratic or Democratic principles." The former could readily "deceive the people," leading to despotism of the few, whereas the latter raised the specter of a tyranny of the majority, "the domination of a riotous mob."[23]

Sometime in late February 1777 John Jay "retired to some place in the country" to prepare a draft of a plan of government. His son William wrote later that his father was chairman of the committee and that the draft reported on March 12 was in his hand, although he was not present to read it. On March 17, Jay returned to the Convention in its quarters over the jail to participate in the debate. The next day the proceedings were enveloped in smoke when members were allowed to light up their pipes in order "to prevent bad effects from the disagreeable effluvia arising from the jail below." On Morris's motion to lift the ban on smoking, "The Convention resumed the consideration of the form of government."[24]

Independent and in defiance of the opinions of his close friends, Morris did not hesitate to tangle with Jay over the article providing for "the free exercise and enjoyment of religious profession and worship." Jay, with a deep, unforgiving Huguenot memory of discrimination, whose family had been driven from

Europe by the Church, proposed that Roman Catholics be denied all civil rights until they had sworn before the Supreme Court that no priest, pope, or foreign power had the authority to absolve their allegiance to the state. He also added that they should renounce the tenet that priests could absolve all men of sin, "a false, wicked, dangerous and damnable doctrine," Jay declared. Fear of Catholicism was epidemic throughout the colonies and "Popery" was exploited on behalf of the American cause by many leaders who should have known better. One hysterical Philadelphia patriot predicted that unless the war was won, the city might "yet experience the carnage of a St. Batholomew's Day."[25]

Unlike Jefferson, who would have agreed with Morris's position but could rarely bring himself to personally address even his fellow Virginia assemblymen in debate, Morris was on his feet and moved to defeat in short order what he considered Jay's affront to tolerance and freedom of conscience. "It was always my opinion," Morris wrote his loyalist friend Peter Van Schaack, "that matters of conscience and faith, whether political or religious, are as much out of the province, as they are beyond the ken of human legislatures."[26]

His challenge could not have been unexpected. During the preceding weeks, Jay, Morris, and Livingston had met regularly in the evenings to thrash out tough constitutional issues. During the debate on the article insuring "the free exercise and religious profession and worship," Jay had proposed that "the liberty hereby granted shall not be construed to encourage licentiousness or be used to disturb or endanger the safety of the state."

Even with revisions, Morris believed that Jay's language still seemed a veiled threat to religious tolerance. When strategy and parliamentary devices failed to defeat Jay's toned-down motion outright, Morris shrewdly turned to language—a tool he knew how to wield as brilliantly as Jay. With his deft revisions, the constitution now limited any broad government persecution of religious groups, the thing that Morris most feared. It read simply that "the liberty *of conscience* hereby granted shall not be *so construed* as to excuse acts of licentiousness, or justify practices inconsistent with the peace and safety of the state" (italics added). It was a brilliant ploy, powerfully strengthening mere "liberty." It passed unanimously.[27]

Morris was not as successful when it came to Jay's efforts to build a similar wall to seriously discourage Catholics from trying to enter New York by requiring new citizens to "abjure and renounce all allegiance and subjection to all and every foreign King, prince, potentate and all matters ecclesiastical as well as civil." Directed at foreign immigrants particularly from Canada, it was another threat to religious liberty, and Morris again fought hard on principle. His motion proposing vague conditions for citizenship to defeat Jay's prejudice, however, was voted down twice, allowing Jay's anti-Catholic prohibitions to become a part of the law. In 1787, however, as a delegate to the Constitutional Convention in Philadelphia Morris saw to it that all powers over citizenship were reserved to the national government, nullifying New York's official bigotry.

Two weeks after the fight over freedom of conscience, without warning, Morris moved to commit New York to the proposition that "every being who breathes the air of this State shall enjoy the privileges of a freeman." There is an interesting genealogical thread to Morris's radical position on slavery. As a judge earlier in the century, his grandfather had issued a writ of habeas corpus for an imprisoned slave rebuking the owner because "being a slave did not alter the case," Lewis Morris declared, "he was a man."[28]

Abolition, which had been left out of Jay's original draft of the constitution, was now placed front and center on the floor for debate. "And whereas a regard to the rights of human nature and the principles of our holy religion, loudly call upon us to dispense the blessings of freedom to all mankind: and inasmuch as it would present great dangers to liberate the slaves within this State: It is, therefore most earnestly recommended to the future Legislatures of the State of New-York, to take the most effectual measures consistent with the public safety, and the private property of individuals, for abolishing domestic slavery within the same, so that in future ages, every being who breathes the air of this State, shall enjoy the privileges of a freeman."

On this progressive issue of human rights, Jay agreed with Morris but was unable to support him because the death of his mother called him away from the Convention. Livingston for some reason questioned the preamble's language. After considerable debate on its wording, Morris agreed to tone down his resolution and it carried thirty-one to five, deferring any further action to future legislatures. By adopting Morris's resolution, the majority had declared its position on slavery. The first legislative act of emancipation was taken in 1781 when it was voted to free slaves serving in the armed forces. Four years later, the state prohibited the sale of any Negro or other person brought into the state.[29]

In May, a month after the constitution had been proclaimed by the Convention, Morris wrote Alexander Hamilton that he thought the work was far from perfect. In a few words, Morris summed up his key reservations. After telling the young artillery captain that he was "very happy that our form of government meets with your approbation," Morris admitted that the "faults in it is not to be wondered at for it is the Work of Men and of Men perhaps not the best qualified to such Undertakings." He was particularly disappointed, he told Hamilton, in the limited power bestowed on the governor. The "want of Vigor in the executive" was likely to create an imbalanced, unstable system given "the very Nature of popular elective government" heavily weighted in favor of the legislature. He thought part of the problem was because "the Spirit which now reigns in America is suspiciously Cautious" and "because a simple Legislature soon possesses itself of too much Power for the Safety of its Subjects."[30]

When he dismissed "a simple Legislature" in his reply to Hamilton, Morris no doubt also had in mind the recently enacted constitution of Pennsylvania, where the popular leadership had pushed through a unicameral legislature. This concentration of power in one body was deeply disturbing to Morris as it was to Jay and Livingston. It would inevitably degenerate into a tyranny of the majority.

Jay's draft called for a senate and an assembly, but the populist mood at the time might well have installed the unicameral Pennsylvania model in New York. When William Duer described the situation in Pennsylvania to Robert Livingston, he replied, "You know that nothing but well timed delays, indefatigable industry, and a minute attention to every favorable attention could have prevented our being in their situation."

But there was something else in the new constitution called a "council of censors," elected every seven years and with the power to call for constitutional changes, that was more dangerous than an all-powerful assembly. If sixteen of the twenty-four members of the council agreed that an amendment was needed, a constitutional convention had to be called within two years. To Morris, this built-in instability was worse than no constitution at all and undermined the very idea of a dependable government that could operate effectively in the face of passing, popular sentiments and pressure. Jay agreed that such weak constitutions produced "cronical disorders in the body politics."[31]

Morris was not alone in urging a strong state executive. It was shared by many leaders who saw a strong government as a bulwark of freedom. Edward Rutledge of South Carolina expressed this view when he wrote Jay in fall 1776 on the proposed New York constitution: "a pure democracy may possibly do, when patriotism is the ruling passion; but when the state abounds with rascals, as is the case with many this day, you must surpress a little of that popular spirit."[32]

To animate the executive with "vigor," Morris forcefully argued that the governor be given a qualified veto over the assembly, one of his essential restraints on a popular legislature. This would mitigate the executive's instability created by his popular election. But Livingston's political instinct told him that it would be defeated. A veto smacked of the arbitrary and all too familiar prerogatives of royal governors. Instead, Livingston successfully proposed, as an inventive arrangement, a Council of Revision consisting of the governor as head, along with the chancellor and the justices of the Supreme Court. By putting the chancellor and judges on the council, the judiciary's dependence on the legislature was reduced, giving it more power than in any other state. The governor, or any two members of the council had the authority to "revise" or veto legislation, an act that could be overturned only by a two-thirds vote of the legislature.

Morris wanted the governor to have sole power of appointment, but this potent tool was also rejected, further curtailing executive influence. After a late night meeting, Jay proposed another innovation, a Council of Appointment in which the governor had only one vote in the council "but no other vote." Morris reluctantly went along with the compromise even though he believed it further limited the power of the governor, who did, however, still retain the command of the state's armed forces.

Just how the will of the people could be translated into a stable republican government was the overriding hurdle for the Convention, an issue that deeply troubled Morris. The demand for the election of both the assembly and senate by secret ballot became a major political issue in the Convention. In an attempt to limit the popular vote, Morris moved to strike out a provision for the election of the assembly and senate by secret ballot. After his motion passed, the old election procedure of the Provincial Assembly of voting viva voce seemed to prevail until Jay later asked for reconsideration. Jay then proposed that after the war, secret voting would be tested. Jay's preamble spelled out the underlying issue: "AND WHEREAS it hath been a prevailing opinion among the good people of this State, that the mode of election by [secret] ballot would tend more to preserve the liberty and equal freedom of the people than the manner of voting *viva voce,* and it is expedient that a fair experiment be made as to which of those methods of voting is to be preferred."[33]

Morris fought Jay's proposal to the end, registering more dissenting votes over secret ballots than any other issue in the course of the debate. From the limited record, it is difficult to know precisely his motives. Voice vote might well represent an excess of popular participation in government, too much "passion." But an open voice vote among citizen-neighbors might also, to his mind, make for a more cohesive, stable government. That it could also lead to a consolidation of the more powerful members of the community can not be denied. Rash and radical measures, however, were more likely to be discouraged by open voting as Montesquieu had advised: "The people's suffrages ought doubtless to be public; and this should be considered as a fundamental law of democracy. The lower class [literally, "little people"] ought to be directed by those of higher rank, and restrained within bounds by the gravity of eminent personages. Hence, by rendering the suffrages secret in the Roman republic, all was lost; it was no longer possible to direct a populace that sought its own distruction."[34]

The same day that the voting issue came up, the related problem of who was entitled to vote for members of the assembly was also thrashed out. On this question, Morris considered ownership of property an important element in any representative system and felt it should be given proper weight. In his sketch on "Progress of Society the Effect on political Liberty," Morris wrote: "Where political Liberty [power of the state] is in Excess Property must be insecure and where Property is not secure Society cannot advance. Suppose a State governed by Representatives equally & annually chosen of which the Majority to govern. Either the Laws would be arbitrary & fluctuating as to destroy Property or Property would so influence the Legislature as to destroy Liberty. Between these two extremes Anarchy."[35]

Morris's suggestion of a twenty-pound freehold requirement or renters of tenements worth forty shillings as qualifications for electors of the popular lower house—one-fifth the requirement for voters for governor and senate— was adopted. This formula embraced all freemen of Albany and New York, the small merchants, artisans, and tradesmen of the state's two urban centers. Tenant farmers who were not simply tenants-at-will usually met the definition of "freeholder." But because they normally paid their rents in kind, their right to vote depended on the fluctuating price of wheat and corn.

As everyone knew, setting up a republican government with vague republican equality at its center was itself a chancy experiment. Aware that the character of the Convention leaned to the populist, John Jay later told his son and biographer that he omitted a number of provisions because "another turn of the winch would have cracked the cord." But Jay, Livingston, and Morris, already seasoned wielders of power, were realists. Perfection in human affairs or in constitutions was not to be expected.

With no time to waste and without waiting for elections, the Convention appointed the principal officials it needed to function as a temporary government until elections could be held. Robert Livingston was named chancellor, John Jay was made chief justice. But "Gouvr. Morris will have no Office," William Smith noted in his diary, "objects his Youth and unsettled Condition in Life.... It gives no Umbrage. He told them plainly he had done enough to hang himself & therefore they need not be jealous of him."

When Morris was later defeated for reelection to the state assembly in fall 1778, Jay wrote him in Philadelphia that his enemies may have intended a compliment. "They said," Jay wrote, "you had so much sense as to be able to do a great mischief and therefore ought not to be trusted." Then Jay added, "I imagine lack-learning Parliaments will become fashionable, to some people I am sure they would be agreeable."[36]

Like Jay and Livingston, Morris found the popular atmosphere of an elected legislature distasteful and tiresome. Unable to dissemble, or play the required petty politics, he understood his prejudices as well as his strengths. A year later, Livingston wrote of his own disenchantment with public office in a confession to Jay:

> My spirits never flagged while our necessities called for great exertions, or while I was impelled by love of my country to contribute to the establishment of a government which was to be the basis of its future happiness. But I feel myself light in the scale of little party politicks. I can not combat a knave with calumnies, and to manage fools (to which I have sometimes submitted) disgusts me when it is no longer justified by some important end.... I converse with men I cant esteem. And I am engaged in a round of little politicks to which I feel myself superior. A happier hour may come, till when with hope for my companion, I will endeavor to jog on.[37]

An interim committee was appointed to act until a governor, senate, and assembly could be elected. Morris was a member of the committee. Peter Livingston told Smith that "RRL, Scott, Jay & G. Morris rule in the Council of Kingston. The Rest seem to leave every thing to them." From his position of temporary power, the young lawyer, with predictable unpredictability, shocked his colleagues by giving notice on May 6 that he would move yet another radical resolution, "remitting all quit rents due, and forever abolishing all quit rents within this state." Like his stand on slavery, Morris's stunning opposition to feudal fees on land originally imposed for the benefit of the crown and later granted to some of the great private estates was far ahead of his time. Disputed land titles, squatters rights, unlawful timber-cutting, and quitrents all added to the confusion and instability in the advancing western settlements, leading to inevitable social and political conflicts on the frontier. Although his foresighted motion was killed in committee, it was entirely consistent with his objection to unreasonable burdens on the rights of private property, rights that nevertheless had to be balanced with the personal rights of citizens. Although entail was swept away by the New York legislature in 1786, quitrents were not abolished by the state until 1846.

Morris was one of five delegates elected by secret ballot to the Continental Congress on May 13. The presumably more elevated atmosphere of the body representing national sovereignty and reaching into international affairs appealed to Morris and fitted his abilities. From the perspective of Kingston, it appeared to be a far more congenial setting than dealing with Livingston's fools and knaves in the New York Convention. But it would be five months before he finally took his seat in Congress.[38]

Little more than two weeks later, on June 1, 1777, General John Burgoyne set off from Montreal with his army of eight thousand seasoned troops, suddenly putting the new state in jeopardy as he launched his campaign to cut it off from New England. The end of the rebellion would be only a matter of time. "Gentleman Johnny" was so sure of the outcome that he bet his Brooks Club pal Charles Fox fifty guineas that he would return to London victorious in one year. Moving south at a stately pace, Burgoyne's army supported by Indians of the Six Nations reached the fortifications at Ticonderoga and Mount Independence on July 1. Four days later the British forced the outnumbered, some twenty-five hundred patriotic defenders under the command of General Arthur St. Clair, to abandon their positions and make a fast retreat. Late in the unfolding of Burgoyne's grand strategy to end the war, he learned that Howe had unexpectedly decided to move south to Philadelphia, leaving Sir Henry Clinton and his smaller forces in New York to support Burgoyne before winter set in. Howe's move seriously undermined the original game plan. Gentleman Johnny would lose his bet.[39]

St. Clair's narrow escape from Ticonderoga alarmed the legislature in Kingston, now reduced to a Council of Safety. On July 10, Morris and Abraham Yates were immediately dispatched northward to meet with General Philip Schuyler, commander of the Northern Department, and make inquiry into "the Misconduct of the Generals" and the reason for St. Clair's humiliating retreat. With typical Morris cheek, he wrote back to the council as he traveled to the scene of action, "having no powers, I shall do what I think best, and trust to the Council to confirm it or hang me."[40]

On the day St. Clair abandoned Ticonderoga, neither Morris nor anyone else understood Burgoyne's real strategy. He wrote to Alexander Hamilton, now an aide on Washington's staff, that he believed Burgoyne's invasion was only a feint to discourage rebel attacks on Howe by the northern army. As for Howe's plans, Hamilton admitted to Morris that he was "such an untilligible Gentleman, that no rule of interpretation can possibly be found out, by which to unravel his designs."[41]

After he and General Schuyler met at Fort Edward, Morris immediately grasped the wisdom of the tactic of retreat before the enemy and wear him out marching through the wilderness as the key to ultimate American success. He strongly supported Schuyler's call for reinforcements if Burgoyne, who camped only twenty miles north, was to be stopped. It is a fair and early example of Morris's cool grasp of military strategy. In his view, New York's defense policy should be to make terrorist war on the civilian population, "to break up all the settlements on our northern frontier, to drive off the cattle, secure or destroy the forage; and also to destroy the saw mills." Although Morris's scorched-earth strategy was grim, it appeared necessary under the calamitous circumstances. "I will venture to say," Morris wrote to the Council of Safety, "that if we lay it down as a maxim, never to contend for ground but in the last necessity, and to leave nothing but a wilderness to the enemy, their progress must be impeded by obstacles, which it is not in human nature to surmount." He gave Schuyler the same advice, warning the council that local support for the cause was tepid and suggested that a company of armed militia might stiffen their backs. Above all, Morris made clear that the northern forces needed immediate help if Burgoyne's advance was to be stopped before the state was lost. William Smith heard the rumor that the tone of Morris's report to the council was "hopeless." Hard truths, however, were not what the council wanted to hear. "We could wish your letters might contain paragraphs for the public," an annoyed Jay complained to his friend for failing to provide an upbeat report on the loss of Ticonderoga. Morris had followed his own advice to Washington earlier in January, when Washington asked for a publishable account of successes in Delaware, warning the general to "take care to say nothing by authority but what is strictly true."[42]

The military crisis in New York grew throughout the late summer. When word reached the Kingston council that Henry Clinton was preparing to march up the Hudson, tensions mounted. Morris candidly admitted to Livingston, "*We are hellishly frightened, but don't say a word of that* for we shall get our spirits again and then perhaps be so full of Valor as to smite the air for blowing in our faces." In August, Horatio Gates replaced Schuyler as head of the northern army, a significant step toward the victory at Saratoga. Schuyler's replacement was announced the same day that Morris and Jay arrived in Philadelphia to plead for reinforcements for the badly depleted northern army, "so dispirited that they hardly dare look the enemy in the face." The self-important Gates, who had spent most of his time in Albany keeping his eye on his rival Schuyler, was not Morris's choice, but it was a compromise that placated Schuyler's loud New England critics, including the Adamses and John Hancock. Later when Gates with calculated rudeness refused to invite Schuyler to his first council of war, Morris pointedly remarked, "The new commander in chief of the Northern Department may, if he please, neglect to ask or distain to receive advice; but those who know him will, I am sure, be convinced that he needs it."[43]

When vain, reckless Johnny Burgoyne, "an Addisonian general in search of a Shakespearean role," crossed to the west bank of the Hudson on September 14, he was prepared to wager all in a smashing victory over the New York rebel forces and collect his bet with Charles Fox. But by the time the British army, under the command of Sir Henry Clinton, had moved up the Hudson and was nearing Kingston to join Burgoyne to take Albany, the ultimate goal, the hapless Burgoyne had already surrendered to "Granny" Gates at Saratoga. Or, as Morris reported in a taunting couplet to his friend Sarah Livingston, now married to the Tory James Ricketts, "Know then, the great Burgoyne's surrounded, His arms magnanimously grounded."

Even before Clinton's army had set a torch to Kingston, the heat was already too much for the beleaguered Convention. Shortly after the legislature abruptly adjourned, Captain Sir James Wallace with "2 gallies one schooner & one little brig" appeared and threatened the town. Morris who had returned from Philadelphia and was helping to evacuate terrified residents before joining the retreat, could not resist regaling his friend Robert Livingston with a ridiculous picture of the desperate state of affairs. "The alarm in the town exhibited more of the Drolerie than the Pathos of Distress. The good Dominie and his Yefrow by the help of the pale and astonished Antoin and the gallant Mr. Bush blowing between Resolution & palid fear laded about half a Ton upon my waggon and then eight of them Children included were dragged only slowly—before they went Willy squealled Sally bawled Adam played tricks and the Yefrow like Hecaba at the taking of Troy [cried] Mou Mou Mou."[44]

Before returning to New York City, a small force of Clinton's disheartened army under General John Vaughn landed troops, captured Kingston, and leveled it. "Escopus [Kingston] being a nursery for every villain in the Country,"

Vaughn later reported, "I judged it necessary to proceed to the town. On our approach they were drawn up with cannon, which we took and drove them out of the place." When firing erupted from the houses, Vaughn continued, "I reduced the place to ashes...not leaving a House." Vaughn's exploits were not finished. He then crossed back to the east side of the Hudson and cheerfully burned Clermont, Robert Livingston's manor. Hearing that Robert might leave the ruined family house as a memorial to British barbarism, Morris immediately penned a stinging epitaph and sent it to his friend. Livingston's defiant Roman gesture was what leaders, without complaint, were supposed to do.[45]

> When the King of Great Britain attempted to establish
> Tyranny over the extensive regions of America
> The Roof of Hospitality
> Sacred to Friendship to Science & to Love
> Was violated by the Hand of War
> To perpetuate the Pleasure he received from British
> Barbarity this Pillar is erected by
> Robert R. Livingston
> Who would have blushed to be exempted
> From the calamities of his country.[46]

Burgoyne surrendered to Horatio Gates on October 17. Five days later, Morris, not yet twenty-six-years old, was requested "immediately to repair to Congress to relieve Mr. Duane" as delegate. Three months would elapse, however, before he would finally take his seat. After signing with Duer, Duane, and Francis Lewis, the Articles of Confederation on behalf of New York on November 15, Morris began his laggardly "jaunt toward Congress," making an extended stop again at Boonton, New Jersey. In a December 14 letter from Boonton to Livingston, he hints that romance had played a part in his delay.

Now in flight, the Continental Congress would not be meeting in Philadelphia when Morris finally joined it as a delegate. The arrival of Howe's army had forced the Congress to beat a quick retreat westward, and it finally settled in the insignificant but safe market village of York, Pennsylvania, on the Susquehanna River eighteen miles from Philadelphia, where it held its first session on September 30, 1777.

On the morning of December 4, the electrifying news of Burgoyne's defeat reached Benjamin Franklin in Paris. Not waiting to print the report of the surrender, Franklin had a handwritten copy quickly made, listing the 9,203 British troops killed, wounded, and captured, and rushed it by courier to the comte de Vergennes, the minister of foreign affairs. On December 17, the minister's first secretary met Franklin and the American commissioners in Passy and informed them that His Majesty Louis XVI "was determined to acknowledge our Independence and make a Treaty with us of Amity and Commerce."[47]

PART III

National Affairs

CHAPTER 6

The Continental Congress,

1778–1779

A N impressed George Washington had already taken the measure of the young New Yorker and wrote to congratulate him on his appointment to Congress when he heard the news. Morris's reputation for a certain genius and eloquence preceded him, but the reviews were mixed. Writing to a correspondent a few days after Gouverneur reached the town of York at the end of January 1778, Robert Morris, the financial juggler who had just met him, thought he had "first rate abilities." He hedged his assessment, however: "I think he will be immensely useful if he pursues his objects steadily (for I have been told his only blemish is being a little too whimsical)." His reputation for doing or saying the unexpected with a mixture of wit and irony gave Morris's personality its reckless edge.[1]

The New York merchant William Constable, who would become Morris's business partner, wrote, "that our Mr. G.M. is a Man of Abilities, but unless intimately acquainted with him you would not be apt to believe that He is also a man of Infinite Industry and strict Attention to his Business." Constable's assessment of Gouverneur's character touches on one of its distinctive qualities, an unusual mixture of phenomenal discipline and imagination disguised by a facade of playboy indolence.

Henry Laurens, the president of Congress, harbored his own reservations and scolded the marquis de Lafayette for taking Morris into his confidence on the proposed invasion of Canada that was being planned when Morris arrived in Congress. "He is," the distrustful Laurens warned Lafayette, "a gentleman who though very Sensible...has given proof, to be often guardless and incautious." Predictably, Morris and the French nobleman who was five years his junior hit it off when they first met at Valley Forge in February 1778 when Lafayette had become an intimate on Washington's staff. "I am deeply surprized at the mature judgment and solid understanding of this *young* man," Morris wrote Laurens shortly after meeting Lafayette. In their first conversations, the romantic, impeccably dressed soldier of fortune, who had arrived in Philadelphia six months earlier, undoubtedly gave Morris a reliable sense of the popular support for the American cause in France. The New Yorker's favorable first impression of the newly minted major general would wear thin by the time both men found themselves together in Paris in the opening days of the French Revolution.[2]

Morris did not fully realize just how close to disaster the patriotic cause was until he got to York, a smoky little hamlet of some three hundred houses. Congress, now in cramped exile, had fled to York just before General Howe entered Philadelphia on September 26, 1777. With a force only slightly smaller than Howe's, Washington's army had lost every engagement in a few short weeks in September and October. The toll of killed, wounded, and captured in this brief fall campaign exceeded two thousand. Support for Washington and his military strategies were at a low point. This state of affairs had to be reversed and given a renewed coherence leading to independence, a policy that certainly had a strong, articulate advocate in the freshman delegate from New York.

All of the business of the government, including running the war, was carried out by congressional committees because there was no executive branch of the jerry-built government. Administratively, it was a nightmare of confusion. Only when the chairman exercised some "energy," one of Morris's favorite words, did things appear to move along. Inevitably, Washington's army was caught up in the clotted mass of congressional inefficiency. To read almost any page of the *Journal of the Continental Congress* makes the final outcome of the war all the more astonishing.

On January 5, 1778, Henry Laurens reported to Governor John Rutledge of South Carolina that no more than "21 members, sometimes barely 9 States on the floor represented by as many Persons." A malaise seemed to engulf the few members that did show up for sessions in the chilly York courthouse, heated by one cast-iron stove. On the same day, the president explained to Washington that the delay of the resolutions announcing "to the world" the surrender terms for General Burgoyne and his troops was because he was short-handed: "the burden of business in Congress lies extremely heavy upon a few Members...necessitated in many Instances to Act in person Commissary general

Quarter master general Clothier general Director general of Hospitals etc. etc. in order to save the Army from dispersion."[3]

On his first day in Congress, January 21, 1778, Morris was summarily named to the Committee at Camp, to meet with Washington at Valley Forge and help him overhaul the organization of his command. "Dear Jay," he wrote shortly after reaching the camp, "Congress have sent me to this place, in conjunction with some other gentlemen, to regulate their army, and in truth, not a little regulation has become necessary." It was fortunate that he had been quickly loaded down with work, for he had been overwhelmed with boredom from the moment he set foot in York, a town no improvement on Kingston. "I would that I were quit of my Congressional Capacity which is in every respect irksome," he confessed to Robert Livingston not long after he arrived. "Stuffed in a corner of America & brooding over their situation," the delegates had become "Disagreeables." Besides, "there are no fine Women here at York Town," he added. "Judge then of my situation."[4]

For Morris, the move to Valley Forge was a sobering three-month introduction into the military and administrative chaos that Congress and its commander in chief now found themselves. For the moment, at least, he was removed from the wrangling, partisan debate surrounding the patchwork Articles of Confederation, approved by Congress earlier in November 1777 and sent on to the states for ratification. If, by a miracle, the army survived the winter at Valley Forge, it had to be prepared for a vigorous spring offensive. Morris assured Jay with his usual self-confidence that "these troublesome fellows," the British, would soon be banished from Philadelphia.

When Morris arrived at the camp, Washington's headquarters was rife with upsetting military politics and insubordination directed at the commander in chief. Pennsylvania politicians bitterly attacked Washington for abandoning Philadelphia to the enemy. There were also disturbing rumors of an "irruption" into Canada. What had been first thought of as a foray of a few hundred volunteers had become a full-scale plan for an invasion of several thousand. The Board of War, chaired by Horatio Gates, had not asked for Washington's opinion on the expanded expedition until it was too late to do anything about it. The cunning victor of Saratoga was not indifferent to the possibility of taking over the position of supreme commander of the army. It was Morris's informal briefing by Lafayette on the details of this secret Canadian adventure that had prompted Henry Lauren to lecture the young nobleman for confiding in the New Yorker.

Lafayette had been put in command of the proposed expedition and the conniving Thomas Conway was named second-in-command. It was a dangerous move, and Morris quickly agreed with Lafayette that Conway's appointment should be blocked. Conway, himself a naturalized Frenchman, was held in contempt by the other French officers. The reconquest of Canada in the name of France might appeal to his ambitions more than the American cause. The Committee at Camp agreed with Morris in opposing the "irruption" as "indigested" and "that Congress had been surprised into it by misinformation." Quickly assuming a pivotal role, Morris drafted a letter to President Laurens on behalf of the committee pointing out the folly of such an adventure. He did not mince words: "What do we build our Hopes of Victory?" he demanded. "Have not Montgomery and Burgoyne demonstrated the Imprudence of distant Expeditions across an inhospitable Wilderness where there is but one Road by which to advance or retire?" Unable to clothe and feed the troops at Valley Forge, the Congress would need to supply an additional four tons of provisions a day to maintain an army advancing on Canada.[5]

All these stratagems and designs were during the first tense days after Morris's arrival at camp, just before "Conway's Cabal" was uncovered. It was not the only intrigue against Washington that was incubating in the log huts of the starving, half-clothed army. Washington professed to be shocked to learn that the pretentious, Irish-born Conway was plotting with Horatio Gates to replace him and confronted Conway with evidence in a letter, one of several that had been exchanged between Conway and Gates. When the letter surfaced, Gates barely escaped with his own tarnished military career intact. The conspiracy against Washington collapsed when Conway resigned. It was the kind of high-stakes Byzantine maneuvering and scheming that kept the New Yorker warm during the freezing weather.

Washington's army, "those dear ragged Continentals," in their makeshift hovels deeply shocked Morris. He described the scene to Jay: "Heu miseros! The Skeleton of an army presents itself to our eyes in naked, starving Condition, out of Health, out of Spirits." Writing to Governor Clinton about desertions and resignations, Morris noted, "when you consider that the poor Dogs are…without Cloathes to wear, Victuals to eat Wood to burn or straw to lie on the wonder is that they stay not that they go." In six months, some 2,500 soldiers out of 10,000 would die in the camp.[6]

Misconduct, negligence, and incompetence played its part in the appalling confusion. "Neglect in the commisaries, worse in the quartermasters, disputed rank and disciplines form the great outlines of the picture," Morris reported to Benedict Arnold, now in Albany and not yet charged with treason. Washington had neither a quartermaster general nor commissary general on duty. Thomas Mifflin, the former quartermaster general and friendly to Conway's machinations, had failed to provide any supplies for months. Laurens thought that Mifflin's "idleness, duplicity and criminal partialities" made him one of the prime suspects promoting Washington's ouster.[7]

A few weeks earlier, on the morning of December 22, after Washington had ordered the army to march against a British force probing in the camp's direction, he was told that the American troops could not stir because they

The "Valley Forge" portrait of George Washington
by Charles Willson Peale, ca. 1780.
West Chester University of Pennsylvania.

lacked basic equipment—shoes and clothes—for even a brief field operation. The next day Washington confessed to President Laurens that he "was...convinced that...a dangerous Mutiny begun the Night before,...with difficulty was suppressed by the spirited exertion's of some officers [and] was still much to be apprehended." There had been no violence, but the sinister chant of "No meat! No meat!" rumbling through the cold night air was an unmistakable warning that the army might disintegrate for lack of supplies.[8]

Finally an alarmed, frustrated Congress moved to reorganize the army at the general's urging. An earlier reorganization had only compounded Washington's problems by entangling the military in a maze of red tape, and there was no reason to think that more congressional meddling would turn out differently. Francis Dana, Nathaniel Folsom, John Harvie, Joseph Reed, and Morris were appointed by congress to a new committee.

When the Committee at Camp sat down to work in the comfortable stone Moore House three miles from Washington's cramped headquarters, Francis Dana as chairman and Morris took charge of the committee's work. Washington had prepared a thorough report on the military reorganization to guide the committee in its work. It included a controversial proposal to guarantee half-pay to officers for life on retirement. The committee accepted Washington's recommendations with few changes and forwarded them to Congress. The finished drafts of the reports to Congress are in Morris's hand.

Morris knew how to get at the nut of a problem, whether financial, administrative, or political and how to define the issues clearly. He also had the ability to master detail without drowning in it. Beyond the discipline of law, it is difficult to pinpoint the sharpening of his natural gift for figures. Under the New Yorker's direction, inventories were taken, new policies laid down, and the states requisitioned for the portion of supplies they were supposed to furnish. The response of the states to share the load was critical, and the committee members returned periodically to York to pressure the Congress to get on with the reforms required to keep the states harnessed.[9]

Financing the war was as urgent as military organization and strategy. Laying it out in the plainest language in a letter to George Clinton, Morris told the New York governor that a pay-as-you-go tax was the only way to finance the war. "The Want of Money in the several Departments is a Complaint reverberated to us from all Quarters and arises, as much as any Thing, from Neglect in those who should have thought a little more of paying while very liberal in contracting debts. The blinkered policy of delaying taxation," he went on, "is so evident that the People ought to take exemplary Vengence upon those whoever they may be who are Causes of such delay."[10]

For all of his bluster, Morris knew that taxation remained so politically explosive that the people would punish any politician who suggested imposing new taxes, especially in a revolution stirred up, in part, over taxation. But he

knew that in order to staunch the depreciation of the currency, the government, as a grown-up state, would sooner or later have to exercise "Power
Method and Firmness" and impose taxes if it were to survive. One reason
Washington could not buy supplies from local Pennsylvania farmers was
because they refused Congress's worthless paper money. Howe in Philadelphia
paid in hard specie.

Not long after returning to Congress from Valley Forge, Morris drew up a
forthright, rational proposal for overhauling the entire financial system of the
national government not beholden to the charity of the states and certainly
not to the disastrous printing presses that had flooded the country with
worthless currency. Sweeping away the state currencies and consolidating fiscal policy in the federal body, his plan boldly proposed that the treasury be
centralized and that individual states give up their western lands to Congress
to be used to secure international loans. The states would in turn receive a
reduction in their future portion of the national debt. Among permanent
sources of revenue would be a national tariff and a per capita tax of one dollar.
All restrictions on interstate trade would be wiped out. As a plan, Morris's
proposal would have nullified the pledge given by the states when they ratified
the Articles of Confederation to levy their own taxes necessary to redeem the
remissions.[11]

The immediate problem, however, was the reorganization of the army.
Working together in the Moore House over Washington's proposal to reorganize the infantry, artillery, cavalry, and corps of engineers, Morris and
Washington deepened their friendship and respect for one another. This did
not mean that the general put aside his natural reserve, an aloofness that set
him apart from his staff as well as from most of his contemporaries. To his
later embarrassment during the Convention of 1787, Morris misread Washington's "most conspicuous visible trait" and discovered the Virginian's limits of
familiarity when he dared to pat him on the back, drawing a chilling, silent
rebuke. A certain territorial distance was central to the genius of Washington's
command of power.[12]

Washington was acutely aware that he lacked Morris's liberal education,
that of a "finished gentleman," and he no doubt valued and admired the
younger man's confidence in handling the fine points of civility in the conduct
of public matters. It is obvious that they shared those values of self-command,
moderation, and dedication to public service. Both revered all those qualities
of "habitual virtue" assumed, without pretense, by a "gentleman," a title
adopted by all homegrown American gentry, which included most of the revolutionary leaders.

Before Morris returned to York in April 1778, the Committee at Camp
forwarded Washington's recommendation to provide army officers half-pay
for life. The proposal involving money, patriotism, and the specter of a stand-

ing army set off a firestorm debate that raged for weeks, "the most painful and disagreeable question that hath ever been agitated in Congress." The absence of a standing army, after all, was part of the definition of a free republic. Writing to Laurens, Washington declared that he "most religiously" believed "the salvation of the cause depends on it." If it was not approved, the officer corps would "moulder to nothing, or be composed of low and illiterate men void of capacity for this, or any other business."[13]

Morris worked closely with Washington to defeat the political maneuvers of the opposition in Congress, which wanted to send the question to the states where it would undoubtedly be killed. After a quick head count, he told Washington that the motion to throw the issue into the lap of the states turned on Pennsylvania's shaky vote, where it was "a mighty flimsy Situation on that Subject having indeed a mighty flimsy Representation." Robert Morris, a Pennsylvania delegate, was away, but the New Yorker's message to the Financier to "think one moment and come the next" brought him back to his seat two days later when his single vote broke the tie, moving Pennsylvania into the majority of six to five. A final compromise involving a seven-year half-pay pension was shortly adopted, along with other reforms Washington had urged. Morris had been the general's staunchest accomplice and floor manager. The plan of reform approved by Congress and forwarded to Washington was written in Morris's hand.[14]

Although Morris supported Washington in most of his negotiations with the camp committee and Congress, he did not hesitate to oppose him over the terms of a treaty of exchange of prisoners with General Howe after the battle of Saratoga. Congress insisted that no British soldiers be released until all expenses of holding the men captive had been paid. Washington wanted soldiers to be given priority as quickly as possible.

Morris was assigned to sort out these complex issues, which he did brilliantly in what amounted to a lecture on statecraft addressed to Washington. While admitting that members of the congressional committee might not have all the facts, "they conceive the Ideas of Citizens may not be quite useless to Gentlemen of the Army now about to determine on the dearest Rights of Citizens at least of unfortunate ones." The subtle irony asserting civilian authority over the military is vintage Morris as was the opening argument stating fundamentals of foreign policy that followed: "Interest alone (and not Principles of Justice or Humanity) governs Men on such occasions," and it was essential in diplomatic negotiations for America, speaking only through Congress, to determine its paramount interests.[15]

Besides the Committee at Camp, other assignments were piled one upon another. That many of Morris's committees involved critical issues of foreign policy made him, in many respects, Congress's foreign secretary. By the end of 1778, he had served on sixty-five committees, a staggering number for someone who denied having "Patience and Industry" and promoted his reputation for "indolence."

"Let me paint my situation," he wrote Robert Morris later in 1778 when he returned to Congress from Valley Forge. "I am on a Committee to arrange the Treasury and Finances. I am on the medical committee and have to prepare the arrangements of that department. I have the same thing to go through with relative to the Commissary's Quarter master and Clothier General's departments. I am to prepare a Manifesto on the cruelties of the British. *I have drawn and expect to draw almost if not all the publications of Congress of any importance.*"[16]

As chairman of these primary standing committees, he did most of the work. Recalling the tiresome grind years later, he wrote, "You must not imagine that the members of these committees took any share or burden of affairs. Necessity, preserving the democratical forms, assumed the monarchical substance of business. The chairman received and answered all letters and other applications, took every step which he deemed essential, prepared reports, gave orders, and the like, and merely took the members of a committee into a chamber and for form's sake made the needful communications, and received their approbation which was given of course." He doesn't mention his accumulating and complex responsibilities growing out of the French alliance and its impact on American war policy.[17]

On April 20, 1778, Congress received a heated letter from Washington enclosing a copy of alarming bills introduced in Parliament by Lord North designed to offer conciliation to the former colonies. Britain was apparently ready to concede the touchy point on taxation and had dispatched commissioners to negotiate with Congress. It was, Washington exploded, a scheme "founded on principles of the most wicked, diabolical baseness meant to poison the minds of the people and detach the wavering, at least from our cause.... I trust it will be attacked in every shape, in every part of the Continent."[18]

Washington immediately saw through the maneuver, as he wrote in a private letter to a friend in Virginia. Even the faint prospect of a negotiated peace might derail public support for a renewed military campaign supported by the French government. General Howe was already circulating copies of the bills according to Virginia delegates, "with a view no doubt of diverting the People of America from their grand object of Preparation and defense."

For once realizing the danger in any delay or hesitation, Congress threw the hot potato into the lap of a special committee, chaired by Morris. Two days later, on April 22, Congress adopted Morris's report of the committee and ordered it published. It was tough, realistic, and inspiring: "that these United States cannot with propriety, hold any conference or treaty with any commissioners on the part of Great Britain, unless they shall preliminary thereto, either withdraw their fleets and armies, or else, in positive and express terms, acknowledge the independence of the said states." When John Jay saw the report, he wrote a friend that it was "too strikingly marked with Morris not to be known by his friends to have been produced by his pen." It was the kind of high-stakes battle Morris relished and knew how to win.[19]

In his argument and zeal, Morris first had to rally Congress, then the thirteen states and a very discouraged public. He also had to make clear to the British ministers and America's allies that there would be no backing down from "the great cause for which they contend, and in which all mankind is interested." Beginning with the stiffening of the congressional back in his opening attack on the "weakness and wickedness of the enemy" to the final, dismissive volley, squarely aimed at the commission, "the sequel of that insidious plan, which, from the days of the stamp act down to the present time, hath involved this country in contention and bloodshed," Morris's denunciation of Parliament's ploy repeatedly hit its target. He set the uncompromising tone that would guide the ensuing peace negotiations in which he played a crucial role, his major achievement in the Congress.

The powerful resolve of Morris's words, read out in the little courtroom in York is a high rhetorical moment:

> The said bill, by holding forth a tender of pardon, implies a criminalitry in our justifiable resistance; and, consequently, to treat under it, would be an implied acknowledgment that the inhabitants of these states were what Britain had declared them to be, rebels....As the Americans, united in this arduous contest upon principles of common interest, for the defense of common rights and privileges; which union hath been cemented by common calamities, so the great cause for which they contend and in which all mankind is interested...must derive its success from the continuance of that union;...The committee beg leave to report it is their opinion, that these United States cannot, with propriety, hold any conference or treaty with any commissioners on the part of Great Britain, unless they shall, as a preliminary thereto, either withdraw their fleets and armies, or else, in positive and express terms, acknowledge the independence of said states.[20]

On the twenty-ninth of April, five days after Morris's committee made its ringing statement in Morris's words, Governor George Clinton reported to John Jay that Simeon Deane the brother of Silas Deane, one of the congressional negotiators in Paris, had suddenly appeared in Fishkill traveling with a cavalry escort of Light Horse on his way to York. Deane carried with him "Dispatches from the Court to Congress of great Importance.... I may venture to tell you as a Truth," he went on, "a treaty is concluded between that Court and our Embassadors."[21]

Morris's own private intelligence network had anticipated the news. On the same day Clinton signaled to Jay the arrival of Deane and his escort, Morris wrote Jay from York: "Our Affairs are most critical tho not dangerously so.... I believe it will not require such astonishing efforts after this Campaign to keep the Enemy at Bay. Probably a Treaty is signed with the House of Bourbon ere this." Then with prescience he concludes, "if so a Spark hath fallen upon the Train which is to fire the World." The day after the treaty and its military escort swept into York, Morris rushed off a note to Livingston telling him that they couldn't have gotten more if "the important word *Louis* had been put in his Thanks at the Bottom of a blank Paper."[22]

Congress quickly ratified both treaties by a unanimous vote on May 4, 1778. France gave the United States an open license to conquer Canada and Bermuda. France, in turn, was at liberty to take the British West Indies by force. Both agreed to respect the other's territorial gains. Neither was to conclude a treaty with Britain without the other's consent. On the day of ratification, Jay wrote Morris cautioning him that "moderation in Prosperity marks great Minds and denotes a generous People," lecturing him like an older brother that his "game is now in a delicate Situation and the least bad Play may Ruin it."[23]

Some of the delegates became giddy over the prospect of the French minister to the United States being received in state by Congress at the same moment that the king's Peace Commission knocked at the door with their olive branch. Solemn steps were taken to publish the news of the treaties far and wide. Fifty copies were rushed to Washington. To underline the importance of the announcement and to reinforce the dangers of falling for London's seductive offer of peace, Morris was asked to write a warning, "Address of Congress to the Inhabitants of the United States of America," recommending that it be read in places of worship throughout the land.

Pulling out all the stops, the New Yorker composed an astute piece of propaganda designed to shore up popular support for the next scene in the drama when American representatives would meet with the King George's agents. Only independence would guarantee security since Britain would never consider itself bound by any treaty negotiated with rebels. Not even a "shadow of liberty can be preserved in a dependent connection with Great Britain."

In the opening paragraph of his address to the British commissioners, the New Yorker set a sharp, impassioned tone of direct assault: "Three years have now passed away, since the commencement of the present war: a war without parallel in the annals of mankind. It hath displayed a spectacle, the most solemn that can possibly be exhibited. On one side, we behold fraud and violence laboring in the service of despotism; on the other, virtue and fortitude supporting and establishing the rights of human nature." He closed with the fervid words of a crusader: "Thus shall the power and the happiness of these sovereign, free and independent states, founded on the virtue of their citizens, increase, extend and endure until the Almighty shall blot out all the empires on earth."[24]

As Morris knew very well, even after two years of war, sentimental attachment to Britain still lurked just below the surface. This nostalgia was exactly what the Peace Commission hoped to exploit. In a letter to Robert Livingston, William Duer hinted that an offer of home rule short of independence might be worth considering. But the chancellor would have nothing of it, wickedly telling Duer, "Our situation is extremely delicate, deliberation would be dangerous to our honor & safety as to a woman's chastity which your own experience will probably tell you seldom survives five minutes hesitation." Although willing to risk all for independence, John Jay admitted to Morris that "the destruction of old England would hurt me. I wish it well; it afforded my Ancestors an Asylum from Persecution."[25]

But the American attitude toward the European players in the drama was not shaped by sentiment or nostalgia, and even less so by idealism. American diplomacy during the revolutionary years in which those power politicians Morris and Jay participated was as hardheaded and calculating as that of any European chancery. They were by no means alone in their realistic appraisals of both friend and foe. Washington had no illusions about foreign relations as revealed in his reaction to the proposed conquest of Canada and the possibility of French participation: "I am heartily disposed to entertain the most favorable sentiments of our new ally and to cherish them in others to a reasonable degree," he wrote Henry Laurens, "but it is a maxim founded on the universal experience of mankind, that no nation is to be trusted farther than it is bound by its interest; and no prudent statesman or politician will venture to depart from it."[26]

Short of a complete capitulation by the enemy, Morris was champing at the bit to scuttle London's badly timed and clumsy peace offering while the news from Paris had a chance to sink in. Every report and response in the crisis carried Morris's distinctive stamp of calm but steely resolve. So did the strategy. As a "man of the world," he was, in Henry Adams's opinion, "cool, even-tempered, incredulous, with convictions chiefly practical and illusions largely rhetorical." Adams's assessments were impeccable credentials for high statesmanship. A contemporary critic of Morris (and he had several who held the same opinion) noted an unequaled amount of "brass" in his makeup.[27]

Before Parliament's gesture of conciliation reached Congress, Morris understood that it signaled a new British strategy. On the American continent, the British army would now withdraw its operations to New York and Rhode Island, while concentrating on the loyalist and neutral civilians left unprotected in the South. Morris immediately saw the dangers the appeal might have to a war-weary population.[28]

When they arrived, and as if the answer was already prepared, the letters from Generals Howe and Clinton accompanying the Parliamentary acts were turned over to Morris's committee on June 6, with directions to "retire into the next room and prepare an answer." Laurens's official reply was ready before the day was out. The reply included Congress's Act of April 22, drafted by Morris, and his crisp addition: "Your lordship may be assured," it curtly announced, "that when the king of Great Britain shall be seriously disposed to put an end to the unprovoked and cruel war...Congress will readily attend to such terms of peace, as may consist with the honor of independent nations, the interest of their constituents, and the sacred regard they mean to pay to treaties." No ambiguous diplomatic fat was allowed to obscure Morris's bristling language stating the American position.[29]

Three days later, while Congress was in the middle of a debate over issuing a passport to the commission's secretary, an express letter from Washington arrived with an impressive packet containing a letter from the British commissioners, who had just landed in Philadelphia. The letter was ushered into the chamber and without waiting, the document was opened in front of all the assembled members and a reading began immediately. When the president got to the second page, the startled delegates heard the French alliance called an "insidious interposition of a power, which has from the first settlement of these colonies, been actuated with enmity to us both." On the next line, "and not withstanding the pretended date or present form of the French offers," an indignant Morris rose to his full height and managed to halt the reading "because of the offensive language against his most Christian majesty." It was a piece of theater that he knew how to carry off to full effect. Samuel Adams, on the alert for any counterrevolutionary blandishments, was pleased to report that the commission's ill-timed language "gave particular disgust to all the Members."[30]

The most sensitive American nerve was touched by the British taunt that the "United" States were not confederated and did not have the authority to speak for the country. After running into Congress's intransigence, they demanded to know by just what powers "you conceive yourselves Authorized to make Treaties with Foreign Nations." Rather than debate the issue with the enemy, an insulted Congress refused to answer. Morris, meanwhile, carried the fight to the press as "An American" addressing the earl of Carlisle: "It is a most diverting circumstance to hear you ask Congress what power they have to treat, after offering to enter into a treaty with them, and being refused. But I shall be glad to know by what authority you will call on them for this discovery. The Count de Vergennes had a right to it, but the Earl of Carlisle certainly has not."[31]

When the commissioners threatened to accept Morris's dare to enter the press war, the New Yorker shot back: "There is but one way to sink you still lower, and thank God you have found it out. You are about to publish! Oh my Lord! my Lord! you are indeed in a mighty pitiful condition. You have tried fleets and armies, and proclamations, and now you threaten us with newspapers."[32]

Since early May 1778, rumors had been circulated in York that Lord Howe was about to abandon Philadelphia. With unbecoming vengeance more in the spirit of the Old Testament than the Age of Enlightenment, Morris brashly advised Washington to move in on the heels of the departing British, put everyone under house arrest, and impose by force a fine of 100,000 pounds sterling "in hard money...apportioned upon the Inhabitants according to their wealth and disaffection." So much for the supposed defender of aristocracy. The New Yorker's uninvited counsel was wisely ignored.

On June 24, after Washington confirmed the evacuation, Congress adjourned in York to reassemble on July 2 in Philadelphia. The British commissioners, who had met with total failure had already been told "whence to take their departure." An understandable euphoria washed over a grand dinner held by Congress in Philadelphia's City Tavern to celebrate "the glorious Anniversary of the INDEPENDENCE OF AMERICA." The timely gift of turtle and wine sent by the British commission to some congressmen as an opening bribe was served to the guests. Thirteen toasts, that magic number, were drunk with heady confidence.[33]

In a stroke, the Paris treaties dramatically set military operations on a new course in the direction of victory. The new British strategy of consolidating its forces, abandoning Philadelphia, and moving to a massive campaign of pacification would play into the hands of the new alliance and its impressive naval presence. But before any peace terms with Great Britain could be negotiated, the war had to be won, and even with French support the struggling government had to put its own administration and finances in some kind of credible order.

To reverse the descent into bankruptcy, an immediate loan had to be found. To secure such a loan, Morris proposed setting aside a portion of the undeveloped public lands to be used by Congress as security for national debts. His single-handed attempt to give the Articles of Confederation a strong national grounding was unsurprisingly defeated.

With growing assurance and the need to show the French that there was an officially incorporated country, on July 9, eight states were ready to sign the long-delayed Articles of Confederation. But now another element in the Paris treaties was triggering a sea change in international relations that would take the American leadership some time to grasp. The vague rhetorical "concern of Mankind" for the outcome, regularly invoked by Americans, was no longer just an inflated cliché embracing the world. Any final treaty of peace would require the very concrete approval of the French government.

No one publicly questioned the motives of the French monarchy coming to the rescue of the fledgling republic. And although the former colonies had been automatically dragged into every European war in which Britain was involved, the new ties with France did not seem to set off any alarms, at least in public. But when Henry Laurens read the advance copy of the minister's remarks and the congressional reply, he told Washington he felt a "reluctance...to acknowledgments of obligations or of generosity where benefits have been, to say the

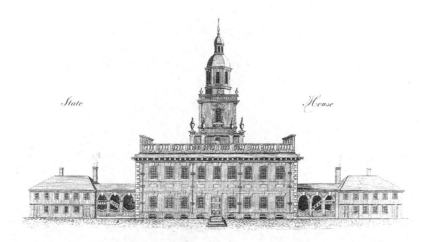

Pennsylvania State House, detail from "A Ground Plan of the City of Philadelphia," 1774 by John Reed, copy by Charles Warner, 1870.
Reproduced from the collections of the Library of Congress.

least, reciprocal." Morris and every other delegate in Congress agreed with the president and would have gladly avoided any French aid if the war could have been won without this entangling of the country in the affairs of Europe. It was, as Edmund Burnett wrote in his history of the Congress, "the great uncertainty that glared Congress in the face... threats of dire consequences to America for having mortgaged herself to France."[34]

The power of the new partnership was revealed when the comte d'Estang with his French squadron of war ships turned up in the Delaware Bay on July 29, 1778. With him on the flagship *Languedoc* was the new French emissary Sieur Conrade Alexandre Gérard. D'Estang's mission was to put the minister plenipotentiary from the Court of Versailles in the hands of Congress before turning his fleet northward toward New York in search of British prey.

It took a month for the British presence to be exorcised from the State House in order to properly receive the French representative. While the place was being cleaned and fitted out for the grand reception, Morris joined Samuel Adams and Richard Henry Lee, an unlikely trio, to work out the ceremonial details for the reception of the country's first official diplomat. Swelling with pride, Adams could hardly believe "that one so little the man of the World" as he "should be joyned to a Committee to settle Ceremonials." Above all, the old Yankee declared, it was important to establish forms reflecting "true *republican* Principles" for future generations.[35]

Morris might pretend to friends that the reception was a "whiffling" inci-

Indépendence des États-Unis, from *Portraits des Grands Hommes Illustres.*
Courtesy of Yale University Library.

dent, but he knew very well that the official panache was as much for the self-esteem and dignity of the Congress as it was to impress the foreign guests. He was also aware of the precedent it would set. He knew that in matters of high seriousness, style was paramount, particularly in the rituals of convention between sovereign states. The orchestration of the reception was even trickier because one party was a republic, the other an ancient monarchy resting on hundreds of years of history and tradition.

What should the seating arrangements be in the chamber of a republic receiving for the first time the agent of a monarch? Should the president's chair be raised above the rest? And if so, how high the minister's chair? In what form were the parties to be addressed? What should be the signal for either the president or minister to stand, sit, or bow? Who should speak first and in what language? Morris knew how to stage-manage these things very well. And he could follow the written scripts of the "public ministers...in the language of their respective countries," as he prescribed. All responses, however, would be "in the language of the United States."

The ceremony was punctilious, performed without any awkward lapses. "The whole," an approving Elios Boudinot, a New Jersey delegate, later reported to his wife, "was plain, grand and decent." Another delegate agreed that it was "conducted with great decorum...grand and elegant." Any lingering fears and anxiety over the new alliance or gauche manners were put aside as everything seemed to "presage a happy Issue to the American Struggle and a growing and undecaying Glory that shall diffuse its grateful Influences thro' the world."[36]

The immediate effect of the French alliance was to give Congress an opportunity to put its "deranged" foreign relations in order. Skeptical European observers now saw the real possibility that the Americans would win the war. Congress was suddenly dazzled by visions of friendly commercial treaties with Lisbon, The Hague, Stockholm, Copenhagen, and St. Petersburg. Henry Laurens complained that there was "not a Book in Town" to guide these missions through what were, from the limited American experience, dangerous uncharted waters. Concerned with its parvenu status in world affairs, Congress resolved in early May that representatives appointed to European courts "should live in such style and manner...as they may find suitable and necessary to support the dignity of their public character." Congress would pick up the tab.[37]

Just as the British peace initiative was winding down with the departure of the battered commissioners, Morris took time out of "the every day minutia" to write an "official" history of the Revolution, called "Observations on the American Revolution," to allow the public to "look over the ground they had trodden." Remarkably, a hard-pressed Congress appropriated $2,986 to have Morris's pamphlet printed.

Morris's "Observations" was soon circulating in London. A second edition was published in Newport. In his three-thousand-word address he conjured up the shining hopes and dreams hinted at in his oration on independence in 1776, that civilization and empire were inexorably moving west, that the future was America. In 1758, the year that seven-year-old Morris arrived at the Philadelphia Academy, a foreigner traveling in the colonies was struck by this same widespread, popular belief in the western trajectory of power: "An idea as strange as it is visionary...that empire is traveling westward."

Morris's optimism and renewed confidence in the war's outcome were tempered with compassion for the losers when he received a farewell letter from his old friend Peter Van Schaack who had been banished to England for remaining neutral. On September 8, 1778, Morris wrote his friend: "I am particularly afflicted that you should be now obliged to relinquish your country, for opinions which are unfavorable to her rights.... It was always my opinion, that matters of conscience and faith, whether political or religious, are as much out of the province, as they are beyond the ken of human legislatures. In the question of punishment for acts, it hath been my constant axiom, that the object is example, and therefore the thing only justifiable from necessity, and from the effect."[38]

In spite of "the heat of this perfidious climate" in Philadelphia, Morris took on his next assignment in foreign affairs, the job of drafting congressional instructions to Benjamin Franklin, the old family friend who had been named minister plenipotentiary at the Court of Versailles. Morris's blueprint for Dr. Franklin would be the first such directive to be sent to an American minister at a foreign post. Morris told Jay that he missed his counsel and experience because there were "many persons whom you know are very liberal of illiberality." The exercise was also useful training for the man who would one day take Franklin's post in Paris. He was careful to add a final admonishing reminder in the instructions that Congress had the last word in foreign policy: "You shall in all things take care not to make any engagements, or stipulations, on the part of America, without the consent of Congress previously obtained."[39]

Realistic about the implications and pitfalls of the new alliance, Morris lost no time in taking the preliminary draft of Franklin's instructions to Alexandre Gérard for his reaction. There was a certain symmetry to his gesture since Gérard had advised in the drafting of the treaties in Paris before coming to Philadelphia. The New Yorker had already caught the minister's eye; he had spotted one of Morris's recent newspaper articles denouncing the British Peace Commission. Sending the article on to the foreign minister in Paris, Gérard told Vergennes it had been written by "a young man of twenty-eight, a delegate from New York, named Gouverneur Morris, descended from a Dutch family...he is a man full of merit and energy, with whom I am trying to become intimate." Having played a central role in negotiating the treaties in Paris, Gérard was looking for someone he could work with in America who would not be suspicious of French interests and advice.[40]

The United States, the draft instructions declared, had already proved its commitment to independence "during three bloody campaigns," but all this was the boilerplate of diplomacy. The proposed conquest of Canada, however, was a potential booby trap. For all the congressional railings against foreign involvement, such a foolhardy move of "emancipation" by the United States would have undoubtedly brought on another Seven Years' War.

Gérard shrewdly did not take a forceful stand against Canadian liberation because the proposed invasion appeared to have strong congressional backing. France, as well as the United States, was let off the hook after Washington reviewed the plan and told Congress that the idea was badly flawed, both in tactics and politics. The general's recommendations were then turned over to Morris's committee, which concurred. Morris had already assured Washington that he "knew more on the Subject than all of us put together."[41]

The most important document in Franklin's diplomatic pouch was Morris's "Observations on the Finances of America," providing the ammunition to make the case for immediate financial aid from the new partner. From the beginning, Morris had grasped the fundamental fact that the art of war was determined by money, a truism not fully understood by some of the more romantic revolutionaries. Simply put, the American cause would evaporate if troops were not paid, fed, and armed. This platitude would take shocking form in fall 1781 when Washington's troops, headed for Yorktown, refused to budge beyond Philadelphia until they were paid back wages. The New Yorker's incisive diagnosis of the patient's economic ills, infecting every other part of the body politic, laid out the argument for the crucial international loans. It also anticipated the ambitious reforms of the new Department of Finance that he and Robert Morris would later attempt.[42]

The basis of Morris's well-timed essay to Franklin on the Revolution's financial straits grew out of an earlier committee assignment. He had focused sharply on the nation's financial problems in the memorial he drew up not long after returning from Valley Forge. To establish a secure financial footing for the long term, Morris urged radical monetary reforms and proposed eliminating all the state currencies in exchange for Continental certificates. "The Torrent of Paper Money," he warned Robert Livingston, "hath swept away with it much of our morals and impaired the national Industry to a degree truly alarming." Permanent funding in the form of taxes and tariffs had to be created. To manage this advanced new system, a central comptroller would have to be named and a treasury board established.[43]

Besides finance, Morris had become embroiled in other noisy Congressional arguments and running quarrels, notably the Silas Deane affair and the embarrassing problem of New England's lust for the "Tomcod" of Nova Scotia waters, issues that would send temperatures up and divide the Congress into hostile camps. These issues and other "little incidents that postpone great affairs" added to Morris's growing list of personal enemies. Jay had warned his friend in the fall: "Your enemies talk much of your Tory connections at Philadelphia. Take care. Some people of importance in your city apprehend ill consequences to yourself as well as the State.... They have informed me in a friendly manner that I might hint it to you." It was an inkling of the opposition that would unseat Morris in the New York congressional election in fall 1779.[44]

Acknowledging the supremacy of the electorate in a republic, an electorate that he had not bothered to cultivate, Morris stoically told Robert Livingston in August 1778, "If the State have not a confidence that their delegates are willing and able to serve them it is time they were recalled. Justice shall be done to us." It was a grudging admission that on the grand scale of revolutions the first principle is that governments are created by "the people," although he had interposed the state's confidence as the final arbiter, not the populace at large.

To Morris, the blessings of a free government meant a republican government dedicated to preserving the liberties of Englishmen, which were now being stepped on. But exactly what form a "republican government" would take and just what the magic formula would be to conjure it into life had not yet been worked out. There was still a wide gap between the rhetoric and reality. The "beautiful and ambiguous ideal" of a government of "We the People" was in the distant Convention of 1787. At this point and in the heat of war, Morris was not inclined to dance attendance on local politicians.[45]

On August 18, Josiah Bartlett reported to a friend, "Mr. Deane has been called before Congress to give an account of our affairs in Europe," adding ominously, "and of his conduct there." Silas Deane, a Yale graduate and ambitious Connecticut Yankee entrepreneur, had been sent to Paris as agent of the Secret Committee of Congress on an undercover mission in fall 1776 to buy military supplies. He was later named one of the three commissioners, along with Benjamin Franklin and Arthur Lee, to explore the possibility of French recognition while continuing to act as agent to secure supplies for the American war.

From the outset, commerce and politics were mixed up in Deane's assignment. After all, Robert Morris, chairman of the Secret Committee, had told him when he left on the mission, "there never has been so fair an opportunity to make a fortune." Before the Deane mission, Robert and his Philadelphia cronies in the Morris and Willing mercantile firms had secretly operated a business to funnel French military supplies to the American cause. Robert Morris was always in the middle of anything where money was involved, and many believed that he had mixed the public interest far too well with his private affairs, generously lining his pockets while advancing the patriotic cause. The same complaint was now made against the Connecticut operator in Paris.[46]

The vital French shipments that followed from Deane's dealings—it is impossible to estimate the extent of French generosity—shored up Washington's army at critical turns. But the new French alliance treaties brought his diplomatic mission to an end, and his complicated accounts were challenged by Congress when he was recalled. Even before he arrived in Philadelphia, members were split over the propriety of his commercial dealings, setting off an acrimonious fight and dragging in the French government and its new minister.

A number of members of Congress held outspoken opinions on the moral and personal virtue required by a successful republic. Samuel Adams saw the Revolution as a holy war to create a Spartan America isolated from European corruption. "Trade," and the merchants who engaged in it, was suspect to men who professed the older American values. Never mind that Adams's small New England merchants and farmers were, in fact, dependent on foreign markets to sustain their economy. So it is easy to see how this Puritan attitude, shared by the anti-Deane faction—frugality, industry, sacrifice for the public good—whether it went under that label or not, entered into the charges against Deane.[47]

In Paris, Deane had antagonized his fellow commissioner Arthur Lee, who accused Deane of "too freely fingering public Money." The scion of the traditions of the family estate of Stratford Hall in Virginia, but incongruously a Puritan manqué, Lee spread the word that the upstart Yankee trader had profited in the private financial arrangements surrounding the covert scheme to secure military supplies from French sources. Working closely with Pierre-Augustin Caron, better known as Beaumarchais, author of *The Barber of Seville,* Deane served as the agent for much of this hugely profitable international trade.

In fall 1778 when Congress weighed into the Deane dispute, a further question was raised. Were these generous war supplies a gift of France in pursuit of its own strategy, or were they, as Deane and Beaumarchais claimed, a charge against the credit of the United States? The question immediately agitated America's new partner, and tensions with an embarrassing international twist hung over congressional debates for months to come.

The day before Deane made his first appearance before Congress, Morris told John Jay that he stood by Deane against the charges of the troublemaker Arthur Lee. "Your friend Deane," Morris wrote, "who hath rendered the most essential services, stands as one accused. The Storm increases and I think some one of the tall trees, must be shorn up by the roots." Having faced the army's dire predicament with Washington at Valley Forge the previous winter, Morris knew just how crucial the clandestine French support Deane helped to organize had been. Without careful management, Morris sensed that the new alliance might be dragged into this domestic political brawl with unpredictable consequences. Gérard had spread the word that the tiresome Lee was persona non grata to the French government, thus putting the minister in the middle of a partisan dogfight that he did not fully understand.

Before the gale subsided, the first tree fell as Morris predicted. Henry Laurens, a partisan of the Lee faction, resigned as president of Congress in order to self-righteously carry on the fight from the floor. His seat was taken by John Jay, who had just arrived as a New York delegate. Like Morris, Jay was an outspoken defender of Deane. Personalities and ideologies so colored the Deane affair that it is even now difficult to fairly judge the issues. Deane's later conduct, with accusations of treason added to charges of war profiteering, has made it impossible to mount a creditable defense.

While waiting for Congress to give him a hearing, Deane published a rebuttal to the charges in the *Pennsylvania Packet* in early December, adding his countercharges against Lee's. Morris who could not resist a war of words— few of his colleagues could—would shortly jump into the press free-for-all.

An outraged Francis Lightfoot Lee reported to his brother Arthur that Deane's supporters had formed "a very dangerous party who think it necessary to their designs to remove all the old friends of Liberty." It is not clear just what he meant by "remove," but the Virginian's use of "party" insinuated the specter of a dark conspiracy drawn from "the new formed commercial Establishments"—led by Morris and his business cronies—advancing their selfish interests while the war wore on. Lee's next line is more explicit: "This party is composed of Tories, all those who have rob'd the public are now doing it." The "old Whigs" like the Lees, who claimed to be the true defenders of Liberty, were shocked by what they perceived to be a new breed of worldly men mixing their private economic interests with their patriotism and the public's interest.

The charge of profiteering rumbles like a basso continuo throughout the Deane affair and beyond. The awkward fact that the Lees lived off the labor, rent, and sale of their slaves, as did Henry Laurens, was ignored in all the moralizing uproar. The rich Maryland planter and merchant Charles Carroll of Carrollton, a supporter of both Morris and old-fashioned virtues, reported that he had even "heard it said that G. Morris is in trade," adding that he trusted the report was "groundless."[48]

Men like the Morrises and Jay, who were cosmopolitan in their perspective and alert to the international world of commerce, expected the United States to take its place among competing nations. They had grown up in the urban trading ports of New York and Philadelphia, where merchants with international interests were a respected part of the establishment. The "sniping diplomacy" of the Lee crowd, attempting to deny American obligations to France, could be a jolt to the incipient and delicate relationship with its new partner. It could cast a shadow over the nation's commercial ambitions as well. The future of the alliance and even the future of the American cause might well be at stake.

In addition to the Lee brothers, Deane's chief antagonists were Samuel Adams, who wore his Puritan values on his sleeve, and Laurens, who though an Anglican had a self-righteous Puritan streak, frowning on card playing, gambling, and even opposed the use of fireworks to celebrate Independence Day in 1779. It is easy to see why Laurens was skeptical of Gouverneur Morris from the moment Morris took his seat in Congress. For the Lees and Laurens united with Samuel Adams, it was a morality play in which they were the victims.

Chaotic economic conditions of Philadelphia added to the acrimony of the Deane quarrel. Skyrocketing inflation throughout 1778 and 1779 created widespread hardship and had made the issue of profiteering a hot public topic. In May 1779, Washington, writing to Jay "on the state of our currency," noted that "a wagon-load of money will scarcely purchase a wagon-load of provisions." Two Philadelphians, Daniel Roberdeau and Christopher Marshall, campaigned against the corrosive high prices and organized a public protest that threatened to become an extralegal political voice of popular opposition.[49]

Deane's enemies were not particularly brilliant when they hired Tom Paine as their chief advocate. He lost no time in making himself the issue. Paine was then acting as secretary to the congressional committee for foreign affairs although grandly "styling himself," Morris charged, "Secretary of Foreign

Affairs." Morris relished the idea of taking on the author of *Common Sense* in public and demolishing his self-serving pretensions. During Morris's earlier press war against the British commissioners, Paine had attacked Morris, accusing him of betraying the interests of the United States by agreeing to give away New England's fishery rights. In his charges against Deane, Paine had also made "insolent menaces," insinuating that some members, such as Gouverneur's friend Robert Morris, had secret financial connections with Deane.[50]

Paine's first salvo, which quickly followed Deane's in the *Packet* during the first week of 1779, claimed that he had official evidence that the supplies furnished by Beaumarchais were a gift of the king of France. The charge contradicted official French assurances given to the British government. Gérard, the French minister, immediately demanded that Congress repudiate Paine's charges. The next day Paine was hauled into the State House and forced to admit before the bar that he had written the inflammatory articles. When Congress then took up the French minister's protest, Morris was ready and moved to dismiss Paine as secretary because he was not fit for the position, "Duty to our ally requires it. Duty to ourselves requires it."

Morris then tore into his prey with savage pleasure. Playing to the French spectators, he demanded, with unbecoming disdain, what would a foreigner think if he accidentally discovered that someone calling himself "our Secretary of Foreign Affairs was a mere adventurer *from England,* without fortune, without family or connections, ignorant even of grammar?" Morris then pushed his resolution that Paine be fired. Reasons to fire him were ample. Quite aside from Deane's problems, foremost in Morris's mind was the damage done to the country's credibility, not to mention the French alliance. Morris also wanted to personally placate Gérard, whose confidence was important to him in their private negotiations. Paine was finished when it was discovered that he had also revealed secrets of the Committee for Foreign Affairs. He was fired from his job on January 16, 1779.

The Deane dispute crossed all lines represented in Congress, but the Lee supporters were mostly New Englanders who were temperamentally isolationists in their hostility to French advice and suspicious of French intentions. They preferred to go it alone. The test came in Morris's resolution, unanimously adopted, that the president assure Gérard and "in the clearest and most explicit manner, disavow the publications," which Congress adopted unanimously. Jay's letter sent with the resolution, also pledged to Gérard "that every attempt to injure the representation of either, or impair their mutual confidence, will meet with the Indignation and resentment of both."

Exhausted with all the tensions of a bitter session, Congress was relieved to recall that February 6, 1779, was the first anniversary of "this union which has taken place between the two nations." To clear the air, it was decided to give His Excellency the Minister Plenipotentiary of His Most Christian

Majesty a banquet to celebrate the anniversary while they tried to repair their badly frayed dignity. The high-flown toasts full of "brilliances" managed to cover up the fact that Gérard had taken sides in the Deane-Lee dispute by leaking unfavorable opinions about Lee to friendly congressmen, helping to finally bring him down. This, of course, insured a hardening of anti-French sentiments. By casting the parties in an ideological mold, laced with conspiracy, as Europeans then and now tend to do, and finding all Francophiles among the moderates of patrician background, while putting all Francophobes in the radical, mostly New England camp, Gérard ignored the shifting composition and allegiance of pressure groups in American politics. As in all simplifications, there was a core of truth in this foreign assessment—after all, Morris occasionally wrote Robert Livingston in French—but what was in question were those dogging labels, "conservative," "moderate," and "radical," that American politics were constantly redefining, to the confusion of European observers.[51]

Two days after the congressional party, Gérard told John Jay that he had been ordered to communicate immediately to Congress on "subjects of the highest importance." Gérard's first secret, divulged to a spellbound Congress was the prospect of Spain joining the alliance, later proved false. But Gérard had other messages to deliver to Congress over the next few days. With clever timing, while spirits were still high, the French minister next asked for and got "a private audience and free conference," the Congress dramatically resolving itself into a Committee of the Whole. On February 15 Gérard, "attending agreeably to his appointment," firmly but politely told Congress that it was now time put aside its usual inertia and face the sobering, complex questions surrounding any peace settlement.

The French minister did Congress a favor by making it face the hard questions it had managed to sidestep. First of all, just how far was the United States willing to go in pressing the war? Which, if any of their priorities were they willing to abandon? What were they willing to fight for to the final blow? What were the territorial limits (and ambitions) to be set at a peace conference? What was, in short, their ultimatum? The possibility of a Spanish alliance was an unknown ingredient in the debate that followed. As had now become the routine, Morris was made chairman of a special committee and asked to provide Congress with possible answers to these tough questions.[52]

Morris's report reached the floor of Congress eight days after the audience with Gérard. The New Yorker maintained his sense of proportion, seeing his job as an attempt to steer a safe course between powerful sectional American interests and the stark fact that the final outcome of the Revolution depended on the good graces of the French government. While the United States would be sensitive to French interests, Morris made clear that it would not be subservient.

As a sine qua non and a preliminary to any negotiations that all agreed on, the irrevocable American position was restated: the absolute liberty, sovereignty, and independence of the new country must be recognized and all forces of the enemy withdrawn. Morris then moved into the divisive issues of territorial boundaries between Canada and Nova Scotia and the Floridas, and between the Atlantic and the Mississippi. American expansion was worrisome to both the French and the Spanish. Congress insisted that its western boundary was the Mississippi. But western interests wanted free navigation of the Mississippi as far as the southern boundary of the United States and a free port to the Gulf of Mexico. Morris assured Gérard that America had no designs on the Mississippi territory of Spain. Many in Congress thought that the West was already filling up with adventurers, bandits, and fugitives from the law and the only way to discipline and civilize them was to first tie them up with industry and property in order to make them "virtuous," that all-purpose measure of a true republican society.[53]

Morris also agreed with the French emissary that the southern line of the Confederation should be fixed because he was persuaded that the virtues needed by a republic could only be bred and cultivated in a healthy climate and a country of a limited size. The Mississippi question would be finally resolved with a proposed trade-off accepting Spain's interest in the Floridas. The United States got the Mississippi rights by default, however, when the Spanish alliance fell through.

On July 4, 1779, the third anniversary of the Declaration, everyone was ready for a truce. Tensions had subsided and the combatants were exhausted. Again the French minister was the center of the celebration. Two weeks earlier, Congress tried to patch any diplomatic rips that might have appeared in the alliance over the language of the peace instructions by requesting portraits of his most Christian Majesty and royal consort—Louis XVI and Marie Antoinette—to be placed in the council chamber, so that "the representatives may daily have before their eyes the first royal friends and patrons of their cause." The supplicants did not hesitate to append a request for a loan in the memorial to the "Great, Faithful and Beloved Friend and ally." Henry Laurens condemned the immoral festivities on the Fourth in his diary: "drinking Media wine from 5 to 9 o'clock then sallying out to gaze at fireworks, and afterwards returning to Wine again." The republic could not survive this display of dissipation.

Realizing that he was under fire among his constituency, Morris around this time began to meditate on a foreign post, a position free of the nuisance of an electorate. On March 24, 1779, Congress had received a report from the committee looking into the charges against all of the American commissioners in Paris. The committee proposed overhauling the entire diplomatic representation and that the appointments of Franklin, Deane, Ralph Izard, and Arthur Lee "be vacated and new appointments made." Thomas McKean of Delaware was close to the mark when he concluded that "the intention of some Gentlemen in Congress appeared to me to be the removal of all our foreign Ministers in order to make way for themselves." Heated sectional intrigue, fired with "envy, malice and every vindictive passion," kept the pot boiling for weeks as each name was brought up, debated, and voted on.[54]

In all this housecleaning, some thought Morris was secretly, but actively, maneuvering for Franklin's job. But Nathaniel Peabody, a delegate from New Hampshire, believed he was angling for the minister's post in Holland. If Franklin had been recalled from Paris, there is no doubt Morris would have leaped for that position. Years earlier on the completion of his law studies, he had declared, quite accurately, that he did not have the temperament or ambition for a sustained career in politics.

By August, it was necessary to draw up a set of instructions for the peace conference with Britain, and Gouverneur Morris produced his final state paper on foreign affairs. Morris's peace proposal, approved on August 14, settled—or rather postponed—the divisive question of New England fishing rights by declaring that the guarantee of these rights was "of the utmost importance yet a desire of terminating the war hath induced us not to make the acquisition of these objects an object of an ultimatum on the present occasion." But no treaty of commerce, it added, would be signed without an agreement on the fisheries.

Written in Morris's hand, the report preserved absolute independence in government and commerce. Morris's instructions also empowered the commissioners, with the consent of France, to conclude a cessation of hostilities during the negotiations. The instructions closed with this carefully drafted passage: "In all matters not above mentioned, you are to govern yourselves by the Alliance between His Most Christian Majesty and these States, by the advice of our allies, by your knowledge of our Interests, and by your own discretion, in which we repose the fullest confidence."[55]

After setting the general terms of peace, the commissioner for Paris had to be chosen. Although partisans tried to push the name of Arthur Lee, the real contest was between John Adams and John Jay. When Adams was selected for Paris in early October, Jay was named minister to Spain as consolation. He would later be appointed to join Adams, Franklin, Laurens, and Jefferson in the peace negotiations. To Morris's detractors, "the Tall Boy" had been too conspicuous in too many bloody political clashes, so when his name was briefly floated as secretary to Franklin in Paris, it was quickly shot down. His adversaries were waiting in ambush when they thought they first detected signs of ambition for the French post. The anti-Deane faction, in particular, was out to get him. One delegate declared that Morris's reputed abilities were greater than his integrity and told John Laurens, Henry Laurens's son and also a candidate, that he would do anything to help him beat Morris. The New

Yorker smoothly claimed that he did not want the post and would not get it, but he privately admitted that he would not have refused it. Franklin's appointment was finally sustained by the narrowest margin.

Morris had become personally ambivalent in the role of a delegate as the business of Congress became more publicly political and as peace became a serious possibility. He always liked a certain amount of limelight but before an audience that he knew and understood. Many of the delegates did not reach his standards.

In late September 1779, Morris learned that he had been defeated for reelection to Congress. It was no surprise. A tie vote had thrown the decision into the New York Assembly where he lost by one vote, charged by the opposition that he had neglected the state's interests while advancing national and international concerns. The long-running fight with New Hampshire over territorial claims was very much a local issue, but it did not particularly engage Morris's interest. Instead, his imagination and energy were increasingly drawn to what he believed would be the emergence of a strong central government, far superior to the Confederation—a topic not foremost on the mind of many Albany politicians.

A solid national structure to unify the vast spaces even if they did not reach from sea to shining sea was his paramount theme. His extended views of building it, his concept of scale, and, above all, the financing of it was second nature in his thinking, putting him far in advance of most of his contemporaries. The ramshackle Congress and its shortcomings provided perfect training for things to come. It would take another eight years for his expansive vision to take form in the Constitutional Convention. Writing to Robert Livingston, Morris told him he had already adopted what some might consider a self-righteous yet accurate motto: "Let Man take a great Line of Conduct and let him take the Consequences."[56]

When news of Morris's defeat reached Philadelphia, William Whipple crowed to his New Hampshire colleague Nathaniel Peabody: "The Tall Boy will not be hereafter to trouble you as he no longer has a seat in a room where he has at least shown a disposition on some occasions to perplex business." The subtext of Peabody's remark was the old boundary dispute between New York and New Hampshire over the Vermont Grants. For years, New York and New Hampshire had fought over the mountainscape wilderness of Vermont. What was believed, by many, to be Morris's indifference to the bickering helped to set in motion his defeat. In the middle of the Revolution, settlers in the area had claimed their statehood and petitioned Congress for recognition. With a residue of family prejudice, Morris was not personally sympathetic to the New Englanders, although he found the sectional issue tedious and not worth the endless feud. It would make New York an "unwieldy dominion," and besides, he told Robert Livingston, to force the issue now would be hypocrisy. After all, "America is now busied in teaching the great lesson, that men cannot be governed against their wills." His "lukewarmness about Vermont and heretical doctrines on that head," Jared Sparks concluded, were "numbered among his sins of neglect." At the age of twenty-seven, Gouverneur Morris was out of a job.[57]

CHAPTER 7

Money Matters

I N November 1779, a relieved Gouverneur Morris moved out of Congress and into the life of a well-connected lawyer about town. "I learn from your quarter," he wrote Robert Livingston, "that I am no longer to be that wretched creature a statesman." Livingston himself had just returned to Congress to take the seat of John Jay. Now that he was free of politics, Morris made it clear that he would resist any attempt to lure him back. "My restoration to the beau Monde," he told Livingston, "is like a resurrection from the grave."[1]

With New York still in enemy hands, Philadelphia was the only place to profitably use his experience in the confused operations of the Continental government. He quickly threw himself into a lucrative law practice, "simply with the View," he assured his cousin Robert, "to eat and drink without burthening Society." Fat legal fees allowed him not only to eat and drink well, they made up for the fact that while his mother lived, his inheritance from his father's estate would be postponed. "I am so thoroughly convinced...that the Goods of Fortune are worth the Attention of a Man of Understanding," he confessed without a trace of dissembling hypocrisy, "but I think so simply because they are necessary to the Gratification of certain Wishes which every Man ought to have."[2]

Morris's frank declaration that the private demands of making a living might be as important as disinterested, uncompensated, and on occasion, bankrupting public service brought into question the classical republican tradition of "virtuous government" run by men willing to sacrifice their private welfare for the public good. In an ideal republic, a virtuous man should take on public service without pay. Morris questioned the premise that "A Man expends his Fortune in Political Pursuits," yet did he do it out of "personal Consideration" or out of a desire to promote the public good? And if one acted to advance the public good like a virtuous Roman, "was it justifiable in sacrificing to it the Subsistence of his Family?" There was another crucial question: "Would not as much Good have followed from an industrious Attention to his own Affairs?" Because greed and improvidence governed all human behavior, he would work to acquire an independent fortune, one not dependent on the virtues and goodwill of others.[3]

Morris had known Philadelphia since his student days, and his impeccable connections made it easy for him to indulge his tastes that ran to the epicurean. Everyone agreed that living in a certain style was a part of a gentleman's "weight and influence." To add to his indulgence, there were several bright, pretty girls within Morris's coterie, whose company he enjoyed. Recognizing his powerful libido, he realized feminine society was an essential part of his life as he regularly hinted to his intimates. And he considered himself a connoisseur of feminine charm. The New Yorker's racy, flirtatious reputation (not to mention his skill with fast horses) was celebrated. The complaints and caviling by his rivals likely concealed jealous innuendoes other than political.

Like any wartime capital, Philadelphia was full of contrast and energy. All ranks of the social and political order were represented: self-righteous patriots, visiting farmers, profiteers, paper millionaires, painted tarts, and sedate matrons of unquestioned standing crossed each other's path at every turn. A fair cross section could be seen regularly in the elegant drawing rooms of the new French minister, the chevalier de La Luzerne, whose house was the center of the city's social life. No moralist, the Revolution's newly appointed paymaster from Paris, replacing Gérard, nevertheless voiced reservations on what he viewed as the capital's reckless, decadent atmosphere. "A rich, commercial city," he remarked in a confidential report, "offering the most frequent opportunities for pleasure and dissipation is not suitable to the representatives of an infant republic which can sustain itself only by economy, activity, and application of work." Although Morris did not agree with La Luzerne's assessment, the old patriots, like the Adamses in Massachusetts and the Lees in Virginia, also saw in the new wartime wealth more than a hint of greed undermining true republican morals.[4]

For Morris, Philadelphia represented a progressive, modern society showing vital signs of enlightenment in its embrace of capitalism, enterprise, and urbanization. It was the kind of society that appealed to him. For all of his patrician roots, Morris had moved beyond the old verities of prerevolutionary traditions expressed in family, land, and a disdain of the world of trade and finance. In many ways, the war had provided excuses for his independent, original development. Besides, his transient romances did not yet suggest the goal of a settled life of marriage, nor had he shown much interest in setting up the conventional household befitting his inherited social standing.

When problems arose during the difficult negotiations for the purchase of the family estate of Morrisania from his half-brother Staats Long Morris, Gouverneur made it clear that he was "not so attached to that Purchase as to walk towards it on bad Ground." He was a man on the move without the slightest qualm when he left for Europe not long after the purchase in spring 1787 and would not see the place again for another ten years.

After leaving Congress, Morris still saw himself very much at the center of things, conscious of the difference he might make in the practical order of the emerging government. By now, both his emotional and rational commitment to forming a unified republican nation out of the old confederation was deep rooted and well known. His intellectual authority in addressing the future nature of the organization of a national government and its financial system had been displayed in impressive expositions, both in Congress and in the press. In the heat of congressional politics and consumed with the problems of the hopelessly underfinanced, improvised Confederation, delegate Morris had regularly lectured his less discerning colleagues on their plight, always proposing a rational solution. But the frustrating problems of Congress—having to fight a war without funds and without the power to coerce either the states or their citizens—seemed at times beyond salvation.

Congressional tinkering with finances consisted chiefly of running the paper money presses full speed, the usual practice of popular and, in Morris's opinion, short-sighted governments facing a financial crisis. The revolutionary governments had issued a staggering four to five hundred million dollars during the course of the war. Other half-measures—new forms of legal tender, price-fixing laws, embargoes, and antimonopoly statutes—were applied with predictable results of failure. In March 1780, Morris wrote Jay, now minister in Madrid, "that Congress have anvilled out another System of Finance the Plain English of which is a Breach of their Resolution to stop the Press. After this the Public Faith is to be pledged etc. on all which I shall make no Comments. In general I tell *you* that it wont do and Money must therefore be had in Europe for however there be Sufficiency in the Country that is of little Importance unless there could be ways and Means discovered to draw it out." He told Jay that he had anticipated the problem and tried to prevent it, but was only politely thanked for his *"fine imagination"* after it was too late.[5]

But Morris, now free from the tedious responsibilities of committee work, was able to take a more extended view of the crisis, which was only partially financial. Questions surrounding the political structure of the Confederation as well as its public finances exposed deep divisions and needed to be reconsidered. The rational, compact analysis on the plight of revolutionary finances outlined in "Observations on the Finances of America" and included in

Franklin's instructions is an example of the diagnostic gift he continued to deploy as a private citizen. The New Yorker's talents deeply impressed the premier financial wizard of the country, Robert Morris.

Beginning in March, Morris launched an expanded version of his earlier "Observations," in an unprecedented series of essays, to educate a wider public on the critical state of continental finance and its relation to the future health of the new nation. Signed "An American," the essays ran in the influential *Pennsylvania Packet.* The core of his argument, one that he had developed over several years, was laid out in the final essay: without a strong federal government, the weak confederation and its forlorn financial structure would lead to the collapse of the Confederation, a likely victim of foreign designs, even if the war was won.[6]

The theme of protecting the rights of property while fixing a sound public policy of financing ran through the argument. There should be minimal laws to interfere with property and this included most of the poorly considered plans Congress had debated, including price controls. His unapologetic defense of monopolies was shameless. Nor should financial schemes be based on patriotic enthusiasm, uselessly "frail and shortlived." Above all, realistic public policy should "be founded in the nature of man; not on ideal notions of excellence."

On May 14, 1780, at the age of twenty-eight, Gouverneur Morris's high-stepping new career abruptly came to a halt. That morning he prepared to leave the city to spend a few days in the country with George Plater, a delegate from Maryland, and his attractive wife Elizabeth. Morris's chaise drawn by a spirited pair of dapple grays was brought to the door of his house, but as he climbed into his seat with a shout, the horses bolted before he could grab the reins, throwing him to the ground. A wheel caught his left leg, breaking it in several places. Doctors were summoned and amputation of the leg just below the knee was recommended.

Morris's stoic acceptance of the verdict and his remarkable humor after recovering from the shock and pain became legend. The leg stories that circulated throughout his life seemed to fulfill his reputation as a daredevil rake with an iron fortitude. Typical is the tale of a friend who assured him that the misfortune would build character and moral temperament because it reduced temptations to pleasure and dissipation. Morris, who had no patience with sentimental parables at his expense, shot back: "My good sir, you argue the matter so handsomely, and point out so clearly the advantages of being without legs, that I am almost tempted to part with the other." A later yarn had Morris swinging the detached wooden member at the mob while hanging on to a lamppost in the streets of Paris during the French Revolution.

The marquis de Chastellux consoled him that his friends were saying he could "now devote himself whole to public business." Sally Jay, also drawing a moral lesson, wrote a friend that the "misfortune will call forth latent virtues that will enhance his merit, and consequently increase the esteem of which he is already the object." Her husband, now in Spain, heard a rumor that the accident happened when Morris jumped out of the bedroom window of his married lover. Writing to Morris, Jay reported he had learned "that a certain married woman after much use of your leg had occasioned your losing one."

Elizabeth Plater played an important (and probably romantic) role in Morris's successful convalescence. She had charmed Chastellux as well: "this excellent female patriot...her taste as delicate as her health: an enthusiast to excess for all French fashions...waiting for the end of this little revolution to effect a still greater one in the manners of her country." On November 25, six months after the accident, Robert Livingston's letter to Morris heralded his impressive recovery at the Plater house. "I congratulate you on your restoration to the Beau Monde and I congratulate the Beau Monde on your restoration to them. I am told you are Master of the Ceremonies to la Belle Madame Bingham. I consider you as enlisted for the season as I am persuaded she will claim all the attention you can possibly spare." The Beau Monde was one thing, but recovery did not inspire any thought of his returning to Congress. He told Livingston that if the question was ever raised, to tell his "Enemies that in losing my Leg, the fever has impaired my Intellect."[7]

Responding to the growing congressional alarm sounded by Washington and others, but without addressing the central issue of national versus state power, New York finally took the lead and called for the reorganization of the congressional machinery. Popular sentiment had finally swung toward a stronger central government, something Morris had been thinking about since at least spring 1774 when British tea was thrown into the harbors of Boston and New York. His vision appears briefly in his address on independence in 1776 when he spoke of future western settlements being authorized "by that body which is the legislature of the Continent," an expanding national state of commerce and wealth with a population, enriched by the "diffusion of knowledge." Morris was never an equivocal, conflicted nationalist. Aware that the habits and culture of the country were singularly democratic, democracy and popular government were simply given conditions that had to be addressed. In an infant republic, many unpopular policies had to be carried out, and in the words of Robert Morris, "the people must be wooed and won to do their duty to themselves and pursue their own interest."[8]

By the end of 1780, delegates with a more national bias were in control of Congress, ready to consolidate and set new terms of authority. Writing to James Duane in September, Hamilton spelled out both the causes and the cure. The causes were obvious: "an excess of the spirit of liberty which has made the states show jealousy of all power not in their hands," their demand "to exercise a right of judging in the last resort" over any act of Congress, and congressional diffidence in asserting its power "to preserve," in Hamilton's words, "the republic from harm." As for the Confederation, it was flatly defective, not "fit for war or peace." Morris could not have summed up his own assessment more succinctly. When Hamilton joined Congress in November of 1782, the "Continentals" had an impressive new ally and spokesman.

In March 1781, when the Articles of Confederation were finally ratified, Morris saw this step as transitional at best. Financially, the central government was still dependent on the goodwill of the states, a naive assumption that could not be relied on when it came to the question of national taxes. The assumption was further weakened by the fact that the states controlled the feeble congressional committees acting as the executive. They were, in the words of Robert Livingston's biographer, "remarkably efficient in the manipulation of inefficiency."[9]

By winter 1780–81, the ominous military and financial situation had so alarmed the comte de Vergennes, French minister of foreign affairs, that he was ready to abandon the American cause altogether. In a confidential memorandum, Vergennes declared that he was prepared to end the war "as far as the United States and Great Britain were concerned, by means of a long truce *uti possidetis* between Colonies and the mother country." He had only to look at the war map at the beginning of 1781 to see that the British controlled the ports of New York, Charleston, and Savannah as well as the Great Lakes and the far northwest. Faced with this geography, such a truce would have put an end to American independence.[10]

Congress never learned of its partner's duplicity, but with the beginning of the new year, steps were finally taken to put its administrative and financial house in some kind of order. Hamilton had actively campaigned for these changes. "Congress," he had reminded Duane, the New York delegate, "is properly a deliberative corps and it forgets itself when it attempts to play the executive." There were simply too many badly informed, constantly changing members ever to act with precision and dispatch as the executive.[11]

On January 10, 1781, the first executive department of Foreign Affairs was established. A month later the departments of War, Finance, and Marine were added, each with a secretary at its head. While the old committee system was still in existence and capable of meddling, to Morris the reorganization offered the possibility that strong leadership in the new departments would bolster the central government. He agreed with the "expedience of making Congress merely deliberative," as Elbridge Gerry candidly put it.[12]

With so much potential power being handed over to the heads of departments, someone needed to think seriously about their credentials and essential qualities. Congress itself was too blunt an instrument and too distracted to perform such a sophisticated, disinterested task. Now fitted out with a new "wooden member" and beginning to regain his old intellectual buoyancy, Morris lost no time in focusing on the qualifications of the new ministers. "It is said," he wrote Governor Clinton, "that Congress intend to deliver the care of the executive business into the hands of ministers, on which I would warmly congratulate you, if I could persuade myself that it would speedily take place," or that the delegates, "in conferring offices…would confer power, or that they would be induced to serve them, or that they would protect their servants."[13]

Morris, like Hamilton, saw these men as great officers of state, and the preface to his sketch of prescriptions of fitness set the high tone for what was to follow: "To determine who should be appointed minister either of Finances, of War, of the Marine, or of Foreign Affairs, may be difficult; but it may not be so difficult to determine the qualities requisite for each of these departments, and having thereby established a rule, the proper persons will be more properly ascertained. These qualities will be classed under the different heads of genius, temper, knowledge, education, principles, manners and circumstances."

Morris's reference to the quality of "genius" did not imply an unusual, inventive personality, a "discoverer of novelty" as one definition put it, but suggested rather the ability and native endowments that fit a person for his particular work, in this case to run a department of government professionally.

> Our Minister of the Finances should have a strong understanding, be persevering, industrious, and severe in exacting from all a rigid compliance with their duty. He should possess a knowledge of mankind, and of the culture and commerce, produce and resources, temper and manners of the different States; habituated to business on the most extensive scale, particularly that which is denominated *money matters;* and therefore, not only a regular bred merchant, but one who has been long and deeply engaged in that profession. At the same time, he should be particularly acquainted with our political affairs, and the management of public business; warmly and thoroughly attached to America, not bigoted to any particular State; and his attachment founded not on whim, caprice, resentment, or a weak compliance with the current of opinion, but on a manly and rational conviction of the benefits of independence, his manners plain and simple, sincere and honest, his morals pure, his integrity unblemished; and he should enjoy general credit and reputation, both at home and abroad.[14]

The problem was that Morris's bundle of qualifications for the head of Finance seemed well beyond the run of achievements of most individuals. His insistence that the minister be "not only a regular bred merchant, but one who has been long and deeply engaged in that profession" described an individual who was also an experienced entrepreneur in pursuit of his own private (some said sordid) interest, indifferent to selfless, enlightened republican virtues. He was calling for a radical new kind of entrepreneurial energy, "a Mercantile Character" to save the state in crisis, a type that had been regularly sneered at by the older patriots who considered themselves the guardians of civic honor. This was a significant shift in the definition of traditional republican virtue, which held that a citizen's public stature grew solely out of public spirit and service to government. Morris implied what others were now arguing, that even commercial experience could be a source of modern virtue and essential to managing the complexity of modern governments.[15]

Morris's standards for the other departments were also notched up to an equally high level but came closer to traditional republican ideals. Impeccable leadership in these key administrative posts and their removal from the vagaries of popular politics was the only way the upstart republic could defy its critics and skeptics or possibly even survive. The new heads were to show the face the nation wanted the rest of the world to see. The qualifications leave little doubt that Morris intended all the departments to be put in the hands of the select, without unduly alarming Congress that some of its prerogatives might disappear as they, in fact, did when Robert Morris and his assistant, Gouverneur, took over Finance.

Now that the French alliance had pulled the country into the stew of European intrigue, the new department of Foreign Affairs had to be equal to Finance in importance.

> A Minister of Foreign Affairs should have a genius quick, lively, penetrating; should write on all occasions with clearness, and perspicuity; be capable of expressing his sentiments with dignity, and conveying strong sense and argument in easy and agreeable diction; his temper mild, cool and placid; festive, insinuating, and pliant, yet obstinate; communicative, and yet reserved. He should know the human face and heart, and the connections between them;...should be acquainted with the history of Europe, and with the interests, views, commerce, and productions of their commercial and maritime powers; should know the interests and commerce of America, and understand the French and Spanish languages, at least the former, and be skilled in the modes and forms of public business; a man educated more in the world than in the closet, that by use, as well as by nature, he may give proper attention to great objects, and have proper contempt for small ones.... His manners strong and polite; above all things honest, and least of all things avaricious.[16]

Morris's requirements for the holders of these high offices were without precedent, the portraits exemplary in their cool delineation, neoclassical in their rectitude. The image conjured in his specifications might complement Houdon's idealized busts of Washington, Franklin, and Jefferson. His own personal values and priorities, representative of the ideals of the age if not the messy reality, resonate in every word and line. Morris, of course, had particular individuals (and friends) in mind who could plausibly fulfill his expectations. Robert Livingston obviously fit Morris's bill and was named head of Foreign Affairs. The appointment of Robert Morris as superintendent of Finance was the predestined and immediate choice, even if the merchant's mixing of private with public business had been for years the subject of sharp attack.

Clever, industrious, and ingratiating, Robert Morris had been a conspicuous figure from the beginning of the Revolution, but he was not accepted in all circles. Benjamin Rush sniffed that he found his manners "peculiar." But a craving for fiscal salvation in the form of a savior overcame the most prejudiced defenders of civic virtue always on the alert for any sign of despotism in the central government. Gouverneur wrote Governor Clinton, "If he accepts the office which Congress against his will conferred on him, I shall hope to see some better modes of raising money... and I shall be morally certain of honesty in the expediter."

Robert Morris's demand that he be allowed to continue his private business while holding public office posed no problem and he was approved. But his demand that he had the right "to remove from office... all persons entrusted with and immediately employed in the expenditure of public money" in any branch of government was harder to swallow. It was obvious that this would make him the most powerful man not only in the government but in the country. "Inexorable" in his demands for such unusual power, the Financier finally had his way. On May 14, 1781, in accepting the appointment, Morris told Congress that he was sacrificing "my interest, my ease, my domestic enjoyment and internal tranquillity." In his diary he admitted that the job was "dangerous" and "contrary to my private interest."[17]

By transferring congressional authority to his new office, Robert Morris had certainly streamlined the work of Congress. "Mr. Morris having relieved them from all business of deliberation in executive difficulty with which money is in any respect connected," one of his detractors caustically remarked, "they are now very much at leisure to read dispatches, return thanks, pay and receive compliments &. For form's sake some things go thither to receive sanction, but it is the general opinion that it is form only."

As soon as he was named, the new financial autocrat asked his young friend Gouverneur to be his assistant, even before that office was approved. It was exactly the cabinet post he had been cut out for at this stage of his twenty-nine years. The marquis de Chastellux concluded that there were few individuals in Europe equal to Gouverneur's "perspicuity and facility of understanding" economics. The superintendent's official, if unpolished, letter to his new deputy makes clear the role Gouverneur had played in his own decision. "I trembled at the arduous task I had reluctantly undertaken aided by your Talents and abilities I feel better Courage, and dare indulge the fond hope that... we may extract [the country] from the present embarrassments. My entire conviction of the great and essential services which your genius, Talents and capacity enable you to render your Country and of that aid, ease and confidence you can and will administer to my own exertions and feelings never left me one moment to hesitate about the choise I should make."[18]

The younger Morris replied that he had no doubt that his mentor would extricate the country from its miseries, but his efforts would have its inevitable price. While "Malice will blacken and Envy Traduce you, I will freely share in this bitter Portion of Eminence." Gouverneur had his own enemies, including Joseph Reed who remarked: "Mr. Gouverneur Morris is the Financier's assistant and censorous people say his director."[19]

Chastellux immediately recognized the American version of the archetypal self-made man of commerce, when he first met the Financier in 1780:

> He is a very rich merchant, and consequently a man of every country, for commerce bears everywhere the same character. Under monarchies it is free; it is an egotist in republics; a stranger, or if you will, a citizen of the universe, it excludes alike the virtues and the prejudices that stand in the way of its interest. It will scarcely be believed that amid the disasters of America, Mr. Morris, the inhabitant of a town barely free from the hands of the English, should possess a fortune of eight million *livres*. It is, however, in the most critical times that great fortunes are acquired and increased. The fortunate return of several ships, the still more successful cruises of his privateers, have increased his riches, beyond his expectations. He is, in fact, so accustomed to the success of his privateers, that when he is observed on a Sunday to be more serious than usual, the conclusion is, that no prize has arrived during the preceding week.[20]

There is no doubt that the Morrises were drawn back into public service by the magnitude of the financial crisis. In spite of the gulf in social rank, education, and temperament, the talents of the two men were complementary, and Gouverneur was prepared to seize the opportunity to put into play some of the finance plans he had already worked out. "His [Gouverneur's] eloquence joined with Mr. R. Morris's judgment," Kitty Livingston remarked, "would ensure success in every cause." She might well have added the senior Morris's substantial personal credit to the formula for predicted success.

Both men were experienced students of the subtler quirks of human nature and privy to most of the political intrigues, but the senior Morris was essentially a skilled businessman and did not articulate underlying political policies or assess motives with anything like the finesse of Gouverneur. Yet his letter to Franklin left no doubt that his plan, and that of his assistant, was to pull "the bands of authority together, establishing the power of Government over a people impatient of control, and confirming the Federal union...by correcting defects in the general Constitution." Throughout their reign, it is next to impossible to separate the strategic thinking and actions of the two men but the daring plan to link the support of public creditors with the military seems most persuasively to have originated with Gouverneur.[21]

To salvage whatever was left of public credit, the first step was to create a national bank, the first commercial bank in the United States. Gouverneur, who had been working for two months before he was officially confirmed, was ready with the draft of the proposal sent to Congress calling for a bank with a congressional charter but funded by private subscriptions. Business cronies of Morris who invested in the Bank of North America were well rewarded for

Gouverneur Morris and Robert Morris by Charles Willson Peale, ca. 1783.
Courtesy of the Pennsylvania Academy of Fine Arts, Philadelphia. Bequest of Richard Ashhurst.

their foresight. This insured that private investors and their resources would now be a part of public finance with a stake in the nation's future. The bank's notes were to circulate as currency, replacing the worthless bills issued in earlier printings. A second currency introduced by the bank were the so-called Morris Notes, backed by the Financier's private fortune. These turned out to be so popular that by September 1781, Morris had advanced "every Shilling of [his] own," which replaced the public credit the country had lost. His terse entry in his day book sums up the crisis: "Congress empowers General Washington to seize flour wherever he could find it, I determine to procure supplies and pledge my private credit."

To supplement the function of the bank, another important ingredient of Gouverneur's financial remedy was to establish a national mint. National coinage would boost national credit and encourage orderly commerce. It would also free the government from dependence on foreign coins. Again, Gouverneur produced the report on coinage for congressional consideration. After consulting Steuart's *Political Oeconomy*, the New Yorker proposed that the system be based on a decimal measure using the familiar Spanish silver dollar. In order to make the new coin exchangeable with state currencies, his analysis determined that the basic unit would be a quarter. The proposal was delayed in Congress and later amended when Jefferson offered a revised plan specifying the dollar as the basic unit, subdivided into one hundred parts.

Before any reorganization could be carried out, the bank chartered, and a mint set up to strike an "American coin," new military operations brought unexpected demands and new anxieties. Seasoned pragmatists, the Morrises were willing to use any creative means to meet the money needs of the army during summer and fall 1781. One unorthodox maneuver to support Pennsylvania's depreciating currency, which had disrupted the purchase of military supplies, has been described as an example of "the most vulgar kind of bill-kiting."

But check kiting, discounting bills of exchange, juggling notes due irate army contractors, and other inventive financial schemes would not solve the lack of hard money, even though expenditures in 1781 had been cut by two-thirds from their peak. As the Financier said afterwards, "The Doctrine then in use was that every pressing occasion must receive a Part of its Demands out of such Funds as could not ward off the Pressure of various Claimants who obtained Warrants, the temporary Discretion of the higher Powers determined the Preference of Payment according to their Idea of the existing Necessity." By clever manipulation, "the higher Powers" slowly began to rebuild public confidence and public credit.[22]

In August 1781, the two men were summoned to an unexpected meeting with La Luzerne and the French commander, comte de Rochambeau. They were told that the French fleet, with some three thousand troops, was momentarily expected in the Chesapeake Bay and plans were afoot to mount a joint Franco-American campaign against Cornwallis's army in Virginia. But a few days later, a disturbing message from Washington arrived saying that the troops under the command of General Benjamin Lincoln headed south to join the critical new campaign threatened to end their march in Philadelphia unless they were given a month's back pay on the spot: "send on a Month's Pay at least, with all Expedition possible," Washington wrote, "I wish it to come on the Wings of speed."

The makeshift Finance Office had already been drained by advances for the Virginia expedition, and in desperation the Morrises turned to La Luzerne for help. Chastellux and Rochambeau joined in the meeting on September 5. The rumor that the French ships carried specie on board proved to be true, but it could only be released by the intendant of the French army, who was then on his way to Head of Elk, Maryland. Without losing a moment, horses were saddled and the stout, middle-aged superintendent with his French-speaking, one-legged assistant at his side rode off in search of the French official. Before they reached him, a messenger reported that he had already been located and had agreed to release 20,000 dollars in hard money for Washington's troops.

Barely six weeks later, on the morning of October 19, General Cornwallis's aide waved a white flag in front of the American and French forces signaling the British decision to negotiate a surrender at Yorktown.[23]

The Morrises had barely headed off financial disaster but for all their frantic energy, it was not adequate to put the country's credit on anything like a solid footing. By fall 1781, the significant element missing in all of the Morris schemes was the means to fund the Confederation and its staggering debt. "As I consider national credit to be an object of the greatest magnitude and importance," the senior Morris wrote to La Luzerne on November 3, "so I think it necessary to bend every possible effort to the establishment and support of it. Provision for our debts is...the first object and therefore must take place of every other demand." The Morrises were momentarily encouraged by the resolution adopted by Congress the day before. Quotas were set for state contributions to the treasury, "separate from those laid for their own particular use...to be subject only to the orders of Congress, or the superintendent of finance."[24]

Besides the creation of a national bank and a mint, Gouverneur's third, and most important, proposal, called the "Report on Public Credit," was introduced in Congress on July 29, 1782. Unprecedented and imaginative in its thrust, Morris had first sketched its outlines in letters on finance published in the *Pennsylvania Packet* in 1780. The object was to establish a federal plan to control money and credit by assuming the total public debt of the war in exchange for government certificates secured by an independent source of federal taxes to underpin the central government's debt. No longer would the Congress be dependent on the fickle kindness of the states. The explosive part of the comprehensive tax plan was the implicit nullification of Article 8 of the Confederation, which stated that the common expenses were to be paid "out of a common treasury, which shall be supplied the several states" by their own taxes and apportioned by their own revenues.

The plan proposed by the Morrises more or less accepted the existing framework of the Articles of Confederation, but this concession was not enough for their opponents in Congress. Both men were realists and knew that their strategy would not be approved automatically by Congress. Their timing was bad. The victory at Yorktown the previous October had deprived the superintendent of his most important card—the call for new patriotic sacrifices for the struggling men on the front lines. The news from London that the North ministry had collapsed in November spread more rumors of peace and further dampened any effort to persuade the states to meet their requisitions. The first step toward a federal tax, the impost tax, that had been proposed a year earlier still languished, and a new request to collect additional revenues through land, poll, and excise taxes was turned over to an unfriendly committee. The Morrises' nemesis Arthur Lee, now a resentful new delegate from Virginia, who blamed them for the collapse of his diplomatic career during the Deane fight, was on the committee and ready for revenge. In March, Lee's committee found the method proposed "for raising a revenue...too exceptional to meet with the approbation of Congress as it would operate very unequally, as well with respect to the different States, as to the inhabitants of each State." Any proposal for new taxes should wait until all national accounts were settled, which would take years.[25]

By fall 1782, the problems created by the expected peace were playing havoc with the Morrises' grand dream of a country of "power, consequence and grandeur." For Gouverneur, an untimely end of the war undermined their strongest argument to shore up congressional power over money matters. "It is not much for the Interest of America, that it [peace] should be made at present," Morris wrote privately to Mathew Ridley in August. To his dismissive eye, the new state constitutions had endowed the people with "freedom in the extreme" just at the moment when the nation was making "a silent but rapid and constant Progress toward Strength and Greatness." What was needed was a strong dose of "Vigor, Organization & Promptitude" and these, he continued, "can only be acquired by a Continuance of the War, which will convince People of the necessity of Obedience to common Counsels for general Purposes." These popular governments, Hamilton told the Financier, were made up of "vulgar souls whose narrow optics can see but the little circle of selfish concern." Without the "Advantages of Union and Decision in carrying on a War," Gouverneur had written Nathanael Greene earlier, in December 1781, he had *"no Hope or Expectation that the Government will acquire Force"* sufficient to save it from "absolute Monarchy" other than the people themselves, who do not have "the Taste and Temper" to accept such an ending.[26]

Except in matters of finance, Robert Morris's program did not envision any serious dislocation of power between Congress and the states as implied in Gouverneur's arguments. It was far more modest and restrained than the goals his young colleague would pursue in the Convention of 1787. He was, it has been said, a statesman by circumstances rather than by bent. Without acknowledging his assistant's dire conclusions, the Financier nevertheless echoed Gouverneur Morris's realistic analysis of the dilemma in a letter Gouverneur had drafted for the superintendent to Washington that "peace is necessary; but if I were to hazard an opinion on the subject, it would be, that war is more likely than peace to produce funds for the Public Debts."[27]

After a series of congressional defeats entangled with complex, divisive questions of exploiting western lands to cover the war debt, the Morrises were running out of strategies. As negotiations on the peace treaty dragged on, the Office of Finance had to face the mounting demands of its private creditors while still saddled with the heavy cost of maintaining the army in the field in case hostilities resumed. After all, the enemy still occupied large pieces of American real estate. Congressional failure to meet the army's payroll for months or to live up to its promise, made in 1780, to establish a half-pay pension for officers had brought unrest in the army to a boiling point.

On December 24, 1782, both Morrises were jarred when they learned that their plan had been derailed when Virginia repealed its earlier ratification of an impost, a tax pledged to solve the army's financial problems. Just as the Morrises were rightly worried that peace would wreck their plans to shore up the national government financed with "certain revenues," the mood of Washington's disgruntled army camped in dismal winter quarters at Newburgh, New York, was becoming explosive, fueled by the prospects of peace and demobilization. The long, cold months had bred a feeling of martyrdom and alarm as the exhausted veterans faced what they believed was an indifferent society now at peace and in pursuit of its own interests, ignoring what it owed its returning troops for their years of sacrifice. For many men at Newburgh, returning to civilian life without pay meant poverty and misery. The bitterest pill was being cheated out of money actually owed them by the government. Early in October, Washington warned Congress that "the patience and long-sufferance of this army are almost exhausted." The smoldering atmosphere convinced the general not to return to Mount Vernon as he had planned. In November, a group of officers decided to confront the delegates in Philadelphia. This was the backdrop to the so-called Newburgh conspiracy and supposed plot of a military coup d'état.

On January 1, 1783, a three-man delegation arrived in Philadelphia, bringing the complaints of the shivering army camped in the hills behind Newburgh. Its mission was to tell the politicians that unless action was immediate, it could expect "a convulsion of the most dreadful nature and fatal consequences." The Morrises were well aware of the turmoil in Newburgh and undoubtedly conferred with the army's committee when it arrived in Philadelphia. In the convergence of the army's anxieties and the political frustrations of the superintendent's office, there suddenly appeared an opening in the congressional impasse over taxes. By joining the army's demands with the public creditors, both men could see a political break in their drive to establish a national tax. Such an obvious conclusion by these two masters of intrigue does not mean that a subversive plot was being hatched, although it is plausible. Neither man was above fishing in troubled waters.

The day the delegation from Newburgh arrived, Gouverneur wrote John Jay, darkly predicting that the army was prepared to take a stand. The timing of the letter has encouraged Morris's critics to conclude that he was in on a cabal.

(The Army have Swords in their hands. You know enough of the history of mankind more than I have said and possibly much more they themselves yet think of.) I will add however that I am glad to see Things in their present Train. Depend on it good will arise from the Situation to which we are hastening. And this you may rely on that my Efforts will not be wanting. I pledge to you on the present occasion, and altho I think it probable that much Convulsion will ensue Yet it must terminate in giving to the Government that power without which Government is but a Name. Government in America is not possessed of it but the People are well prepared. Wearied with the War, their Acquiescence may be depended on with absolute Certainty and you and I my friend know by experience that when a few Men of Sense and Spirit get together and declare that they are the Authority such as few as are of a different Opinion may easily be convinced of their Mistake by that powerful Argument the Halter.... On the Wisdom of the present Moment depends more than is easily imagined and when I look round for the Actors—Let us change the Subject.[28]

Taking the lead in a dicey, covert strategy to manipulate Congress with the help of the army, the Financier informed Congress "explicitly" that the coffers were bare and the treasury was already dangerously overdrawn. Two months after Yorktown, Gouverneur may have tipped his hand to Nathanael Greene, writing that "to reinforce the reasonings" to enlarge the power of Congress, "to impress the arguments, and sweeten the persuasions of the public servants, we have that great friend to sovereign authority, a foreign war."

While the superintendent convincingly spread his gloom in the right places, Gouverneur Morris baldly proposed in a letter to Henry Knox, now in Newburgh, that the army should unite with the creditors to force Congressional action: "The army may influence the Legislatures, and if you will permit me a Metaphor from your profession after you have carried the post the public Creditors will garrison it for you." His theme was similar in a letter to Nathanael Greene. He admitted it might be "imprudent" that he sound the same note, but "if the army, in common with all other public creditors, insist on the grant of general permanent funds for liquidating all the public debts, there can be little doubt that such revenues will be obtained," funding the national obligations with "a solid security."

With his close ties to Washington as a former member of his staff and outspoken champion of nationalist views, Hamilton also wrote to Washington outlining the strategy to secure the army's cooperation in pressuring Congress. This move was undoubtedly coordinated with Gouverneur's efforts to spread the rumor that the army would not disband until its demands were fairly settled. Hamilton had also met with the Financier over the army crisis, and although there was pushing and shoving and plots within plots of this whole dangerous business, the chief goal was clear and Hamilton spelled it out. "The Great *desideratum* at present is the establishment of general funds which alone can do justice to the creditors of the United States (of whom the army forms the most meritorious class)." He warned that it would be difficult "to keep a complaining and suffering army within the bounds of moderation" and cautioned Washington to act discreetly as the sage mediator in the approaching crisis to "guide the torrent and bring order perhaps even good, out of the confusion." Arthur Lee complained to Samuel Adams that "every Engine is at work here to obtain permanent taxes.... The terror of a mutinying Army is played off with considerable efficacy."[29]

If all this was not enough to start rumors of "a most violent political storm," the Financier got everyone's attention when he announced without warning, on January 24, 1783, that he would resign if permanent funding of the public debt was not made. He would not, he declared, be "the minister of injustice." Their strategy was transparent: the Morrises wanted the army to look to Congress, not to the states, for satisfaction of their demands.

"This letter," Madison, who was not involved in the army negotiations, noted, "made a deep and solemn impression on Congress." No longer would the Morrises work toward incremental gains, beginning with the impost tax, to finance the government. Not only had the situation become "utterly insupportable," now Congress was confronted with the superintendent's ultimatum.[30]

Shortly after the Financier's bomb was delivered, the Newburgh affair reached its climax when two pamphlets were circulated in the camp, one calling for a meeting to discuss a petition to Congress without the authorization of the commander in chief, the other equally mutinous declaring that the army would not disband until "justice" was done. Cooler heads insisted that Washington attend the meeting. With his rank and prestige, he managed to keep things under control, and a committee, headed by General Knox, drafted resolutions condemning the inflammatory addresses. In the end, the officers were given five years' pay in lieu of pensions. The Newburgh settlement separated the army's demands from the national government's financial crisis. The Morrises and their circle of supporters had failed to get congressional endorsement of their fundamental agenda calling for comprehensive national taxes.

In the heat and rancor, combined with the suspect motives of some of the players in the Newburgh drama, Washington became disenchanted with the nationalist leadership, though he shared many of their political sentiments. He thought the Morrises, in their single-minded drive to fund the Confederation, were willing to sacrifice the army's just claims to secure federal taxes independent of the states. In the general's opinion, the army was "a dangerous Engine to Work." At one point, he even suspected that Gouverneur and Robert Morris had secretly manipulated the crisis in camp. In a letter to Hamilton two months later, Washington still harbored a wariness of Gouverneur's particular role in preparing "the ground work of the superstructure which was intended to be raised in the Army by the Anonymous Addresser."[31]

The end of the war brought an end to demands for a stronger national government. Hamilton retired from Congress in disgust. Madison returned to Virginia. Livingston resigned as secretary of foreign affairs, and Robert Morris came under heavy fire by his enemies in Congress. Gouverneur's omen of the "bitter Portions of eminence" had been on target. A committee reopened the case of the Financier's role in the old Deane affair and, in March 1784, he quit his office.[32]

To some, the Office of Finance was an "Aristocratical Junto" in the making. With the departure of the Morrises, and with them their network of accomplices, Stephen Higginson could not contain his relief: "Their schemes are now entirely defeated; their web is broken, which they have with so much art and industry been for several years spinning."[33]

Even before the war ended in the spring of 1783, both Gouverneur and Robert were making plans to reestablish themselves in private business and make the most of peacetime opportunities. Gouverneur, for all of his advantages of social status and education, accepted the fact that as his father's youngest son he was on his own. His was only a slight advantage over the Nevisian immigrant, Alexander Hamilton, now beginning to practice law. Hamilton's ambition and success on Washington's staff probably offset much of Morris's advantage of family and connections.

The resilience of the American society was remarkable in its rapid recovery from seven years of war. But this did not mean that the Philadelphia government had begun to solve its debilitating financial problems. Many believed the economic anemia of the central government had precipitated a decline that would end in disunion. The public debt had passed into the hands of the states and the servicing of this debt with uncertain state resources simply meant that Congress was left out of the fiscal system. Because the states still resisted a federal impost or other supplementary taxes, Congress had very little income to meet the payments on its foreign loans. The inevitable result was that beginning with France, Congress defaulted on its foreign loans, and its credit with Dutch investors became shakier than ever. Dutch bankers would not excuse a late payment. A single default would have brought the whole house of cards tumbling down.

From Gouverneur Morris's consistently long-distanced, progressive outlook, time would correct these problems of national sovereignty and financial stability. "True it is that the general Government wants energy, and equally true it is that this Want will eventually be supplied," Morris optimistically wrote John Jay at the beginning of 1784. "A national Spirit is the natural result of national Existence, and altho some of the present generation may feel colonial Oppositions of Opinion, that generation will die away and give place to a Race of American." Later historians confirm Morris's confidence "that the world was still open, that young energetic, daring, hopeful, imaginative men had taken charge and were drawing their power directly from the soil of the society they ruled and not from a distant, capricious, unmanageable sovereign."[34]

Morris had become deeply and profitably involved in the Financier's extended private affairs while acting as his assistant. The astute antennae of the pair were quick to pick up enticing signals from the emerging new world as peace approached. Like other prominent leaders—Washington, Jefferson, Adams—both Morrises shared an earlier generation's attitude of ambivalence toward public office and were looking forward to putting politics behind them once and for all. With peace assured, Gouverneur's "energetic" taxation schemes seemed less urgent, and resistance to his bold continental thinking too entrenched. Samuel Osgood was accurate when he said that although the Office of Finance judged well in money matters and public credit, neither Morris had believed it was "necessary to secure the Confidence of the People by making measures palatable to them." The ability to cultivate and secure the trust of the people had certainly never been one of Gouverneur's conspicuous qualities.[35]

In fall 1782, the Financier, with unseeming haste, replied to an overture from a New York trader still living under the British flag that he saw no "impropriety in laying a foundation for a plan to be executed upon the conclusion of peace." By March of the following year, the Morrises managed to put together enough venture capital to enter into several large investments in western land, and in ships, naval stores, and American produce. The new business partners were also attracted by the large profits in the newly opened and risky China trade. Substantial investments were added to the portfolio. This compounded to the complexity of what was now a global enterprise.

Political disputes about the army still smoldered in the spring of 1783 when Robert and Gouverneur dispatched John Vaughn to Europe to borrow several hundred thousand dollars to finance their complex private enterprises. In 1784, the Morrises made a another deal with the New York merchant house of William Constable and Company, a firm already focused on the lucrative future of the port of New York. Robert put up the money for Gouverneur's share, the loan to be paid out of future profits. The partnership was to continue seven years. In July and August of the same year, Gouverneur enlarged his business interests further with the purchase of eight hundred acres of land in Northumberland County, Pennsylvania.[36]

Speculation in public land was one of the great sources of economic energy in postrevolutionary America. Beginning with George Washington, nearly everyone dabbled in land. With commerce disrupted after the war, land speculation offered the most creative means of investment. For the new American capitalists and for Morris, as he had written in his essay on Liberty, the development of the wilderness was the true measure "of Progression from a State of Nature to that of Society. Till Property in land be admitted Society continues rude and barbarous." But even after the development of the wilds and the establishment of government, "a long Space intervenes before perfect Civilization is effected." During the various experiments in government, society will move forward or wither. "The Progress will be accelerated or retarded in Proportion as the Administration of Justice is more or less exact." The history of European society confirms this and "if the foregoing Reflections be just their Conclusion results that the State of Society is perfectly in proportion as the rights of property are secured." For Morris, this recognition of the rights and security of property was a keystone of civil liberty. His constant attention to society's need to balance political liberty (the right to participate in government) against the requirements of civil liberty (the right to be left alone) informed his constitutional views in the Convention of 1787.[37]

In the early postwar years, the pursuit of his business and law practice were not Morris's only concerns. He also found time to help former loyalists obtain pardons and recover their fortunes and property. Taking up the cause of defeated Tories was not exactly the way to advance one's popularity at the time, but it was consistent with his deep belief in civil rights of individuals. He had a patrician indifference to public opinion, and this commitment was one of his most admirable qualities. Quakers, Catholics, slaves, American Indians, former loyalists—enemies of the state—as well as the beleaguered king and queen of France were strongly defended by this one-man council of civil liberties.

Gouverneur was thirty-four when his mother died, in 1786, and only then did the small capital bequest of two thousand pounds from his father's estate appear near at hand. Up to this point, his substantial investments had been funded mostly with generous loans advanced by friends, a true measure of the optimism generated by the country's new-found energy. Morris's natural talent for planning and making large, sophisticated business decisions placed him in the fast lane of Philadelphia entrepreneurs. But he had not yet laid much of a foundation for a fortune. His income was mostly from his law practice. In 1781, when he had the opportunity to buy stock in the Bank of North America, he could afford only one share worth $400. Morris's name does not appear as an owner of any shipping vessels in any American port during the 1780s.[38]

A month before peace was officially declared, in March 1783, Morris had taken time out from his growing law and business affairs to make his first visit in seven years to Morrisania. The war had taken its toll, on both his ailing mother and the family estate. The property had been ravaged by British troops and friction, resulting from his father's second marriage, lay just below the surface of the family reunion. Richard Morris was ready to settle old scores. In May 1784, he abruptly demanded in court an inventory of their father's estate, raising the ugly question whether Gouverneur's mother had fairly administrated her trust. He even questioned whether Sarah Morris had spent too much on the funeral of her husband, Judge Morris. Richard's pettiness reached into Sarah's expenditure on wine for the mourners.

In a moving letter to his half-brother, Gouverneur begged him to put to rest "past Animosities." The note of compassion in his plea that the two men join "to support each other" reveals one of the strongest elements in Morris's character, a quality that surfaces time and again, not only in dealing with family and friends, but with enemies as well. "I do not expect that you will ever entertain for my Mother any Affection. Perhaps I myself may be viewed with equal Indifference; but let it rest there. If Love cannot exist, still there can be no Necessity for Hatred. It is at best, a bad Passion, and between near Connections rather ungraceful. Believe me Brother we shall serve ourselves quite as well and all our friends infinitely better by joining to Support each other."[39]

While the legal dispute was pending, Sarah Morris died, passing her life interest in Morrisania to Staats Long Morris, now a retired, gouty general and member of the British Parliament. With no ties to America beyond his dysfunctional family, Staats offered to sell the 1,400-acre estate to either his brother Richard or his half-brother Gouverneur, making a hurried trip to New York to negotiate the transfer of the property. Euphemia Ogden, Gouverneur's sister was sure that Richard was out to "poyson" Staats's mind against the "second children." When Richard decided not to bid on the property for reasons now lost, Gouverneur offered Staats ten thousand pounds, even though he had no cash in hand. Two thousand pounds were due Gouverneur from the estate, so the other heirs (after the usual bickering, which prompted Gouverneur to threaten to walk out) finally accepted his notes for the balance, requiring him to place no immediate money up front. At some point, the general's wife, the former duchess of Gordon had invested in the Jersey flats, and Gouverneur also took over this "Raritan Tract." The purchase of all the real estate added some seven thousand pounds to his already impressive, swelling indebtedness.

On April 4, 1787, Gouverneur became the owner but not the "lord" of Morrisania. There was, however, no sign that he was prepared to settle down to the retiring life of a country squire. Nor was he ready to marry and establish a new feudal line of Westchester County Morrises on his part of the family manor. The image of privilege built on family land would remain a part of his makeup, but such a nostalgic existence for Morris represented a pastoral world of appealing agrarian values founded on outdated laws and institutions, including slavery. His willingness to turn his back on his stepbrother Richard during negotiations and renounce sentimental family ties to Morrisania suggests that his was a quite different agenda. He had, after all, declared war on both the feudal institution of slavery and New York's property laws of quitrents during the New York Constitutional Convention, the time-honored underpinnings of aristocratic ambitions on both sides of the Atlantic.

Unlike the Virginia Junto, held captive by their thousands of acres and hundreds of slaves, Morris had moved beyond this prerevolutionary, agrarian tradition. The traditional order of things—manners, position, an elevated notion of personal comfort—occupied an important place in his private life just as much as it reinforced the sentiments of his southern contemporaries, but he seems far more emancipated and uninhibited in maintaining these accustomed measures of a civilized life without compromising his personal values and moral standards. Long before the phrase was coined in the twentieth century, he believed that "living well was the best revenge," preferring a fair "remuneration" for his energy and imagination as the ultimate measure of personal liberty, a freedom so long as it did not infringe on the liberty and rights of others.

The Protestant ethic of hard work, frugality, and self-denial was not a visible part of Morris's character. When provident John Jay expressed concern over rumors of the spread of luxury in Philadelphia, Morris had a ready answer: "With respect for our Taste for Luxury," he wrote his friend now finishing up the peace treaty in Paris, "do not grieve about it."

"Luxury is not so bad a Thing as it is often supposed to be," he continued, "and if it were, still we must follow the Course of Things and turn to Advantage what exists since we have not the Power either to annihilate it or create. The very Definition of Luxury is as difficult as the Suppress of it, and if I were to declare my serious Opinion, it is that there is a lesser Proportion of Whores and Rogues in coaches than out of them. If I am mistaken, I shall say, with the poor roman Catholic, it is a pleasing error, for my intimate Acquaintance lies among those who ride in coaches."[40]

For Morris, the late eighteenth century that engaged his adventurous imagination was a watershed, a historically unprecedented environment involving new experiences, new relationships, and new institutions. His America was part of the first society, transatlantic in its reach, dedicated to science and driven by the commercial and industrial revolutions already underway. The American experiment in self-government itself was only the most conspicuous development portending the surging, unknown changes ahead. The signs, symbols, and signifiers of this emerging world, which Morris freely embraced with such obvious pleasure—the world of banks and checks, national budgets and debts, international travel and international friends—signaled a break with the past. It was a divide just as definitive as the political crises and uncertainties faced in drafting constitutions, forming new states, raising public revenues, and organizing commercial enterprises.

On Friday, May 25, 1787, the thirty-five-year-old lawyer took his seat as a Pennsylvania delegate to one more extralegal gathering, a convention in Philadelphia called to revise and repair the Articles of Confederation. But on the morning of the thirtieth, with a bare quorum of seven states present, Morris deftly helped to maneuver the Convention in another uncharted direction: away from the dilapidated Confederation toward a totally new experiment in the making, "that a *national* government ought to be established consisting of a *supreme* legislative, executive, and judiciary." Ignoring the mandate to reform the Confederation, the subversive resolution carried by a vote of six, New York having divided over the radical, alarming course.[41]

CHAPTER 8

The Convention

——————

MORRIS maneuvered in and out of public and private affairs with seamless ease, fitting into the exclusive enclaves of power. After resigning as Robert Morris's assistant secretary of finance at the beginning of 1784, at the age of thirty-two, he was ready to invest his energy and talents in his own private interests. Business, banking, and his legal practice, centered in Philadelphia now absorbed much of his time.

In 1786, he was the youngest member to join with the decrepit Ben Franklin, a near contemporary of his grandfather; James Wilson, an ambitious Scottish lawyer with literary tastes; Robert Morris; and Benjamin Rush to form the Society of Political Inquiries. Sociable and private, the group represented a concentration of the town's enlightened establishment. Morris's still youthful élan gave a lift to what would otherwise have been stodgy affairs.

Washington was made an honorary member of the society, signaling the nationalist leanings of the group. Remarkably, the quirky, dogmatic Tom Paine was also invited to join. His fame as the author of *Common Sense* gave him a passport into the more respectable circles even though he remained an outsider. Paine had redeemed himself somewhat in the eyes of Morris and Wilson after he had worked for them as a hired flack on behalf of the Bank of North America.

The society met once a week in Franklin's library, designed for forty thousand volumes. Rush "commonly took the lead," but he had tough competition from Morris who never hesitated to express an opinion, no matter how contrary to those around him. The society's charter claimed that it was founded to discuss "general politics only," but the timing of its organization suggests that there was an anticipation of bigger things behind those bland words. The record is silent as to whether this clubby little group went beyond the familiar themes and theories of reform in their discussions and discussed the possibility of a national constitution, but there was at least a consensus that a cool, rational assessment of the accomplishments of the Revolution and the future of the country was long past due.

In May 1787, a number of the members of the society—Washington, Franklin, James Wilson, and Morris—were elected delegates to join an unprecedented meeting of the former colonies to be convened in the State House. It was not clear exactly what if anything would be accomplished, but Morris's old criticisms and complaints about the ineffectiveness of state governments had become widespread and had grown louder throughout the country. As Madison would later reflect after the meeting in Philadelphia, "the evils issuing" from the states "contributed more to that uneasiness which produced the Convention," than any other factor.[1]

The prologue of what in retrospect became known as the Constitutional Convention is well known. In January 1786, the Virginia assembly issued an invitation to a conference in Annapolis, Maryland, to "take into consideration the trade of the states" and consider the possibility of giving Congress the power to regulate commerce. Earlier, in 1784, Morris had written his friend John Jay, reflecting on the future of the country in transition: "True it is that the general Government wants Energy, and true it is that this Want will eventually be supplied. A national Spirit is the natural Result of national Existence, and altho some of the present Generation may feel colonial Oppositions of Opinion, that Generation will die and give way and give Place to a race of Americans.... You will find that the States are coming into Resolutions on the subject of Commerce, which if they had been proposed by Congress on the plain Reason of the Thing, would have been rejected with Resentment and perhaps contempt."[2]

A discouraged James Madison supported the Annapolis meeting to solve problems of interstate trade as "better than nothing," even though he thought it would "probably miscarry." But when commissioners from only five states turned up in the Maryland capital, rather than admit defeat, the rump group called for a second convention nine months later in Philadelphia. In ambiguous words, the purported aim was "to devise such further provisions as shall appear to them necessary to render the constitution of the federal government adequate to the exigencies of the Union." For all of its calm tone, it was an act of audacious desperation, yet one even a reluctant, enfeebled Congress could endorse. It is not surprising that wary politicians in Massachusetts, and Patrick Henry in Virginia, "smelt a rat" in the vague language of the invitation and demanded ironclad instructions that the Philadelphia convention was to meet "for the sole and express purpose of revising the Articles of Confederation."

As Morris and others who took the lead at the Philadelphia convention realized, the huge, emerging country, with no clear boundaries to the west, had no collective identity as a nation beyond the common struggle of the war years. The fact that Washington was called "the father of his country" even before there was a country, made him the only enduring, unifying symbol. Morris believed that the "jarring, jealous and perverse" atmosphere that had grown thicker since the Treaty of Peace in 1783 would never supply the cohesive traditions, history, leadership, and dignity that any self-respecting government required to survive and make its way in the world. The government's inability to force the British to live up to the treaty or to compel states to observe its provisions was humiliating.

But the sacred dogma of the sovereignty of the separate states proclaimed at the beginning of the Revolution held state governments enthralled. Paranoia lay just beneath the surface of the faith of many of the old Revolutionaries who were still powerful in the state councils and still haunted by the specter of imperial oppression. They believed that the principles of the Revolution had inexorably transferred power from the few to the many. Any tinkering with the Articles might reverse that sacred course.

Mercy Warren can always be relied upon to state the Anti-Federalist position—the men of 1776 "were jealous of each ambiguity in law or government, or the smallest circumstance that might have a tendency to curtail the republican system" they believed was embedded in the holy text of the Articles of Confederation. According to the most suspicious, there were "artfully laid, and vigorously pursued" plans in the works to transform "our republican Governments into baleful Aristocracies."[3]

The debates over Robert and Gouverneur Morris's revenue measures in 1783–84 had revealed the deep divisions within the old Congress. The Anti-Federalist opposition to any reform declared that if Congress ever "obtained a Perpetual permanent revenue at their disposal, will it not be a Temptation to that August body...either to vote themselves Perpetual, or apply to the states for such a grant[?]" Attacks on the Morrises' financial schemes to fund the national government, including the controversial military pensions, invoked emotional images of "lordly aristocrats" threatening the people's liberties, rhetoric designed to exploit parochial prejudices against the slightest hint of concentrated power supported by standing armies. The Articles' mandate requiring unanimous approval by the states of any amendment made even the limited financial program proposed by the Morrises impossible. To Gouverneur, the narrow-minded leadership of the states lay at the heart of the Confederation's problem.[4]

The authority claimed by the states was not the only structural problem of government during the Confederation. The ill-defined character of the Continental Congress acting as a "deliberating executive assembly" had also contributed to the malfunction. Even the most mundane business had to be taken up in the daily sessions, and layers of committees on which Morris served were set up to carry out the administrative details. In the name of administrative efficiency, Morris had promoted a plan to create four executive departments. But the prevailing antimonarchical sentiments left over from the Revolution had prevented giving these offices enough power to operate effectively, let alone check the excesses of the legislature. To the Old Revolutionaries, Robert's and Gouverneur's purported attempt to manipulate the public creditors and a mutinous army at Newburgh in order to persuade Congress to back their financial program was proof that the executive and its ministers could not be trusted.

Morris had asked not to be named as a delegate to the Philadelphia convention, claiming that he had his hands full with promising business ventures and reorganizing his newly acquired Morrisania estate. Like other leading politicians, he had no faith in the prospects of reform or, as James Varnum put it, "that the Convention at Philadelphia will frame and recommend a system that will be federally adopted." Ever cautious John Jay told John Adams, "I do not promise myself much further immediate Good from the Measure than that it will tend to approximate the public Mind to the Changes which ought to take place." As late as April 1787, Madison wondered whether Washington should "postpone his actual attendance, until some judgment can be formed of the result of the meeting."[5]

Morris was surprised when he heard he had been elected by the General Assembly of Pennsylvania, writing Henry Knox ten days later, when he heard the news: "Had the Object been any other than it is I would have declined. The Appointment was the most unexpected Thing that ever happened to me for have I not only declined in general my unwillingness to accept of any Thing under this State but in this particular Instance objected to being named but it was done while I was in Trenton."[6]

As everyone in Philadelphia knew, Morris "did not," in Madison's understated words, "incline to the democratic side." He barely made it under the wire; Pennsylvania's Assembly accorded him the fewest votes of any of their delegates. His contempt for the radical state government of Pennsylvania is palpable in his letter to Knox. Morris was particularly indignant that the state's legislatively controlled government allowed the majority to harass minorities and particularly the Quaker minority for refusing to take up arms on religious grounds, leaving no doubt of his scorn in a letter to Robert Livingston suggesting that persecuted Quakers take refuge in New York: "If the State of Pennsylvania will not only be mad but add Persecution to Folly they certainly must not Wonder if wise Philanthropists [New York] who love their Specie & Country equally should profit from their Misdoing."[7]

If, as Morris later claimed, "the passions of the people had been lulled to sleep" during the four months of debates in the convention by what Franklin called "*une assemblée des notables*," it was largely because the Convention decided to meet in secret and keep no minutes. An instinctively secretive Jefferson sitting in Paris, complained to John Adams, "I am sorry they began their deliberations by so abominable a precedent as tying up the tongues of their members." Even after a month of meeting, Edward Gould of New York was amazed to see "with what indifference people in general speak of the [Convention] and how little anxiety they betray for an event that in *all* probability must produce some very important Changes in the Government of this Country."[8]

Like many of the "demigods" present, Morris could draw painful lessons from his own impressive experience in state and national governments. Sometimes "abrupt" and "abrasive," he did not bother to conceal his animated presence or opinions, taking the floor 173 times, more than any other member. "Mr. Morris is one of those Genius's in whom every species of talents combine to render him conspicuous and flourishing in public debate," a delegate from Georgia grumbled. "He winds through all the mazes of rhetoric, and throws around him such a glare that he charms, captivates and leads away the sense of all who hear him." A worldly French observer called Morris an "*avocate célébre...mais sans moeurs, et, si l'on en croit ses ennemis, sans principes.*"[9]

With his skeptical, if often irreverent, appraisal of human nature, Morris clearly relished the rhetorical clashes provoked by the attempt to establish a successful republican government. He quickly found that his opponents could respond in kind with their own brand of skepticism. Madison referred to him on the floor as "a member who on all occasions, had inculcated so strongly, the political depravity of men, and the necessity of checking one vice and interest by opposing them to another vice & interest."[10]

Unlike James Madison, Morris did not arrive at the State House with an agenda. But Madison lived up to his reputation for doing his homework thoroughly. Someone remarked that the ascetic gloomy little Virginian with a forgettable face appeared to have entered public life with a book under each arm as he pursued his "researches to the sources ancient & modern" of government's fundamentals. By the time he arrived in Philadelphia on May 5, Madison's imagination and reading of history enabled him to define, in his mind at least, the scope of the assembly's central issues. In letters to Jefferson, Edmund Randolph, and Washington during the spring of 1787, he displayed "the first shoot in his thoughts of a plan of a Federal Government." The results of all this dogged work would be incorporated into what became known as the Virginia Plan.

After George Mason arrived, bringing the Virginia delegation to full complement, they began to draft a formal plan of government with Madison's guidance while they waited for a quorum. Mason had written the Virginia constitution and its bill of rights so he had some definite ideas to contribute. On May 25, with a quorum of seven states present, Robert Morris nominated

Washington who was unanimously elected president of the Convention. Two days later on the twenty-ninth, Virginia's outline of a new government was placed before the delegates, dramatically widening the perspective of the gathering into what Jack Rakove has called the "Madisonian Moment."

Madison's first resolution, introduced by Governor Randolph, diplomatically proposed that the old Articles be "corrected and enlarged." But the form, scope, and tenor of the fourteen resolutions that followed proposed a government so radically different than the Confederation that no one present could have been fooled. It was a call for a new constitution of the United States, "a durable edifice," in Morris's words, to be placed on a popular but solid foundation.

It appears that Madison, Morris, James Wilson, and a few other nationalists had prepared their strategy well when, after Randolph's presentation, it was moved that the "House would resolve itself into a Committee of the whole House to consider of the State of the American Union" the following day. There is no record of talk between Madison and Morris "out of doors" or at Philadelphia's best inn, the Indian Queen, that evening. But the next morning, Morris was on cue, poised firmly on one good leg and the new wooden member, standing a head taller than the diffident, unassuming Madison. The New Yorker needed no prompting when he boldly moved to postpone any debate to repair the exhausted Articles. With the scraping of his chair as he pushed it back and the rap of his new leg calling attention, the balance was tipped in the direction of Morris's vision of a strong central government. Anti-Federalist opposition hardly existed in the body to challenge the maneuver. The Virginia Plan, he argued, envisioned "a *national, supreme,* Govt...having a compleat and *compulsive* operation" on individuals, not states, invoking the principle that "in all communities there must be one supreme power, and one only."[11]

During the opening debate on whether or not to repair the Articles, Morris quickly supported the Virginia resolution that "a Union of the States merely federal will not accomplish the objects proposed by the articles of Confederation, namely common defense, security of liberty, & genl. welfare." The maneuver worked, pushing to the center of the debate the critical Virginia proposition "that a *national* government ought to be established consisting of a *supreme* legislative, executive and judiciary."[12]

After grasping the initiative with such ease, Morris had managed to put himself in the forefront to launch the Virginia Plan, the blueprint that would guide the sessions over the next crucial two weeks. But things did not move very far into uncharted territory the next day when uneasy members questioned the meaning of those loaded words "national" and "supreme." Randolph said his plan envisioned "a strong *consolidated* union" rather than a "federal government," the word "federal" meaning confederation. Morris and George Mason then deftly provided some definitions recorded in Morris's words: "1. We are not now under a federal government. 2. There is no such thing. A federal government is that which has a right to compel every part to do its duty. The federal gov. has no such compelling capacities, whether in their legislative, judicial or Executive qualities."[13]

The force of Morris's argument comes through the abbreviated staccato notes of delegate James McHenry, when Morris appropriates the very words of the worn-out Articles to justify the sudden radical course that the Convention was now taking to move on to a wholly new form of government:

> The States in their appointments Congress in their recommendations point directly to the establishment of a *supreme* government capable of "the common defense, security of liberty and general welfare.
>
> "Cannot conceive of a government in which can exist two *supremes*. A federal agreement which each party may violate at pleasure cannot answer the purpose.... We had better take a supreme government now, than a despot twenty years hence—for come he must."[14]

Consistent with his view that the country had to have a government of a truly national character, Morris's political philosophy had not changed since the eve of the Revolution when he observed the contending crowd gathered in the streets of lower Manhattan. In Morris's estimation, no party or class held all the answers. The Few would always try to deceive its democratic supporters while the populists would attempt to disenfranchise the Few. A successful republican government had somehow to harness these two powerful competing forces.

This did not mean in Morris's judgment, that a republican government had somehow to embrace direct, widespread participation of the people. He acknowledged that the ordinary people had what might be called a conceptual place in the structure, as in the popular election, of the House of Representatives. He wanted to make sure, however, that these egalitarian elements, particularly in state government, did not subvert the national authority established by a constitution or undermine the role of the able, experienced wielders of political power. If the states controlled the national legislature, then the country would continue to disintegrate, as it had under the Confederation. Along with the independence of the executive and judiciary, this was for Morris the defining issue, particularly as it related to the qualifications and composition of the two legislative bodies.

During ratification, Patrick Henry thought he saw through the sinister web that Morris and the nationalists were weaving: "The Constitution," he growled, "reflects in the most degrading and mortifying manner on the virtue, integrity, and wisdom of the state legislatures; it presupposes that the chosen few who go to Congress will have upright hearts, and more enlightened minds than those who are members of individual legislatures." The irascible old Virginian had rightly detected that Morris's objections were not so much to the power of the states but rather to the character of the people who held it.

On July 2, 1787, Morris returned to the Convention after a month's absence at Morrisania, ready to make up for lost time. He discovered that in his absence a serious division had emerged between the small and large states over the representation in the national legislature. The Virginia Plan and the heart of Madison's program called for proportional representation in both houses. But by the end of June, it was apparent that equal representation, at least in one body, was necessary to keep the whole thing from falling apart over the small states' fear of domination by the large.

The day before Morris reappeared, Washington expressed in a letter to a friend in Virginia his gloom over the biased, sectional wrangling he was witnessing from the chair of the presiding officer. The question of proportional representation turned out to be the most divisive issue, and at times it seemed that the meeting might break up. Morris said later that "the fate of America was suspended by a hair." Even Franklin's surprising motion that "prayers imploring Heaven...be held in this Assembly every morning" was opposed because it might cause public alarm that things were not going well. There is the story that Hamilton opposed Franklin's motion on the ground that the Convention did not need "foreign aid."[15]

It was finally settled by the eight larger states and their strong nationalist leaders that "the people," rather than state legislatures, elect the first chamber. This followed the Virginia Plan. George Mason of Virginia, an unlikely defender of the people, dismissed the concern of Elbridge Gerry of Massachusetts for the "danger of the leveling spirit" and insisted that the popular branch of the national legislature should "be the grand depository of the democratic principles of government."

If the House of Representatives was to represent proportionately the people, there was a growing belief that the second branch must somehow represent the states regardless of the discrepancy between their sizes. And since the Continental Congress under the Articles gave an equal vote to each state, large and small, the same formula should prevail in the new government.

To complicate matters, the Virginia Plan proposed that the first branch would elect the Senate from nominations made by the state legislatures. To no one's surprise, Morris exploded that such arrangement was wholly unacceptable, exposing individual liberties to the whims of local majorities. "Is not here a Govt. by the States. This is going back to mere treaty. It is no Govt. at all. It is, altogether dependent on the States," according to Madison's notes of Morris's first speech on his return, "and will act over against the part which [the Continental] Cong. has acted. A firm Governt. alone can protect our liberties."[16]

Morris proceeded to argue the classic theory of a mixed constitution reflecting not only the realities of society, but also insuring a strong government that, in Morris's steadfast view, supported the "dignity and splendor"—a constant image on his mind—of the country's future. A confederation of state or "federal" representation in the government would perpetuate the flaws of the Articles and remain an insidious threat to the future glories of a powerful nation. "It had been said...that the new Governt. would be partly national, partly federal; that it ought in the first quality to protect individuals; in the second, the States. But in what quality was it to protect the aggregate interest of the whole. Among the many provisions which had been urged, he had seen none for supporting the dignity and splendor of the American Empire."[17]

For Morris, the Senate should represent the higher interests of the nation expressed most effectively by the Few, to give stability to the lopsided majority in the House. He told the Assembly that he himself had come as "a Representative of America...and in some degree as a representative of the whole human race" who would be affected by the outcome of the proceedings. Above all, he wished that the delegates would somehow "extend their views beyond the present moment of time; beyond the narrow limits of place from which they derive their political origin." If the House was to be popular and transient, Morris insisted that the second house had to be entirely different in character. "To obtain anything like a check on the rashness of democracy," he confessed, "it was necessary not only to organize the legislature into different bodies, (for that alone is a poor expedient) but to endeavor that these bodies should be animated by a different spirit." Somehow, the Senate had to reflect the natural divisions and hostile interests of the established, wellborn, and rich in order to act as an effective balance against the force of the great masses. Morris frankly admitted that he also feared the influence of the rich who had always strived "to establish their dominion & enslave the rest.... The proper security agst. them is to form them into a separate interest."[18]

Placing the natural aristocracy in the Senate with appointments for life, would not only "check the precipitation, changeableness and excesses" of the other branch, but they themselves could also be controlled and checked in their "proper sphere." Without this segregation within the bicameral legislature, the "result will be a violent aristocracy, or a more violent despotism." To allow the state legislatures to nominate the Senate would only compound the evil. "If the members of [the Senate] are to revert to a dependence on democratic choice, the democratic scale will preponderate. All the guards contrived by America have not restrained the Senatorial branches of the Legislatures [in the states] from a servile complaisance to the democratic. If the 2nd branch is to be dependent we are better without it. To make it independent, it should be for life."[19]

To Morris, the critical realist, inequality was simply the condition of mankind, and a republican constitution had to take it into account. The new government should face up to this inexorable political fact even if it meant accepting social inequality as immutable. While he might agree with Jefferson that a new chapter in human history was opening, he did not believe that it would be classless, a vision that he, like Adams and Hamilton, thought illusory.[20]

The debate on the composition of the Senate exposes some of Morris's deepest—some would later call them reactionary—feelings and reservations on the republican experiment. It also exposed his obsession with aristocracy and what he admitted was its insatiable appetite for power. Morris's patrician elite was not a hereditary aristocracy but the natural variety produced by material advantages, leisure, learning, and those qualities of the mind demanded of the classical Few. The true elite would always be recognized by the Many. On this point, Morris's passion was similar to that of Adams, whose fixation has been called "enlightened perversity" challenging the very concept of equality, "the most alluring idea of the age."

It did not help Morris's cause when he waved the red flag of "aristocracy" in his audacious definition of the qualities of the Senate. As a branch "it must love to lord it thro' pride, pride is indeed the great principle that actuates both the poor & the rich." It should be not only an appointment for life by the executive, but "be composed of men of great and established property—*an aristocracy*, Men, who from pride will support consistency and permanency." These were his code words for civic virtue—"consistency and permanency," all in the name of the public good. His plan to corral and isolate the aristocratic interest exclusively in the Senate was, he believed, to keep it "from doing mischief." If the "rich mix with poor and in a commercial country, they will establish an Oligarchy."

Morris's intellectual honesty and his refusal to twist and subvert the meaning of words in his pointed, unpopular analysis of the oligarchic nature of American society insured that he would be seen as outside the mainstream, an exotic in the intellectual development of the country. Yet he was vindicated by history. The post–Civil War period saw the rich establish a commercial oligarchy as Morris predicted, buying state legislatures, congressmen, and any other popularly elected official that would help the robber barons consolidate their economic power.[21]

His proposal that there be a freehold property requirement for the members of the House as well as the Senate was also rejected with the argument that Morris, once again, favored government by the propertied and the select. To him, even a token amount of property would help ward off the corruption that inevitably engulfed rootless democracies with no stake in the society. His reply that the "ignorant & dependent" would sell out (or give away their vote by not voting) to "the designing rich" remains startlingly pertinent in an advanced industrial society with few restrictions on the buying of elections, making individual qualifications for office irrelevant. Quoting from Madison's note, Morris had long learned not to be duped by words. "The sound of Aristocracy therefore, had no effect on him. It was the thing, not the name, to which he was opposed, and one of his principle objections to the Constitution as it is now before us, is that it threatens this Country with an Aristocracy. The aristocracy will grow out of the House of Representatives. Give the votes to people who have no property, and they will sell them to the rich who will be able to buy them. We should not confine our attention to the present moment. The time is not distant when this Country will abound with mechanics & manufactures who will receive their bread from their empires. Will such men be the secure & faithful Guardians of Liberty? Will they be the impregnable barrier agst. aristocracy?...The man who does not give his vote freely is not represented. It is the man who dictates the vote."[22]

It is not surprising that Morris's most enduring contribution to the Convention was in the debates over the nature, selection, and function of the presidency. More than anyone else, he helped to mold the office into a strong counterforce to the legislative branch. Morris believed that an energetic, independent executive could be the most effective damper on legislative sovereignty. He wanted a national executive just as he wanted a national Senate, directly elected by and accountable to the people. "It has been a maxim in the political Science that Republican government is not adapted to a large extent of Country because the energy of the Executive Magistracy can not reach the extreme parts of it," he argued in his long discourse on the office. "Our Country is an extensive one. We must either then renounce the blessings of the Union, or provide an Executive with sufficient vigor to pervade every part of it....It is necessary then that the Executive Magistrate should be the guardian of the people, even the lower classes, agst. Legislative tyranny, against the Great & wealthy who in the course of things" will control the legislature. The very freedom of legislative power required an "active and vigorous" executive to restrain its excesses. All subordinate powers of the executive, such as finance and foreign affairs, must be "tied to the Chief," anticipating Truman's homely dictum the "the buck stops here." The issue was of central importance to Morris and would continue to flare up in different forms during the deliberations until the last days of the Convention in September.[23]

From the outset, the Convention showed little inclination to approve the election of the president by the people. The Virginia Plan proposed that he be elected by the national legislature, but this raised its own set of problems. When questions intensified over direct election by the people, James Wilson quickly threw out a variation: divide the states into districts, and let the voters qualified to vote for the House choose individuals to serve as electors of the national executive. The electors would then meet and elect by ballot.

Wilson's tentative solution was turned down, and three more months of contention—even over the matter of compensation of the executive—followed before a formula could be agreed upon. A tentative agreement evolved on the election of the president by the national legislature into a term of seven years, ineligible for reelection.

In the debate on executive power, Morris was adamant with his astounding proposal that the president be elected by the people at large. "If the people should elect, they will never fail to prefer some man of distinguished Character, or services; some man, if he might so speak, of continental reputation." Morris declared that the "one great object of the Executive is to control the Legislature." If he was appointed and impeachable by the same body, it would generate more intrigue and abuse than a conclave of cardinals electing a pope. It was a blueprint for disaster and could lead to either monarchy or chaos.

To Morris, the president should serve during good behavior without a term limit. When the charge of "monarchy" was hurled at him, he replied that he was "as little friend to monarchy as any gentleman," adding that the way to avoid such an institution "was to establish such a Repub. Govt." that the people would never want to change it.

When the proposal to limit the president to one term seemed to gain support, Morris argued that ineligibility for a second presidential term only compounded the flaw in the method of selection by the national congress. "Cabal and corruption," he railed was "attached to that mode." He had little problem detecting hidden vices in his opponents' schemes. Prohibiting a second term would encourage the president to sacrifice his executive rights in order to court popularity in the legislature so that he could "go into that body, after the expiration of his Executive office and enjoy the fruits of his policy." Or as he interjected at another point in the debate, "It was saying to him, make hay while the sun shines." Worse yet, his rivals would always be plotting his ouster. It was in the middle of this debate on the election of the president that Morris proposed that the president "shall be chosen by Electors to be chosen by the People of the Several States." His move was in opposition to the president's election by the senate, the worst of all solutions. He had planted the seed of the electoral college system, incorporated in the final draft.

In the report of the Committee on Postponed Matters, on which he served, Morris urged that the Senate settle any vote deadlock in the electoral college. The question on the election of the executive and the term of office had appeared to have been fixed earlier by the Committee on Detail, appointed to smooth out the text of resolutions already agreed on, "after which it will undergo one revision more." Morris's argument to change the term of office from seven to four years and to elect by an electoral college was accepted. In the end, the power to resolve a tie vote was given to the House, a power first used in the Jefferson-Burr tie in 1801.

As the summer of 1787 moved into the dog days of August, attempts were made to further define executive power. Morris finally agreed with Wilson, Madison, Franklin, Mason, and Randolph that the executive could be impeached, but he insisted that the president be armed with the power of veto. Earlier, Morris had effectively argued that impeachment should be enumerated and limited to bribery, treachery, and incapacity. When Madison proposed that the Supreme Court conduct the trial for impeachment, Morris countered that only the Senate could be trusted. "The Supreme Court were too few in number and might be warped or corrupted." While any dependence of the executive on the legislature might encourage "legislative tyranny...there could be no danger that the Senate would say untruly on their oaths that the President was guilty of crimes or facts, especially as in four years he can be turned out."[24]

Morris also insisted that impeachment require a vote of two-thirds of the members present. As in the case of the approval of treaties, the reversal of an election could not be left to "a mere majority of Senators present." A coup d'é-tat of "cunning men" united in a faction could overthrow the choice of the people. Expressing public will numerically in the legislature was perverse. People who followed such reasoning "are the tools, which usurpers employ in building despotism." "That numerical majority not only may but frequently does, will what is unwise and unjust...in order to please the people...regard-less alike of what conscience may dictate or reason approve." It was, in his opinion, a sure step to tyranny.[25]

The Convention did not spell out the authority of the Supreme Court to declare laws unconstitutional, but Morris took it for granted that it had the power. "Legislative alterations not comfortable to the federal compact," he told the delegates, "would clearly not be valid. The Judges would consider them null & void." In his objection to a congressional veto of state laws proposed by Madison, Morris stated that he believed the federal courts were the appropriate place to sort out constitutional disputes. But he strongly agreed with Madison that the president, rather than the Senate, should appoint judges. Senatorial appointment, he argued, would have undermined the independence of the judiciary since the Senate had also been given the power to remove.

Morris's sensitivity to the differing opinions on the precise role of the judi-ciary is reflected in a letter to Timothy Pickering of 1814. Morris wrote briefly about the language of the document he had drafted for the Convention's Committee on Style. His words were "as clear as our language would permit," redundant and equivocal terms had been avoided except in the matter of the judiciary. He had, however, gotten in the last word on the subject within the text of the Constitution itself; in his Preamble, he called "a declaration of motives." There was no doubt in Morris's mind that it was the people who enacted constitutions and who were ultimately sovereign. After establishing "a more perfect union" it was the people's intent and the object of the compact to "establish justice," then would follow "domestic tranquillity."[26]

Although the method of electing the president has been called "the longest and hardest fought battle in the whole convention," Morris considered the fight over slavery just as critical. The issue of slavery had become entan-gled with the question of future expansion into western territories and the admission of new states. To add further complications, these two incendiary subjects reached into the disruptive question of representation in the House. The tensions between the North and the South that had been apparent from the outset were further aggravated by the turbulent disagreements between the large and small states. Before the Convention was over, the volatile mix of slavery and western expansion was added to the stew, rankling and alarming the increasingly testy delegates, including Morris.

On June 11, James Wilson resurrected an old formula, first proposed (but not approved) in the Continental Congress, to apportion taxes among the states as a way to resolve the problem of representation in the House. Known as the three-fifths compromise, five slaves were to be counted as three white men in determining the number of seats each state would hold in the popular body—"in proportion to the whole number of white and other free citizens and inhabitants of every age, sex, and condition...and three fifths of all other persons."

Backed by Charles Pinkney of South Carolina, Wilson now urged the formula as a way to restore harmony to the Convention, that both representatives and direct taxes would be proportioned according to the scheme. But the use of the invidious word "slave" in the text was carefully avoided. Wilson disingenuously claimed that slaves were "indirectly only an ingredient in the rule," although he could not have failed to know Pinkney's real goal to protect the South's vested interests. A periodic census would take into account three-fifths of the slaves, and Morris believed that this periodic census, in turn, would translate into a devious formula of representation to protect the southern states in the national councils as the country grew.

With proportional representation in the House approved, counting slaves to fix the representation in the lower body insured that slavery would then be mirrored throughout the national government. There were a number of other proposals, but with mounting tension, the smaller states held firmly to their position that all states should be equal in the Senate. With the later admission of new states, the Great Compromise of July 16, giving each state an equal number of seats in the Senate would make that body key to the South's eventual control. To Morris this meant slave interests would determine the blueprint for the inevitable catastrophe that lay ahead.[27]

Morris was the only member of the Philadelphia convention who had fought to abolish slavery in a state constitution. With John Jay, he had also founded the New York Manumission Society to work for immediate abolition. He was not prepared to buy any of the arguments giving slaves, the South's "peculiar objects," a protected footing in the new government and used all of his lawyer's skills, indignant rhetoric (of which he had plenty), and strategies to attack any further incorporation of slavery into the political fabric of the country. "He never would concur in upholding slavery." It was, as the abolitionists would later declare, a nonnegotiable issue, a moral blight on the states where it existed. His direct, no-holds-barred assault on the southern delegation and its "peculiar institution" was relentless. The combined holdings of the nineteen slave-owning delegates present in Philadelphia alone represented approximately fifteen hundred slaves. The American census of 1790 revealed a total of seven hundred thousand blacks held in bondage throughout the country.

The suggestion that the three-fifths ratio was a compromise to garner support for a direct tax was a subterfuge, Morris charged. Given the implications of the South's formula of representation, maybe it was time for the nonslave and slave states to "at once take friendly leave of each other." Even "ye vicious principle of equality in the 2d branch" would be better than giving slaves non-voting representation. Because there was no such thing as a "direct" national tax, the scheme's only purpose was to increase the representation of the slave states in Congress. More taxes would be collected on "the bohea tea used by a Northern freeman" than "the whole consumption of a miserable slave, which consists of nothing more than his physical subsistence and the rag that covers his nakedness." The three-fifths clause simply insured slave masters extra seats in the Congress. "He would sooner submit himself to a tax for paying for all the Negroes in the U. States," he asserted, "than saddle posterity with such a Constitution."[28]

What was worse, the provision rewarded those states for importing more slaves. When admitted into the plan of representation, the slave trade would suddenly have a bright new future: "the inhabitant of Georgia and S.C. who goes to the Coast of Africa, and in defiance of the most sacred laws of humanity tears away his fellow creatures from their dearest connections & dam[n]s them to the most cruel bondages, shall have more votes in a Govt. instituted for protection of the rights of mankind, than the Citizen of Pa or N. Jersey who view with laudable horror, so nefarious a practice." Morris then took the label of "aristocrat" so often thrown at him, tossing it back in the face of the defenders of slavery seated around him. To claim that the three-fifths clause had anything to do with taxation was errant hypocrisy, for it exposed to the world "that Domestic slavery is the most prominent feature in the aristocratic countenance of the proposed Constitution. The vassalage of the poor, the favorite offspring of the Aristocracy," was a sacrifice "of every principle of right, of every impulse of humanity."[29]

When Morris returned to the Convention from Morrisania, the tense dispute over slavery had spilled into the equally volatile questions surrounding the status of the vast western territories and the new states that might be carved out of it. The organization and development of the extended national domain had long been a smoldering problem in the old Congress. Finally, in July 1787, the celebrated Northwest Ordinance was passed. That triggered a new urgency to the arguments over the political future of the original thirteen states and the ones yet to be created.

From the beginning, Morris had held ambivalent reservations on western expansion. When Jay was trying to persuade Spain to support the Revolution, Morris dismissed Spain's concern over the potential American threat to control of the Mississippi. "The Territory we cannot occupy," he wrote Jay in Madrid, "the Navigation we cannot enjoy...an immigration from the whole world, whereof one hundredth or perhaps not so much shall be our descendants, will claim Title under us to a Part of the Soil, then set up an Independence and hold [it] under the King Christ of Heaven," justified by the very precedent of the Revolution that secured American liberty. Fundamentally he doubted the compatibility of great territory and republican government. The threat of the spread of slavery only compounded the problem of an expanded dominion.[30]

In his travels through Virginia and Maryland, Morris had been shocked by the destructive impact of slavery on the physical environment. The dismal landscape of scarred and rutted tobacco fields now abandoned to scrub pine and broom sage, to Morris, was an appalling indictment of the system. Here and there, shanty slave villages housed their "wretched beings" in subhuman conditions. In the Convention, he raised in a political setting, for the first time in the nation's history, the condition of the manmade environment and its victims as a national, moral issue. Madison's abbreviated notes capture the compassionate emotion of Morris's prophetic concern, an indictment unmatched by any other delegate:

> It was a nefarious institution—It was the curse of heaven on the States where it prevailed. Compare the free regions of the Middle States, where a rich & noble cultivation marks the prosperity & happiness of the people, with the misery, & poverty which over spread the barren wastes of Virginia, Maryd. & the other States having slaves. Travel thro' ye whole Continent & you will behold the prospect continually varying with the Appearance & disappearance of slavery. The moment you leave ye E. Sts. & enter N. York, thye effects of the institution become visable; Passing thro' the Jerseys and entering Pa— every criterion of superior improvement witnesses the change. Proceed Southwdly, & every step you take thro' ye great regions of slaves, presents a desert increasing with ye increasing proportion of these wretched beings.[31]

Morris argued that there should simply be future legislative discretion to evaluate both population and wealth in determining representation. He could see that the counting of heads (black and white) by census would fuel the spread of slavery westward, and he was deeply alarmed by the prospect. If the new states were admitted on an equal footing with the original thirteen and with the same distorted three-fifths formula, it would not take long for them to outnumber the Atlantic states.

In the debates on representation, the West, and slavery, Morris's rhetoric reached its most extravagant register. He did not hesitate to spell out what he perceived as an insurmountable cultural and political gap between the urban, commercial society of the progressive East and the agrarian South and West built on human bondage. The older states should keep close control of the territorial governments, and that meant excluding new states as well. Slavery was the ulterior and driving thrust of the census and the three-fifths clause.[32]

> Among other objections it must be apparent they [the new states] would not be able to furnish men equally enlightened, to share in the administration of our common interests. The Busy haunts of men not the remote wilderness, was the proper school of political Talents. If the Western people get the power into their hands they will ruin the Atlantic interests. The Back members are always most averse to the best measures.... Another objection with him agst. admitting the blacks into the census, was that the people of Pen [Pennsylvania] would revolt at the idea of being put on a footing with slaves. They would reject any plan that was to have such an effect.[33]

Madison immediately taunted Morris for accepting future legislative discretion of apportionment contrary to his normal skepticism and for his uncharitable appraisal of westerners. The Virginian was surprised that a man who "had inculcated so strongly the political depravity of men" was willing to accept their future judgment on something as critical as representation. "With regard to the Western States, he (Madison) was clear & firm in opinion, that no unfavorable distinctions were admissible either in point of justice or policy."[34]

When the South continued to block outright prohibition of the slave trade, the debate led by Elbridge Gerry of Massachusetts then turned to the possibility of a tax on imported slaves. Any concession to the institution was going against the grain, but the relentless pressure from the slave block finally forced Morris to give ground. His sharp eye saw the glimmer of a way. "These things," he reluctantly conceded in the middle of the debate, "may form a bargain among the Northern & Southern States," and he recommended that the question of slavery be sent to a committee. Two days later, the committee reported a compromise, as Morris had foreseen, proposing that Congress be barred from prohibiting slave trade until 1800. Morris finally went along with the provision amended to extend to 1808.

On August 6, after Morris and Washington returned from inspecting the site of the camp at Valley Forge, during a brief recess, the Convention took up the report of the Committee of Detail, including the three-fifths provision in Article 4. Morris made his last strike at the immoral declension of human beings into fractions. "Upon what principle is it," he demanded, "that the slaves shall be computed in the representation? Are they men? Then make them Citizens & let them vote. Are they property? Why then is no other property included?" Morris moved to insert the word "free" before the word "inhabitants" in the third section of the article, which would effectively scuttle it.[35]

Having earlier proposed that the territories remain under the control of the Atlantic states, Morris gave ground but argued that the Congress should at least set conditions of future statehood. The reality was that the West was going to grow regardless of what was decided in Philadelphia. When the Committee on Detail inserted a provision that new states "be admitted on the same terms with the original states," Morris then offered a substitute wording: "New states may be admitted by the Legislature into this Union; but no new State shall be erected within the limits of any of the present States, without the consent of the Legislature of such State, as well as the Genl. Legislature." Sixteen years later, at the time of the Louisiana Purchase, Morris told Henry W. Livingston that he believed that his artless words did exclude new states in the territories but confessed that it should have "been more pointedly expressed" and would have been but for the strong opposition.[36]

Concerned that time was running out, in late August Morris pushed the framers to finish their business as soon as possible, so that states could arrange their ratifying conventions. He also urged state conventions to be called as quickly as possible "to prevent the enemies to the plan, from giving it the go by." The question of the mode of ratification had, of course, come up early in the Convention but was left unresolved. Ratification was not seriously addressed again until the last two days of August and the first part of September. By then, the impatient nationalist majority had stepped up the pressure to finish the job. When the Committee on Detail reported, some members of the Convention said that they might not be signers. From the bare notes that have survived, a rising sharpness of the tone of the debate comes through over the method of ratification just before turning everything over Morris's Committee on Style. A defeated article said that the Constitution was to be "laid" before the old Congress for its "approbation" and then submitted to conventions chosen in each state. Morris was opposed to submitting it to the Confederation for its approval, and his move to strike the word "approbation" was accepted. There was also a critical agreement that nine states would be sufficient "for the establishment of this Constitution between the States so ratifying the same."[37]

In cold fury, George Mason moved for postponement of the final vote saying he would rather cut off his right hand than submit the document as it then stood. Morris cheerfully accepted the threat by announcing that he was "ready" to bring the whole affair to a halt—"He had long wished for another Convention, that will have the firmness to provide a vigorous Government, which we are afraid to do." Mason's motion was defeated eight to three. Ten days later, Morris joined Madison, Rufus King, Samuel Johnson, and Hamilton as members of the "Committee for revising the stile and arrangements of the articles agreed on." All the members and certainly Morris had their reservations. Madison admitted that in addition to the "brilliancy of his genius," Morris could forthrightly surrender his opinions if he was satisfied with the opposition's argument. Hamilton, who had given a six-hour speech during the Convention and then gone off to New York for several weeks after it was ignored, bluntly expressed his "dislike of the scheme of government" when he returned. But he agreed to support it "as better than nothing."

James Madison has immortalized Morris's most enduring contribution to the framing of the Constitution as the member of the Committee on Style who consolidated the Convention's intent into a solid structure. Morris characterized his role in the Convention, and he no doubt saw a similar role as a member of the committee, "to further our business, remove impediments, obviate objections, and conciliate jarring opinions." His language did all of this brilliantly. The former president wrote Jared Sparks on April 8, 1831: "The *finish* given to the style and arrangement of the Constitution fairly belongs to the pen of Mr. Morris; the task having probably, been handed over to him by the chairman of the Committee, himself a highly respected member, and with the ready concurrence of others. A better choice could not have been made, as the performance of the task proved."[38]

Although Morris had been defeated on many of his proposals, a number were included when he began his work on the finished draft, but both his support and opposition left important marks. His words in the debate on the suspension of the writ of habeas corpus only "in Cases of rebellion or invasion the public safety may require" passed into the final version. In the provision for impeachment of the president, after reciting the causes "treason, bribery, or other high crimes and misdemeanors," he eliminated the words "against the United States." His strong and successful opposition to sumptuary laws of any kind—he argued, contrary to his stereotyped reputation, that it would "create a landed Nobility by fixing forever in great-landholders and their posterity their present possessions"—was successful.[39]

Four days after its appointment, the Committee on Style submitted its revisions, written more for clear direction than for inspiration. Rhetorical distractions were not allowed to cloud its "simple and precise language." In its unadorned, muscular phrasing, its vigor and thrust, the fact that it was a makeshift affair was well disguised. Neither Morris nor anyone else was exactly rhapsodic about the results, but the new constitution achieved far more than he and the other framers had dared to hope. Even Washington was guarded with his expectations, writing Henry Knox that he was "fully persuaded that it is the best that can be obtained at the present moment under such diversity of ideas as prevail." The survival of the Constitution would have astonished everyone at Philadelphia, lasting so well, Leonard Levy has written, because the government that emerged would have the power to achieve its goals, but also because it would be a government properly "bitted and bridled."[40]

The weight and dignity of the document was increased when the original twenty-four articles turned over to the Committee on Style were edited into seven, introduced by Morris's new Preamble, setting out the high command of a responsible national government. The opening words, "We the People," literally describing the people's role in the ratifying town meetings of Massachusetts, were taken from the Massachusetts constitution of 1780. As a rhetorical embodiment of both the people and the separate states embraced in the words, they remain the most significant words in the document. Even if it does not support the same critical analysis as the Declaration of Independence, it captured the essence of national unity, lifting the Convention's work onto the moral plane of the Declaration.

When Morris's Committee on Style received the working draft from the Convention, the Preamble had read "We the people of the New Hampshire, Massachusetts, Rhode Island, etc...." an awkward list naming each of the other states, hardly the right note to begin on. It ended on an equally pedestrian note to "ordain, declare, and establish the following Constitution for the Government of Ourselves and our Posterity." This earlier version had its origin in the question of who exactly would ratify it. It was assumed that all the states of the Confederation would have to give their approval before the new government was established just as they had all originally approved the articles. After it was decided that only nine states would be adequate to form a new government, no one could then predict and name in advance the members of this radical, unprecedented coalition. The fate of the old Confederation was sealed.

On September 14, during the Convention's final review, it accepted without discussion the committee's new language that no state could pass any "law impairing the obligation of contracts." The following day, and just before the worn-out delegates signed off, Morris's acute antenna picked up "the circulating murmurs of the small states," still worried about their ultimate survival. At the last minute, he generously offered "to annex a further proviso," which was accepted "that no state, without its consent, shall be deprived of its equal suffrage in the Senate." With that, the small-staters appeared satisfied.[41]

On September 17, "the engrossed Constitution being read" to the delegates gathered in their final session, most seemed prepared to sign. But a shaky yet alert Benjamin Franklin was worried that some of the "Grumbletonians" might delay unanimity at the last minute. The day before, he had written out an address to be presented to the Convention, which he reviewed with Morris. Too unsteady to read it himself on the morning of the seventeenth he handed it to Wilson who read it for him. The ancient statesman's words spoke for many present when he said that there were "several parts of this constitution which I do not at present approve," but he seriously doubted if another other Convention would be able to make a better one. Franklin ended with the inspired "wish that every member of the Convention who may still have objections to it, would with me, on this occasion doubt a little of his own infallibility—and to make manifest our unanimity, put his name to this instrument." He then offered a resolution, shrewdly written by Morris, as an umbrella for the fainthearted. The signing would be "as a convenient form viz. Done in Convention, by the unanimous consent of *the States* present the 17th of Sepr. &c-In Witness whereof we have hereunto subscribed our names."

At the last moment, a jittery Edmund Randolph got cold feet in the closing debate, making the pusillanimous excuse that he could not sign because he needed more time to think about it. Morris answered him in his last recorded remarks on the floor. While frankly admitting that "he too had objections, but considering the present plan as the best that was to be attained, he should take it with all its faults. The majority had determined in its favor and by that determination he [Randolph] should abide. The moment this plan goes forth all other considerations will be laid aside—and the great question will be, this must take place or a general anarchy will be the alternative."

Then he offered to clear up any ambiguity in the wording of his resolution, attached to Franklin's speech, adding that "the signing in the form proposed related only to the fact the *States* present were unanimous." Hamilton rose and gave his reluctant support to Morris's argument, saying that while "no man's ideas were more remote from the plan than his," he agreed that the stark choice was "between anarchy and Convulsion."[42]

Morris knew that the Constitution was a "bundle of compromises" without much logic to it and was without precedent. In the official letter he wrote for Washington to transmit the document to Congress, he admitted that it had been extracted from a resistant nation faced with no alternative. While acutely aware of the rumbling discord between the states, "their Situation Extent Habits and particular Interests," the Convention had, Morris wrote, "kept steadily in our View that which appears to us the greatest Interest of every true American. The Consolidation of our Union in which is involved our Prosperity Felicity Safety perhaps our national Existence." Above all, the Constitution now presented was, in Morris's best diplomatic gloss, the "Result of a Spirit of Amity and of that mutual Deference & Concession which the Peculiarity of our political Situation rendered indispensable." He knew the importance of compromise and the role it had played in Philadelphia, a role it must continue to play in the process of popular government.[43]

With all the mythology that has grown up around the Constitution, it is sometimes forgotten that the framers were practical, imperfect men out to solve real problems. Some claimed it "the work of Heaven," but Morris was under no such illusion, writing an acquaintance in France that "it was the work of plain honest men, and such, I think, it will appear." If John Adams had been in the Convention with Morris, those plain words of the New York patrician could have been written by the cranky sage from Quincy. The delegates in Philadelphia, Morris insisted, "were Rep[representatives] of America ney human race" who "ought to extend our view beyond the moment of the day" and beyond in the broiling, transient passions and fleeting sentiments of that abstraction called "the people." Transcending his worst premonitions and against all odds, he had helped to test and reinforce the structure, as well as giving the final form to the emerging edifice "now open wide as an Asylum to mankind" ready to "receive to her bosom and comfort and cheer the oppressed, the miserable and the poor of every nation and every clime."[44]

Morris took no part in the battle over ratification although he had insisted that it be in special conventions in each state rather than in the elected assemblies. He was "warmly pressed by Hamilton to assist in writing *The Federalist*" but turned him down. He claimed he was not "inquisitive about political opinion," but he quietly took the temperature of public sentiments toward the Constitution, optimistically reporting to Washington that the "preachers are advocates," and with the support of "property...makes the current set strongly, and I trust, irresistibly," in its favor. Oddly, and contrary to popular opinion, the Anti-Federalists who opposed the Constitution did not hold views radically different from Morris's expressed reservations of majority rule dictated by the darker view of human nature generally. They, like Morris, expressed no great faith in "the people." If, in fact there had been fewer checks and balances and more direct democracy in the finished draft, the Constitution would probably not have been ratified. What Morris and his cohorts in Philadelphia had were the faith and the vision to see the new government on a monumental scale and firmly placed in a strong, national framework that would accommodate the later rise of democracy.[45]

After a few weeks of rest at Morrisania, Morris was back on the road, riding off to Philadelphia and then to Virginia were he spent the winter and spring of 1788 on behalf of his business partner and law client Robert Morris. Sometime after leaving the Office of Superintendent, the elder Morris had entered into large contracts to supply the tobacco monopoly in France. Under contracts with the farmers-general, which held the monopoly, Morris had received a large advance for the exclusive shipment of 20,000 hogsheads of American tobacco each year for a period of three years. Gouverneur Morris's job was to reorganize affairs that had been neglected during the Philadelphia meeting and to collect some of Robert Morris's old debts.

During his visit to Virginia, he attended the Virginia Ratifying Convention in the sweltering heat of June 1788, staying with Thomas Mann Randolph at Tuckahoe, his plantation just west of the village of Richmond. The large house at Tuckahoe stood in the middle of the plantation, flanked with neat rows of slave cabins and looking down across the James River. Randolph had "one of the best fortunes in this country," the New Yorker believed, but like so many of the Virginia gentry he was seriously indebted. Like his cousin Thomas Jefferson, Randolph was held ransom to a "thralldom of debt." The "thralldom" was some twelve thousand pounds sterling owed to British creditors, making it increasingly difficult to keep up the generous, expected standards of Tuckahoe hospitality and the education of his children. The Randolph household included Thomas Jr., aged twenty; Judith, sixteen; and Anne Cary, called Nancy, who was fourteen. Later that summer, Thomas returned from studies in Edinburgh with a Scottish tutor for his sisters. Nancy is not mentioned by the New York guest, but twenty years later she would suddenly and dramatically enter Morris's life.[46]

Morris carefully watched the Virginia convention, evenly divided with "one half of her crew hoisting sale for the land of *energy*," in the words of a delegate, "the other looking with a longing aspect on the shore of *liberty*." A young delegate with an impressive military record in the Revolution—John Marshall—listened intently to Madison's opening defense of a stable, respected national government. Morris dismissed Patrick Henry's populist diatribes, calling him a master of "Action Utterance . . . to stir Men's Blood," but his "warm and powerful" demagoguery against ratification did not hold up to examination, even if it raised the temperature and tempers in the packed convention hall. At one low point in the debate, the old rabble-rouser was heard to shout, "They'll free your niggers!" Marshall skillfully replied to Henry's "violence of opinions, the prejudices and animosities," intended to undermine "a well-regulated democracy." Marshall the chief justice would become a friend and confidant of the New Yorker.[47]

Like contagious diseases, Morris told Hamilton, Henry's arguments were "only known by their Effects on the Frame and unfortunately our moral like our physical Doctors are often mistaken in their Judgment and Diagnostics." Then, with vintage Morris optimism, he assured his anxious friend in New York, "Be of good Chear. My Religion steps in where my Understanding falters and I feel Faith as I loose Confidence. Things will yet go right, but when and how I dare not predict. So much for this dull Subject." Virginia became the tenth state to ratify the Constitution by a vote of eighty-nine to seventy-nine. New York would reluctantly follow on July 26. "The people of America" had finally "bound the States down" with the new compact.[48]

By the end of 1788, Robert Morris's tobacco customers in France had grown increasingly nervous over late deliveries, and it became clear that Gouverneur's abilities as a troubleshooter were needed in Paris. There were also serious political problems surrounding the Philadelphian's contract with the French tobacco monopoly. Jefferson, serving as minister to France, had been doing everything in his power to scuttle Robert's arrangements as exclusive purchasing agent for the farmers-general. Morris was also to act as Robert's agent in unloading huge tracts of western lands the overextended Robert had acquired in speculation.

Among Morris's other ventures in France was the prospect of organizing private investors to purchase the American debt of some thirty-four million dollars from the strapped French government at fifty cents on the dollar. The assumption was that the United States would eventually redeem the debt at full value, yielding a nice profit to the investors, including Gouverneur Morris.

Writing Washington to request a few letters of introduction on the eve of his departure to Paris, Morris told him it would be as good as gold, a bill of exchange wherever he went. In particular, he asked for an introduction to Jefferson, whom he barely knew. Continuing the banker's metaphor, but with the usual tone of familiarity, he cautioned the general not to give him more credit than he was worth "least proving a bankrupt, you be called on by my creditors." Washington, in turn, asked the New Yorker, with his customary detail, to buy him a gold watch in Paris for his own use, "not a small, trifling, nor a finical, ornamental one, but a watch well executed in point of workmanship, large and flat with a plain, handsome key." On December 18, 1788, Morris boarded the *Henrietta* at Philadelphia and sailed for France.[49]

PART IV

Europe

CHAPTER 9

Paris, 1789

THE convulsions of the North Atlantic in the winter of 1789 were the prelude to the turbulent world Morris was about to enter, a society on the verge of a nervous breakdown. The crossing to France took forty days "at a Season," the traveler noted, "when the greatest Part of the twenty four Hours was clothed in Darkness." The heavy sea also served as a metaphor for Morris's complex private life in Paris, a tangle of money, politics, and romance. Admiring rumors of his success in finance, "gallantry" and constitution-making had preceded him.[1]

The New Yorker's ability to think and then nail his thoughts down with his pen even under the most distracting conditions was put to the test in his cramped quarters on the *Henrietta.* "When the howling winds would not permit repose," he told Robert Morris, "maritime meditations" on American finances allowed him to weather the rough trip in his dark cabin, sketching out a three-thousand-word essay he would discuss with Thomas Jefferson when he arrived. Morris landed at the port of Harve on January 27, 1789, and called on Thomas Jefferson, the American minister, ten days later at his elegant little Hôtel de Langeac on the western edge of Paris. Jefferson reported to his secretary, William Short, who was traveling in the south of France, that Morris had arrived "deputed as is supposed to settle R. Morris's affairs which continue still deranged."[2]

The very air of the Paris that Morris entered had the feeling of a modern city, even though its medieval ribs still showed. To Morris, the giddy capital appeared to be in a "fluctuating uncertain State," a city in the throes of dynamic change extending from the architecture in splendid new buildings to the salons and bedrooms of the men and women he would meet. They, like the society, were also improvising and testing out new relationships, codes, and manners in their often reckless private lives. "Indeed Pleasure," he reported to Robert Morris, "is the great Business."

The key to the Parisian beau monde was that at its core its scale was intimate and manageable, a place where all the leading figures—political, cultural, entrepreneurial—were able to know each other without difficulty. The metropolitan center was in the districts around the Place Louis XV, the city's new western entrance, the Palais Royal and the Tuileries on the Right Bank. Smart residential districts across the river on the Left Bank were reached by several bridges.

Invitations, mostly casual, often by word of mouth, to the best houses, more than filled Morris's daily and evening hours from the moment he arrived. Lady Sutherland, the wife of the British ambassador, apologized to him when he found himself barred from her house, but she was so annoyed with "Frenchmen who break in on her" at all hours unannounced that she had ordered her butler to shut her doors. But few doors were closed to the new man in town.[3]

The march toward *liberté, fraternité, and égalité* in Paris was well underway in the slow, chilly spring of 1789, even if no one was sure where it was leading. While intellectual transformation was examined in polite exchanges in the salons, hidden from public view, much of the visible change in the streets was driven by crass real estate speculation, spawned by new buildings in new streets cut through the medieval sections. A new capitalism, in collaboration with the government, had taken command. Morris understood the signs, remarking, "Here, every Thing is Expedient and Circulation." The journalist Louis-Sébastien Mercier estimated that fully a third of the city had been rebuilt in the past twenty-five years. In a certain way, the new geography was the map of modernity, a network of smaller more intimate private spaces bounded by large ordered public territory, an interconnected topography of unstable worlds of novelty, fantasy, imagination, and risk.[4]

One of the most conspicuous real estate developers was the duc d'Orléans, whose Palais Royal was close to Morris's Hôtel de Richelieu in the street of the same name. Pressed for funds to maintain his extravagant living and love affairs, the duke, a cousin of the king, had remodeled Cardinal Richelieu's old palace complex, turning it into the hottest real estate development in the city. The duke's enterprise was in the vanguard of the commercialization of leisure. Around the perimeter along the promenades were shops, gambling dens, private clubs, brothels, and cafés promoted by the duke "to serve a quotidian of carnival appetites." Within its demotic arcades and gardens could be found a revolutionary fraternity drawn from every class. "There you can see everything, learn everything," Mercier announced. "There is no spot in the world comparable to it. Visit London, Amsterdam, Madrid, Vienna, you will see nothing like it: a prisoner could live here free from care for years with no thought of escape."

Standing at the "center of a big city's chaos"—the words are from Restif's *Les Nuits de Paris*—the Palais would become the underground intelligence hub of the Revolution. While the New Yorker remained tempered in his impressions of the place, he was regularly drawn into the Palais's milieu as a part of his daily and evening rounds. As he put it, "to know all one must see all." With his instinctive cosmopolitan tastes, Morris was attracted to the erotic, exuberant atmosphere. "Go to the Palais Royal to walk a little," is a typical, laconic diary entry: "Take a view of the Circus, which is said to have cost the Duke of Orleans 3,000,000# and which he rents for 80,000#. It is vast and an elegant building underground about 120 to 130 Yards long and 30 to 40 wide."

The duke's shopping mall also became a place where Morris could sharpen his ability to observe and translate the social, cultural, and political shifts taking place around him. He was far from an indifferent spectator, but the pace was something he had not encountered before. "A Man in Paris lives in a sort of Whirlwind which turns him round so fast," he wrote a friend in Philadelphia, "that he can see Nothing. And as all Men and Things are in the same vertiginous Situation you can neither fix yourself or your Object by regular Examination." The New Yorker was impressed with how Parisians had overcome the problem and could, in a flash, pronounce judgment on both people and places "from the first Glance, and being thus habituated to shoot flying they have what Sportsmen call a quick Sight.... They know a Wit by his Snuff Box, a Man of Taste by his Bow, and a Statesman by the cut of his Coat."[5]

It may well have been this perception of these still detectable French qualities that inspired Morris to buy a notebook shortly after he arrived and, on March 1, 1789, to begin a diary. Each night he would record the major themes of his Paris life—politics, finance, and romance—in straight, even lines, leaving few signs on the pages of any hesitation or uncertainty in sorting out fleeting impressions of people, places, and events. But this is not the only reason Morris turned to the diary form. Because he had no intention of sharing it with others then or later, the candid daily entries offered him an avenue of psychological liberation with unprecedented possibilities. It was a new way for him to discover and understand his own unique, "modern" sensibility, his inner identity. One comes away from the diary feeling that in the churning, uprooted, emotional times he was living through, his dedication to the formality of a journal somehow gave order and meaning to the confusion around him. The act of writing always in the present tense allowed him to replace a fragile, passing experience with the recorded order of his feelings and intellect. Unlike most Americans on their first trip to Europe, there are few signs of the awestruck "innocent abroad."[6]

Morris's considerable reputation as a statesman, lawyer, and financial expert was well known in the higher levels of Paris society and the government. Close dealings with French emissaries in Philadelphia as a member of the Continental Congress and his important post in the Office of Finance had put him in touch with a number of the city's leading characters. His engraved portrait was among the American patriots published by Du Simitière in Paris in 1781, a collection that included George Washington, John Jay, and Horatio Gates.[7]

Some of the newcomer's most influential connections came through his acquaintance with the marquis de Chastellux, whom he had first met in Philadelphia. The marquis had been chief of staff of Rochambeau's army and although much older was immediately struck by the New Yorker's "exquisite wit and excellent understanding." In his journal of his travels in America, Chastellux first noted the young man's remarkable ability to adapt himself successfully "to business, to letters, and to sciences" with few equals in Europe. A philosophe, a member of the French Academy, and a man of the salons, the "amiable" marquis was also in a good position to spread the word of Morris's role in drafting the Constitution. As a measure of the impression the New Yorker had made, early in 1788 Chastellux confided to Morris his plans to marry at the age of fifty-four, "a revolution wrought in my destiny." But the marquis had died suddenly the previous October, just before his son was born. Morris would make one of his first calls in Paris on the marquis's widow and infant son.[8]

Madame de Chastellux, a charming Irish woman, was lady-in-waiting and confidant of the duchesse d'Orléans. Their intimate circle of friends quickly adopted the American, a camaraderie that did not include the duchess's notorious husband, later called Philippe Egalité. After Morris had met the grieving widow "who is not the less lovely for the Tears she sheds," he reported his visit to Washington suggesting he send her a note of condolence, which he would personally deliver as a gesture of thanks for her husband's contribution in the American cause.

Morris carried a number of letters of introduction from the comte Elie de Moustier, the French minister in America. One of his first letters from Paris was to thank Moustier for his introductions. As usual, Morris cut to the central political issue, summing up his first impressions to the minister: "Your Nation is now in a most important Crisis, and the great Question, shall we hereafter have a Constitution, or shall Will continue to be Law." But Morris added that he believed Louis XVI, unlike former monarchs, had shown positive signs of a desire for reform. Then, quoting Horace, that men change only their climate and not their souls when they cross the sea, he gave the Roman's words a polished spin: "I say what he could not, that I find on this side of the Atlantic a resemblance to what I left on the other; a nation which exists in hopes, prospects, and expectations."[9]

Morris's politic words at the close of his letter did not make up for the tinge of unease he had expressed in an earlier paragraph, that there were signs of hubris among his new circle of acquaintances hiding the actual state of affairs. "Your nobles, your clergy, your people, are all in a motion for the elections. A spirit, which has been dormant for generations, starts up and stares about, ignorant of the means of obtaining, but ardently desirous to possess its object—consequently, active, energetic, easily led, but also easily misled. Such is the instinctive love of freedom, which now grows warm in the bosom of your country."[10]

Whatever "hopes, prospects and expectations" the New Yorker detected in the cold, wet spring of 1789 had been dampened by the sobering realization that the nation was broke, the treasury empty. The treasury's shortfalls of revenue compounded by the enormous costs of the American Revolution had pushed the government to the brink. Slogans, pamphlets, and passionate debates in well-appointed drawing rooms were not going to solve the problem. "Republicanism is a moral Influenza from which neither Titles, places nor even the Diadem can guard its Possessor," Morris wrote La Luzerne, now posted as ambassador in London. To his friend William Carmichael in Madrid, Morris went even further but tempered his words with his good humored irony:

I have here the strangest Employment imaginable. A Republican and just as it were emerged from that Assembly which has formed one of the most republican of all republican Constitutions, I preach incessantly Respect for the Prince, Attention to the rights of the Nobility and Moderation not only in the Object but also in the Pursuit of it. All of this you will say is none of my Business, but I consider France as the natural Ally of my Country and of Course that we are interested in her Prosperity— besides (to say the Truth) I love France and as I believe the King to be an honest and good Man I sincerely wish him well, and the more so as I am persuaded that he earnestly desires the Felicity of his People.[11]

There had been ugly riots in Paris, Brittany, and Grenoble the summer before, in 1788. People had been killed and more violence promised. A desperate government, careening toward bankruptcy, asked the powerful Parliament of Paris to approve new loans. In return the king promised to convene a more representative Estates-General at some future date to sort out other issues. Parliament refused, and when the king commanded the Parliament to act on the question of loans, Parliament issued what Jefferson optimistically called a "bill of rights" asserting that it was the prerogative of the Estates-General to levy taxes. The defiant Parliament then announced its decree to call the Estates to meet in Versailles on May 1, 1789.

When scattered bursts of turbulence erupted again in fall 1788, the Swiss banker Jacques Necker was brought back into the government as minister of finance. He had first been forced to resign in 1781 after he had failed to finance the American war without taxes, sinking his "economical reforms." It was the first of three royal ministries from which he was dismissed during the decade of the 1780s as the French government slid into bankruptcy. During the weeks leading up to the convocation of the Estates, an intense debate developed over a declaration of rights and a written constitution that might be adopted by the assembly when it met. By March 1789, Jefferson believed that these sanguine moves, which he had discussed with his most intimate, enlightened friends, promised nothing less than a "complete revolution in this government." The Virginian naively saw these developments as democracy in action, comparable to what he had witnessed in the country courthouses of Virginia and in Williamsburg on the eve of the American revolt. It was all happening "merely by the force of public opinion, aided indeed by the want of money which the dissipations of the court had brought on. And this revolution has not cost a single life, unless we charge to it a little riot lately in Bretagne."[12]

Morris did not share the American minister's optimism that "the public mind is manifestly advancing" and the people would bargain over their rights in exchange for paying higher taxes, which the government desperately needed. "This is the agent," Jefferson declared, recalling the Stamp Act of 1765, "by which modern nations will recover their rights." Making a corrective to Jefferson's overconfidence and concerned that things might get out of hand, Morris noted that "the Ton of Society seems to be that it was not worth while to call the States General for such a Trifle as the Deficit in the Revenue amounts to." To Morris, it would be foolish to make any prediction on the outcome. "If any new lesson were wanting to impress on our hearts a deep sense of the mutability of human affairs," he reminded Jay, "the double contrast between France and America two years ago, and at the present moment, will surely furnish that important lesson."[13]

The Estates-General had not met since 1614 when Marie di Medici called a meeting following the assassination of Henri IV. One hundred and seventy years later, no one had a clue about its potential role and power to reform the government, nor could anyone predict how it might all turn out. Of equal importance to the gratin, they did not know how to dress for the occasion.

By the ancient ground rules favoring the status quo, voting in the reconvened Estates-General was to be by bloc, with each of the three orders—the nobility, the clergy, and the Third Estate—making its own decisions separately. The nobility and the clergy, Germaine de Staël, Necker's daughter, called them "obscure eminencies," would control the show. Then on December 27, Louis XVI did the unthinkable: he agreed to doubling the number of the lowest estate "by order of the [king's] council." Public opinion generated by "the Patriotic Part" had triumphed, giving the Third Estate control of the proceedings. A pessimistic John Adams wrote Richard Price in London: "Too many Frenchmen, after the example of too many Americans, pant for equality of person and property. The impracticality of this, God almighty has decreed, and the advocates for liberty who attempt it will surely suffer for it."

With the dramatic act to double the Third Estate, the country's attention and political energy quickly shifted to the provincial elections: "This country presents an astonishing Spectacle," Morris reported to Washington. Even their friend the marquis de Lafayette was on the hustings in Auvergne "attending his Election.... Everything is *à l'Anglois* and a Desire to imitate the English prevails alike in Cut of a Coat and the form of Constitution. Like the English too, all are engaged in Parlimenteering."

In spring 1789, Jefferson's friends in the new Patriotic Party, led by men like Lafayette and the marquis de Condorcet, along with Talleyrand, the bishop of Autun, and the abbé Sièyes were in no mood for restraint in the direction of major reform. A worn-out nobility, or part of it, nevertheless tried to resist in its rearguard attempt to protect its ancient privileges. "The *Noblesse,* who at this day possess neither the force, the wealth, nor the talents of the nation, have rather opposed pride than argument to their assailants," Morris told William Carmichael. "Hugging the dear privileges of centuries long lapsed, they have clamored about the court, while their adversaries have possessed themselves fully of the public confidence everywhere." The comte de Puisignieu, a staunch reactionary confirmed Morris's hunch, telling him over dinner one evening that the French were "incapable of Liberty." Morris recorded the count's conversation later that night. "They can bear nothing long and will not even stay at their Regiments above three Months. Thus he [the count] takes the Noblesse for the Nation and judges the Noblesse from those Members who from Idleness and Dissipation are the least Consequence in Revolutions."[14]

Many volatile issues surrounding the convocation of the Estates had not been resolved before the May meeting. Tensions had escalated earlier in December over the king's "Order of the Council" when it failed, as it turned out fatally, to specify whether the votes would be counted "*par Ordre ou par Tête,*" allowing that issue to consolidate the lower Estate. Sièyes's radical pamphlet, "What Is the Third Estate?" was published in February. With icy disdain of the nobility, the abbé went further and publicly called for the organization of a truly national republican assembly selected from the Third Estate. This incendiary proposal was all the more serious because the method of voting was still in the hands of each of the Estates themselves.

On March 16, in his new diary, Morris made his first skeptical prediction on what would happen in the crisis: "In Effect, as the Constitution of this Country must inevitably undergo some Change which will lessen the Monarchical Power, it is clear that unless the Nobles acquire a Constitutional Sanction to some of their Privileges it will be the Power of the Ministry afterwards to confound them with the People... and the result will be a Tyranny of one in the *first instance,* or as a *Consequence* of Anarchy which would result from giving the wretched Constitution of the Pennsylvania Legislature to the Kingdom of France." Morris's scorn for the Pennsylvania constitution was because it concentrated all the legislative power in a single chamber and substituted a popularly elected council of twelve for the office of governor.[15]

Jefferson was of course also following the developments closely and believed, like Morris, that all sides must show restraint. But he disagreed with Morris that the Estates should vote by orders. Both men, however, had concluded, as Morris had written John Jay, that the country was not yet ready "for the uncertainties of freedom." In Jefferson's words, by the end of the year the French would have "as full a portion of liberty dealt out to them as the nation can bear at present, considering how uninformed the mass of their people is."[16]

The contrast in personality and philosophy of Morris and Jefferson could not have been greater. Given the political divisions between the two men later, their reactions to the dilemmas presented by the French Revolution, particularly at its beginning, is instructive. During the eight months they were both in Paris, before Jefferson returned to the United States in early October 1789, Morris was a regular guest in Jefferson's house. They shared many interests, including a good table and good wine, for which the New Yorker gave the Virginian high marks, Jefferson filling him in on his recent travels through the wine country of Burgundy, Champagne, and Bordeaux. They, of course, talked a lot about the political scene and finance, the American debt, and Dutch loans, but after one such visit, Morris made a telling observation in his diary: "I think he does not form very just Estimates of Character but rather assigns too many to the humble Rank of Fools, whereas in Life the Gradations are infinite and each Individual has his peculiarities of Fort and Feeble."[17]

Taking a clue from Dr. Franklin's calculated style of sartorial understatement, both men had made a point of dressing the part, as Morris noted "in the tone of republican equality." He claimed that Paris domestics at elegant levees did not know what to make of him. The Americans' simple, dark, well-made suits without ornament also made them conspicuous on the streets as they enjoyed walks and rides together around the city.

Jefferson, the aesthete, never missed an opportunity to instruct Morris on taste and point out important works of architecture that had caught his eye, an interest the New Yorker did not share. Although he managed to move with ease all over the city in spite of his wooden leg, he claimed that even if he lived for twenty years in Paris, he "would continue in ignorance of the length of the Louvre, the breadth of the Pont Neuf." He did make one shrewd and penetrating comment that the "splendor" of Parisian architecture "is owing entirely to despotism," adding that it will inevitably "be diminished by the adoption of a better government." In Jefferson's optimistic assessment this was the exact opposite of his undying faith that a perfect, rational government would be, must be reflected in its public buildings, but he believed they could simply be copied from examples produced, in fact, by a corrupt and despotic past.

In their rounds together, Jefferson took Morris to the studio of Houdon, "the first statuary in the world," and introduced him to the sculptor who was working on a full-scale sculpture of Washington. It had been commissioned by the state legislature of Virginia on Jefferson's enthusiastic recommendation. The sculptor had traveled to Mount Vernon to make the bust of the general, and he was now ready to work on the body of his famous, imposing subject. When he met the well-proportioned Morris, with his commanding posture just short of six feet four, Houdon knew he had his model. As Benjamin Rush said of the general, Morris also had so much natural "dignity in his presence that there is not a King in Europe that would but look like a valet de chambre by his side."[18]

The sculptor subjected the New Yorker to two uncomfortable sessions, but Morris took it with his usual good humor: "I stand for his Statue of Genl. Washington, being the humble Employment of a Manakin. This is literally taking the Advice of St. Paul to be all Things to all Men." Houdon proposed to Morris also to allow him to make a plaster cast of his face, the first step in making a bust as he had done of Jefferson, John Paul Jones, and Lafayette. He had traveled to Mount Vernon to make a cast of Washington. At first Morris suspected that he was being conned into a commission, which he politely turned down, but he agreed when Houdon assured him it was only for his personal pleasure.[19]

For all of their surface affability, the question still remains whether there was any genuine rapport or feeling of friendship between the New Yorker and the Virginian. Morris thought Jefferson's understated, American style as minister set the right diplomatic tone in Paris, yet there is a guarded formality on both sides, without any signs of intimacy or candor. Jefferson's total lack of humor or sense of irony, two important qualities in Morris's makeup, posed a real barrier. They were not simpatico. "You seem surprised, that our minister here does not mention my name; but *cui bono?*" Morris confided to William Carmichael, "You suppose that he has introduced me to the *Corps Diplomatique*. In this you are mistaken. I hinted that matter to him shortly after my arrival. He told me they were not worth my acquaintance."[20]

It might appear that the company of men of affairs and the boiling political scene consumed most of Morris's attention during his first months in Paris. His diary makes clear in every entry that this was not the case. He was constantly on the move and the society of women, mostly rich, wellborn, and often beautiful, became a significant part in his Paris life. He was particularly impressed by their political savvy, which they did not hesitate to display. In a playful letter to William Short during the constitutional debates of the National Assembly in 1790, the New Yorker suggests the best solution for compromise would be to put the women of one party in charge of the men in the other: "By Way of Addition and Amendment I would humbly propose that the Male Aristocrats should be put into the Custody of the female Whigs and I daresay they would come out much less fierce than they were."

Morris's confident social manners and his comfortable relations with women distinguishes him from Jefferson's more conflicted, uncertain nature. While the Virginian's relationships with women in Paris appear convincingly chaste, several of Morris's friendships, by his own uninhibited confessions in his diary, were not. It would be impossible to imagine Morris writing the scolding letter Jefferson sent to their Philadelphia friend Anne Bingham, telling her that "the empty bustle" of her life in Paris was too frivolous and she should be back home "enjoying the society of your husband, the fond cares for the children, the arrangements of the house." The Virginian also warned another friend, Angelica Church, that "the French ladies miscalculate much their own happiness when they wander from the true field of their influence into that of politics." Even more unimaginable from Morris's point of view was Jefferson's complaint to Washington that the alarming liberation of women in France, at least at the higher levels of society, threatened to undo the holy cause of liberty. He was shocked, Jefferson told the president, that they were allowed "to visit alone all persons in office to solicit the affairs of family or friends"—he might have added lovers—"in defiance of laws and regulations."[21]

Still, for all of his sophistication, the first weeks of introduction into the strange, rarefied world of the upper echelons of Paris society were a startling revelation to Morris. At first, he kept up his American guard while adding bemused diary entries that capture the small, but telling, cultural differences, particularly the role of women in politics. The diary becomes a kind of album of sharply focused snapshots of his first encounters, revealing his natural respect for their independence and their opinions. This sympathy comes through in an altercation with an empty-headed abbé who opposes all "Moderation in Politics." When Morris asked him what he wants, "he says a Constitution. But what Constitution?"

As Morris recorded the episode in his journal: "A tedious Argument is commenced to which I pay no attention but find that the ladies [present] are vexed at it because the Orators are so vehement that their gentle Voices cannot be heard. They will have more of this if the States General should really fix a Constitution. Such an event would be particularly distressing to the Women of the Country for they would be thereby deprived of their Share of the Government; and hitherto they have exercised an Authority almost unlimited, with no small pleasure to themselves."[22]

Morris had met the seductive, Madame de La Suze, mistress of Baron Besenval, shortly after he had arrived in Paris, and by his first diary entry on March 1, 1789, they "sup'" together. He obviously found her interesting and, while she was not at the top of his growing list of lady friends, her lively banter touching on politics makes her worth following for a few diary entries as her American *ami* moves in and out of her life. A month after the first entry, their intimacy had advanced, and he accepted her compliment of allowing him to sit "with her an Hour at her Toilet." During another visit the conversation over tea "turns as usual upon Politics" and the price of wheat. Four days before the Bastille falls, "Walk with Madame de Ségur and converse on the Situation of their Public Affairs." A conversation with a feminine companion who could hold her own on his favorite subjects was a heady experience. Days pass and he does not find madame home. Then a chance stop found her again eager to see him. She told him she is "just going to dress but this is nothing. *'Mons. Morris me permetta de faire ma Toillette—Certainly.'*—So we have the whole dressing except the Shift, and among other Things, washing the Arm Pitts with Hungary Water."

At one of his first dinner parties, Morris was introduced to Phillippe de Ségur, French ambassador to Catherine the Great and an intimate of Catherine's lover Prince Potemkin. The Ségur family was a regular part of the Palais Royal ménage presided over by the duchesse d'Orléans. Morris had already met Ségur's vivacious wife, who makes her seductive appearance in the diary's second entry. She coyly complained that the newcomer failed to visit her earlier: "These are mere words of course, but the Look, the Manner and the Tone of Voice are perfectly in Unison with the Sentiment…whispers to the Heart."[23]

The ambassador's conversation and the scene that followed took Morris deeper into the private, uninhibited world of the gratin where the rules of love and play represented a society that seemed to be on a different planet compared to provincial New York and Philadelphia. After dinner, the count "applies to me on the Subject of Gallantry," and when a suddenly flustered, dissembling Morris assured him that there was "nothing of the Kind in America," the Frenchman was incredulous. Ségur then asked the New Yorker about his love life, to which he replied that he had none, and when he lamely confessed that, being new in Paris he might offend "a virtuous Woman," the count laughed and reassured him that "no woman is offended at a Thing of the Kind, that it will frequently succeed and could do no Harm if it fails." Morris must not have known that through his mother, the count was the grandson of the celebrated *debauché* regent, Philippe, duc d'Orléans.

This "Rare Morality" seemed to have given Morris pause—reflective, fleeting moments of "Meditation and Edification." "Everybody agrees that there is an utter prostration of morals," he piously wrote Washington, "but this general position can never convey to an American mind the degree of depravity." Morris continued:

> A hundred anecdotes, and a hundred thousand examples, are required to show the extreme rottenness of every member. There are men and women who are greatly and eminently virtuous. I have the pleasure to number many in my acquaintance; but they stand forward from a background deeply and darkly shaded. It is however from such crumbling matter, that the great edifice of freedom is to be erected here. Perhaps, like the stratum of rock, which is spred under the whole surface of their country, it may happen when exposed to the air; but it seems quite as likely that it will fall and crush the builders.[24]

Morris did not tell Washington of his amazement when, after this conversation Ségur suddenly invited his hostess, "with great Sangfroid," into an adjoining room and bolting the door in front of the guests, left no doubt what was going on. When the couple rejoined the party "after a convenient time," the ambassador embraced his hostess and having, "as Sterne says, gratified the Sentiments in a few minutes takes Leave and steps into his Cabriolet."[25]

For all of his dissembling repartee with Ségur, Morris had indeed arrived in Paris with a reputation for "gallantry." When a Paris friend mentioned this in front of his wife, Morris said to himself that the subject should be dropped as it inspired women "to examine a Man more narrowly," making comparisons and asking themselves "foolish questions." He was not indifferent, of course, to his reputation or to the serendipitous possibilities it encouraged. "Madame Rully, another of the Duchess of Orleans' Women of Honor comes in,"—he was now at another soirée of his new friend, the attractive widow Chastellux—"and with very fine Eyes which she knows very well how to make Use of seems to say that she has no Antipathy to the gentle Passion. Nous verrons."[26]

Adelaide de Flahaut had heard the same fascinating rumors of the New Yorker's charm, and she lost no time in asking her friend Madame de Corny to invite him "to sup with her next Thursday" at her apartment in the Louvre. Her quarters were separate from her ancient husband who lived on the floor below, and with the help of the clever, obsequious former abbé de Talleyrand now the bishop d'Autun, Adelaide had established a small but select salon where men of letters, science, and politics gathered with women of fashion and intellectual pretensions. The apartment represented, and not only for Morris, a private center of information, gossip, and intrigue. Bertrand de Molleville and the comte de Montmorin, ministers of the king; the comte Louis de Narbonne, a rival of Talleyrand; Chastellux; the abbé Delille suggest the stylish, select society the countess had attracted.

In her apartment, Adèle, as she was known, had created a space for her own independence far in advance of the conventional roles of most Parisian women. She received whom she pleased, freely participated in conversations on an equality with her gentlemen guests, and she controlled her sexual life. "Platonics," a Morris descendant wryly remarked, "were not in the Flahaut tradition, continence was not among the age ideals." An outfoxed Morris later captures, in one candid image, her subtle manipulation of the two rivals vying for her affection. "My friend's Countenance glows with Satisfaction in looking at the Bishop and myself as we sit together agreeing in Sentiment & supporting the Opinions of each other. What Triumph for a Woman! I leave her to go Home with him and thus risque heroically the Chance of Cuckoldum."[27]

The New Yorker had first seen the countess at a dinner at Versailles, and there may have been an exchange of glances: "Madame Flahaut enters shortly after Madame d'Angivilliers. She speaks English and is a pleasing woman." Morris then sharpens his skill as a "quick sight," concluding, "If I might judge from Appearances, not a sworn enemy of Intrigue." This impression was no doubt sig-

Adélaide Marie Emile, Comtesse de Flahaut with son Charles de Flahaut
by Adélaide Labille-Guiard, 1785. The three-month-old infant
is believed to be the son of Talleyrand.
Cliché Bibliothèque nationale de France, Paris.

naled by the countess's witty eyes, "*des yeux de velours*." For Morris, gallantry was
not always shaded with skeptical speculations on the fidelity of female virtue. The
crowded Flahaut apartment did not encourage such reflections. Seemingly, Adèle
was never without callers or lovers in her drawing room or when she was in her
bed or bath, and in spite of all this constant attention, she was secretly working on
a novel, another sign of her liberation. Her novel's heroine, called Adèle, is like
her creator, carefree, self-willed, and tender, the ambiguous themes of virtue, liberation, and adultery seem translated from the author's own experiences.[28]

Born in 1761, Adèle Filleul, the comtesse de Flahaut, was nine years younger than Morris. Her mother, Cathrine de Buisson Longpré, although of a minor aristocratic family, was no stranger to Louis XV's Parc aux Cerfs. She had once been the king's mistress, and he was the father of Adèle's older half-sister Julie, wife of marquis de Marigny, the brother of Mme. de Pompadour. Adèle's putative father was Charles-François Filleul, who had married Adèle's mother after she had received a royal pension for her service, but her actual father was most likely Michael Bouret, a rich farmers-general with an uncertain pedigree. His extravagance eventually led to suicide. Her mother died when Adèle was six, and she was placed in a convent where an English nun taught her the perfect English that first caught Morris's attention.[29]

At eighteen, Adèle was married to Charles de Flahaut of Boulenois nobility, who was thirty-five years her senior. It was a marriage of a certain prestige but without money, security, or love. Charles-Maurice de Talleyrand-Périgord, who had taken orders and would become the father of Adèle's son, performed the marriage ceremony. Through the influence of Flahaut's brother, the comte d'Angivilliers, superintendent of the king's buildings, academies, parks, and manufactures, Flahaut had been made keeper of the *Jardins des Roi* succeeding the great Buffon. The sinecure gave the count a modest salary, the small apartment in the Louvre, and very few responsibilities. Some have claimed that the apartment was originally a gift to Adèle's mother by the crown as a reward for her "frailty." The crown paid part of the couple's small pension; the comte d'Artois, the king's brother, paid the rest. Madame Vigée-Lebrun, the painter, remembered Adèle around the time that she and Morris met, describing her as if she had stepped out from one of Lebrun's enameled portraits: *"une jolie taille, un visage charmant, les yeux les plus spirituels du monde et tant d'amabilité qu'un de mes plaisirs était d'aller passer la soirée avec elle."*[30]

In spring 1789 after two months in Paris, Morris was more than ready for a little feminine intrigue. He needed company and hated dining alone. The weather did not improve his disposition, as he noted—"Wind, Rain & of course Mud without and Dampness within," stoically adding, "but this is human Life." He never complains of his *jambe de bois,* but there were a couple of humiliating falls: one in the treacherous streets, another in the narrow stairwell of Adèle's apartment. Even after the weather improved, there were still signs of passing loneliness. At the end of a pleasant day visiting Malmaison, he was puzzled by his homesick mood: "I am in Health and yet there is more Melancholy than Gaiety about me." Walking in the gardens, he was surprised how he enjoyed the solitude, a place where "I can dream of my own Country and converse with my absent friends."

When he was not dining out, Morris frequented the Club Valois in the Palais Royal, which he had just joined. The abbé Sièyes, the explorer Bougainville, Talleyrand, the duc d'Orléans, and the philosophe the marquis de Condorcet were among its sophisticated members. At that moment, the club was probably one of the best listening posts for social and political gossip in town now that, as Morris put it, the Palais had become the city's "Liberty Pole." Condorcet no doubt found the New Yorker's independent views congenial as they both shared advanced positions on every form of discrimination in society. Abolishing slavery and achieving equal rights for women were at the top of the philosophe's list. Morris would not have disagreed, even if he might not have stated his position as plainly as the marquis: "He who votes against the rights of another, whatever be his religion, color, or sex, has at that moment abjured his own rights," Condorcet declared in his radical attack on slavery. These same words had made Jefferson deeply uncomfortable when he attempted to make a translation of Condorcet's essay, causing him to finally drop the project. At that moment, living with Jefferson in his house on the Champs Elysées were two slaves, James Hemings and his young sister Sally. Under French law, both could have been freed from bondage by simple application to authorities if Jefferson had informed them of their rights. Sally later told her son Madison that she had become Jefferson's "concubine" while living with the minister in Paris. She was fourteen when she arrived in Paris from Virginia with Jefferson's daughter in 1787.[31]

Throughout the spring, Adèle de Flahaut was on Morris's regular rounds of calls, but so was Madame Ségur, Madame de La Suze, Madame de Chastellux, and the duchesse d'Orléans, "affable and handsome enough," Morris thought, "to punish the Duke for his Irregularities." Unlike Jefferson's aesthetics that concentrated on art works and architecture, Morris, the unabashed sensualist, was a connoisseur of beautiful, intelligent women and in the case of the duchess, her seductive arm as well as her face. "She has," he carefully noted, "perhaps the handsomest arm in France, and from habit takes off her glove and has always occasion to touch some part of her face as to show the hand and arm to advantage."

When he was first introduced to the duchess by the marquise de Chastellux, he thought he detected an interesting signal from her: "A Look from her royal Highness opens the idea that *Mons. Morris est un peu amoureux de Madame la Marquise.*" But the New Yorker adds, "Madame la Duchesse is mistaken. However, this Mistake can do no Harm to any Body." The vicomte Ségur had already suggested to Morris that he might consider "an Affair with the Widow" Chastellux while hinting that he, too, was prepared "to console her for the Loss of her Husband."[32]

Morris, like everyone in Paris, knew that the duchess was badly treated by her husband, and he signaled both sympathy and interest in a charming piece of poetry he sent to her. The duchess, in turn, was clearly attracted by the adventurous New Yorker. When politics heated up in anticipation of the meeting of the Estates-General, she sent him a program and arranged for a ticket to the opening. She also expressed some independent political opinions, and Morris went out of his way to "congratulate her on this Employment for her Mind which has contributed already to her Health."

For all of their fashionable elegance and expensively maintained beauty suggesting subordination, the women in Morris's circle enjoyed an independence that he admired. His words of encouragement to the duchess were salutary. On another occasion, he sensed a deeper void in her life and he gave her counsel that underlined their growing friendship: "I make an apology for her husband's wildness, by advising her to raise her son, M. de Beaujolais, as a bourgeois businessman, because, otherwise at five and twenty, having enjoyed all which rank and fortune can give him, he will be unhappy from not knowing what to do with himself." This sound advice on the education of the future "bourgeois king," Louis-Philippe, also subtly articulated his own sensitivity to the seismic rumbles portending the great shifts that were occurring beneath the duchess's world, predicting far more devastation than the duke's infidelities.[33]

Morris had no idea of the extent of Adèle de Flahaut's intrigues when they first met. As spring advanced, there are few signs that anything was developing except for Morris's dogged persistence in making regular, polite appearances at the Louvre. She stands him up frequently, says that she "is not well" or that she is "troubled with Indigestion." Once, and one supposes without irony, he found her recovering with her feet in hot water. Morris is clearly fed up with all this diplomatic dodging, and on occasion he drinks too much wine with friends out of frustration. He was adept in the skillful, psychological game lovers or would-be lovers play, but with Adèle, there were none of the usual sexual politics as they were equals. Beneath the glittering surface of a setting out of *Les Liasons Dangereux,* there was an emotional tension between the two, created by a shared need to control what would mature into something else.

On April 20, the New Yorker casually noted in his diary meeting the bishop of Autun at Adèle's apartment. Lame, cynical, and full of malaise, the pasty-faced Talleyrand had been elevated from abbé de Talleyrand to bishop only a few months before, when his and Adèle's son was six years old. Injured in infancy when he was dropped by a careless nurse and unfit for a military career, Talleyrand had been made a bishop by the king who had granted his father's deathbed wish. The day after he had knelt and vowed to obey the successor of Saint Peter in Rome and "preserve, defend, augment and promote the authority, honors, privileges and rights of the Holy Church," the new bishop, richer by fifty thousand livres a year, had dinner as usual with Adèle in her apartment.

Following several encounters with the devious Autun, a master of the *sous-entendu,* Morris decided that while he might as a connoisseur of intrigue admire the Machiavellian side of the *monstre mitré,* at close range, he did not personally like him. He concluded that he was a "sly, cool, cunning and ambitious Man." The portrait of the bishop that the New Yorker sent to Washington was sanctimonious, however, saying that Talleyrand was criticized in Paris for his adultery but more "for its variety" and lack of discretion than because he was a high ranking member of the clergy, adding sanctimoniously that he thought the charges "unduly aggravated."[34]

The wretched weather in Paris continued throughout the spring of 1789. The prolonged winter, the coldest in memory, had killed countless thousands. The streets of the capital were littered with the homeless and starving. During a visit with a friend to Hôtel Invalide, which he found to be "a most magnificent Piece of Architecture," Morris was depressed by the number of mutilated veterans it housed with "no hope this side of the grave." When his companion remarked that several of the inmates expressed sympathy that "so fine a man" had also lost his leg in battle, Morris did not admit that he had been slipping coins into the hands of the old soldiers along the way.[35]

Around midday on April 29, a sharp explosion rattled shops and houses in the Faubourg Saint Augustine. After setting a fire, several hundred workers in the nearby Réveillon wallpaper factory and in a saltpeter plant had marched off the job and taken to the streets, shouting threats against the rich and privileged. The Réveillon factory was gutted and the owner's house ransacked. To those who saw the milling crowds armed with sticks and stones, it looked like a full-scale uprising of the proletariat. Before it was put down by troops, there were perhaps as many as one hundred fifty casualties, one of the bloodiest single days in the entire revolution. An indignant Jefferson reported to Jay that the demonstrators were a "mob" of "the most abandoned banditti...unprovoked and unpittied." It was a misreading of a sign of bigger things to come.

At first, Morris also thought the affair was trifling, but he changed his mind as he heard more alarming reports. Two days after the riot, two men caught looting were hung outside the Bastille. Later that evening, at supper with friends, Morris had a firsthand report from a guest who "entertain[ed] the Ladies with a Description of the Magnificence of the hanging Match." Madame La Suze's lover, Baron Besenval, in charge of Paris security who gave the orders to crush the mob, "was very pleased with his Work....It is therefore agreed on all Hands that the Baron is a great General, and as the Women say so it would be Folly and Madness to controvert the Opinion."[36]

"While in Paris, people were cutting each other's throats," the marquis de Ferrières, a delegate to the Estates-General, reported to his wife, in Versailles they were deciding the details of the delegates' costumes. After repeated delays, on May 4, the last royal procession to be staged in Versailles got under way, and Morris was on hand, watching with Adèle from "Part of a Window" she had offered him. It is a subtle and revealing detail of the old order that the daughter of a former mistress of Louis XV had received a coveted window to view the proceedings, as the court and Holy Sacrament moved to the Cathedral of Notre Dame at Versailles for a special mass.

"Neither the King nor the Queen appear too well pleased," Morris noted later that night in his diary. He also observed how the crowd ominously withheld any applause or recognition of the queen when she passed by. By contrast, his friend, the duchesse d'Orléans, and her husband, walking as a representative of the Third Estate rather than a Prince of the Blood, were loudly cheered. It was all a part of the pattern of public insult reserved for "l'Autrichien." "I cannot help feeling Mortification which the poor Queen meets with for I see only the Woman and it seems unmanly to break a Woman with Unkindness."[37]

The next day, the Estates-General finally opened with all the panache the exhausted regime could muster. The court's creaking stage reflexes went through the motions with impressive style. Morris was up early and on the road to Versailles with Jefferson by 6 A.M. to get a seat in the redecorated, crowded *Salles des Menus Plaisir*. The walls of the hall had been covered with richly colored Gobelin tapestries, the more voluptuous pagan scenes discreetly hung in the room's shadows. The New Yorker, moved by the pageantry, again was touched by the forlorn queen he noticed quietly weeping during her husband's address. "Here drops the Curtain on the first great Act of this drama," Morris wrote later in a letter to Mrs. Robert Morris, the courtiers feeling what the king "seems to be insensible of, the Pangs of Greatness going off."[38]

By the first of June Adèle's health appeared to have recovered, and she told Morris that she had finally decided that he "suit[ed] the Taste of the Country." A few weeks later on a warm, humid June 20, their conversations took an unexpected turn to Adèle's "domestic Affairs," Morris's words but she, in fact, initiated. "She talks to me of certain Affairs of Gallantry which she has been told I once engaged in. I assure her that these are idle Tales, unworthy of Credit. She nevertheless persists in her Belief. I tell her that I have a perfect Respect for the Lady supposed to be the principle Object. She questions me of the Term *Respect* and I take that Occasion to assure her of a Truth that (without Reference to any particular Person) I never lost my Respect for those who consented to make me happy on the Principles of Affection."

Morris closed this entry on the countess's education with practiced confidence that his description of "Tenderness and Respect with Ardency and Vigor go far toward the female Idea of Perfection in a Lover." Adèle would shortly prove to him that he was right. The very complicity of their powerful sexual imaginations is impressive. Played out against the lurid spasm of a world expiring, the details of the affair in the New Yorker's candid words somehow defuses any temptation to make moral judgments.[39]

The two did not know that in the morning of the twentieth, the members of the Third Estate had barricaded themselves in the royal tennis court close by the palace in Versailles, where the Estates-General were meeting. In a scene immortalized by David's unfinished painting, the heroes of the moment "swore to form a Constitution before they part." It was a brilliant gesture of defiance, setting the assembly free from any particular location and, in Simon Schama's words, sending "the state off in a sea of abstraction. Wherever they were gathered was to be the National Assembly."[40]

The night before, the members of the Third Estate had found the doors of their meeting hall barred and a notice posted that their meetings were suspended. This had triggered the retreat to the Jeu de Paume in defiance of the king's orders. Jefferson rushed to assure James Madison in a letter that "Commons" as he called it, had all the country's talent, "cool, temperate and sagacious," but he did not mention that their friend Lafayette was not among them.

Three days later, Morris was again in Versailles but found it difficult to know just what was happening. Madame de Tessé, Lafayette's liberal-minded aunt whose estate Chaville was nearby, invited him to dinner, a good place, he knew, to take a reading of the approaching storm. At Chaville he learned that the king's Séance Royale—the official audience earlier in the day, where the king addressed the three orders—had annulled the rump proceedings in the tennis court. In closing the audience, Louis declared "I command you, Messiers, to adjourn directly and tomorrow assemble in your separate chambers to resume your sessions."

When Morris heard that the nobility was pleased with the king's performance, he concluded that they "have less Cause, for Exultation than they imagine." At dinner, he found himself seated next to a preoccupied Lafayette and did not hesitate to criticize him to his face for failing to assert leadership in the Patriot party. "I seize this Opportunity to tell him that I am opposed to the Democracy from regard to Liberty." The liberals were rushing "Headlong to Destruction." Their democratic ideas were hopelessly at odds "with the materials" they had to work with. Under the circumstances "the worst Thing which could happen would be to grant them their Wish" by turning the government over to them.

A few days later Morris expanded on his misgivings in a letter to John Jay. "The States-General have now been a long time in session and have done nothing.... The commons, who represented by a number equal to both the others...insist on forming a single house." Meanwhile the soldiers who were supposed to guard Paris were drinking in the streets declaring that "they will not act against the people." Some men around the Palais Royal, believed to be agents of the duc d'Orleans, were seen slipping money freely to the soldiers. Morris accurately detected in all this confusion a dangerous turning point, "the sword has slipped out of the Monarch's hands without his perceiving a tittle of the matter."

In his letter to Jay, Morris once again restated his fundamental misgivings: "All these things in a nation, yet not fitted by education and habit for the enjoyment of freedom, gives me frequent suspicions, that they will greatly overshoot their mark, if indeed they have not already done it.... Having never felt the evils of too weak an executive, the disorders to be apprehended from anarchy make as yet no impression." Only a few days before, Jefferson in his eagerness to paint an idealized picture of a successful democratic revolution carried to conclusion with little bloodshed—just enough to water the Tree of Liberty with the blood of patriots—assured Jay that with the Third Estate safely in the hand of the majority, "the great crisis" was over. He ended by writing, "I shall not have matter interesting enough to trouble you with as often as I have done lately."[41]

Contrary to Jefferson's visionary predictions, but no surprise to Morris, things continued to slip beyond anyone's control. On the afternoon of Sunday, July 12, alarm quickly spread through the city that Necker had been abruptly dismissed the evening before. The Palais Royal, headquarters of the duc d'Orléans's hired troublemakers, erupted. When Morris heard the news, he concluded that the king was in far greater danger "than he imagines." The sovereignty of the nation had now passed to the self-appointed and newly named National Assembly.

While the American example had been inspiring, Morris told William Carmichael of the French, "liberty runs away with their discretion, if they have any.... They want an American Constitution, without reflecting, that they have not American citizens to support that constitution." Then he makes clear his profound reservations of attempting to impose a system of government borrowed from another experience "by the standard of preconceived notions" where differences may be insurmountable. "Different constitutions of government are necessary to the different societies on the face of this planet. Their difference of position is, in itself, a powerful cause, as also their manners, their habits.... Those who look to America for their political forms are not unlike those tailors in the island of Laputa, who, as Gulliver tells us, always take measure with a quadrant. He tells us, indeed, what we should naturally expect from such a process, that the people are seldom fitted."[42]

Morris remained calm when, later, he actually witnessed the first clash between defiant Parisians and the king's mercenary German troops. The prince de Lambesc, in command of troops in the Place Louis XV (Place de la Concord), was ordered to clear the square. When the crowd ran into the Tuileries gardens they collided with the prince's cavalry. Jefferson was riding in his new London carriage, hidden behind its Venetian blinds near the scene of "the little Affray," as Morris put it, but missed by minutes the main encounter. The Virginian's illusions of the French Revolution would remain unsullied. Without illusions, Morris recorded his impressions and more accurate predictions that night in his diary. "Success or a Halter must now be their [the *noblesse*] Motto. I think the Court will again recede, and if they do, all further Efforts will be idle. If they do not, a Civil war is among the Events most probable."[43]

Through the mounting tension, Adèle de Flahaut's anxiety for her son and herself increased. She was also concerned for the safety of her husband who might be a target even as a minor court *fonctionnaire*. Her growing alarm made her increasingly dependent on Morris's advice and his reassuring presence in her apartment.

Looking at the only evidence we have—Morris's remarkable diary—we are, in A. S. Byatt's words, faced with the impenetrable "mystery of the known facts," puzzled by the true nature of the relationship between Adèle and Morris. To begin with, love (or love-making), to them and their set, short of a permanent commitment, was a highly refined game that both were skilled at; resistance by either party weakened or overcome by a sudden turn of phrase, a line of verse, or feigned emotion. A gesture, a fleeting glance, or a touch advanced or stalled the ultimate objective. The threat of discovery, reinforced by the greater threats in the streets, a threat that constantly surrounded their sparrings and pairings, increased the couple's passion.

The two enjoyed discussing sex frankly, Adèle often taking the lead, once dividing the subject into "pleasure," "desire," and "love." But given the entanglements of Adèle's love life, the New Yorker reminded himself more than once that love, whatever it meant to her, was transient. After a family dinner with the bishop, their son, and Morris, she grew despondent about her son's future following Autun's departure and began to cry. When Morris wipes away the tears, his "silent attention mingles by Degree with maternal Affection" and her profession of "endless love," which he is convinced she means every word. This is followed by the two accepting "Adam's first Commandment." But the entry closes with Morris's pensive words, "nothing here below can last forever."

Morris records another frank exchange when he tells her of one of their acquaintances who had boasted of having committed "the Crime agt. Nature" with a Capuchin friar. After Morris added some observations on the subject, Adèle matter-of-factly replied that a friend of hers, Madame Vetris, "received the Embraces of her lovers in no other manner."[44]

At another level beyond the sexual gamesmanship, Morris made it evident to Adèle that he respected her intelligence and individuality, unlike Talleyrand who thought women were incapable of serious thought or any responsibilities beyond their traditional role. His warm, sympathetic attraction to her as a person gives a clue to the New Yorker's undoubted emotional advantage in his competition for Adèle's attention. In one revealing diary entry, the bishop, Adèle, and Morris are in her apartment discussing a pending reorganization of the government. While Morris silently disagrees with Autun's scheme, Adèle forces the cleric to give up his point with her own superior argument, to the admiring New Yorker's wonderment. "She has infinite good sense," Morris readily admits. Defeated in the debate, the bishop then left the two alone, Morris finishes the diary entry with satisfaction, "we pick up the Shreds of Conversation and close as Lovers what we had commenced as Politicians." This line deeply enriches what can only be conjecture on what is essentially unknowable of their powerful attraction for each other.[45]

Throughout Sunday and Monday, July 12 and 13, 1789, the Palais Royal and surrounding streets near Morris's hotel were a boiling pot of public agitation. Baron de Besenval, who was responsible for the city's military forces, could not control the gathering crowd. On the morning of July 14, under low, ominous clouds while Morris was in the office of his banker M. le Coulteux discussing the American debt, the old fortress of the Bastille was attacked. The prison's ancient governor along with the Prévôt des Marchands were taken captive and later beheaded. Controlling his emotions, Morris noted in his diary, "They are carrying the heads in triumph through the city." Then he admitted, with wry irony, that while the event "is among the most extraordinary things I have met with...I presume that this day's transactions will induce," at Versailles, "a conviction that all is not perfectly quiet."

Within days of the fall of the infamous Bastille, the city, in spirited Gallic style, was back in a festive mood. Dinner parties resumed and Morris went with Adèle and her dinner guests, including the bishop, to an exhibition of paintings. Always ready with advice, he told the artist that a view of "the Storm of the Bastille" would be a more fashionable subject than his pastoral landscapes. Later he recommended to a man already working on the history of the Revolution, that the papers of the Bastille ought to be gathered up to produce "the Annuls of that diabolical Castle from the Beginning of Louis the fourteenths Reign to the present moment."

On July 20, while the dust drifted above the rubble of the dismantled fortress, Morris made "a long Visit" to his friend, "at first tête à tête." After giving her some verses, "with infinite Coolness and Seriousness tell her that I cannot consent to be only a friend...that I know her too well. That at present I am perfectly my own Master with Respect to her, but that it would not long be the Case. That having no Idea of inspiring her with Passion I have no idea of subjecting myself to one." She replied, quite frankly, that she found it "a very Strange Conversation." Believing that his gesture would have a delayed effect, he closed the entry with the now familiar "Nous verrons." The next day the two went off together to see what was left of the stinking prison.[46]

Walking in the arcade of the Palais following the visit—he cautiously now wore a green leaf on his hat for safety, a badge of the Third Estate—Morris was suddenly confronted with that signature image of the Revolution, a head carried in the streets on a pike, its mouth stuffed with hay, announcing "to tyrants," in the words of one report, "the terrible vengence of a justly angered people." Monsieur de Foulon's only "crime is to have accepted a Place in the Ministry." After showing his son-in-law, Bertier de Sauvigny, the remains, the crowd dispatched Bertier on the spot, "cut to Pieces, the Populace carrying about mangled Fragments with a Savage Joy." The New Yorker then closed this bloody little vignette: "Gracious God what a People!" It was the kind of ghastly scene that prompted Jefferson's quip to Maria Cosway that "the lopping of heads is à la mode." That night, a shaken Morris wrote a friend in America: "I was never till now fully apprized of the mildness of American character. I have seen my countrymen enraged and threatening. It has even happened that in an affray some lives were lost. But we know not what it is to slay the defenseless who is in our power. We cannot parade the heads of our fellow citizens and drag the mangled carcasses through the streets. We cannot feast our eyes on such spectacles."[47]

Morris's increasingly complex business affairs, which he had somehow been able to juggle for all of the political and romantic distractions, now required his attention in London. Before he left, a member of Estates-General asked him to put together some thoughts on a constitution for consideration by a committee of the Third Estate. Adèle was aware of the request and urged him to do it. He agreed on condition that she would translate it. The next day, on July 27, when he went to the Louvre intending to work "with the best Disposition imaginable" he found that M. Flahaut had conveniently left the two alone, so "instead of a Translation" the two made love for the first time. They repeated the experience the following day. Two days later, ready to depart for London, he finally "takes Leave of Madame de Flahaut. Perfectly platonic. In this I do myself Violence, but it is right."[48]

On his way to London, Morris sent Washington his pointed impression of the storm that had swept through France. He told the president that there was a dangerous plan afoot for the king to flee. "He is a well-meaning Man but extremely weak...being absolutely and entirely a Cypher....There are some able Men in the national Assembly, yet the best Heads among them would not be injured by experience, and unfortunately there are a good number who with much Imagination, have little Knowledge, Judgment or Reflection." He closed by accurately predicting that the king "does not know a single Regiment that would obey him."[49]

During the six weeks that Morris was in London, the National Assembly made several critical moves. On August 4 all feudal privileges were renounced, and on August 26 a Declaration of the Rights of Man, largely taken from Lafayette's draft, was adopted along with decrees outlining a constitution. The details of the document had actually been cooked up around Jefferson's dining table at the Hôtel de Langeac with Lafayette and a few Patriot members of the assembly.

To Morris, adopting a bill of rights before establishing a constitution was getting the cart before the horse, as he had argued in opposing such a bill in the first New York constitution. First of all, there had to be an ordered system of government firmly in place before unleashing the unpredictable energy of the people. From the American perspective and in contrast to the French experience, its revolution meant freeing the country of a distant despot and unfair taxes while preserving many of the historic legal and constitutional rights of its citizens.

This limited American objective on the other side of the Atlantic was in sharp contrast to the radical French ideal where all of the nation's political, social, and economic problems were to be solved from top to bottom and for all time, transforming every citizen in the country. Unlike Morris and his American experience, the French believed that the entire French society had been freed from time itself. In Michelet's words, "Time no longer existed; time had perished." Having miraculously escaped from history, their revolution would go on forever, liberated from the curse of a discredited past.

When Morris returned to Paris, Adèle was in the country, but she rushed back in spite of "feeble Health, a wretched Carriage, a bad Road and worse Weather" to meet her lover. For the next three years, their affair was caught up in the erratic energy of desire, a metaphor for the equally unpredictable passions in the streets. The two made love whenever and wherever possible, sometimes at considerable risk. "After Dinner visit by Appointment Madame de Flahaut. She is fatigued...*Exige des Ménagemens, mes enfin*—The Rites performed we go to visit her *Religieuse au Couvent*," where they met the old English nun who had tutored her. On another visit to the convent, a year later, they are overtaken with passion but find all the parlors occupied with visitors except that of Madame l'Abbesse. "We proceed thither and while Madᵉ. de Trant is sent for we sacrifice to the Cyprian Queen in the retreat of Chastity.... 'In those deep solitudes and awful Cells where heavenly pensive Contemplation dwells.'" More sedately, after dining "in the Style a Man would wish who wishes to be Happy" at Adèle's apartment, the two were overcome "with mutual Desire." Before the dishes were removed, they lost no time to "join in fervent Adoration to the Cyprian Queen," a favorite of several of Morris's private code words. One morning, the pair even resorted to the cramped privacy of Morris's carriage while driving in the Bois, when no better place presented itself.[51]

Adèle's beauty was not her only attraction for Morris. He was fascinated by her cultivated, knowing political brain. At the end of September, a major shift in the government leadership was underway, and he asked her for her opinion on possible candidates. "We have L E[vêque] d'A[tun], premier and in Finance, M[ontesquiou] in the War." He disagreed with her choice of Biron to replace Lauzon in London, but he admitted that "the Measures to be pursued and this amiable Woman shews a Precision and Justness of Thought very uncommon indeed in either sex."[52]

After reorganizing the government, the two conspirators then turned their attention to the unhappy queen. That evening, Adèle planned to see Marie Antoinette's doctor and have him work on "her Majesty's Prejudices." Morris agreed that this was an inspired idea since the Queen "is weak, proud, but not ill tempered, & although lustful yet not much attached to her Lovers, wherefore a Superior Mind would take that Ascendancy which the feeble always submit to though not always without Reluctance." Adèle coolly answered "with perfect confidence. *'Je lui donnera[i] un Homme chaque Nuit et un[e] Messe chaque Matin.'"* It was a solution that not even the New Yorker, at his most cynical and witty, had thought of. He had more than met his match in the fine art of royal diagnostics.[53]

After the comte de Flahaut left on a long trip to Madrid, just before the tense October days when the royal family was brought by force to Paris, the electric atmosphere, both in the streets and in Adèle's apartment, threatened to get out of hand. Early on the morning of October 5, 1789, hunger and anger coalesced into a volatile compound that suddenly ignited exposing in its glare the abyss just ahead. A crowd of six or seven thousand, mostly women, gathered in place de Grève in front of the Hôtel de Ville, demanding immediate action on the part of the government. By midday when an unnerved Lafayette finally reached the square, part of the mob was already moving on the rainswept road toward Versailles. What was more alarming, the *poissardes*—fishwives and marketwomen—were joined by members of Lafayette's own National Guard. The Guard's participation represented a mortal challenge to the government's authority. To Lafayette's credit, he decided to lead the way on his white horse, in Morris's words, "the prisoner of his own troops," desperately attempting to give the appearance of command.

The events at Versailles the following day are a part of historical memory—the assault on the palace, the murder of the Swiss guards outside the queen's apartment, the insult to the queen on the balcony, Lafayette's chivalry, kneeling before her in an effort to restore calm, finally the bedraggled cortège bringing the king and queen captive back to Paris. The bizarre procession was led by National Guards with loaves of bread stuck on their bayonets. The National Assembly now moved to Paris to sit in the hastily redecorated riding school in the yard of the Tuileries palace. Then, suddenly the hurricane seemed to subside. At Adèle's apartment, Morris heard from his lover that the queen was "obliged to fly from her Bed in her Shift and Petticoat with her Stockings in her Hand to the King's Chamber for protection."

The same afternoon, when the Revolution had taken this jolting pitch forward, the lovers fell into an argument in the chill dim light of Adèle's apartment. She had suddenly asked Morris to marry her even though her husband was only away on a short trip and, of course, had not been consulted on her plans. There are laughs and jests between the two, but she "returns to her Point with all the Arts of wily Woman working to her purpose. I see the Game but yet appear the Dupe." Madame de Corny had already tipped him off, if he didn't already know, that Adèle operated under her own rules of morality.

With the world crashing down around them, Adèle's idea was preposterous. There would be "time enough to talk of that matter when we are both free," Morris told her. Tears follow. Anguish, fractured expressions. Morris then teasingly taunts her that he would not be party to her "engagement by which she was bound to her Lover," the bishop. When she protests that she

Lafayette as Commandant of the National Guard by P. L. Debucourt, 1789.
© Photothèque des musées de la ville de Paris (ou PMVP)/Cliché: GIET.

was not "wicked enough to enjoy Pleasures which violate the Principles of Honor," Morris puts her to the test. In a few moments the two "are again at our sentimentals.—This becomes then a Case of Conscience on both Sides."[54]

After "sentimentals," Adèle returned to her proposal of marriage, vowing "eternal Fidelity," whatever that meant. Momentarily taken aback, Morris then asked her point blank if she would go with him to London "next Monday." She replies: "If you command, I obey. I am yours." That night the weary New Yorker conceded in his diary; "So I find I have a Wife upon my hands indeed....I submit." Then he added a footnote: "This day has been rainy, windy, and I believe (at sea) a high gale if not a storm." Two days later, Adèle took Morris to a jeweler to buy her ring, after her lover had mingled "sweet Discourse with Kisses" to "teach my lovely Scholar all I know," then marveling that "my lovely Scholar has very little to learn on any Subject."

The background to the growing intensity of their relationship in fall 1789 was Adèle's fear that, while her husband was in Spain, she had become pregnant. She was also worried that Autun, who still insisted on sleeping with her, might eventually abandon her. With an extraordinary nonchalance that may have been studied, and was certainly irresponsible, the New Yorker tells her that if "nothing happens, we are to take care of the future until the Husband returns, and then exert ourselves to add one to the Number of human Existence." Morris seemed pleased with his elegant, if perversely irregular, "Mode of conciliating *Prudence* and *Duty*."[55]

On November 9, after taking his friend to the Manufactory of Sevré to buy some tableware, they returned to her apartment where he "hastily pays his devotions in which she enjoys with a pious fervor." Afterwards, the bishop stopped by to report on the assembly. Later that day, Morris dined with Necker and his daughter Madame de Staël, to whom Talleyrand was now making calculated advances. The New Yorker did not like Necker any better than Autun, finding Necker deeply flawed both as a man and as a public servant: "His education as a Banker has taught him to make tight Bargains.... But tho he understands Man as a covetous Creature, he does not understand Mankind, a defect that is Remediless.... The Plans he has proposed [in the Assemblée] are feeble and ineptious."

At dinner Morris found himself seated by the flamboyant Germaine de Staël who asked him to speak in English so that her husband, the Swedish ambassador nearby, could not understand their flirtings. There was "much conversation about the Bishop of d'Autun" who was seeking a ministerial post. "I desire her to let me know if he succeeds because I will in such Case make Advantage of the Intelligence in making my Court to Madame de Flahaut. A Proposition more whimsical could hardly be made to a Woman but the manner is every Thing and so it passes." His fascinated dinner partner then told Morris that he might also become her "Admirer," to which he smoothly replied that "it is not impossible," even though he noted in his diary that she reminded him of a housemaid.

With his instinctive generosity, after dinner Morris made a point of speaking to the plainly afflicted husband, who Morris sensed still deeply loved his faithless wife. In a burst of emotion, the ambassador "inveighs bitterly against the Manners of this Country and the Cruelty of alienating a Wife's Affections. He says the Women here are greater than Whores with their Hearts and Minds than with their Persons." Morris does not challenge him but on that uncomfortable note wisely decides to close the conversation: "I regret with him on general Ground that Prostration of Morals which unfits them for good Government."

The test of virtue, so often invoked in America and by Morris as a ritual sine qua non of a righteous and successful republican government, was now applied to a decadent, disintegrating society cut loose from all moral moorings. But as he well knew, adultery and other sexual indiscretions had nothing to do with sound republican constitutions any more than the other "romantic ideas of government" now prevailing in France, "which happily for America," he reminded Washington, "we were cured of before it was too late."[56]

Following the October Days, Lafayette assumed the role of the royal family's protector, "the mayor of the palace," after rescuing them and installing them in the Tuileries. But they detested him. With his showmanship as a great and liberal lord, always out in front offering benign command, he impressed the people whose cheers he could not resist, but he did not impress the New Yorker. As for the assembly, it could not agree on a single issue. Rampant revolutionary passion dismissed all discipline, and Morris could see that Lafayette was unable to lead the political factions to form a stable constitutional government. After all, he could not even discipline his own troops. Earlier in September, at Jefferson's farewell dinner, Morris concluded that if the storm subsided, the general "will be infinitely indebted to Fortune, but if it happens otherwise the World must pardon much on the Score of Intention."

Uninvited, Morris finally went to the general's house and confronted him with the desperate urgency of establishing a ministry of "Men of Talents who have Principles favorable to Liberty" and an executive with authority. Given the enormity of the crisis, a forceful executive was the crux of the New Yorker's argument. He admitted later that, if asked, he himself would have accepted the assignment "of restoring Order to this Country." When Lafayette objected to some of the individuals Morris suggested for a new ministry because of their questionable rectitude, Morris told him quite frankly "that Men do not go into Administration as a direct Road to Heaven." When Lafayette wanted to keep the ineffective Necker because he could trust him, "as if it were possible," Morris told himself, "to trust a timid Man in arduous Circumstances." With growing exasperation on both sides, the argument was broken off. Morris later vented his frustration: "am vexed to find that by Littleness the little are to be placed where greatness alone can fill the seat." It was a cheerless assessment of the general and the government he could never shape.[57]

CHAPTER 10

Business as Usual

L IFE in Paris tested Morris's bent for self-indulgence precariously balanced by an inner discipline. But for all of his love-making and political
intrigue, Morris never lost sight of his primary mission, to carry out an
audacious plan to buy the American debt from the royal treasury and at the
same time straighten out Robert Morris's troubled tobacco business with the
farmers-general. The first was grandiose, the second mundane. Until he succeeded Jefferson as minister in 1792, business affairs continued to press him
relentlessly and are noted in virtually every entry of the diary. His private commercial correspondence conveys in numbing detail the projections of profit and
loss, schedules of meetings and land surveys, documenting not only his own
zigzagging fortunes but also those of his friend the Financier, whose steadily
accumulating bad luck would lead him to the Prune Street Jail in Philadelphia.

As a businessman, Gouverneur was more conservative than Robert, his
growing land speculations handled with greater care. He was also far more
adept than Alexander Hamilton and James Wilson at avoiding the perilous
financial shoals that eventually wrecked both men. Although Morris's goal
was to amass sufficient means to support a comfortable style of living with all
the essential amenities, he was clear that it should be kept in proportion to an
American or republican standard of restraint. He had no intention or desire to
build a marble palace like the one Robert Morris started in Philadelphia but
never completed. He had seen the same extravagance in Europe, stimulated by
the new commercialism. While traveling in Flanders, he passed a huge, vulgar
new château, which he learned had been commissioned by a successful snuff-

maker. To the New Yorker, the builder had misapplied human labor from the proceeds of such a "trifling useless article" to construct "one of the most striking monuments to human folly" he had ever seen. It was another example of the mindless greed and luxury that would undermine any society. Writing to a business partner, Gouverneur stated his belief that "our country and Government do not require and hardly forgive immense Property.... Learn then early and teach your Children the Poet's maxim Est Modus in Rebus."[1]

Throughout his life, the New Yorker believed that both private and public prosperity in America must be grounded, in principle, on high standards of conduct in the best Calvinist tradition. Those precepts, of course, were not always reflected in the political and business ethics of the times. During the current French and British conflict wholesale privateering turned international waters into a guerrilla war, for some a very profitable one. Neutral American vessels were regular targets. But he was concerned that some American entrepreneurs and those drawn to privateering might take a short-term advantage preying on the belligerents in order to reap a windfall. "I am sure," he wrote Jefferson, "that the United States will strictly observe the Laws of Nations and rigidly adhere to their Neutrality." But he coupled his warning with more fundamental moral considerations: "I know of Nothing so dangerous and I might say fatal to Morals as sudden Acquisition of Wealth by bad Means. Industry is thereby discouraged and Honesty discountenanced. The Vulgar are soon dazzled by the Glare of prospering vice and the Young are seduced from the Paths of Virtue. And Virtue once gone Freedom is but a Name for I do not believe it among possible Contingencies that a corrupt People should be for one moment free. Excuse I pray my dear Sir these Observations which I cannot restrain. They flow from the Conviction of my earliest Reason and are strengthened by the Experience of twenty years."[2]

Morris frankly confessed to William Carmichael that acquiring property had given him a taste for more, "but with the same frankness with which I avow that desire," he explained that when he referred to property, he meant investments with a "lively" return that might in the end support him at Morrisania as "an American farmer." More important, to Morris, the honest accumulation of a solid economic footing was a central element of his moral philosophy. In an oration on "The Love of Wealth," he declared: "Let us not be ashamed to love Wealth as it ought to be loved and seek it as it ought to be sought, that we might possess the Comforts which become our Station in Life, the means of that Independence which is essential to Freedom and the Power of indulging a generous Mind in Acts of Benevolence."[3]

Although his ultimate goal, his "great *disideratum*," may not have differed much from Thomas Jefferson's at Monticello, he was far more realistic and moral in his means and strategy. The profits from the monopoly the farmers-general held in the tobacco trade had nothing to do with a free market any more than slavery had anything to do with republican ideology. In his judg-ment, the slave economy in Virginia was worse than the tobacco monopoly of France (in which it was now entangled), not only in its human toll but, as he had often pointed out, in its destruction of the environment and soil by encouraging tobacco cultivation. "Notes respecting Tobacco," which he drafted for Lafayette's education in 1791, begins with this indictment as the crown's ruthless tax collectors, the Farm, as it was known, also collected custom duties and taxes on tobacco. With a paramilitary police force of some twenty thou-sand, the Farm's enforcers protected the monopoly on the commodity while collecting taxes. The journalist Mercier called the Farm an "infernal machine which seized each citizen by the throat and pumps out his blood."[4]

In spring 1785, Robert Morris had secured an exclusive contract to supply American tobacco to the farmers-general, which held the private monopoly on tobacco imported from America. The Farm had held the tobacco monopoly in France by license from the crown since the time of Louis XIV. Before the American Revolution, France was forced to buy American tobacco from British agents, but this was ended in 1783 when Benjamin Franklin made a deal with the Farm to bypass London and sell directly to France.

Gouverneur's efforts to salvage Robert Morris's troubled tobacco contract with the farmers-general was made more difficult by Jefferson's determination to destroy it. The Virginia envoy, a large tobacco planter himself and deeply indebted to London factors, believed the arrangement with the entrenched farmers-general was corrupt, unfair, and ideologically insupportable. The ancient corporation was, in Jefferson's view, a closed body of privileged, unen-lightened businessmen who held their exclusive rights from the king, adding moral indignity to his personal economic injury as one of its victims.

Both Morris and Jefferson understood the Farm's reactionary economic system very well, but Morris was more realistic in assessing its power and its true influence on American tobacco prices. He also held strong moral reserva-tions about Virginia's production system, in which Jefferson was hopelessly implicated. Although Jefferson had condemned slavery's corrosive effects in his *Notes on the State of Virginia*, his personal complicity in the system undercut his moral attack on the farmers-general. To Morris, this was hypocrisy. Not only was slavery "a curse of Heaven" on society, as he had told the Constitutional Convention, its environmental effects through destructive agricultural practices led to "misery & poverty" in the tobacco states, making "barren wastes" of Jef-ferson's state where the effects of slavery had turned his pastoral mirage into a desert in "increasing proportion to these wretched beings." Nor did he endear himself to Jefferson, the scientific farmer, when he bluntly told the Virginian that prolonged cultivation of tobacco was simply "bad Husbandry."[5]

Morris had met a number of the principle partners in the farmers-general when he first arrived in Paris and fully understood both the deep roots and the ambiguity of the Farm's position in French society. While the Farm was a pillar of the ancien régime with connections to the crown—John Jay told Jefferson these links were "golden Rivets"—by the late eighteenth century the new generation of partners in the Farm represented some of the country's most liberal and enlightened figures, distinguished for their intellectual interests and cultivation. Like Jefferson, they too seemed blind to a system that generated the wealth that gave them unlimited leisure to follow their dilettante interests. Morris's good friend Antoine Lavoisier, who had inherited his financial position in the Farm, was not a unique example. Like most of these *grands,* Lavoisier was not a businessman. With a large and secure income from the Farm, he was able to spend most of his time in his elegant private laboratory carrying out scientific research in chemistry. This would lead to the his discovery of the role of oxygen in chemical reactions. The partners in the Farm's exclusive club, as tax collectors, naturally became early targets of revolutionary forces. Lavoisier and most of the members of the Farm ended their lives under the blade of the guillotine in November 1793.[6]

Because of disputes with the Farm over late deliveries, by 1789 payments on Robert Morris's tobacco contract were in arrears. He believed that he had claims of 1.2 million *livres tournois,* and given his stretched credit, he was desperately squeezed for cash at the very moment when the Farm refused to pay. He also wanted a new contract to supply to the Farm an additional 20,000 hogsheads of American tobacco a year, but at a price higher than the current market. Gouverneur proceeded in a lawyerlike way and succeeded in reaching a compromise settlement on past payments, but negotiations on the new contract broke down.

As early as 1784, before Robert had secured his first contract with the Farm, Jefferson had decided that he would do everything in his power to destroy the Farm's monopoly. Jefferson believed that it was in Robert Morris's interest to buy tobacco as cheaply as he could from the Virginia farmers by manipulating downward the price. Writing to James Monroe in cipher, Jefferson declared his clandestine crusade, "The *monopoly* of our *tobacco* in the hands of the *Farmers General* will be pushed *by us* with all *our* force. But it is so interwoven with the very foundations of *their* system of *finance* that it is of doubtful event." This covert admission by the American minister to involve himself in the internal economic and political affairs of the host country lay at the heart of Gouverneur's difficult negotiations on behalf of Robert Morris.[7]

To carry out his strategy and yet avoid being accused of direct interference with the Farm's affairs, in 1786 Jefferson persuaded Charles Alexandre de Calonne, the comptroller general, to set up an "American Committee" to study the tobacco issues. He then managed to have Lafayette put on the committee as his clandestine agent. A day after the committee was formed, Lafayette wrote Washington that his goal was nothing less than the destruction of the Farm, "the greatest obstacle to Franco-American trade." Throughout these negotiations, crosscurrents of political and commercial interests, and conflicts of high-powered economic policies, Jefferson covered his tracks in his efforts to dissolve the Morris contract.

To break the impasse created by those who wanted to abolish the monopoly, as well as Morris's contract with the Farm, on May 11, 1786, Calonne accepted the proposal of the Farm to buy 15,000 hogsheads from the open market, provided that the Morris agreement remained untouched. Faced with Calonne's fait accompli, the "American Committee" indignantly demanded an emergency meeting held at Calonne's country house south of Paris near Berni where it was agreed that the Morris contract would run its course to the end of 1787 but would not be renewed. When Jefferson got word of the "Berni Agreement," he considered it at least a partial victory—the Farm was still in business—and immediately notified the governors of Virginia and Maryland. Although Jefferson had told Gouverneur that he had "constantly insisted on Compliance" with Robert's contract, his letter to John Adams after the Berni meeting tells another story. In July, he wrote Adams in London, revealing the depth of his true feelings as a tobacco grower about the Morris contract: "The monopoly of the purchase of tobacco for this country which has been obtained by Robert Morris had thrown the commerce of that single article into agonies. He had been able to reduce the price in America from 40/ to 22/6 lawful hundred weight, and all other merchants being deprived of that medium of remittance the commerce between America and this country, so far as it depended on that article...was absolutely ceasing."[8]

Following these arcane transactions, Jefferson's letter appears to be more opinion than factual analysis because it is difficult to see how Robert Morris's purchases on behalf of the French could drive the price down when the French took less than 10 percent of American tobacco. Furthermore, the real monopoly consisted of the well-established British and Scottish factors who historically had bought most of the American product. To Morris, it was once again an example of mixing, in his words, "metaphisical Ideas into the Business of the World." The New Yorker spelled this out in plain English to William Short who had little business experience: "I tell him that Morris's Contract with the Farm, which Jefferson considered as a Monopoly, was the only Means of destroying that Monopoly of Tobacco in Virginia by the Scotch Factors which really existed."[9]

Immediately after the Berni order, the problems for Robert Morris's tobacco trade mounted and his financial condition deteriorated even though French purchases went up briefly both in price and quantity. By 1789, American imports dramatically fell because of overstocking. By the time Jefferson returned home in fall 1789, his work and agitation to establish a healthy French-American trade had utterly failed. Britain had recovered its prewar dominance of the American trade. Too late, the Virginian realized and admitted, just as he left Paris in September, that if the Farm was put out of business and the market opened to the forces of free trade as he had advocated, "more tobacco will be raised in Europe and less demanded from America."[10]

By fall 1789, when Morris realized that nothing more could be done, he wrote his friend in Philadelphia, accurately predicting the results of Jefferson's efforts: "Before I close this letter I must wander a little from the Object of it to repeat an Observation I had frequently occasion to make in America, and which seldom met with assent from any one. Experience however the great Test of all human opinions must decide whether I was right in the Idea that the Determinations of the Committee of Berni must lower very considerably the Price of Tobacco in America and give Great Britain the Monopoly of that Article."[11]

From Gouverneur's personal interest and fortunes, his audacious plan to buy the American debt from France was far more important and complex than Robert Morris's tobacco business in which he had no financial stake. The very scale and daring of the speculative scheme is impressive. Gouverneur cared deeply about the future of both countries and not just their financial welfare. Knowing firsthand the critical importance of French financial support to the American triumph over Britain, the New Yorker and others saw their private efforts to replenish the treasury of their old ally as a patriotic responsibility quite aside of the likely private profits their rescue might produce. By helping at this critical juncture, it would remove a major source of tension and lead to improved trade relations, something both countries wanted. Writing to Washington, Morris noted that further delay in paying the debt was no way to treat a friend. He then outlined his practical argument for a "Bargin with Individuals," the purchase of the debt by a private consortium. It would have the "Advantage of bringing in the Aid of private Interest to support our Credit, and...it would leave us at Liberty to make use of that Credit for the Arrangement of our domestic Affairs."[12]

As everyone knew, French support of the American Revolution had plunged the country deeply into debt. It had seriously weakened the French nation and further deterioration might well lead to civil unrest, even revolution. By 1787 matters had reached a crisis and bordered on desperation when Congress defaulted on installment payments of the principle. According to Morris's plan, he and his partners would attempt to buy the total debt of 35 million *livres tournous*.

Besides defaulting on principal installments in 1787, interest had been in arrears for some time. That same year, treasury commissioners of the American government told the bankers in Amsterdam that there would be no further interest payments until the new government was installed under the Constitution. Furthermore, the loan made by the French government on America's account in Holland was to be paid in guilders, worth much more than the original loan in livre. The squeeze in the rate of exchange would come out of the French pocket. This state of affairs drove Necker, the French minister of finance, to attempt to negotiate the sale of the entire American debt to relieve the cash shortage. Comte de Saint-Hérem-Montmorin, who had become minister of foreign affairs in 1787, summed up the pending bankruptcy when he told Gouverneur plainly in November 1789, "they want now to receive Money," without further delay.[13]

The idea of an international consortium of financially sophisticated and experienced men considering a plan to buy the American debt was not wild-eyed speculation. The motive would be a reasonable profit combined, as in Morris's case, with a desire to find a practical solution that would help both parties. The debt would be bought at a discount and the profit would be made on repayment. Because the loans were in livre and the payments were to be made in Dutch guilders, the profit could be made in the difference of the rate of exchange.

All business transactions at this early and primitive stage of international finance, and in particular when it involved the politics of public debt, makes the evidence, such as it is, seem conspiratorial, reeking with conflicts of interest. Increasingly chaotic conditions at all levels of French society, guarded remarks, hints of intrigue, and cryptic passages in both Morris's diary and in other scattered documents make it difficult to get a clear picture of the exact nature of these schemes and plans surrounding the American debt or an accurate reading of some of the characters moving in and out of the dim and shifting scene. Throughout all the ups and downs of Morris's daily encounters there is a stimulating mix of politics, finance, and regular attention to the comtesse at her apartment in the Louvre.

Morris's plan to acquire the debt rested on the backing of the American bankers in Holland: Willink, Van Staphorst, and Hubbard. Both French and American investors would participate in the purchase. To make it financially possible, Morris's strategy called for deferred payments on the principle for five or six years, and this would have to be sold to Necker, who as director general of finances, controlled the government's policy to liquidate the debt.

Morris held a low opinion of Necker's abilities as a financier. The minister's musings on finance, he told Washington, "teem with the sort of sensibility, which make the fortune of modern romances," adding that it "exactly suited this lively nation who love to read but hate to think." The New Yorker's conclusion that Necker's wobbly leadership, like Lafayette's, floated "upon a wide ocean of incidents" accurately describes his dithering management of the debt negotiations. The minister was no match for Morris's self-assured style. In one exchange with Necker in his own house, Morris carries on a lively exchange over terms of the "Bargin" and raises his voice when the minister insists on security, telling him that security on such a large transaction was impossible. When Necker proposed payments of ten million per annum for three years, Morris preemptorily cut him off, backing up his position with his superior knowledge of the attitude of the Amsterdam bankers. Hearing the heated exchange, Necker's daughter, Germaine de Staël, intervened and asked Morris to send her father over to sit with her. With a flash of wit to clear the air, Morris replied that those, like the king, who had once before tried to send the minister away, lived to regret it.[14]

As in the tobacco business, there is reason to believe that Jefferson played a backdoor role in helping to torpedo Morris's "Bargin" to buy the debt. This would have been consistent with his ideological prejudice against what he saw as immoral speculation, a naiveté that grew out of his agrarian antiurban, antibusiness background as a Virginia planter. In August 1789, while Morris was in London, Jefferson received a letter from the Dutch bankers Willink, Van Staphorst, and Hubbard, asking him to secure the power to pay the American debt in full, funded by loans to be raised in Holland. In their letter that carried with it a definite tone of urgency, the bankers make clear that there had been earlier discussions with the American envoy, saying that the "object We Know Your Excellency and believe the United States to have much at heart." It is probable that Jefferson had initiated the proposal from Amsterdam, knowing that he would soon be returning to the United States where he could discuss the matter with the new government. He had earlier urged such a plan in letters to Jay, Madison, and Washington but had received no response. On September 24, the bankers sent Jefferson a detailed memorandum with the evident idea that Jefferson would personally carry it to the American treasury commissioners on his return.

When Morris received "intelligence which affects deeply our Plan about a purchase of the American Debt" in London, he was on his way back to Paris within twenty-four hours. His first call was at Jefferson's house, and finding the Virginian out for a walk, he caught up with him and, as Morris put it in the diary, "cast about to know if any Thing has been done respecting the Debt to France but cannot perceive that there has." Then he adds, "Avoid mentioning it to Mr. Jefferson for the present."

Morris and Jefferson discussed the debt from time to time, but it is not clear how much the New Yorker revealed of his strategy. Knowing that he had both competitors and adversaries, Morris believed that his negotiations should be kept as secret as possible, although the diary shows that many people knew at least some of his plans. He no doubt suspected that the American minister was part of his opposition. Jefferson did not know that Morris discussed with Lavoisier the possibility of bringing the farmers-general into the partnership, placing the United States' obligations in the Farm's hands, a move that certainly would have given Jefferson heart palpitations. In the end, Jefferson's maneuvers played a part in fatally delaying getting cash into the hands of the bankrupt French government.

By December 1789, Europe, Morris told Washington, was "like a mine ready to explode," yet he still believed his negotiations on the debt to be back on track and moving in his favor. Both Montmorin and Necker seemed to favor his plan, but something told him that there was a problem.

In the middle of all of this confusion and uncertainty, Morris took time out to do some shopping for his friend, who was settling in as president. Washington always had an eye for projecting the right image as a public figure. Now as head of state, these details became critical. He was concerned about the correct furnishings for his official residence in New York, and he wrote Gouverneur asking him to buy and "send by the first ship" fittings for his dining room—"mirrors" for the table, some ornaments and several wine coolers "for *at* and *after* dinner.... Should my description be defective, your imagination is fertile and on this I shall rely." On January 24, Morris shipped off three cases containing "a Surtout of seven Plateaux and the Ornaments in Biscuit." There were twelve figures and two vases in the group. He instructed Washington on how to place the surtout in the middle of the table for "large Companies" and as "ornaments to the Chiminey Piece" in a drawing room. He added directions for cleaning the bisque with warm water and a watercolor brush. By the time the cases arrived in New York, the president had moved into a new and larger house, the former residence of the French minister, recently vacated by the comte de Moustier, and had purchased some of the minister's handsome furniture and Sevres porcelain.[15]

By the beginning of 1790, Morris had become uneasy over the debt negotiations: "I have for some Days past," he tells himself, "had disagreeable forebodings about the Affair negotiating in Holland." On January 30, Mr. Van Staphorst delivered the bad news. The Dutch bankers had turned down Morris's plan and had, as an alternative, opened an account of three million florin on behalf of the United States to be used to pay down a portion of the debt. They had also written Necker and Hamilton, urging them not to agree to Morris's proposal, piously insisting to the secretary of the treasury that they deemed themselves "the natural Guardians of the Honor and credit of the united States." Even though Morris continued to hope he could reverse what he believed to be the "misconduct" of the bankers in Amsterdam, this would not be the case.[16]

Three days before Morris shipped the table decorations to Washington, he received an unexpected letter from the president instructing him to carry out a private mission to the Court of Saint James to explore the possible resolution of unfulfilled British commitments contained in the peace treaty. These commitments included the removal of the still occupied British military bases on the Western frontier and the payment for slaves who had escaped during the war. There was also the possibility of laying the groundwork for a commercial treaty with the former enemy. Taking on this diplomatic task would bring to an end, for the time being, any further private negotiations on the debt as inconsistent with his role as a public official. Morris even refused to put his commercial correspondence in his diplomatic pouch because, as he wrote Robert, "I do not chuse even in Matters of indifference to make my Public Character subservient to private Purposes for I have observ'd that Men slide easily into a Practice of that sort and seldom stop at the Point which on cooler thought they might wish."[17]

CHAPTER 11

A Presidential Mission

O N the morning of January 21, 1790, before celebrating "the connubial Misteries" with Adèle in her Louvre apartment, Morris received three letters from the president of the United States all written on October 13, 1789. In a private letter, Washington reported to his friend that the paper government Morris had left in New York was now organized at the top. He had appointed Edmund Randolph attorney general, Hamilton to the Treasury, Jay as chief justice, and Henry Knox in the War Department. Jefferson, now on his way home from Paris on leave, was asked to be secretary of state but had not yet accepted the post. John Adams was already boiling because Washington considered him part of the legislative branch rather than the executive since, as vice president, "the most insignificant office," he was also the presiding officer of the Senate. Morris's words in the finished Constitution were now to become all-too-human flesh in the personalities and ambitions of these men as they gave meaning to the document through their divinations and often ugly clashes.

The two other official letters spelled out the president's request for the New Yorker to take the temperature of British-American relations and assess "the sentiments and intentions of the Court of London" to fully carry out the terms of the peace treaty. In a brief reply the following day, Morris said that he would head for London as soon as possible.

Two days after this official exchange, Morris wrote the president privately assuring him that the table ornaments "of noble simplicity," which Washington had asked Morris to buy, were on their way. He did not, however, confide to Washington that his friend Madame de Flahaut had helped him select the porcelain at the Angoulême factory. Reporting that the purchase came to a stunning 2,384 pounds, he assured Washington that the quality of the service was well worth the extravagance. Besides, he insisted, choosing the best quality was in the national interest: "I think it of great Importance to fix the Taste of our Country properly, and I think your Example will go far in that Respect. It is therefore my Wish that every Thing about you should be substantially good and majestically plain: made to endure." In this same letter with the shipping details, the New Yorker went on to say that he knew the president was "not liable to the Dupery of false Hopes and groundless Expectations" for the new experimental government he now headed. Then, echoing his description of the presidential tableware, the New Yorker confidently praised the Constitution with the same aesthetic metaphor he used for the china, commending it for its simplicity and utility: "the new Constitution is such a plain, calm, sensible Appeal to the interest, Feelings and Common Sense of our Countrymen that it must by its own Weight bear down all Opposition."[1]

The president no doubt agreed on both counts. Having put his cabinet together he was ready to move into the former residence of the French minister, fitted out to stage his presidential levees. The all-important question of just how many receptions a week there would be was taken up with key cabinet members. Washington finally settled on two. Calling them "unexceptional" affairs, he nevertheless secretly monitored and noted in his diary their popularity—"attendence at Levee thin today...a pretty numerous crowd this evening."

Beyond the newly invented ceremonies with all the right appointments of state, including powdered lackeys at receptions and a coach and six on call, the president also believed that it was important to add weight to the emerging government by making its first diplomatic move into foreign affairs. For Morris it was the first step leading ultimately to his appointment as minister to France. Without a secretary of state, the president decided that the appointment did not require Senate approval. He did not want their advice or need their consent.

The background to Morris's mission was Washington's intuition that it was time to improve relations with Whitehall or at least determine its real intentions. "It is in my opinion very important," he cautioned Morris, "that we avoid errors in our system of government respecting Great Britain; and this can only be done by forming a right judgement of their disposition and views." "Forming a right judgement" firsthand were the careful, operative words in Washington's instructions. What was central to national interest from Washington's perspective was the need to avoid a major clash at this fragile stage of national development. It was imperative not to become embroiled in the running world conflict between England and France. England's continued presence on the American frontier, and her naval power, made it critical to his for-

China and table decorations purchased by Gouverneur Morris in Paris
for George Washington.
Courtesy of the Mount Vernon Ladies' Association.

eign policy to know what her real intentions were. He could rely on Morris
not only to read between the lines of the written exchanges of negotiations but
to detect any signals given by the personalities, even the body language of his
diplomatically well-disguised antagonists in London.

Specifically, the president asked Morris "to press for a speedy performance
of the treaty" requiring the removal of all military installations. The presence
of British military posts still functioning on the American western frontier
was an insult to national dignity and authority. Not only was national honor at
stake, the posts prevented orderly settlement in the Northwest and in the
Ohio Valley where the Indians had been stirred up by British fur traders operating out of Canada. Since the new Constitution agreed to compensate British
creditors, Whitehall could no longer refuse to honor the peace treaty by holding on to the posts as leverage for payment.

The treaty had provided for compensation for slaves lost during the war,
and this, too, had been ignored. Washington also wanted to know the government's true attitude toward sending a minister to the United States. He gave
Morris the discretion to let Whitehall know that its earlier failure to send a

minister, when John Adams was posted in London, "did not make an agreeable impression on this country."

The Navigation Acts of 1784, requiring all American goods entering British ports to be carried in British bottoms, had seriously curtailed American trade with the West Indies. "The privilege of carrying our productions in our vessels to their islands, and of bringing in return the productions of those islands to our ports and markets," Washington told Morris, "is regarded here as of the greatest importance." Great Britain's refusal to enter into a commercial treaty with the old Congress in 1785 was still a festering issue. In the recent Congress, Madison had, in retaliation, introduced legislation discriminating against British shipping and trade because there was no commercial treaty. Washington cautioned Morris that the opening of West Indian trade was a sine qua non and he was "not to countenance any idea of our dispensing with it in a treaty."[2]

Madison's efforts to restrict free trade with Britain of course collided head-on with Hamilton's grand design to fund the national debt, founded on a firm and visible tax base, a stable revenue generated by a system of duties or imposts on foreign trade. Since 90 percent of this trade was from Britain, a trade war or any disruption of relations would undermine Hamilton's entire system. To Hamilton, a commercial treaty was absolutely essential and could not wait for a resolution of the long-running disputes over the peace treaty.

The secretary of the treasury's ambitions, however, were more complex than the mere balancing of the national budget. Born in the West Indies, Hamilton in many ways remained an alien, psychologically tied to his native British citizenship and roots. Morris's keen observation at Hamilton's funeral is starkly apropos: "the first point of [Hamilton's] biography is that he was a stranger of illegitimate birth." The secretary's vision of ever-closer relations with the mother country, extending to "political friendship," seemed to overlook the very fact of the Revolution and emboldened him to promote by whatever means a comprehensive reconnection between the two countries. In many ways, Hamilton suffered as many illusions about Anglo-American ties—"*we think in English,* and have a similarity of prejudices and predilections"—as Jefferson harbored of an idealized republican France, an illusion that would later prevent his grasping the terrible realities of their Revolution. He would never achieve Morris's nuanced understanding of the gulf that separated the Old and New Worlds. America "has never been known to Europe," Morris told Jay even before he set foot there, "and God knows whether it ever will be so."[3]

But Washington's decision to ask Morris to carry out the sensitive mission to London encountered resistance when he discussed it with James Madison. Madison thought the president should wait for Jefferson's return from Paris. He was afraid that such a trip might be read as a commitment to appoint the New Yorker later as minister to London or Paris, without Jefferson's approval.

Shy and provincial, Madison was probably suspicious of Morris's urbane self-confidence, smelling of money, and went out of his way to express reservations about Morris's suitability. Madison told the president, "He thought, with Colo. Hamilton, and as Mr. Jay also does,... that Mr. Morris is a man of superior talents—but," he went on, "his imagination sometimes runs ahead of his judgment—that his manners before he is known, and were known, had created opinions of himself that were not favorable to him, and which he did not merit." Beneath this personal, and barely veiled, attack was Madison's conviction, shared by Jefferson, that Britain should make the initial move toward an exchange of ministers before they considered the question of any commercial treaty. Jefferson had spent his entire five years in France trying to cut down Britain's monopoly of American trade by expanding commercial ties with France, the country's true friend.[4]

It so happened that the same morning he spoke with Madison, Washington sounded out Hamilton, who had told him that he thought "Mr. Gouv'r Morris well qualified." As for Jay's views, he believed the trip was advisable but offered Dr. Edward Bancroft's name as envoy. Washington, of course, knew Morris better than any of his cabinet. He had been impressed with Morris's keen appraisal of the growing instability in Paris and was confident in his own judgment that he was making a choice that required "abilities, address and delicacy." Washington also knew from Morris's aggressive, tough handling of British arrogance as a member of the Continental Congress, that the New Yorker would not be intimidated by a country that held its own dignity to be paramount. Both men also appreciated that, as a novice on the world scene, the new republic had to maintain "a due respect for ourselves." "I shall readily acknowledge," Gouverneur wrote Robert Morris, "that these national attentions, like the exterior ceremonies of good breeding, do in fact mean nothing; but, in both cases, the omission means a great deal."[5]

Alexander Hamilton, in his zeal, to put it charitably, attempted to take over or at least monitor Morris's negotiations from the beginning, using the dubious means of a secret go-between. Major George Beckwith, an unofficial representative of the governor general of Canada, Lord Dorchester, became Hamilton's conduit to undercut Morris's integrity at Whitehall as the president's personal agent. While Morris's appointment was still being weighed by Washington's cabinet, Hamilton revealed to Beckwith his desire to establish commercial relations, without reference to Washington's concern for British violations of the peace agreement: "We wish to form a Commercial treaty with you to Every Extent, to which you may think it for Your interest to go." Hamilton's back-channel assurances were hardly a way to strengthen the American negotiating hand. He warned the major to keep their high-risk conversations secret. But in the end the secretary's scheme would have little real effect on the results of Morris's mission. American interests, as Morris soon found out in London, were of little concern to the Pitt government's imperial perspective.[6]

As he prepared to leave Paris, Morris had deep qualms about leaving Adèle, but he writes no conflicted dialogue of the "Head and the Heart" to her or in his diary. The president's mission could run on for months, and their relationship had reached a critical stage. And there was always the bishop, still an annoying, smirking presence and with his family ties, a threat as a rival. On a chilly morning in Adèle's apartment not long before departing for London, her speechless lover looked on as she again soaked her feet in hot water while "the Bishop employs himself in warming her bed," adding wryly, "It is curious enough to see a Reverend father of the Church engaged in this pious Operation." But he had found from experience that "a little Kindness in Tone and Manner" did more good than her foot bath or the doses of ether she regularly took when things threatened to spin out of control.[7]

During the month before leaving for London on February 17, he continued to work overtime to get Adèle pregnant, apparently with the idea that this would somehow preserve their affair while he was away. His optimistic rationale ignored how little her son had, in fact, tied her to the bishop when Morris had first appeared on the scene. It would be nearly eight months before he would see Adèle again and she would not be *enceinte*.[8]

Two days after arriving in London, on March 29, 1790, Morris met with the duke of Leeds, the foreign secretary, at the London house of Jefferson's friends Maria and Richard Cosway. Angelica Church had told Morris that the Cosways' stylish residence located on the Mall was "considered as one of those where, from the very mixed companies which frequent it dangerous connections may be formed." Morris was both amused and disappointed when he found the Cosway crowd to be totally unlike his French circle, stiff and chilly, a *"froideur anglais"* underlined by the "ladies ranged in Battalia on the opposite side of the Room."[9]

While waiting for his first official audience with Leeds, Morris had dinner with his old friend La Luzerne, now the French ambassador in London, telling him that his mission was to insist on the performance of the peace treaty. Because there was no way to keep the negotiations secret, Morris had not been enjoined to do so. Taking the French into his confidence was an astute move, although it would later be used by his critics in Congress as poor judgment. Given the role France had played in securing independence, Morris rightly believed that it was diplomatically prudent to keep America's most important ally posted on the negotiations to enforce the treaty. More to the point, the spirit of the treaty required it. Writing to Washington on April 7, "the thing itself cannot remain a secret; and by mentioning it to him [La Luzerne], we are enabled to say with Truth, that in every step of the Treaty of Peace, we have acted confidentially, in regard to our ally." Besides, La Luzerne's experience with the British and his counsel might prove useful. The ambassador told him, quite accurately as it turned out, that Britain would not give up its western posts.[10]

Morris immediately reported to Washington the details of his first meeting with Leeds. The New Yorker found the atmosphere diplomatically cordial, but by constantly changing the subject, Leeds avoided making any specific commitment. When he used the lame excuse that the government wanted to send a minister but could not find anyone qualified, without hesitating Morris retorted that it was a transparent dodge. "Wherefore, as it was not worth while to discuss the winds and the weather," he stiffly told his lordship. "I observed that he might probably choose to consider the matter a little and to read again the treaty and compare it with the American Constitution."

After meditating on this first meeting, Morris dashed off a second letter to Washington, reflecting on Leed's personal demeanor and manner when he read the president's letter. By his eager expressions, Leeds seemed to be personally relieved to have the issues with the former colonies out on the table. Morris, however, was a bit puzzled by this and speculated that the recent tensions in Europe had "excited some disquietude" about the role the United States might play in a general war between Britain and France.[11]

Just before he left Paris, he had, in fact, brashly urged Montmorin to consider declaring war on Britain because a foreign war, as he had argued in 1781 when the Continental Congress became paralyzed, was "a great friend of soveignty." He reported "for yourself alone" what must be called his not-so-subtle war mongering to Washington. In his highly venturesome, dangerous diplomatic strategy, an offensive war would cure France of "the french disease, Revolt" and might even replace "*Aristocrat*" in the dictionary with "*Anglais*." Ignoring the risk, he even advanced the plot with the Spanish ambassador in London, believing that the calculated strategy could well force the British to reach a fair accommodation with its former colonies. An embargo in the West Indies, he argued, would invite privateers eager to disrupt British commerce. Writing to Lafayette, burning with desire for military glory, Morris the agent provocateur's imagination took flight: "Secure their seamen and never exchange them, and you will by that Means ruin both their Marine and Finance, and if you send those Seamen into the interior Parts of the Kingdom and employ them in public Works upon the Highways &ca. &ca. they will cost you Nothing and by Degrees loose their Habits of Seamanship."[12]

After his first meeting, Morris heard nothing further from Leeds for a month. When he finally received the foreign minister's dissembling response, Morris concluded that matters were seriously stalemated. "It seems pretty clear," he wrote Washington, "that they wish to evade a commercial treaty, but not peremptorily to reject it; and, therefore, I have construed into rejection his Grace's abstruce language, leaving him the option to give it a different interpretation." He also understood the British bargaining strategy over the western posts and continuing to "withold payment for the negroes" carried off during the war. Always the realist, Morris recognized the simple fact that America had little leverage to gain British attention on issues of so little consequence to its global ambitions. It had even less power to enforce its rights within its own territory in the Northwest.[13]

The underlying problem was that after seven years of calibrated indifference to American complaints, the Pitt ministry was comfortably prepared to do nothing. Washington's government and Morris's mission were frustrated by what Stanley Elkins and Eric McKitrick call "the enormous disparity between the level of American attention upon Britain and that of Britain upon America." The month's lapse between Morris's first meeting exposed the extent of the lopsided relationship.

On May 5, Morris heard that trouble was brewing between Spain and Britain in a remote corner of the world—Nootka Sound, later called Vancouver. He actually learned of the incident before leaving Paris but thought it of no consequence. Spain had seized two British merchant ships that had trespassed on its territory. In the diplomatic fracas that erupted over the release of the vessels, the Spanish ambassador charged that a British ship had tried to "take possession of Nootka Sound in the name of the British king." In fact, the owner of the seized ships admitted building a trading post at Nootka, which the world knew Spain claimed as its lawful territory under a papal bull issued in 1493, declaring that most of the New World's real estate belonged to Spain.

The confrontation in Nootka was insignificant, but it gave the Pitt government a useful excuse to challenge Spain's claims to the Pacific coast of North America. By the time the affair was disclosed, the prime minister had a squadron of ships of the line fitted out and ready for action. "If Spain submits," Morris told Washington, "she may as well give up her American dominions; for the position advanced here is that nations have a right to take possession of any territory unoccupied." Spain's submission was exactly what Pitt had in mind. By October, the Spanish were ready to cave in and on October 28, Nootka Sound was occupied by British forces. Territorial sovereignty in the Pacific would be completely remapped by Pitt's action.[14]

Using the serious pretext to complain of the "hot Press" of American seamen during British preparations to challenge Spain, Morris finally got the brief attention of Whitehall and secured another audience with Leeds. At this point, he seemed overconfident in the prospects of war with Spain, forcing the British to pay a good price for American neutrality. The envoy had not been authorized to raise the issue of impressment, but, as he told Washington later, "I could not be an indifferent witness to the injuries sustained by my fellow citizens." To Morris's surprise the prime minister unexpectedly joined the meeting and took the lead in the animated exchange. Pitt had shown little interest in American affairs and except for the Spanish dispute with its potential risks, he was perfectly content to let matters drift in that department. The exchange, recorded in Morris's letter to Washington, shows the New Yorker at his most dazzling, an impressive match for the seasoned Pitt, who had been in office since 1783 when he was all of twenty-four.[15]

In spite of what some of his critics were saying back home, Morris was no Anglophile, giving his personal negotiating posture an edge that his experienced diplomatic adversaries respected. Years later, Morris summed up his distaste for the dull, boring English society: "Recollect that a tedious morning, a great dinner, a boozy afternoon, make a sum total of English life. It is admirable for young men who shoot, hunt drink.... I respect...the English nation highly, and love many individuals among them, but I do not love their manners...they are certainly too cold for my taste."[16]

Unlike Hamilton, who in his anxious, deferential state, was willing to go to any length in the name of friendship to secure England's cooperation, Morris understood that diplomacy required an adversarial stance even with a friend. He outlined his strategy to Washington: "I thought it best to heap coals of fire on their heads, and thereby either bring them into our views, or put them most eminently in the wrong.... If, as is not improbable, they should give us no answer, or one so vague as to mean nothing, I shall pursue, according to circumstances, my object of compelling them to speak plainly, or refuse absolutely."

As in Hamilton's personal attempt on his own account to form an alliance with England, Jefferson also had crossed the line from a correct diplomatic position to that of a direct participant, with Lafayette and other friends, in attempting to organize the constitutional forces in the French Assembly in the fall of 1789. Like Hamilton, Jefferson was making a rational projection of his personal vision onto the future of France and his mind, also like Hamilton's, was fueled by illusory probabilities, not by official American policy or diplomatic protocol. Morris's respect for diplomatic conventions and his unblinking, realistic reading of the diplomatic landscape made him, by far, the more reliable statesman to represent national interests in international affairs.[17]

At the first meeting with Leeds near the end of March, the foreign minister had dangled a glimpse of carrot, vaguely expressing a willingness to enter into a commercial treaty. Morris "answered cooly that...it appeared idle to form a new treaty until the parties should be thoroughly satisfied with the already existing one." When Pitt complained of American delays in compliance, Morris calmly reminded the prime minister "that delay is always a kind of breach" and then proceeded to discuss the substance of the complaints. When the New Yorker raised the question of compensation for lost slaves, Pitt exclaimed that the loss was exaggerated. "I at once acknowledged," to the prime minister, "my belief that in this, as in all similar claims, there might be some exaggeration on both sides.... As to the compensation for negroes taken away, it is too trifling an object for you to dispute, so that nothing remains but the posts I suppose, therefore that you wish to retain those posts." Pitt shot back "Why, perhaps we may." Then Morris's parry: "They are not worth the keeping, for it must cost you a great deal of money, and produce no benefit. The only reason you can desire them, is to secure the fur trade, and this will centre in this country, let who will carry it on in America."

Pitt then suggested that if the posts were of no consequence, why fight over them? To this, Morris pointed out that, while the posts were of little importance to the British empire, they were essential to America to "preserve this boundary," which was necessary "if you wish to live in amity with us.... Those who made the peace acted wisely in seperating the possessions of the two countries by so wide a water.... Near neighbors are seldom good ones, for quarrels among borderers frequently bring on wars."

Pitt wondered whether progress might be made "if, on general ground, some compensation could not be made mutually," suggesting a horse trade of the posts in exchange for a monetary settlement of debts. But such an agreement would not only have been contrary to Morris's instructions, it would have removed any future leverage to force Britain to abandon the posts. Morris was quick with his response: "I immediately replied, 'if I understand you, Mr. Pitt, you wish to make a new treaty instead of complying with the old one.' He admitted this to be *in some sort* his idea. I said that, even on that ground, I did not see what better could be done than to perform the old one."

Taking a final tack, the prime minister said that the former colonies might at least offer special privileges, which they now enjoyed in British commerce. "I assured him," the New Yorker lightly replied to his startled adversary, that he knew of none "except being impressed, which of all others we least wish to partake of." The heavy double entendre, referring to British impressment of American sailors, was picked up by Leeds, who tried to clear the air just before the meeting ended by weakly saying both were "favored" nations each treating the other the same.

With things going their way in the confrontation with Spain, Pitt and his minister never bothered to make further contact with Morris. Neither Washington, Adams, nor Jefferson was surprised by the turn of events after reading Morris's detailed reports. The president expressed his "entire approbation." Adams added that "their conduct was of a piece with their conduct towds. him whilst Minister of that Court; and just what he expected; and that to have it ascertained was necessary."

Hamilton, however, was not willing to give up his dreams of "connections" and refused to accept Morris's version of the negotiations or his pessimistic conclusion. While the British continued to deliver their message of indifference simply by ignoring Washington's representative, the secretary of the treasury continued to promote the notion that the British were, contrary to Morris's letters, still interested in a "connection" with the United States. He went so far as to tell Washington and Jefferson that his supposedly superior information from Major Beckwith confirmed Whitehall's willingness to enter into a commercial treaty, and a possible military alliance as well. The president asked Hamilton to put his information into a memorandum and in doing so, he seems to have misrepresented what his informant had told him. Washington, however, was not misled. After reading the memorandum, he entered in his diary a summary of Morris's accurate appraisal of British intentions to maintain the status quo. Washington directed Hamilton to be wary of Beckwith, but to "extract as much as he could...without committing any assurances whatever, [of] the Government of the U. States."

At this stage, Hamilton began a subtle campaign of character assassination to undermine Morris's effectiveness and bring about his eventual removal. After Hamilton read Morris's lively report to Washington on his encounter with Pitt, he told Beckwith there was "something in his [Morris's] conduct on that occasion, which I do not altogether approve." Beckwith then asked Hamilton if he knew of any circumstances that might explain Morris's unsympathetic reports. When Hamilton mentioned Morris's friendship with La Luzerne, Beckwith recalled that he had heard disturbing gossip that Morris had also been friendly with the opposition leader, Charles James Fox, while on the presidential mission. But Beckwith added, "it is for Your consideration, how far a gentleman in [Morris's] situation ought to form intimacies with persons in public political situations, excepting they are in administration." Without any authority whatsoever and without the knowledge of his president, the secretary of the treasury replied, "I am quite of Your opinion, and this among other causes led me to remark, that it is greatly desirable, that this negotiation be transferred to our seat of Government."

Hamilton recast this secret exchange with Beckwith and put it into a letter to Washington, charging that Morris's reports were inaccurate and his firm demeanor had somehow been an embarrassment to the American government. Hamilton's indictment of subtle defamation began with a varnish of truth: "I had lately a visit from a *certain Gentleman,* the sole object of which was to make some observations of a delicate nature, concerning *another Gentleman* [Morris] he employed on a *particular errand.*" He then went on to detail his charge that Morris "was upon terms of great intimacy with the representative of a certain Court [La Luzerne] at the one *he* was employed and with the party [Charles James Fox] opposed to the Minister," a condition that "cannot be calculated to inspire confidence or facilitate free communication." Hamilton closed his message with a chilling disclaimer: "It is to be hoped that appearances, which admit of so easy a solution will not prove an obstacle to any thing which mutual interests dictate."[18]

While Hamilton continued his Machiavellian efforts, the silence between the negotiating parties in London grew louder through the cold and rainy English summer. Things remained in limbo for nearly four frustrating months. The New Yorker's social life, however, continued unabated except for bouts of sickness, evidently brought on, or so he thought, by the heavy English cuisine. Morris also kept his hands in his private business affairs, the promotion of the sale of his American lands and the purchase of a splendid "indianman," the *Goliath* fitted out for the India trade. On July 4 he wrote to his New York partner, William Constable, telling him of the new ship, costing thousands of pounds, and assuring him that "a finer vessel there is nowhere than she will be" when she receives her copper bottom. He also discovered a "leg maker" who could made copper legs so he spent most of one day having a plaster cast made of his right leg as a model. A cast was made of the stump in order to have the new member fitted without having to spend time in the shop later.[19]

In September, around the time Hamilton was concocting his letter for the president, Morris wrote Leeds, saying that since no new grounds for negotiations had appeared, he was preparing to return to Paris. This drew a confidential letter from Leeds privately apologizing for the government's intransigency. Morris sent Washington a comprehensive report on where things stood at the end of his mission. From Leeds's vague letter, Morris correctly understood that those in the government advancing better relations with America were "outnumbered by those, whose sour prejudices and hot resentments render them averse to every intercourse, except that which may immediately subserve a selfish policy. These men do not yet know America," adding a private, accurate observation: "Perhaps...America does not yet know itself." The New Yorker then expressed to the president his informed reservations of the Hamiltonian policy of pledging the nation's fiscal welfare and possibly more to the tender paws of the British lion. Some Americans "believe that British credit is essential to our commerce. Useful, it certainly is, at present; but let our public credit be well established and supported, and in a few years our commercial resources will astonish the world. We are yet in a seedling time of national prosperity, and it will be well not to mortgage the crop before it is gathered."

After receiving Morris's detailed reports, it was clear to Washington and Jefferson that further negotiations would be futile. In September, Morris reported to the president that American sailors had been impressed on the high seas by British warships. It was an insult, and he lost no time in informing Leeds that the affront bordered on a breach of the Treaty of Peace. "Having acted without Authority," he immediately reported the events to Washington and enclosed a copy of his firm, but graceful, letter to the minister of foreign affairs. In writing the letter to Leeds, he told the president that he had followed his own rule "to support your pretensions with Spirit."[20]

When Morris's enemies blamed his personal style for the breakdown of negotiations, he made his own defense in a letter to Robert Morris. "I will suppose it to be a very good Reason to be given to America for not conferring a *Favor* on her that the Man sent to ask it was disagreeable, no Matter from what cause, but I trust they will never avow to the british Nation a Disposition to make Sacrifice of their Interests to please a pleasant Fellow."[21]

Far from being rudely antagonistic in his dealings with Whitehall, Morris had, as he learned from Jefferson in December, managed to smoke out the true intentions of the British cabinet now that the threat of war with Spain had dissipated. In February, the president sent Congress excerpts from Morris's letters, leaving no doubt of the British position, a devastating blow to Hamilton and the "British interest" in the Senate. Madison's Navigation Bill, promising American retaliation against British commerce, was revived. These efforts, supported by Jefferson, immediately set off alarms in Whitehall, and later in the spring of 1791, London abruptly decided it was time to send the first minister to the United States, the ironic result of Morris's reports to Washington, which had now been made public.[22]

CHAPTER 12

Minister to France

This unhappy Country, bewildered in the pursuit of metaphisical Whimsies, presents to our moral view a mighty Ruin. Like the remnants of ancient magnificence, we admire the Architecture of the Temple, while we detest the false God to whom it was dedicated. Daws and Ravens, and the Birds of Night, now build their Nests in its Niches.

GOUVERNEUR MORRIS TO GEORGE WASHINGTON,
November 22, 1790

AFTER a month's side trip through Flanders and Germany looking at both paintings and architecture, Morris arrived back in Paris on November 6, 1790. His traveling companion was a large Newfoundland dog he had ordered from America while in London. It was to be a present for his friend the duchesse d'Orléans. He called on Adèle on his first day back but left abruptly when he found a handsome young Englishman, Lord Henry Wycombe, at the apartment, "*un peu enniché.*" When Adèle assured the New Yorker of her fidelity and chastity, he said to himself that he was "obliged to doubt both a little." He did not know that in Adèle's secret novel-in-progress, Wycombe would become "Lord Sydenham," the heroine's English lover. Morris's four-word diary entry the following day, "At the Louvre *denied,*" said it all.[1]

On November 10, the day he planned to make his presentation to the duchess, he had his first serious meeting at the Louvre after nearly eight months of separation. Following the usual sparing games of estranged lovers, which they both seemed to enjoy—arguments over the bishop's role in what now appears to be a quadrangle, followed by "a Scene of Sentiments, Caresses and some Tears"—Adèle suddenly asked him to "possess her." When he told her that it will be "*pour la dernière fois,*" she teasingly baited him, calling him "a cheat for telling her it is the last time." She was, of course, right.

Louise Marie Adélaide de Penthievre, Duchess d'Orléans,
by Elisabeth Vigée-Lebrun, 1789.
Réunion des Musées Nationaux/Art Resource, N.Y.

That night after their first post-London reunion, Morris walked his stylish, dignified gift around to the Palais Royal, but by then the duchess's title no
longer existed officially. While Morris was in London, titles and all other signs
of the hereditary orders in France had been dramatically erased by the
National Assembly. On June 19, 1790, William Short, now the American
chargé d'affaires, had reported to Morris that the night before "a new scene
opened. It was decreed that all titles should be abolished—such as Dukes,
Counts, Marquises &c—that no coats of arms, liveries, & other distinctions of
that kind should be used."[2]
On August 4, 1790, the Assembly moved to begin voting on the Declara-

tion of the Rights of Man and the Citizen. Without debate, the Assembly, "by a kind of magic," according to Morris, adopted equality of taxation and the redemption of all manorial rights except for those involving personal servitude. All titles of nobility were abolished. Other resolutions followed, among them freedom of speech, the right to assemble, equality of legal punishment, admission of all to public office, abolition of the sale of public offices and freedom of worship. The final decree grandly declared, "The National Assembly destroys the feudal regime in its entirety." The words were far from accurate, but for a bright moment, "liberty and equality thus worked irresistible charm upon imaginations.... The mythic character of the French Revolution unfolded."[3]

On July 14, 1790, an extravagant piece of revolutionary theater, the Fête de la Fédération, was staged in the Champs de Mars, setting the stage for the revolutionary actions of the Assembly that shortly followed. This first anniversary of the fall of the Bastille was an emotional climax to the creation of the new order and its hybrid state religion. Both Talleyrand and Lafayette had central roles. Like the opening of the Estates-General, it was the kind of "metaphisical whimsy" Morris hated to miss, a spectacle that would have inspired in his diary acerbic, skeptical observations missed by most of the participants. He would not be fooled by the grand illusion that a united nation under a sovereign fiction had been created by the master choreographers of the Fête, intent on overwhelming its awed audience.

After describing the festival in his letter to Morris, then still in London, a worried William Short raised the question of Jefferson's successor, saying that James Madison was often mentioned in Paris as the likely candidate. Having shipped off Jefferson's remaining luggage, crates of furniture and plate—it would total eighty-six pieces—he told Morris that the Hôtel de Langeac had "the appearance of a bankrupt" after the creditors had cleaned it out. Short deeply coveted the post of minister but, of course, could not refurnish the house until an appointment was confirmed. He was also apprehensive that Morris might be picked instead. The young Virginian's anxieties were further compounded by his secret love affair with Rosalie de La Rochefoucauld, wife of Jefferson's friend the duc de La Rochefoucauld d'Enville.

Morris's own private feelings about remaining in Paris were ambivalent, colored by his increasingly rocky relations with Adèle. It seems odd and certainly out of character for a man who considered himself an expert on the ways of the world and of women to be surprised, much less annoyed, by Adèle's racy life, which she had continued to pursue during his absence. To Short, he confessed to an unusual malaise: "Objects of business are suspended by Circumstances and this is disagreeable because I wish to close all my private affairs so that I may go hence whenever it may be proper. Pleasurable affairs also go badly. My Circle is too much narrowed and I am loath to extend it just now because twenty years Converse with Mankind have not yet given me the

Festival of the Federation by Cornu, 1790.
Bevalot

needful insensibility. I attach myself easily and leave always with Regret those to whom I am attached."[4]

To himself, Morris ruefully admitted that Adèle "has just now much the advantage of me" after he discovered both the bishop and "her Lord" vying for her attention. But as the political strain intensified, coupled with growing violence during winter and early spring 1791, their affair picked up with a renewed heat mixed with the usual quarrels and misunderstandings. There was also an alarming recklessness in their pairings, an atmosphere of capricious sensuality permeating the apartment. Once while Adèle's niece was playing the harpsichord in the drawing room, they "take the chance of interruption and celebrate in Passage." On another occasion, to the niece's background music—this time a fortepiano—and her convenient nearsightedness allowed the two to "almost perform the genial act" in the same room.[5]

As for his business affairs, they too had taken a dangerous turn. A shady London business partner of his and Daniel Parker, "a devilish slippery fellow," had suddenly failed and decamped leaving 15,000 pounds of unpaid bills owed mostly to William Constable, whose partnership included both Morrises. To deal with the crisis, Morris rushed back to London as the crisis threatened to take everyone down in its collapse. With effort, he managed to head off financial disaster, but his business ventures for the entire year of 1791 were lackluster. Constable's books in New York, however, continued to add substantial profits to Morris's private account, keeping him afloat in his comfortable Parisian style.

Morris's extended interests in the sale of land in America—his own and others—had continued while he was Washington's personal representative in London and on his return to France, well into 1791. But foreign land sales had been badly hurt by the king's secret attempt to flee France. Arrested at Varennes, he was brought back a captive to Paris in July 1791. The debacle had produced a decree by the Assembly banning all emigration, and this in turn had wiped out the speculative American market targeting desperate French émigrés planning to flee to the Promised Land. Morris described to William Constable just how the royal family's capture at Varennes had wrecked the overseas real estate market: "The Evasion of the King and Queen has among other Things produced a decree against Emigration which damps the Sales of land & the Accounts of Scioto each one worse than the other have a similar Effect. Indeed they have brought the Scioto upon the Stage and these frenchmen who once supposed that all the people of America lived in Boston seem now to imagine that all the Land of America is on the Scioto."

The Scioto Company had been formed in 1787, in connection with the Ohio Company. It was, as Morris told Jefferson, "a Plan for colonizing the Banks of the Scioto with the inhabitants of the Rue d'Honoré and others who might think proper to go to the Land of Promise." The organizers of the company planned to sell preemption rights to purchase American public lands between the Scioto and Ohio rivers in what is now southern Ohio. The original design cooked up by the shady William Duer, secretary of the board of the United States Treasury, was to buy depreciated American securities held by European banks and investors then use them at face value to buy the Scioto land to resell, "promising freely," in Morris's words, "what in the Nature of Things could never be performed." It was another one of those smoke and mirrors schemes of early capitalism that suffered from the public's lack of a clear understanding of what it was all about beyond the usual dreams of large profits. When the value of American securities suddenly rose on the unexpected adoption of the American Constitution, the whole scheme began to unravel.[6]

One of the Scioto promoters and victims was the self-important American poet Joel Barlow, who had been sent to France to help sell the Scioto Company land. He arrived in Paris in fall 1788, and when Morris first met him, he was not impressed. The New Yorker did not bother to hide his reservations of Barlow either as a poet or businessman. A sign of his subtle disdain was his refusal to sign the poet's high-flown effusions read in tribute to Jefferson at the envoy's Fourth of July party in 1789. Later, when Morris heard about some of Barlow's naive promotion letters back to the United States touting the golden opportunities for American land sales in France, he warned his partner

William Constable that "the highly colored Pictures drawn by Mr Barlow were not taken from Life and [I] observe that the mischievous Consequences of this Business will be felt by others who are in pursuit of a similar Object."[7]

The new company, which included General Duportail, the French minister of war, intended to buy the entire Scioto tract and then sell parcels to émigrés directly. Without any authority, Barlow misled his clients to believe that he would arrange transportation and materials to build the settlements for the pioneers. When the first group arrived in southern Ohio, to their shock, they found that they had no title to the land and few resources to survive the first winter. The reports back to Paris blew the scandal open, to no surprise of Morris, who had often expressed his skepticism.[8]

It is easy to see that Morris had in Barlow a new enemy in the making. After the Scioto fiasco, Barlow remained in Paris and became a passionate admirer of the Revolution, a defender of many of its radical outrages. He later sought retaliation against the leery New Yorker who had helped to expose the Scioto scam, writing Jefferson to oppose Morris's appointment as minister. "It is really unfortunate for our interest as well as the cause of liberty in general, that he [Morris] does not accord better with the principles which do and ought to govern the people of France."[9]

For all his misgivings on the dangerous path "the cause of liberty" was taking, which were eloquently voiced in his letter on his return from London in November 1790, Morris nevertheless saw in the "failed" revolution "some foundation of future prosperity." He applauded the nationalization of church property and the abolition of feudal property rights, "by which the tenure of real property is simplified, the value reduced to money, rent is more clearly ascertained, and the estimation which depended upon idle vanity, or capricious taste, or sullen pride, is destroyed. And [a]bove all," he added with words ignored by most of his biographers, he looked forward to "the promulgation and extensions of those principles of liberty, which will, I hope, remain to cheer the heart and cherish a nobleness of soul, when the metaphysical froth and vapor shall have blown away. The awe of that spirit which has thus been raised, will I trust, excite in those who may hereafter possess authority a proper moderation in its exercise, and induce them to give to this people a real constitution of government, fitted to the natural, moral, social, and political state of their country."[10]

Morris watched with foreboding the alarming path taken by the Revolution, a direction that largely confirmed his earlier predictions when he arrived in Paris. As early as fall 1789, he had seen the problem and told the president of the Assembly that "it was simply impossible for such a Mob to govern this Country...the executive Authority is reduced to a Name. Everything almost is elective and consequently Nobody obeys."

Reporting this conversation to Robert Morris, he added that the enlightened leadership, particularly among the nobility and upper bourgeoisie had "by romantic Notions picked up in Books and who are too lofty to look down upon that Kind of man which really exists, and too wise to heed the Dictates of common Sense and Experience, have turned the Heads of their Countrymen and they have run amuck at such a Don quixote Constitution as you are blessed with in Pennsilvania. I need say no more. You will judge the Effects of such a Constitution upon a People supremely depraved. They are devilish wicked."[11]

As the Assembly continued to flounder in the name of liberty, Morris was not surprised by Lafayette's failure to organize and lead a firm, energetic government. He had "left America...when his Education was but half finished," he told Washington, "but had not learned to be a Government Maker." The New Yorker's judgment that the Lafayette was basically mediocre was not new; he had first expressed serious reservations, after a meeting at Jefferson's house to hear Lafayette explain how he was going to deal with the mounting crisis the fall of 1789.[12]

In his theatrical performance before the altar on Champs de Mars at the Fête de Fédération, "the hero of two worlds" had, in fact, reached the high point in his dream to restore unity and order to the Revolution. But his romantic optimism, which grated on Morris's pragmatic sensibilities, and his misplaced confidence in his own abilities appeared to be leading to disaster. Suffering, in Morris's words, from "the Consequences" of "too great Elevation," Lafayette blithely assured Washington a month after the fête that the Revolution would be over shortly, a constitutional monarchy would be in place, and he would be back in private life. Almost at the same moment, Short wrote Jefferson that the marquis "has sworn enemies in all the parties, owing to his having endeavored to conciliate them all."

Unlike Short, who did not have the self-confidence or experience to offer Lafayette advice and who regularly flattered him, Morris had frankly cautioned the general on his crowd-pleasing missteps. "I lately told him some Truths which offered so much from the Style of Flattery, he has been accustomed to," Morris told Madame de Montmorin, "that he is not well pleased with it." This was about the time that he candidly told Washington that Lafayette's "Authority depends on Incidents and sinks to nothing in a Moment of Calm." It is not surprising that Lafayette much preferred Short—or anyone else—over Gouverneur Morris as Jefferson's replacement as minister.

One theme that did not go down well with Lafayette was Morris's argument of "the necessity of restoring the Nobility" to a significant role in the government, "at which of Course he flinches and says that he should like two Chambers as in America. I tell him that an American Constitution will not do in this Country & that two such Chambers would not answer where there is an hereditary Executive. That every Country must have a Constitution suited to its circumstances." To Morris, the love of liberty was shared by both bourgeoisie and the nobility. Given France's historic condition, he believed some way should be found to bring together the liberal nobility and the enlightened middle class of the Third Estate to reflect what he considered the historic reality of the nation.

In other words, a powerful hereditary monarchy and a strong popular legislature had to be counterbalanced with an equally powerful senate, but this did not mean the restoration of the aristocracy. Morris had no love for the nobility or confidence in its leadership, yet he did believe that a government should mirror its own organic, historic condition, requiring, as he had told Washington, "a real constitution of government, fitted to the natural, moral, social, and political state" of the entire society with all its flaws. This was at the heart of Morris's deeply humane, civilized, and sensible constitutional philosophy. He knew that inflated declarations and elevated rhetoric could be torn up in flash by the same people who drafted them. As he pointed out to Robert Morris, after the Assembly proclaimed that every man had a right to go where and when he pleased, it immediately turned around and passed a law, aimed at the aristocrats, prohibiting all emigration by the new citizens.

Morris believed that for all of its reputation for inept cupidity and incompetence, the nobility was an old and significant element of the country's fabric and as such it should somehow be accommodated in the framework of government. Ignoring the popular stereotypes and beyond their privileges and ranks, he recognized that in many ways the aristocratic and bourgeois codes of personal morality and manner of living were not all that different. Personal relations between nobles and commoners had become more relaxed, and even the once telltale class distinctions in dress had become blurred. On the eve of the Revolution, there were complaints that it was impossible to distinguish lords and those without pretensions of birth merely by their appearance. Far from being idle and useless, the nobility's professional and bureaucratic roles in government administration and in commerce and industry had become critical to the country's future welfare. To read it out of the social contract was an act of incalculable violence with serious consequences.[13]

After Jefferson's departure, the New Yorker was the only figure in France with practical experience in constructing and organizing a constitutional government. He was regularly asked for advice and he did not hesitate to give it. Nor was he as dogmatic as his critics claimed. In a letter to Jefferson supporting the administration's independent policy toward Britain, he admitted that among those who considered the subject, "there must be a variety of opinions, because dispositions Differ, because Prejudices exist, because Interests sway, in a Word, because Men are Men." The same balanced, considered judgment informs his critical assessment of the French Revolution.[14]

In summer 1791, when it appeared that after two years the Assembly would finally produce a constitution for the king to accept, Montmorin, still foreign minister, asked Morris for his opinion of it. In the form of a proposed speech to be delivered by the king when he was asked to uphold it, Morris laid out a detailed critique, recommending that Louis qualify his acceptance of the constitution by spelling out its fatal flaws as a condition of agreeing to it, particularly the internal discrepancies between the inflated "Rights" of the people and the provisions that followed. Louis could later throw it out when it failed. "Let the people become disgusted with the novelties of which they are so fond," Morris had earlier advised the queen. "Time changes everything...tranquility will be in its turn the object most earnestly desired."[15]

Speaking for the king, Morris used the opening lines of the speech, as in any good theater, to set the stage. Adèle de Flahaut, who was now a *dame d'honneur* to the queen because others were afraid to accept any post in the captive court, helped him with the translation. "It is no longer your King who addresses you. Louis the Sixteenth is only a private individual. You have just offered him the crown, and informed him on what conditions he must accept it." Then the New Yorker in the king's words, applying his own powerful scalpel, proceeds to lay the document open, to expose its defects, beginning with the opening Declaration of the Rights of Man. The Declaration's contradictions at the outset, followed by the constitution, were apparent. If "*men are born and exist free and equal in rights,*" then any subsequent limits on those rights, such as voting qualifications, taxation, and governmental participation, set out in the body of the constitution posed a conflict that would paralyze the government. At this point in the crisis, a bold move by the king, backed by capable ministers, which he still had the power to appoint, and military leaders, could reorganize the government and steer the course of events away from disaster. With little confidence in the outcome, Morris saw it as a last-ditch effort by the king to hold on to his dwindling "reserves of symbolic and moral capital." For the king's vacillating advisers, Morris's scheme implied a brazen tactical cynicism they could not swallow. But the king himself, in reflecting on the constitution after he had signed it, seems to have accepted, at least in spirit (and after it was far too late), the New Yorker's recommendations that complemented the king's detached "don't blame me" posture.[16]

John Hardman, biographer of Louis XVI, has, like Morris, concluded, that the constitutional provisions were either "too general to be applicable or too topical to endure." The lack of checks and balances and the power of the legislature placed both the judiciary and the executive under its control. If, as Morris argued, a faction took over the legislature for its own "dangerous designs," there was no mechanism by which the executive could appeal directly to the people. Morris believed that the legislative assembly remained the ultimate master of the state, even though the king still had a limited veto and the power to appoint ministers. To Morris, the inevitable tyranny of the legislature was even worse than the old Continental Congress in which the states could at least exercise a veto over congressional despotism, which, of course, created its own insurmountable problems. It reminded him of the benighted state of Pennsylvania, a "republic with no real government." "Where there is no authority," he told the king, "there can be no accountability, Where the executive power is feeble, anarchy must ensue and where anarchy long prevails, despotism must succeed," warning with grim prescience, that "the descendants of your ancient Kings...will probably be the earliest victims."[17]

It did not take long for Morris's criticism of the constitution to reach the press. Identifying "Monsieur Morris" as "an American who participated in the famous Philadelphia Convention," on October 4, 1791, the *Gazette Universelle* commented that the New Yorker's reflections on the constitution "exude the intolerable aristocracy." It went on to note that he might even have the "vain insolence" to express his views to the king. William Short, of course, lost no time in sending the article on to Jefferson in his effort to derail Morris's appointment as the American minister. This publicity continued to color the New Yorker's reputation, even after the fall of the monarchy, and was later used by the French government to demand his recall.[18]

On January 28, 1792, George Washington sent a private letter to his friend to accompany the official communications, signed five days earlier by the secretary of state, naming Morris minister plenipotentiary to the French Court. Washington told Morris that both the nomination and appointment had been made with "*all my heart*," but the Senate's "*advice and consent*," an untested concept, had been another matter. The president laid out with stark candor the arguments advanced by his enemies in their attempt to defeat Morris. He not only had been accused of "levity, and imprudence" in conversation and conduct but had shown "a hauteaur disgusting to those who happen to differ from you in sentiment." The president then went on to say that there were those in France who believed the New Yorker to have shown himself by his associations in favor of the old order and "unfriendly to its revolution," making him unfit to promote the interests of the United States.

Without revealing his source as the secretary of the treasury, Washington spelled out in general terms Hamilton's accusations that it was Morris's fault that the British had not agreed to a commercial treaty. The wily New York senator Aaron Burr, for his own purposes, appropriated Hamilton's charges on the floor of the Senate during the confirmation debate. "I merely state a fact. It has been asserted and without any injunction of secrecy, that Mr. Morris conducted himself so offensively in his intercourse with the Eng. Ministers, that they were offended & refused, after an abrupt breaking up of an interview, to renew it."[19]

Madison's fine hand—he was also a rumored candidate—can be detected in the criticism Washington repeated of Morris's "sallies...and of that ridicule of characters which begets enmity." The naive little Virginian was still smarting from some of Morris's "sallies" in Philadelphia. The president closed by saying that it was a proof of his personal friendship and confidence that he was laying out the charges so that if any of them was accurate, Morris would have an opportunity "to effect a change" in order to silence his enemies.[20]

That such an opinionated man as Morris had drawn both political and personal fire is hardly surprising. He had never had difficulty collecting adversaries, many of whom, like Hamilton and Short remained covert. Morris was well aware that his conversational indiscretions and his inability to resist a bon mot could cause trouble. "In conversing about public Men and Measures," he candidly admitted to himself, "I am so weak and absurd as to express many Opinions which I ought to conceal and some of which I perhaps find reason to alter." Morris's reply to the president's stern lecture was contrite: "I *now promise you* that Circumspection of Conduct which has hitherto I acknowledge form'd no Part of my Character. And I make the *Promise* that my Sense of Integrity may enforce what my Sense of Propriety dictates." He also asked that he be able to "communicate to you many Things which I should willingly entrust to others," meaning the secretary of state. Washington readily agreed to this private arrangement. Morris also set up a similar private channel with Hamilton, even before he received official word of his nomination.[21]

The bombardment of attacks on Morris's appointment from Short and others further undermined Jefferson's opinion of Morris. They reinforced the secretary's growing belief that Morris's candid letters had planted skepticism about the French Revolution in the mind of Washington. In spring 1792, the secretary met with Washington to discuss sending a warm presidential letter to Louis XVI to congratulate him on the new constitution. To Jefferson's surprise, the president cautioned him to avoid in the draft "saying a word in approbation of the constitution, not knowing whether the king approved of it or not." Jefferson then notes Washington's next stunning words: "Why in deed says he [Washington] I begin to doubt very much of the affairs of France." In his memorandum recording the conversation, the secretary concludes that Washington's "want of confidence" in the Revolution was due to Morris's deliberate bias in his letters. "The fact is that Gouverneur Morris, a high-flying Monarchy-man, shutting his eyes and his faith to every fact against his wishes, and believing every thing he desires to be true, has kept the President's mind constantly poisoned with his forebodings." James Monroe had used the same words, "monarchy-man," when he also weighed in against Morris's nomination in the Senate. Monroe told St. George Tucker that he was against Morris because "his manners were not conciliatory and his general moral character wh. precluded all possibility of confidence in his morals... his known attachment to monarchic govt. & contempt of the Republicans." Worst of all, Monroe sniffed, "He went to Europe to sell lands and Certificates."

Roger Sherman, who was the kind of self-righteous Connecticut Yankee Gouverneur's father loathed, also attacked Morris's moral character, charging that he was "an irreligious and profane man—he is no hypocrite and never pretended to have any religion." As a Philadelphia delegate, Sherman was among those who had not been amused by the New Yorker's humor in the Convention. "He makes religion the subject of ridicule and is profane in his conversation," warning that it was wrong "to promote such characters."[22]

When Lafayette heard of Morris's appointment, he wrote Washington that the New Yorker's "aristocratic, and indeed counter revolutionary principles" made him ideologically unsuited for the job. "I cannot help wishing," he told the president, "the American and French principles were in the heart and on the lips of the American ambassador to France." By the time Washington received Lafayette's letter, the general had been arrested while trying to escape from France.[23]

No one would dispute that Morris's American version of urbane manners would set well with the rising *sans-culottes* of Paris. Degree was instinctive with him from the capitalized nouns in his letters to proper enunciation, so to some his nature seemed condescending or as Washington put it, "imperious." Nor was Morris's imperiously beaked nose reassuring to the less confident. The Virginians—Madison, Short, and Monroe—had also libeled Morris for being "in trade." The subtext of the charge was that his attacks on slavery in the Constitutional Convention still rankled the Virginia Junto.[24]

It was, of course, Jefferson who resolutely closed his eyes to "every fact" contained in Morris's firsthand reports detailing the violence that would engulf France and destroy many of his friends. He refused to acknowledge the account of the murder of his friend the gentle duc de La Rochefoucauld, written by his widow, and when Short gave him graphic accounts of wholesale massacres, "too horrid and disgusting to behold," the secretary of state was livid. He told Short that he, too, was exaggerating the savagery. "The liberty of the whole earth," he chillingly told Short, "was depending on the issue of the contest, and was ever such a prize won with so little blood? My own affections," he went on, "have been deeply wounded by some of the martyrs to this cause but rather than it should have failed, I would have seen half the earth desolated." Then in the words of a fanatic, he famously adds, "Were there only an Adam and an Eve left in every country, and left free, it would be better than it now is." Laid against the compassion repeatedly expressed by Morris throughout the Revolution, no words more unmistakably separate politics, ideologies, and, indeed, the inner character of the two men.[25]

Morris was on a business trip in London on April 6, 1792, when he received his credentials to the Court of France. But that ancient institution of the court had not existed for nearly a year. After its capture and humiliating return to Paris from Varennes in July of 1791, the abject royal family had been held under house arrest in the old Tuileries palace, ending all pretense of constituted monarchy.

In his official letter, Jefferson made clear that the improvement of commerce between the two countries was to be the New Yorker's principle mission. The secretary advised the new minister to avoid any expression that would either please or offend the French government. If any such expression was unavoidable, "they would naturally be in conformity with the great mass of our countrymen, who having first, in modern times, taken the ground of Government founded on the will of the people, cannot but be delighted on seeing so distinguished and so esteemed a Nation arrive on the same ground, and plant their standard by our side." Jefferson may have tried obliquely to justify his own deep ideological entanglement with French politics and policy while serving as minister, suggesting that it was "in conformity" with the American public opinion. In his reply, Morris urged the secretary to write regularly on developments in the United States that might affect his mission. "Changes are now so frequent, and Events seem fast ripening to such awful Catastrophe, that no Expressions on the Subject, however moderate, would be received with Indifference."[26]

The American government's slow communication with its representatives had been a problem from the beginning, drawing regular complaints from its diplomats. In his letters of thanks for their support to well-placed friends like Oliver Ellsworth, Rufus King, and Hamilton, Morris urged them to promptly send him their frank, private views. "Intelligence Opinions *Advise*" was essential because "a Minister who knows not those Affairs of his Country which are known to many others is placed in an Awkward Situation; besides there is always a kind of Traffic in Articles of Intelligence among Members of the diplomatic Body in which Beads and Wampum are sometimes given for Gold to the satisfaction of both Parties."[27]

The New Yorker knew that he had been thrown into a hopeless predicament. "To stand *well* with both Parties is impossible," he told Robert Morris. And if he had "consulted only my feelings and my own Interest I should certainly not accept it." As for the shots fired at him in the Senate, Gouverneur told his brother-in-law Samuel Ogden that he would "fairly stand forth and challenge the World to produce a single Instance of mean or cruel or dishonest or dishonorable Conduct." When one of the first attacks was made by Aaron Burr, Morris said nothing at the time but, as his revenge, coolly opposed Burr in the presidential showdown in 1801.[28]

Before Morris's fitness as minister had been questioned in Paris or New York, the astonishing transformation of an ancient ceremonial society into a radical new political state appeared to be a consummated miracle on September 18, 1791. On that day, Gouverneur and Adèle, dining at her apartment, saw a hot-air balloon trailing tricolor ribbons float lazily over the roof of the Louvre. The balloon and the illumination of the Tuileries later that evening signaled the king's formal acceptance of the constitution. Four days earlier, Louis had sworn in the Constituent Assembly, as the king of the French, "to maintain it at home and defend it against attacks from abroad and to use all the means which it places in my power to execute it faithfully." The extreme monarchists claimed his act was invalid because it had been signed under duress. For their part, the political left believed that it was defective because the king had not acted in good faith. Neither side would agree to maintain royal authority under the constitution in the name of the nation.

While an aura of unreality hung over the government and the imprisoned court as the fall of 1791 stretched into winter, Morris continued to express his gloomy opinions. From the beginning, the republican wing, the Girodins, led by Jacques-Pierre Brissot, Jérôme Pétion, and Pierre Vergniaud, pushed for a showdown with the king by marginalizing his authority, introducing harsh legislation against émigrés, and promoting war with Leopold, the emperor of Austria and brother of the queen. When Morris was asked at a party near the beginning of the new year to cast a horoscope for France, he answered "that it might be done in three words *Guerre, Famine, Peste.*"

By fall 1791, the Revolution had moved well down the road to war with Austria and possibly Britain. After the king accepted the constitution, the Constituent Assembly was dissolved and was replaced by the Legislative Assembly. Both the Girondists and Jacobins then began an attempt to replace the monarchy with a republic launched by a patriotic war against outsiders that to many sounded like the popular efforts of the American Revolution. In December, fifty thousand French troops were ordered to the frontiers to confront the anticipated Austrian and Prussian forces. Morris's regular predictions to Washington that had "appeared like the wanderings of exaggerated fantasy" now seemed "within the coldest limits of truth." Still, even the remote possibility of a reenergized monarchy, he confessed to the president, seemed the only alternative to civil war.

During the "fatal commotions" in the dark December days of the Paris winter, the New Yorker sketched out his own private concept of a constitution for France, a government centered on the king. The powers of the executive, legislative, and judiciary branches reflected the accumulated traditions that had evolved in French government over the centuries, including the preservation of the hereditary monarchy. Morris saw his plan merely as an essential stepping stone of order and stability, an interim move to a more enlightened arrangement, established later in a calmer and more reflective atmosphere. But the thrust of the document lacks Morris's usual pragmatism and seems more of a willful effort to reinforce his own rational sanity in a world increasingly unhinged, cut loose from all civil moorings. He knew that there was no way that his words could be translated into an operating regime, and they remained an undebated and untested experiment, buried among his papers.[29]

In January 1792, the Assembly issued a stiff ultimatum to the Austrian emperor demanding that he declare before March 1 whether he would stay out of the European alliance being organized against France. What was not known in Paris was that Austria and Prussia, historic enemies, had already made plans for a military partnership in February to intervene in France. Morris's foreboding was once again on target. Talleyrand, too, was accurate when he told Morris that French belligerence was because "the Nation is *une parvenue* and of Course insolent." He said that "their Situation is such that Nothing but violent Remedies can operate and these must either kill or cure."[30]

Pale and ill at ease, the king stood before the Assembly on April 20 and read in a faltering voice the declaration of war against the king of Austria. Armed conflict, which all sides wanted and Talleyrand predicted, would destroy the very basis of the constitutional monarchy. Or, as Morris put it, while "a great Part of the Nation is desirous of overturning the Government in order to restore its antient Form," another part is "desirous of introducing the Form of a federal Republic"; the moderates caught in the middle "contend alone against an immense Force," scuttling "the finest Opportunity which ever presented itself for establishing the Rights of Mankind throughout the civilized World."[31]

During the nearly three years Morris served as minister, the tumultuous French government, at war with its neighbors and at war with itself, appointed no fewer than seven different ministers of foreign affairs. With typical irreverence Morris called it "the electrical Chairs of office kicking Breeches." Three died on the guillotine, four were condemned as traitors, one of whom fled to Austria for asylum. These convulsions made the American envoy's job all but impossible.

The newly appointed minister arrived back in Paris following his business trip to London on May 6, 1792, in the middle of rumors from the frontiers that France was about to be invaded. After he and his friend celebrated his return, Adèle asked his permission and blessing to join Talleyrand in London where he had gone to wait out the storm. Taken aback, he replied that she could go if she liked but his approval was impossible. The following day the two went shopping for a ministerial residence to rent, eventually selecting one at 488 rue de La Planche in the smart Faubourg Saint-Germain. Morris had bought a proper coach in London, ordering a set of bespoken harness to complete the stylish turnout. Plate was also purchased at the London auction of the effects of his late friend the marquis de La Luzerne who had died not long after Morris heard that he had been nominated minister but before he was actually confirmed. He also purchased the late ambassador's "Orders of the Cincinnati" out of respect for the society. Like Jefferson and Washington, Morris believed that these outward signs of distinction, the correct equipage and tableware, was important in maintaining ministerial dignity, the honor of the republic.[32]

The couple returned to the Manufacture of Angoulême to order some porcelain, the same factory where they had earlier selected table ornaments for Washington. The day before Morris was to meet the foreign minister, Charles-

François Dumouriez, on May 15, they selected more plate from a goldsmith. But for all of this domestic activity and with regular sacrifices "on the Cyprian Altar," there were growing spats and scenes as the affair gradually cooled.

At his first meeting with Dumouriez, Morris asked to be presented to the king without a sword at his official audience because of his wooden leg. Dumouriez replied this would be no problem because he already knew the king, but the New Yorker assured the minister that he had only seen him briefly on public occasions and had not been presented. While he had indeed hoped for some changes to the constitution in support of the king, "essential to its' Existence," he had failed. Now as "a Public Man," he added, "I consider it my Duty not to meddle with their Affairs." It would be impossible for Morris to keep his word, particularly to Dumouriez. The king fired him a month later, on June 16, just two days after Morris had enjoyed a pleasant dinner with him at Adèle's apartment. Earlier in June the New Yorker had been invited to dinner at the minister's house, and Morris's keen eye noticed a telltale deterioration in ministerial entertaining, to him a bad sign of deeper disorders in the ministry. "The Society is noisy and in bad style. The Dinner is still Worse." Dumouriez assured Morris that there was "no Danger to the constitution at present, that it will triumph over every Obstacle and must amend itself." "I think," Morris recorded in his diary, "I cannot believe one Half of what he says."[33]

Six days before Dumouriez was dismissed Morris gave Jefferson a full report on the state of things and told him that his presentation at court had been postponed because of the alarming chaos in Paris. The "best picture I can give of the french Nation," he confesses, "is that of Cattle before a Thunder Storm." After most of the king's ministers resigned on the sixteenth, Morris updated Jefferson: "we now stand on a Volcano, we feel it tremble and we hear it roar but how and when and where it will burst and who may be destroy'd by its Eruptions is beyond the Ken of mortal Foresight to discover." He correctly told Jefferson that the outcome would depend on immediate military force, but since it also depended on Lafayette to act, "the precious moment will be suffered to pass away."[34]

During the summer of 1792, a number of plots to rescue the royal family were hatched. Morris's composed, affable manners, as well as his official position, carefully disguised his role. In late June Morris reflected "on the state of things" after a visit with the ex-minister Montmorin, still a close adviser to the king. They had been joined by two moderate politicians, Mallouette and Bertrand de Moleville. The New Yorker's account of what was said is guarded, but it has a strong conspiratorial tone: "in order to see what Stuff they are made of I tell them what Measures would put an End to all Troubles; but these Measures are deep and dangerous and when we go into Mr. de Montmorin's closet he sickens." Montmorin's unhappy involvement in the abortive flight to Varennes made him resist another rescue attempt. Moleville, also a close adviser to the king, however, had more than one plan to get the king out, and he took Morris into his confidence. Two days later, the plot thickened when Morris met with Terrier de Monciel, minister of the interior, to discuss the use of Lafayette in bringing off "the *Sortie* of the King." Morris believed that this "Part of the Plan is the most reasonable." The following day Morris met Lafayette briefly and in "the Ton of antient Familiarity" told the general that unless he fights "for a good Constitution," in six weeks it will be too late. Later, Morris sent a note to Monciel, now his fellow conspirator, insisting that the king make a decision. The plan was to bring the king out during routine troop movements of Lafayette's Army of the Rhine and Luckner's Army of Flanders on July 15 and for him to travel to Compiègne near Paris while Lafayette and Luckner went to Paris and distracted the Assembly. But in the confusion of conflicting advice and uncertainties, the royal family was divided and the plot collapsed. The king himself was immobilized and in Morris's opinion displayed "an uncommon firmness in suffering," adding that he believed he did not have "the Talents for Action." In the end it was the queen who had to tell Lafayette that his scheme would not work.[35]

The king was to make his final decision on July 10. Morris signaled Jefferson he expected that "this Day the King will commence a new Career." But the next morning he ruefully admitted that "their Majesties flash'd in the Pan." The ministers compromised in the escape plot had no choice but to resign. In spite of Morris's oblique message to the secretary of state, he was hardly surprised. "I think there is a Want of Mettle," he admitted in his diary, "which will prevent them from being truly royal."

Near the end of July, the king sent his thanks to Morris for the advice he had given him and his regrets for not having followed it. Then in an extraordinary endorsement of confidence, Louis asked the New Yorker to "supervise what was being done in his service and to become the guardian of his papers and his money." On July 22, Monciel gave Morris 547,000 livres of the king's money. Some of this money was later used to finance yet another, even more desperate, attempt to rescue the king "from his perilous situation," this time taking him to Rouen. Morris had taken precaution and secured a passport "for the Interior of the Kingdom." The implication of this step and its timing suggest that Morris intended to follow the king when he escaped. But again, the queen vetoed the plans. August 9 would be the last full day of the monarchy. That day Morris received from Monciel another delivery of money from the king. In the evening he spent what would be his last "happy moment" with his friend in the Louvre. Later he closed his diary entry: "Paris is in great Agitation."[36]

On the blistering hot morning of August 10, the storm finally broke over Paris. An attack on the Tuileries forced the royal family to take refuge in the hall of the Assembly. Morris heard the cannon and musketry as the Swiss Guard, whose orders to defend the king had not been countermanded, briefly stood off the attackers. By the time Louis belatedly sent word to stop firing, the Guard had been butchered in the palace. Morris tersely noted: "the King & Queen are in the National Assembly who have decreed the Suspension of his Authority." Not officially deposed, the king's fate would be settled later by a new assembly. That evening, Adèle and her son fled from the Louvre and took refuge in Morris's house in the rue de La Planche.

With the city at the mercy of the mob, others crowded into the envoy's house for protection. Throughout those terrible August days the New Yorker insisted on maintaining his routine of serving dinner to guests, a defiant sign of civility and courage in the middle of an imploding world. One refugee was an American visitor who had watched the sack of the Tuileries. As the American visitor left after an oppressive, sleepless night, Morris took him aside and admitted that he would be criticized by the revolutionary government for protecting his uninvited company. "Whether my house will be a protection to them or to me, God only knows; but I will not turn them out of it, let what will happen to me; you see sir, they are all persons to whom our country is more or less indebted, and had they no such claim on me, it would be inhuman to force them into the hands of the assassins."[37]

At six o'clock in the evening on August 13, the bedraggled royal family was driven through a sullen, menacing crowd to the Temple, once the grim headquarters of the Knights Templar. When the party reached the Temple, representatives of the city of Paris, without removing their hats, addressed the king as "monsieur." It was in fact the city council that had forced the Assembly to move the captives to the Temple. That same day, Morris wrote one more metaphoric passage trying to capture the shocking events in words: "a ship badly ballasted has overset. Experienced Seamen knew that it must happen, before she went out of Port. The fresh Water Sailors by whom she was fitted and equipt are many of the drown'd and more of them will be drown'd. They would not be advised and they pay for their Presumption."[38]

The attack on the Tuileries on August 10 had announced a second revolution. Morris lost no time spelling out the possibility of a bloodbath to Jefferson. He also told the secretary that all would depend on the army under Lafayette's command but, once again, concluded that he would allow "the precious moment" to pass away. The victors of the insurrection moved quickly to establish their dictatorship. A seething populace was now stirred up to take vengeance. Marat, "the people's friend," who had been calling for the slaughter of the aristocracy en masse found a ready army in the streets to begin the First Terror. The blood-letting quickly spread to the countryside and did not stop until it, too, was purged.[39]

In an attempt to consolidate their gains and their control of the government, leaders in the Assembly opposed to all compromise called for the election of a National Convention. By law and by fact the convention, meeting for the first time on September 20, 1792, was invested with dictatorial powers as Morris had repeatedly predicted. The legislature, with its power concentrated in a single, unruly chamber was, in Morris's words, "under no Control except Maxims and Popular opinions." It could do what it pleased without the restraint of a solid constitution or a system of government, a prescription for disaster.[40]

Within days, members of the diplomatic corps who had not already left were scrambling for passports. Morris's friends the British ambassador and his wife, Lord and Lady Sutherland, had been ordered back to London. The Venetian ambassador already on his way to safety was brought back to the city and roughed up. After repeated late night searches of his own house, Morris himself thought of departing not from fear but "to shew Resentment." However, when Washington named him to the embassy, "it was not," he told Jefferson, "for my personal pleasure or safety but to promote the interest of my country."[41]

With the National Convention's declaration of a republic "one and indivisible" on September 21, the Court of France to which Morris was appointed was abolished, leaving him in a dangerous quandary, to stay or go. When local vigilantes broke into his house looking for arms, he firmly ordered them out but with impressive poise. He was careful not to take offense "by what is done by the people, because they cannot be supposed to understand the Law of Nations and because they are in a State of fury which is inconceivable and which leaves them liable to all Impressions and renders them capable of all Excesses."

Deserted by the rest of the diplomatic corps and with no instructions from his own government, Morris had to break new ground in American foreign policy. "Going hence" he told Jefferson, "would look like taking Part against the late Revolution and I am not only unauthoriz'd in this Respect but I am bound to suppose that if the great Majority of the Nation adhere to the new Form the United States will approve thereof because in the first Place we have no Right to prescribe to this Country the Government they shall adopt and next because the Basis of our Constitution is the indefeasible Right of the People to establish it."[42]

Still trying to make some diplomatic and political sense of the country's convulsions, while sparring with the new masters, Morris told Hamilton the ship of state had overturned because it was "all Sail and no Ballast.... Some Gentlemen who considered it as the Achmé of human Wisdom must I suppose find out Causes which Persons on the Spot never dreamed of, But in seeking or inventing these Causes what will be their Opinion of present Powers what the Conduct they wish to pursue. These are to me important Questions.... The Flight of Monsieur de la fayette the murder of the Duc de la Rochefoucauld and others with many similar Circumstances have, I know, affected the Ideas of some. But what will be the republican Sense of the new Republic?"[43]

When Lafayette fled towards Holland with plans to catch a boat for America on August 19, Morris, with caustic irony, told the general's friend Jef-

Unloading Victims after a Revolutionary Journée by Étienne Béricourt.
© Photothèque des musées de la ville de Paris (ou PMVP)/Cliché: LADET.

ferson that he had lasted longer than he expected. His aborted escape was triggered by the mass arrests in Paris and throughout the country. Three thousand suspects were rounded up and thrown into the already crowded jails of the capital. With the Prussian advance and the threat of an enemy at the gates, hysteria swept through the streets, fed by Danton and his henchmen. On September 2, the mobs began breaking into the prisons and for the next five days, carrying out the wholesale slaughter of their inmates. Montmorin perished, as did the queen's close friend the princesse de Lambelle, sister-in-law of the duchesse d'Orléans. Her corpse and severed head were taken to the Temple so that the king and queen could view the mob's ghastly handiwork. Morris did not spare Jefferson the unspeakable details, "she was beheaded and embowelled, the Head and Entrails were paraded on Pikes thro the Street and the body dragged after them."[44]

At noon on September 5, crowds gathered in front of the Hôtel de Ville, headquarters of the Paris Commune. They were preparing to march on the Convention, then meeting in the Tuileries palace, to demand the organization of a people's army to secure provisions while establishing the egalitarian principles of the Revolution. Suddenly, as if on signal, the city turned ominously dark. It was only an eclipse, but there were those who saw the darkness as a sign of what lay ahead. After the tumultuous meetings with the Convention, a renewed resolution seemed to grip both the people and their leaders. Marat proclaimed that the only way to save the Revolution for "the people" was by the elimination of its enemies. The Reign of Terror had begun.

Morris's intimate circle was already disappearing in the maelstrom, not all by the blade or garrote. Talleyrand made it safely to London in September. Adèle and her son also found safety there in a "little lodging in Half Moon Street," using forged passports Morris probably supplied. Lord Wycombe paid for her London apartment. As soon as she was settled, she resumed her work on her novel *Cècil de Senage*. With time on his hands, the bishop, stopped by regularly and helped her correct her proofs. Madame de Staël fled to Switzerland after helping the comte de Narbonne, the former minister of war who had replace Talleyrand as her official lover, to hide.

Even in the face of all the horrors committed in the name of liberty, in late October Morris managed to give Jefferson another measured report, although he could not predict whether authority could an be reestablished after so much devastation. Throughout the fall of 1792 the new envoy was increasingly annoyed by the delay in receiving instructions from his government. This breakdown in communication at a moment of civil anarchy left him in a dangerous, equivocal spot with the new and suspicious French leadership. Through no fault of his own, the failure of the American government to respond to his alarming narratives would have personal repercussions for him later in Philadelphia.

Beginning in fall 1792 and continuing into 1793, French military forces scored some important victories over the allies but failed to restore stability. "Tis true," Morris wrote Carmichael, "that the french Arms are crowned with great success. Towns fall before them without a blow, and the Declaration of Rights produces an effect equal at least to the trumpets of Joshua." But, he continued, "as, on the one hand, I never questioned the force of France if united, and her natural enthusiasm, warmed by the ardor of new-born freedom, so, on the other, I was always apprehensive that they would be deficient in that cool reflection which appears needful to consolidate a free government." There was no cool reflection in the voice of Tom Paine, who had gotten himself elected a "*Membre de la Convention nationale*" and unsurprisingly, Morris reported to Pinckney, had loudly called for the abolition of the monarchy.[45]

On January 25, 1793, with his unfailing compassion, Morris reported to Jefferson that the king had been executed and had "died in a Manner becoming his Dignity." His last words, Morris added, were deliberately cut off by the roll of drums, his neck mangled by the excited executioners. Morris's letter, a month earlier, describing the king's trial, however, did not conform to the secretary's settled image of a despot he had already decided was guilty. "It would seem strange," Morris wrote, "that the mildest monarch who ever fill'd the french Throne, one who is precipitated from it precisely because he would not adopt the harsh Measures of his Predecessors, a Man whom none can charge with a Criminal or cruel Act, should be prosecuted as one of the most nefarious Tyrants that ever disgraced the Annuls of human nature." Morris told Hamilton that the king's only crime was "of not suffering his throat to be cut." To the émigré the comtesse d'Albani he correctly predicted that the assembly's death sentence was only "the forerunner of their own destruction."[46]

Jefferson could hardly contain his satisfaction when he got the news of the king's death, writing a friend that "should the present ferment in Europe not produce republics everywhere, it will at least soften the monarchical governments by rendering monarchs amenable to punishment like other criminals, and doing away with oppression, the inviolability of the king's person." The Virginian conveniently ignored the fact that Louis XVI and his government had been the decisive benefactor of the American Revolution. The king was, Morris told the secretary of state, the victim of a "sanguinary proceeding apparently unnecessary and unauthorized by that Constitution which till his dethronement (since which he is accused of no crime) was by the Nation established as the Rule of conduct."[47]

When the Convention declared war on England and Holland on February 1, 1793, a week after the king's execution, Morris's headaches intensified. Both countries stepped up their interception and seizure of American commercial ships. Within a few months French ports were filled with captured ships along with their crews. In June, the Convention placed an embargo on the rebellious port of Bordeaux, and ninety-two American ships were trapped in the harbor. The American captains, of course, were outraged, but there was little that Morris could do to rescue them. With the help of Citizen Paine, they presented a petition to the Convention and sent word back to Philadelphia that Morris was negligent or, worse, indifferent to their plight. Writing to the American consul at Bordeaux, the New Yorker did not dissemble, which was cold comfort to the American hostages. "Those who come to a country torn by the Paroxisms of Revolution must calculate on the inconveniences attending such a State of Society. If they come in the Character of Spectators they must be as the other Cases gratify their Curiosity at the Risque which attends it. If they come in the Character of Merchants they must set the probable Gain against the probable Loss and if they have made a bad Calculation, they must be content, and try new Plans."[48]

After being arrested and briefly detained in spring 1793, "because I had not a Carte de Citoyen," Morris decided it was time to move from the center of action, hoping "to avoid those Accidents which are almost inseparable from the present State of Society and Government and which should they light on the Head of a public Minister might involve Consequences of a disagreeable Nature." "Republican Virtues," he confessed to Jefferson, were "not yet of gallic growth." He bought a "little Country Box" on the riverside in the sleepy rural village of Seine-Port, remaining there until fall 1794 when he was recalled.[49]

The strain of the past few months momentarily wore off in his rural asylum, where he spent time reading, writing, and gardening, while managing his ministerial duties with regular trips to the city. "If Peace were restor'd" he told his brother Staats, "I would press you to enjoy a french Air on the Banks of the Seine in my Hermitage where you would be in the Neighborhood of many Objects worth riding to look at if only to gain Appetite for a Bottle of good Claret and a slice of small Mutton."

For all of his city tastes, beneath the polish in the New Yorker's makeup was the genetic strain of a country man. This is apparent in the natural way he settled into the routines of his comfortable rural estate, anticipating his "retirement" at Morrisania when he returned from Europe. "At this moment, I look out of my window and see the pear and plum trees in full bloom," he reported to Robert Morris in spring 1794. "The peaches and apricots and almonds are already formed. The apple trees are advanced. We have had hardly any winter.... This is the best farming country I ever saw, taking it all in all; but it is badly cultivated. Our country is capable of producing much better fruits, and with far greater certainty."[50]

He claimed that his new country house was "humble," not a "chateau" but with additions it had evolved from a modest seventeenth-century beginning into an elegant and substantial establishment. He had no problem furnishing its rooms with the impressive collection he had quickly assembled from the revolutionary fire sales now taking place in Paris and Versailles. Like Jefferson, Morris had an eye for luxury, surrounding himself with superb furniture, porcelain, and silver, finding in their acquisition a genuine aesthetic pleasure. In Paris, collecting also offered an escape from the mounting tensions that encircled him and his friends. His eye was impeccable. Nor did he bother to apologize for or attempt to hide this sensual side of his makeup under what a Hamilton partisan called Jefferson's "cloak of humility...a flimsy veil to the *internal* evidences of aristocratic splendor, sensuality and Epicureanism."[51]

With a house in the rue de La Planche and one in the country, Morris could indulge his taste on a generous scale. When the revolutionary government ordered the sale of the contents of Versailles, the furnishings of "the last tyrants of France," the minister of the American republic bought at bargain prices some of the finest pieces of royal furniture and silver to add to his growing collection. His Versailles purchases included part of the suite designed for Marie Antoinette's private apartment in 1779. On the eve of his departure from France in fall 1794, he reported to his successor James Monroe that the plate he was shipping from Seine-Port alone weighed thirteen hundred and sixty-two marks along with twenty-seven marks of vermeil he valued at one thousand louis. When he sent his library, plate, royal furniture, and carriages to Morrisania in October 1794, on the ship *Superb,* he instructed his overseer to take special care of the liquor and wine. In the shipment were several cases

Morris's house outside Paris at Seine-Port, photographed by Adelaide de Menil.

of Imperial Tokay sealed in wax with the double-headed eagle of Austria. It had been a wedding present of Maria-Theresa to her daughter, the future queen of France, in 1770.[52]

Throughout the summer and the fall of 1793, the Revolution had veered further off course, racing wildly out of control. With the fall of Danton "at the feet of Robespierre," the slaughtering in the Place Louis XV, renamed the Place de la Révolution, picked up speed. Even Samson, the chief executioner, complained of overwork and demanded more pay. There were now, Morris noted dryly, "abundant Executions at Paris and the Guillotine goes on smartly." In October the queen followed her husband to the scaffold. "Insulted during her trial and reviled," Morris wrote to Washington, "in her last moments, she behaved with dignity throughout." To his dying day, Jefferson believed that it was Marie Antoinette who had "plunged the world into crimes & calamities." If there had been no queen, there would have been no French Revolution. By this reckoning, he might well have added Marie Antoinette to his cabinet of worthies at Monticello.

To Short in The Hague, Morris confessed that "Providence alone (who directs the Affairs of Men) can determine in what Way this One is to operate. In the mean Time we stretch in vain our Idle Vision to pierce the Clouds which the Hurricane has blown together and which shut our political Horizon to a narrow Circle." The gale, now reaching full force, had accelerated earlier in July when Robespierre took charge of the Committee of Public Safety and the Police Bureau as its instrument. The government in his and the Committee's hands now claimed all power. Terror was the order of the day. Quite often Morris seemed unwilling to continue the terrible accounts, telling his correspondents like Jefferson, Washington, and Jay that they could read it all in the newspapers he enclosed. Only an occasional satirical image such as liberated Parisians dancing "the *carmagnole* in holy vestments" and "performing other mummeries" lighten his narrative of carnage.

With a religious fervor, a brutal attack on Christianity swept spontaneously through the country. Vandalism was carried out on a massive scale. The churches were stripped bare of all official icons and evidence of sacred worship. Donkeys, as well as *sans-culottes*, paraded through the streets grotesquely dressed in clerical robes. Morris reported to Hamilton that the Church had joined the nobility and bankers "in the crusible" of violence. The Catholic religion was "now expiring," he told Jefferson, "under wounds from the true French weapon, ridicule." But "the burning of Legs and Arms and Fingers of Saints Male and female with Relicks from the wood of the original cross to the paring of St. Anthony's Nail must," wryly adding his own gibe, "have the good effect of undeceiving those who imagined there were miraculous qualities inherent in those crumbling materials." To make the new religion official, the president of the Convention had actually knelt to the Goddess of Reason, a former opera star not known for her "*sage*" (chaste) qualities, who danced before the high altar in Notre Dame.[53]

Anticipating this anticlerical furor, Morris had reflected on the dangers of religious intolerance expressed in a letter from Lord George Gordon, Staats Long Morris's eccentric stepson. Gordon had enclosed a virulent anti-Catholic pamphlet, in keeping with his central role in the disastrous Gordon Riots against Catholics in London in 1780, which landed him in jail on charges of high treason. Skeptical of Gordon's motives, Morris replied that he could not "estimate the Operation of religious Sentiment on the political System" of England. "But I have liv'd to see a new Religion arise. It consists in a Denial of all Religion and its Votaries have the Superstition of not being superstitious. They have with this as much Zeal as any other Sect and as ready to lay waste the World in order to make Proselytes."[54]

The September Law of Suspects, in 1793, had flooded the Paris prisons with some seven thousand inmates. In this sweep, continuing into spring of 1794, the government's net brought in more of Morris's friends and acquaintances, some marked for jail, others for the guillotine. Tom Paine, who had become a French citizen and member of the Convention was thrown into the Luxembourg prison. Morris wrote Jefferson that Paine had amused himself in prison by writing "a pamphlet against Jesus Christ." This was to be Paine's savage attack on Christianity, *The Age of Reason*.

The Convention had decreed that all Englishmen living in France were to be arrested. Paine was born in England and no allowances were made. The paranoid Jacobin government was also afraid of Paine's open criticism of the government's increasing authoritarian policies. The desperate troublemaker turned to Morris for help even though he admitted that they had never been "on the best terms of harmony." But given that Paine had claimed French citizenship and in light of the fragile diplomatic relations between France and America, there was little the envoy could do beyond writing a diplomatic letter to the minister of foreign affairs.[55]

In Paris alone, more than 1,500 people perished during the first six weeks of the "Great Terror." On April 22, 1794, Morris' friend Chrétien-Guillaume Malesherbes, the distinguished statesman whom Morris admired for his "serene Gaiety...and good Heart," followed his two daughters and a son-in-law to the guillotine. On May 8, the brilliant amateur scientist Lavoisier joined other farmers-general to be sacrificed. Condorcet sidestepped the blade by taking his own life on March 19 after being trapped by his enemies. Madame de Lafayette, along with Morris's friends Madame Chastellux and the duchesse d'Orléans, was held prisoner in the Luxembourg. Morris immediately wrote an "unofficial" letter to the government warning that any harm to Madame de Lafayette would have international repercussions. She was later released.

The New Yorker confessed to Washington "that four years of convulsion, among four and twenty millions of people" had not produced a leader "whose head would fit the cap which fortune has woven." He actually found Robespierre in his ruthless objectives the most plausible candidate: "There is an imputation against him for corruption," he told the president, yet "he is far from rich, and still farther from appearing so. It is said that his idol is ambition; but I think that the establishment of the Republic would, all things considered, be most suitable to him."

It is a balanced judgment, and it is ironic that Morris's enemies in Philadelphia thought that he was far too sympathetic to the counterrevolutionaries to effectively represent the United States. Morris also understood the precarious balance of intimidation that existed between the Committee of Public Safety, the Committee of General Security, and the Convention itself. He saw that Robespierre did not have complete control of the government or the Terror. The committees were vying for control and as he predicted, they would eventually come to blows.[56]

In the middle of the continuing horror, Gouverneur reported to Robert Morris in April 1794, that the bursting promises of spring in Seine-Port were "a miracle of nature and the expected bumper crop might well turn the country's crisis around. Heaven seems to have decided in favor of the Republic against those who would by famine deprive her of freedom," he told his old friend. The guillotine, however, continued during the fine spring weather and had, in a few weeks, dispatched Danton and other popular leaders, placing the Committee of Public Safety under the control of Robespierre's faction. "Danton, when condemned, or shortly before it," Morris wrote, "told his judges that he had observed in reading history that men generally perished by the instruments of destruction which they themselves have created. 'I,' says he 'created the Tribunal Révolutionnaire by which I will be destroyed.'" Morris then quotes the chilling lines Macbeth spoke to predict his own death: "But in these cases we still have judgment here; that we but teach bloody instructions which being taught, return to plague the inventor: this even-handed justice commends the ingredients of our poisoned chalice to our own lips." Morris reflects that it is hard to know who will "drink out of the same cup," adding that "there is no want of liquor."[57]

From October 1793 to July 1794 the New Yorker received no instructions from Jefferson or anyone else in the government, a gap covering the most savage months of the Revolution. Without directions and with growing exasperation, he reminded Jefferson, in March 1794, that in the catastrophic upheavals "that vex this hemisphere, the opinion of the United States is the polar star, which should guide my course, but which," he added with veiled chagrin, "is totally concealed from my view." He closes an earlier letter with a swipe at the secretary's seeming indifference to the growing hardships of American citizens in France. "Happy they who contemplate them at a distance. A view of what our country men suffer in this respect so torments me, that it is very difficult to be patient."

On January 3, 1794, when he resigned as secretary, Jefferson turned all of Morris's accumulated letters dealing with these divisive issues over to his inexperienced, indecisive successor, Edmund Randolph. As the murderous French drama continued to unfold, Randolph wrote Morris, on April 29, a long, convoluted letter finally getting to the point: the French government had presented its request for the New Yorker's recall. The reasons were sparse but sufficient for Morris's superiors: "His principles, his liaisons, all his conduct reveals the sentiments which undoubtedly influence reports which he transmits to his constituents and we must fear that they serve to confirm hostile insinuations of the English, Spanish, and Dutch ministers in Philadelphia."[58]

When Randolph's letter arrived telling him he was to be replaced, Morris wrote to Short, "I of course thank God am quit." While he had heard reports of his recall earlier in March, he told Robert Morris that he was determined to continue to uphold "what I conceive to be the true interests of America, in spite of Faction and Calumny in either Hemisphere or in both; saving always my Obedience to the Instructions I received." Disregarding the damage that his frankness might do to his own reputation at home—"I know that the Language of flattering Hope would be more agreeable"—he was not willing to mislead his government or misrepresent his own judgment as some would do in more recent American conflicts. The record of his intelligence, courage, and honesty in the face of one of history's major political earthquakes remains with few counterparts in American diplomatic history.[59]

Randolph admitted to Morris that there was political pressure on the American side to replace him and that the Senate had earlier asked to review his official correspondence. He assured the New Yorker that the "result, I believe, was much to your reputation." The secretary did not tell him that it was an unfriendly Madison who had called for the review. Nor could Morris have known that in Jefferson's scathing attack on the French envoy, Edmond Charles Genet, that he had sent to Madison in July 1793, he claimed that with Morris in Paris, "we have no channel of our own" to make a complaint to the French government without appearing to criticize it, implying that Morris was unpopular and ineffective. The impossibility of dealing with the Convention's shifting, divided leadership somehow did not penetrate Jefferson's mind.

Jefferson's friend and neighbor James Monroe had made several attacks on Morris, both privately and in anonymous newspaper articles. Before he resigned, Jefferson added fuel to the fire by passing on to Washington reports of the French government's dissatisfaction with Morris, making it difficult for the president to resist the pressure to replace him. To complicate matters, Washington had at the same time appointed the Federalist John Jay, whose sentiments were perceived as pro-Whitehall, as minister to London. The results of his negotiations would be the Jay Treaty, an agreement that deeply offended France and almost produced a break in relations. The treaty increased the bitter rancor between the Federalists and Jeffersonians at home.[60]

The request to replace Morris had been triggered by Washington's indignant demand that the French minister, Genet, be recalled. In the face of American neutrality, the first envoy of the French Republic, inept and poorly informed, had, in short order, alienated Washington's government by promoting both commercial and military confrontations with Britain. Morris had warned the president that Genet was a bit of an "Upstart" and talked too much. When Morris later read Genet's accusations against him, he told Edmund Randolph they were unworthy of a reply "and the more so, as the falsity of some, and the folly of others are evident from facts in possession of your office, and from the style and nature of the complaints themselves."[61]

On July 29, 1794, four days after Robespierre and seventeen of his loyalists went to the rattling machine, surrounded by puddles of blood in the Place de la Révolution, James Monroe arrived in Paris as the new minister. To Morris he was "a person of mediocrity in every respect." A more naive, ill-equipped appointment for the French post could not be imagined. A number of the members of the National Convention that noisily embraced Monroe on his arrival at an elaborate ceremony had, in fact, taken an active part of bloodletting of the Terror in collaboration with Robespierre before turning on him.

In little more than a year after leaving France in the fall 1794 Morris saw that Napoleon's brilliant military campaigns were leading the country into the personal rule of one man, as he had predicted. A passage from a letter written in 1796 captures his political philosophy and the American experience, with implications that reach into the country's contemporary foreign policy. To him, the American Revolution, unique to its time and place, was an experiment that would take a long time and endless testing to prove.

> In effect Time is needful to bring forward Slaves to the Enjoyment of Liberty. Time. Time. Education. But what is Education? It is not Learning. It is more the Effect of Society on the Habits and Principles of each Individual, forming him at an early Period of Life to act afterwards the Part of a good Citizen and contribute in his Turn to the Formation of others. Hence it results that the Progress towards Freedom must be slow and can only be compleated in the Course of several Generations. The french Nation jumped at once from a mild Monarchy to wild Anarchy and are now in Subjection to Men whom they dispise.[62]

PART V

Settling Down

CHAPTER 13

The Long Journey Home

Left Paris at 10 o'clock.... In how many ways Reflection and Experience inculcate the important Maxim not to govern too much.... Constantly successful in the Field, she [France] is running to Ruin with a Rapidity that is as yet unknown in the History of human Affairs.

DIARY ENTRY,
Sunday, October 12, 1794

MORRIS remained in Paris long enough for James Monroe to present his credentials to the National Convention and to prepare for his own departure. He had shipped his furniture, books, wine, and carriages back to Morrisania, which he had not seen for five years, but any homecoming was indefinitely on hold. Over the next four years, his business affairs and curiosity carried him on a long, slow journey around Europe, visiting Switzerland, the Netherlands, Germany, Prussia, Austria, and England—and always well received wherever he went. Many of his Parisian friends, now fugitives, were scattered like leaves by the revolutionary storms across his path from London to Vienna.

The New Yorker had planned to travel only briefly to Switzerland before returning to France to embark for America. Monroe reported to Washington that Morris wanted to see where "John James Rousseau" lived. There is usually a whiff of amorous or political subterfuge in Morris's activities, and Monroe's naive reference to a literary pilgrimage sounds like a cover Morris had planted.

It is impossible to know if his intelligence network had yet tipped him off that Adèle had left London and was staying in Switzerland, near Zurich, and in close touch with the duc d'Orléans's son, a potential heir to the French throne. Morris had not seen her for more than two years and their affair had run its course, but a strong tie of friendship remained. Having left London and finding herself adrift in the uncertain and dangerous territory of the Continent, Adèle still depended on her New York friend for encouragement and security as she struggled to survive the deluge that was washing away her world. Her name, however, does not appear in Morris's diary for another six months. Morris may have avoided direct communication with her for fear of revealing to French agents the hiding place of the young Orléans, the future Louis-Philippe.

There were last-minute problems with the former minister's passport before he left Paris. The Committee of Public Safety decided that because of his "well-known political principles," he would not be allowed to return to France to catch a ship at Harve for the United States if he traveled to Switzerland. When he abruptly canceled his plan to leave from France, the passport was issued immediately. Heading for Switzerland, he would never set foot in France again.

At the age of forty-two, the prospect of restless wanderings expressed Morris's renewed personal sense of liberation after being exhausted with both the beauty and horror of Paris. From the beginning, he had not been taken in by the city's seductive allure and expressed no knowing regrets when he left never to see it again. Jefferson had, in more peaceful times, also enjoyed travel as escape but preferred the anonymous freedom of traveling alone, staying in ordinary inns and using public relays for transportation. Morris's entourage—his large carriage and driver, a baggage wagon, his valet and postillions—was quite conspicuous. The wanderer, without a home, a job, or family, carried out his explorations in fitting comfort, which he could afford. At the Swiss border he declared four hundred louis d'or in his trunk, a small fortune to be carrying in such perilous times.

The late eighteenth century shares with our own time, as one scholar has observed, both "the rhetoric of freedom of commerce" and "the sense of living in a society of universal commerce and universal uncertainty." For Morris the capitalist, the new ideal of individual independence was personified by the modern world in which he now found himself, a world of daunting risks, speculative adventures, and a vision of prosperity. It was not simply to get rich or to better his condition, rather it was to ultimately secure the creative freedom he considered essential to his well-being. This "active, unquiet, innovative society"—to appropriate Tocqueville's words—in which he moved, seemed to capture his imagination and animate his inner drive.[1]

If his plans seem vague and ambiguous in his correspondence, it was because his existence itself was unstructured, unpredictable, reflecting all the possible opportunities that had been opened up by the revolutionary upheavals. His nomadic life embodied the new era of economic opportunity as a process of emancipation, linked with the liberated individual's imagination, marking a watershed in the way the modern world would work.

Aside from any hidden agenda, he was now free to pursue his private financial interests, to play with bonds, notes, shipping, real estate; transactions that, in turn, supported his unstructured travel in a society increasingly in motion. Although he would later grow weary of the endless, existential gyrations that now defined his life, the dynamics of commerce, suffused with a rush of uncertainty, announcing a new order of things, stimulated Morris's open, confident disposition. Time itself had become an indeterminate measure as he moved on an impulsive, indefinite schedule. As days and months, even years, piled up, new reasons to delay returning to Morrisania regularly appeared. There are stretches when all this uncertainty and rootlessness caused Morris emotional pain, a feeling of uncharacteristic loneliness and depression, but at this stage of things, that was far more acceptable than settling down to the boring routines as squire of Morrisania.

He told his brother-in-law two years after leaving Paris that "Affairs...in which Reputation as well as Property are concerned" had to be taken care of before leaving "precipitately." He was concerned, he went on, that he might be "called again in to public Life were I in America, but so long as I continue abroad, I can trust to the Industry of my Enemies for keeping me in a private Station." Neither excuse seems completely convincing.[2]

Tired before he left Paris, and suffering from a painful attack of gout during the long trip, Morris arrived in Lausanne on October 20, 1794. The Swiss town had become one of the many hubs for revolutionary exiles throughout Europe. The next day he called on Jacques Necker, the former minister of finance now living at his gloomy château of Coppet on the shore of Lake Geneva, where he had fled in 1790 after his final fall from power. Necker's daughter, Gouverneur's Parisian friend Germaine de Staël lived nearby in the rented château of Mézery. It had been the residence of the historian Edward Gibbon, who had earlier carried on an affair in the house with Germaine's mother, Madame Necker. Those same rooms now received her liberated daughter's grab-bag assortment of friends and several lovers. Germaine's husband, the melancholy Baron de Staël, had gone off to look for solace from a mystic Lutheran divine in Germany to restore his marital harmony.

When Morris arrived at Coppet, he was immediately invited to dinner with the retired minister. Unimpressed with Necker's abilities during his service in the French government, Morris thought his effusive greeting was suspiciously too cordial. In fact, later that evening the financier took the New Yorker aside to talk confidentially about possible investments in American lands, everyone's fallback in case things got worse.

The next day, Germaine entertained the visitor at Mézery. He found the dreary little French gathering of exiles "as gay as circumstances will permit," not the garrulous, bubbling salon Germaine had presided over in the Faubourg Saint-Germain. Germaine spent the evening boring him with her history and plans for life, and he later confessed to his diary that his pillow would have been far better company.[3]

He could not wait to escape from the de Staël-Necker ménage, and in a few days he was off again, his next stop at his friend Madame de Tessé, the aunt of Lafayette. Passionately for the Revolution at the beginning—Morris called her "a republican of the first feather"—the ancient countess did not put all her eggs in one republican basket, shrewdly transferring money to Switzerland just in case the revolution did not work out. Now safe but bored, living the life of a lonely refugee, she was delighted to see Morris and to talk of the good old days at Chaville, her château near Versailles. When she told him that she had a small fortune of twelve thousand pounds and was thinking of leaving Switzerland, Morris advised her to put her savings in "American three per cents."

On November 12, Morris wrote to his friend the American consul and banker John Parish in Hamburg. Parish's banking house was a worried creditor of Robert Morris. He told Parish that he was now on his way to the German city, the most important neutral port in northern Europe, with shipping links to England and the United States. An easy escape route by sea made it a popular gathering place for wealthy refugees on the run. The free port was also a mercantile and banking center with a liberal bias toward free trade, an attitude congenial to the New Yorker's sentiments.

Morris reached a gray, freezing Hamburg in December. Soon after his arrival he wrote to Washington, in response to a letter he had received the previous June but had not replied to it before he left Paris because the mail was unsafe and routinely opened by the authorities. In his letter, Washington, with heavy irony, had assured his friend that for all of its problems, the new government could not go "*amiss*" because there were "*so many guardians*" and "*infallible guides* that one is not at a loss for a director at every turn." But the president wanted and needed Morris's independent, measured opinion of American foreign policy from a European perspective, something he had come to depend on. "My primary objects, and to which I have steadily adhered, have been to preserve the country in peace if I can, and to prepare for war if I cannot; to effect the first, upon terms consistent with the respect which is due to ourselves, and the honor, justice, and good faith to all the world." The former envoy completely agreed and had been guided by the president's concern for national respect when he had confronted the hauteur and indifference of the British government in London in 1790.

After explaining that his delay in returning to America was due to the risk of a winter crossing and because he had business in London, Morris gave Washington his views of France. His assessment that the country was worn out with all the strife and was ready to restore the monarchy, however, was off the mark—wishful thinking on his part. He again cautioned the president against reading the American experience into the French picture. "We were in actual enjoyment of freedom, and fought not to *obtain* but to *secure* its blessing. The people elected their magistrates during the continuance of the war...."

But in France they have been lured by one idle hope after another, until they are plunged in the depth of misery and servitude." He repeated his regular prediction that if order was not restored, France would be saddled with "a single despotism." The only reason that it had not happened earlier was because of "the want of mettle" on the part of potential usurpers.[4]

Early in February 1795, Morris received a long letter from Adèle who was still in Switzerland. She had met the young duc d'Orléans, who had been hiding there incognito. The possible heir to the throne—his father Philippe-Égalité had been executed in 1793—was without funds but wanted to travel in Europe and possibly move to the United States "to forget the grandeur and sufferings of his youth." Adèle asked her former lover and good friend of the young man's mother, the duchesse d'Orléans, for help. Morris immediately sent funds for the pair to travel to Hamburg. Having moved to the nearby town of Altona at the mouth of the Elba River, which was also a haven for refugees and a hotbed of émigré politics, the New Yorker surreptitiously found lodgings there for Adèle and the duke she had given the code name of "cousin."

During the next few weeks before he left for London, he saw a good deal of Adèle and her "cousin." At one dinner, she asked him to sign a note to secure additional funds for the duke's European travels. Later when he learned that Orléans was planning to leave for America, Morris generously arranged for credit during his wanderings with his brothers, who joined him after their release from prison in Marseilles.[5]

Morris left for London that spring, arriving in the middle of June 1795. His normally robust health had been undermined by the cold, miserable climate of northern Germany, and he continued to suffer from what he called "augue and fever." But he soon rebounded and was off on tours of southern and northern England and Scotland. At the same time, he was also restlessly making plans for a trip to Vienna and Italy later in the year. While military actions by the allies against France seemed to have settled down to French advantage, American shipping was still threatened and harassed, particularly by the powerful British navy. This gave Morris an opportunity to urge Washington to support the creation of an embryonic navy, the argument he had already made to Edmund Randolph.

On his return to London in November, Lord Grenville presented Morris to the king, a diplomatic gesture of goodwill toward the United States. A year earlier, on November 19, 1794, the British foreign secretary and John Jay had signed the treaty that would carry his name, finally settling critical issues between the two countries. As a sign of the new alliance, Grenville also arranged for Morris to be seated at a grand dinner in the city between himself and John Quincy Adams. At the age of twenty-eight, Adams was on his way to The Hague as American minister. During the banquet, Adams was not impressed with what he sourly called the New Yorker's "parade of sagacity."

For his part, Morris found Adams "deeply tinctured with suspicion...sees design in everything...and will always go obliquely." When a toast to John Jay was roundly applauded, Morris whispered to Adams that this would not play well at home where the treaty remained under attack. "Adams pricks up," Morris noted later in his diary, "and his countenance (in general insipid), overflows with joyful expression." From this, Morris concluded that "his father and Mr. Jay are at political variance," a bad omen for the treaty's future.[6]

Washington was all too well aware of the international crisis facing the United States and his administration. In December 1795, the president wrote Morris and again asked his private envoy to convey personally his deep irritation to the British government and to Lord Grenville, the foreign secretary, who was still creating major problems for American shipping. Since the beginning of the conflict, both Great Britain and France had each taken their share of neutral American commerce, especially cargoes that would likely end up in enemy ports. The angry public debate in America over Jay's treaty throughout the spring of 1795 had been divisive and bitter. Then in July, the president had learned that the British were again seizing American grain shipments headed for France. At the same moment, Congress was taking the treaty apart line by line in an acrimonious debate. All this had rekindled popular revolutionary sentiments toward France and against England, the old enemy. The new insults by the Grenville government were an outrage that Washington could not comprehend.[7]

While the president was still weighing whether to sign Jay's treaty, he learned that his secretary of state Edmund Randolph apparently was working behind his back to advance French interests and to reject Jay's work to improve relations with London. Randolph's confidential dispatch friendly to the French government had been intercepted at sea by the British navy, turning the public debate over the treaty into a partisan battle led by Jefferson's new Republican party. This partisanship was, of course, anathema to Washington. After he had digested all of these explosive developments, on August 17, 1795, the disillusioned president signed the treaty and fired the hapless Randolph. The treaty was still threatened by the refusal of the House to appropriate funds to carry it out.

All this and more, regarding British misconduct, was very much on Washington's mind when he asked Morris to protest "the impolite conduct—for so it strikes me—of the British government toward these United States." Morris's old friend from Valley Forge was again expressing his unwavering confidence in his loyalty and judgment. The president restated to Morris, in no uncertain terms, his foreign policy, a policy that was central to his presidency. This policy "has been, and will continue to be, while I have the honor to remain in the administration, to maintain friendly terms with, but independent of, all nations of the earth; to share the broils of none.... Nothing short of self-defense, and that justice which is essential to a national character, ought to involve us in war; for sure I am, if this country is preserved in tranquillity twenty years longer, it may bid defiance, in a just cause, to any power whatever; such, in that time, will be its population, wealth, and resources." It was a vision Morris had anticipated in his Independence address of 1776.[8]

Morris had a good vantage point for closely following the international problems of the Washington administration, and he was very sensitive to the president's domestic headaches with the threat of being dragged into the running war between Britain and France. Alert to "the noisy folks" back home, "loud in our obligations to France" and long in their list of complaints against England, Morris gave Hamilton sensible, practical diplomatic advice that cuts through the growing ideological warfare stirred up by Jay's treaty:

> As to the former [France], I think we should always seek to perform acts of kindness toward those who, at the bidding of their Prince, stepped forward to fight our battles. Nor would I ever permit a frigid reasoning on political motives to damp those effusions of sentiment which are as laudable in a nation as they are desirable in a private citizen. But would it be kind to support that power which tyrannizes over France and reduces her inhabitants to unheard of misery?...As to the conduct of Britain towards us, although I see as clearly as others the grounds, which we have for complaint, and can readily account for the resentments, which have been excited, yet I give due weight to the causes by which that conduct was instigated; and if in some cases I find it unjustifiable, I cannot consider it as in all cases inexcusable.... I am so far from thinking, that the injuries we have endured should become the source of inextinguishable hatred and war.[9]

The same day that Morris wrote to Hamilton, in March 1796, Washington was writing Morris, saying that while he expected more attacks on Jay's treaty in the House, the country was beginning to support it. There was a new prosperity in the air, and Republican ideology against England and in favor of France was no match for the bright economic picture that was beginning to emerge. "We have settled all our disputes," the president told Morris, "and are at peace with all nations. We supply their wants with our superfluities, and are well paid for doing so. The earth generally for years past has yielded its fruits bountifully. No city, town, village, or farm, but what exhibits evidences of increasing wealth and prosperity; while taxes are hardly known, but in name."[10]

At the beginning of the new year, Morris repeated his pretext of business to friends to explain why he was still not ready to return to New York. There are only scattered references in the record to confirm his excuse. "I am sure I could live more comfortably at Morrisania than I can any where else," he admitted to Samuel Ogden. But the European demands on "my different concerns" came first. If all worked out and he successfully wound up his "private transactions," he would be able to return with enough resources to retire "quietly to enjoy the advantages of those two Constitutions which I have had some share in framing, forms the summit of my ambition."[11]

On May 16, 1796, Morris wrote Washington from London that some "indispensable circumstances" had called him to Switzerland and that he would, out of a "sense of propriety" reverse his round-about way, traveling through Germany to avoid going through unfriendly French territory, where, in fact, he was still persona non grata. That same day he mentions Adèle in his diary for the first time in nearly a year: "I walk out to Kensington. Madame de Graave tells me of an intended marriage between Madame de Flahaut and M. de Souza, also of a coldness between him and her respecting the Duke of Orléans. I presume that he [the duke] has been *un peu mystérious* and she *un peu légère à cet égard.*"[12]

Adèle was still at Altona when Morris heard the news of her pending marriage. The New Yorker lost no time in arranging a reunion in the German port. During a drive, she told him of "her whereabouts with her Portuguese lover M. Souza" who was the dashing Portuguese minister to Denmark. Whatever was on Morris's mind when he left London, their brief reunion was only that. Adèle had made her decision to marry, and it took only a few days of repeated messages at her house in Altona that she was "abroad" for her former lover to understand that there would be no revival of the now burned-out affair.

By midsummer Morris was in Berlin and renewed his friendship with Madame de Nadailac whom he had met at Adèle's Louvre apartment in February 1791. She attracted him when they first met, and after Adèle's Altona brush-off he was ready to explore new fields. But again, he made no progress with serious romantic plans, and by August he was on his way to Dresden and Vienna where the British ambassador arranged for him to be presented to the Austrian emperor. He was touched when two "ancient valets de chambre" to Louis XVI, liveried ghosts from a lost world, recognized him and introduced themselves after the ceremony. The Austrian winter was cold and disagreeable. Neither business, love affairs, nor the stuffy Viennese court held him long. By the end of the year, the lonely, cultivated, and now increasingly portly wayfarer in his coach-and-four was headed for Prague.

During the fall of 1796, Morris learned that a resentful Monroe had been recalled and that Washington had given his Farewell Address. During his travels, he now wrote long letters to Lord Grenville on the state of Europe, the extent of various military buildups, and the shifting alliances. These confidential reports, both in their detail and length, were very valuable to Grenville and have led to the speculation that the New Yorker had been secretly commissioned by the British foreign minister as a paid agent. Morris later sued James Duane for making such a charge.

John Quincy Adams reported to his father, now president, that he had heard that Morris had been "wandering about some of the small German courts." It was an accurate if unrevealing summary of the New Yorker's erratic travels. Moving from Prague to Leipzig and on to Altona, he found Adèle still

living there but not yet married. Once again, he attempted to renew the relationship, obsessively making calls day after day. The record of steady, if gentle,
rejection in the diary makes sad reading. By September 1797 this singular,
brave woman decided that it was time to to return to Paris with her son, whatever the risks, and continue her writing. September 21, 1797, marks her last
mention in Morris's diary. Her second novel, finally published in 1799, was
well received and helped her to survive financially. Called *Emile et Alphonse,* its
ironic subtitle was *The Dangers of First Impressions.*

On October 14, 1797, Morris was present with the imperial minister of
Austria in Hamburg when Lafayette and his companions were delivered over
by his Austrian jailers after five years of imprisonment. The transfer was made
to Morris's business partner John Parish, the American consul. The prisoner
believed that he had been liberated by Napoleon Bonaparte instead of by a letter from Washington, the emperor of Germany, and Morris's private negotiations on his behalf in Vienna.

In August 1792 when Lafayette found his troops abandoning him, he had
fled over the Belgian frontier where he was captured. Morris wickedly told
Jefferson that he had "taken Refuge with the Enemy," a view the French government also took, charging him with treason. Thrown into prison, he had
ended up in the grim castle of Olmutz, where the jailers were even forbidden
to use his name. He had remained there until he was brought to Hamburg.
Distressed by his arrest, made more complicated because of Lafayette's ties to
the American cause, Morris was not surprised by the turn of events. "Thus his
circle is completed. He has spent his fortune on a revolution, and is now crushed
by the wheel which he put in motion." As Morris explained to William Short,
Lafayette's claim to American citizenship was no help given the circumstance
as he was a Frenchman fighting in the French army against the allied forces.
"Can the United States interfere in an Affair of this Sort without making
themselves Parties in the Quarrel?"[13]

American efforts to free Lafayette, including a letter from Washington to
the Austrian emperor, were unsuccessful. When Morris heard that the general
was destitute in the Austrian prison—his possessions had been reduced to a
watch and one change of clothing—he immediately ordered his American
banker in Amsterdam to forward ten thousand dollars to the prisoner, pledging his own private security for the amount. His efforts on behalf of the financially pressed Madame de Lafayette and her children were gestures of old-
fashioned Morris chivalry. From his own private funds he sent her one
hundred thousand livres, and when she was thrown into a Paris prison, he
managed to save her from the guillotine. In his letter to the Jacobin authorities, he made clear that his interest in her cause was not official but was done
out of his friendship as well as the American people's patriotic attachment to
the family. The seriously devout Madame de Lafayette had been no fan of the

New Yorker, but she was deeply touched by his generosity and wrote him a letter of gratitude.[14]

On his release, Lafayette told Morris that he planned to go immediately to United States, but he was still in Europe nearly a year later when he called on the New Yorker. Asking Morris if he should now leave, the New Yorker told him that it was apparent that he had already made up his mind to stay. The former prisoner loved the limelight and still imagined that he would soon be asked again to step onto the political stage mounted on a white horse. "Always declaring his resolution to lead a private life," Morris mused, "he sighs still for an opportunity of appearing again on the public theatre."

The Lafayettes later took advantage of a French law to avoid paying interest on the money their friend had advanced. Morris was deeply shocked but philosophical when he wrote his agent handling the disagreeable business: "The ungrateful man never thinks of his benefactor without a pang, and how should one not detest the object that causes such suffering and lowers one in one's own eyes? Having pardoned the first wrong [not fully repaying the loan], I pardon the second one in advance." Long after Morris's death, Lafayette actually accused the New Yorker of helping to bring about the downfall of the French monarchy by personally undermining the general's superior advice to the king and queen during the crisis.[15]

Reading the details of Morris' 1798 itinerary, his last year in Europe, is as tedious as the travels themselves must have been. Each entry becomes more compressed with few private reflections, as if the inner dialogue had run its course. After nearly ten years of living in continuous tumult, he was worn out by the unspeakable follies and stupidity of the human race. "Indeed, we live in a time," he wrote John Parish, "not to be surprised by anything."[16]

In March, after Napoleon had sacked Rome and invaded Switzerland, Morris assessed the implication of the ruthless French campaign now unleashed on a terrified Europe: "The french are in Berne. From the German ocean to the head of the Adriatic, including everything round the British Channel, the Atlantic and the Mediteranean, except Portugal and Naples.... His empire is too rapidly and widely extended to put on a solid existance but there is every means of extensive mischief."

While waiting out a sudden storm that had delayed his departure, on October 2, 1798, Morris read the details of Horatio Nelson's great victory over the French in the Battle of the Nile. Two days later, on October 4, a weary, wiser, and sated New Yorker began the long journey back across the dark Atlantic to Morrisania.

CHAPTER 14

On Native Ground

―――――――

A FTER eighty days of a rough ocean crossing, Morris arrived at New York City on December 23, 1798. A few days were spent seeing old friends and family members and adapting his wooden leg to solid ground. Hamilton lost no time in giving him a political briefing. "Colonel Hamilton, now General Hamilton . . . tells me the state of our affairs." Morris's disagreeable half-brother Richard also paid a call. Morris charitably thought him less foolish than he had remembered, forgiven of "the past for he is always the Son of my Father."[1]

At dusk on January 5 of the new year, he reached the cold, drowsing rooms of Morrisania. The ground was covered with snow. On the thirty-first he turned forty-seven. Ten years of neglect had taken its toll on the old family house, now "leaky" and "ruinous." But beyond the carelessness of hired managers, the silent white fields and woods of Morrisania, reaching north toward the hills of Westchester, appeared little changed. Unsurprisingly, the estate he called a "farm" had produced little income in his absence. He had always been interested in scientific agriculture and naturally threw himself into the predictable demands of the farm, managing it with a firsthand knowledge that surprised some of his city friends.

With that decisive Morris manner, before the month was out he had an architect on hand to begin planning a new house on the foundation of the old one, eventually laying out some $60,000 in improvements. As he unpacked his papers and books, he was surrounded by carpenters and masons. With his usual ability to stand to one side and clarify his life, he realistically confided to John

Parish that he "should provide himself with a helpmate" as "the long evenings may grow somewhat dull and force me into town." At least one young lady in the neighborhood let it be known through friends that she was a candidate.[2]

By the time Morris arrived in Manhattan at the end of 1798, an international crisis had developed with the French government over its attacks on American shipping as a part of the war with Britain. With the war going badly, in desperation the Directorate stepped up its seizure of American vessels. A new decree of the government placed all American maritime commerce at risk. Finally the aggression and insults forced John Adams to call a special session of Congress recommending negotiations backed by stronger measures of maritime protection if negotiations failed. In fall 1797, Adams sent a special mission to Paris to iron out diplomatically the French problems. A few days after their arrival in the French capital, the commissioners, who included John Marshall, were visited by three strangers who claimed to represent the ministry of foreign affairs. This was the beginning of the infamous XYZ Affair—code name for the attempted shakedown by the mysterious agents identified by letters. It quickly became clear to the Americans that the visitors were, indeed, acting as mouthpiece for a shady scheme manipulated by members of the French Directory. The exposure of the plot in spring 1798 gave the more militant Federalists the upper hand as they pushed the country toward an all-out war with France.[3]

The characters in the Paris drama were all familiar to Morris. The central figure in the scandal was none other than Morris's old rival Talleyrand. True-to-form, the bishop had wheedled himself into the post of foreign minister under the new Directory with the help of Germaine de Staël, his former mistress who had used her considerable influence to get him the job. Talleyrand's avarice and that of his cronies came to a stunning $250,000, which they tried to extract as the price to enter into any negotiations with the Directory. Aside from the money, it was a diplomatic insult the fledgling republic could not tolerate.

The unassuming but blunt Marshall, "tall, meagre, emaciated," was more than a match for the slippery minister. The Virginia lawyer, who had made himself the reporter for the commission and chief negotiator, wrote the report to the president on the whole squalid business, setting off a firestorm.[4] The news of this high chicanery suddenly turned the Adams administration into a war party throwing the pro-French Republicans into a tailspin. Jefferson's unrequited love affair with the French Revolution would be sorely tested. "You know what a wicked use has been made of the French Negotiation, and particularly the...XYZ dish cooked up by Marshall, where the swindlers are made to appear as the French government," Jefferson fumed to Edmund Pendleton.[5]

Congress was ready to put the country on a war footing and in June and July had passed the Alien and Sedition Acts, "the inglorious measures" that would mortally wound the Federalist party. By July 4, it looked like the war hawks in the Federalist camp with the sword-rattling help of General Hamilton would get their war. Adams's bête noir, Hamilton, had his heart set on the army he would lead under the titular command of George Washington. But in November, word came that Nelson had destroyed the French fleet in the Battle of the Nile that August, followed by other reverses, so things began to cool down. Two months after Morris's return in December, Adams sent a message to a flabbergasted Congress that he was "ready to embrace every plausible appearance of probability of preserving peace or restoring tranquillity" with the French republic. Just before he had left Europe, Morris told Necker that if the French government sincerely wanted peace, it no doubt could have it, in spite of Jefferson's efforts to scuttle Adams's commission. "For myself," the New Yorker confessed before hearing about Talleyrand's indignities, "I would have it at any Price, except the loss of Honor."[6]

Before he left Europe, Morris concluded that he would not be at all surprised if Napoleon's Directory tried to "force us into a little war," Morris sighed, sounding quite world-weary and tired of wars. "It is vain to cite history, or example, to accommodate reasoning, or lavish arguments. Each new generation will see, hear, feel, taste, smell, and suffer for itself."[7]

Having "got safe into the port of private life," the overarching theme of the New Yorker's life was to put his rootless, gypsy wandering behind him and settle down into an condition that, up to then, had held little appeal. His seasoned view of politics and life were now well fixed, and he had no interest in becoming "a moral Quixote," trying to make converts to his particular principles. Yet the prospect of a staid, sedentary existence had never figured in his plans before. He confessed in a letter to Germaine de Staël that he had decided that the ideal life would be four months in a city like Philadelphia or New York, a few months in a country summer retreat (like Morrisania), and the remainder of the year traveling, "a mode of life," he added, "by no means repugnant to common sense." Urging her to join him for a visit, she could "gather peaches, take walks, make verses, romances," adding that, in a word, she could do whatever she pleased.[8]

Morris continued his diary routine, but the homespun details bear no resemblance to the European volumes: "It rains hard the greater Part of this Day. I walk in the afternoon but the frost not being yet out of the ground, it is deep and muddy.... Walk out this Day with Mr. Edmonston and in the Course of our ramble trim up several trees. A great number of fruit trees particularly Apples are scattered about by Storm." One of his diary entries, shortly after his return, records his supervision of butchering hogs and laying down hams for the winter, a scene that would have amused his gratin intimates at the Palais Royal and Versailles.

When the work on his new house was completed, Morrisania's generous public rooms fitted out with furniture from Versailles displayed the cultivated taste of a man who knew how to live very well and could afford it. The "squire" carried on his correspondence and kept his meticulous accounts at a Louis XVI *bureau à cylindre,* a polished mahogany desk with finely chased ormolu mounts. A Louis XVI longcase *régulateur* surmounted by a small bust of a Republican Roman, designed by Jean-Antoine Lépine, stood nearby marking time that had dramatically slowed for its owner since his days in the rue de La Planche and at Seine-Port.

The subtheme of Morris's new life now encompassed the management of his fortune, including Morrisania, and taking the leadership in visionary projects—canal building and laying out a plan for New York City topped the list—that formed a part of his confidence in the future of the country and the new century. From his earliest days, he had understood the geographical phenomenon that made New York City and its port a commercial emporium unique in the world. If it had been known to the gods of antiquity, he declared, they would "have reared to commerce a golden throne on the granite rock of Manhattan" instead of the temple to Jove they built on the peak of Olympus.[9]

The country had undergone dramatic changes during Morris's ten-year absence. The census of 1800 recorded a national population of 5,308,483, an increase of 1,379,279 since the first census ten years earlier. One-fifth of the American people were slaves. New York had gained the lead in population over Massachusetts to become the most populous state in the Union. Jefferson confidently reported to Morris that he calculated that the country would double its population "in 22 y 3 m."[10]

Given those figures, New York's political landscape was also altered probably more than any other state but the public was still intent on serving its own interests, particularly the commercial. Its moral and intellectual landscape also showed signs of a compulsive, perpetual newness unburdened by the Puritan doctrine that still lingered in Boston. Although New York society appeared aristocratic, down deep, as Henry Adams remarked, its instinct was democratic. Morris, however, did not seem alarmed by radical populist influences from the recent French experience. "The dizziness which French principles had produced in some heads," he reported to Necker, "is cured." The country had a fund of common sense and "a calmness of character" that would avoid dangerous excesses. "We are free; we know it, and we know how to continue free," he declared. Even if the military defense budget was growing as a result of Anglo-French tensions, it was of no consequence because the country had "arrived at a situation where a few millions more or less may be disregarded."[11]

With the presidential election just ahead, Jefferson the idealist was busy making a deal with the New York politicians Aaron Burr and DeWitt Clinton, the new Republican idols of the ward bosses of the city. What appeared to outsiders to be a strange political partnership was, to most New Yorkers, nothing more than another commercial deal to be pulled off without undue concern as long as it did not interfere with business as usual.

During Morris's absence, the political coalitions of the 1790s had produced sharply different perceptions of the constitutional settlement Morris had powerfully helped to put in place in 1787. As John Marshall described it in his biography of Washington, the country had been divided into two great political parties, one that "contemplated America as a nation" working to preserve the union. The other was attached "to the state authorities" and "viewed all the powers of congress with jealousy." Marshall modestly concluded, "Men of enlarged and liberal minds," members of his and Morris's party, "arranged themselves generally in the first party."[12]

The national government, firmly in the hands of the national or "Federalist" party when Morris left, was now torn by internal discord and sectional animosities. Altercations within Washington's administration had surfaced as early as 1791 when Jefferson and Madison tried to block Hamilton's grand design for the nation's fiscal policy. The treasurer's vision that alarmed the Virginians was his blueprint for government to systematically encourage the development of industry, raising the specter of speculation and public debt, an anathema to the emerging Republican leaders. By nature Hamilton was incapable of any reasonable compromise with his opponents. "One marked trait of the General's [Hamilton] character," in Morris's tart judgment, "was his pertinacious adherence to opinions he had once formed."[13]

Even without Jefferson's and Madison's opposition, Hamilton's abstract projections, couched in classical, orotund phrases, were not the kind of bright goals that appealed to or could be grasped by the mass of voters who were not members of the lofty and exclusive Federalist club. Made up of intelligent, strong individuals endowed with what one of the anointed called "generous feelings, delicate, noble and disinterested sentiments," who were used to running things their way, they were clueless when it came to communicating with the ordinary run of people who now seemed to be in the political ascendancy.

Proclaiming themselves the party of "enlarged and liberal minds" and displaying conspicuous "aristocratic" pretensions in everything from their dress to the books they read and the tables they set, the Federalists, with their superior tastes and manners, were easy targets for their opposition. That old issue of class, an education based on Latin and Greek, which had divided Morris's academy forty years earlier in Philadelphia was now back on the Federalist agenda. Yet as the authors of *The Age of Federalism* point out "there are elites and elites." In fact, a striking number of the Federalist leaders, such as Robert Morris, James Wilson, Theodore Sedgwick, William Cooper, and, of course, the immigrant Alexander Hamilton, were self-made men with unorthodox education and none of the visible signs of inherited position and wealth in their background.[14]

Morris's years in a chaotic Europe had only reaffirmed his skepticism of popular, direct democracy and its threat to his notion of an ordered society. But he still held firmly to those two liberal tenets of a republic: that political power ultimately derived from the people, and that all shared an equality before the law. Although his personal bias may have been reinforced by the European experience, in spirit he remained very much a confident American, devoted to national honor. A monarchy, he admitted to the princess de La Tour et Taxis, might produce mild, civilized manners, but society would lack energy and drive. In a republic of commercial persuasion where dynamic change was the norm, "freedom and tranquillity are seldom companions." Having made a choice, he was willing to accept, not always with perfect grace, the inevitable conflicts and instability. While the course of his return to Morrisania may have been laggard and at times wayward, not once in all those years after he had left Paris did he seriously think of becoming a permanent European expatriate.

To some, Morris's European patina seemed alien and slightly *démodé*, at odds with America at the turn of the new century. While his style of oratory could still stir an audience on state occasions—he was the speaker of choice in New York City—there were signs that it too might be fading. To many, the Federalist discourse had become suspect—words of men who "talk so finely and gloss over matters so smoothly." Hamilton told Morris that the Anti-Federalists thought his classic funeral eulogy of Washington was "too cold." Morris admitted to himself that he was not up to his old form. In fact, a feeling of being out of touch had begun to trouble many of the revolutionary old guard. Nor did Morris's brief tenure in the United States Senate suddenly reveal a politician for all seasons eager to make his way in the uncharted sea of popular sovereignty by immersing himself in local issues and the petty squabbles of local politicians. It had never been his métier, insuring that all of his elective offices would last hardly more than one term.[15]

The national and state sovereignties of the federal system turned out to be far more complicated than the drafters, in 1787, could ever have imagined, nor did Morris and his brethren of the true faith understand just how complex and unpredictable their federal system was in practice. Tensions between the states and the national government remained, as Alexis de Tocqueville later pointed out, demanding "the daily exercise of a considerable discretion on the part of those it governed." Morris lacked discretion when it came to controversial public issues or patience in educating ordinary citizens in the fine points of a system that was constantly undergoing tests. The system also required, in Tocqueville's words, a vast amount of information and understanding "in the people whom it is meant to govern" if they were to grasp its "limits and extent." It was this widening gap that Morris and his fellow Federalists were unable or unwilling to close.[16]

Until he retired from the political battlefield after two terms, Washington had been the chief prop of the nationalist party. His towering presence, overwhelming any opposition, had made it unnecessary for the Federalist party to build a popular base. John Adams had taken Washington's place in 1796 and was now preparing to run for a second term. The New York Federalists, in particular, were outspoken in their opposition to Adams. Their problem was that they had no alternative candidate or platform to rally the voters. Hamilton and others argued with Morris throughout the summer and fall of 1799, insisting, Morris recorded, "that I *must* take an active part in our public affairs, for that the Anti Federalists are determined to overthrow our Constitution." This was an argument that touched home. The Adams-Hamilton feud had a long, bloody history, and Hamilton, a driven man, would do anything in his power to defeat "His Rotundity." He would take even Jefferson over the New Englander. Hamilton knew that although Morris had not been directly involved in the notorious cabinet fights, he had never been drawn to the Yankee from Quincy and would be a willing ally. This split in the Federalist party spelled its doom.[17]

Morris quickly grasped the potential disaster looming but had nothing to offer beyond a last-minute appeal to the ailing Washington to reunify the fractured party. On December 9, 1799, the New Yorker wrote what would turn out to be his last letter to his friend at Mount Vernon, begging him to come out of retirement and resume his reign. The fact that he would write such a letter reveals the desperate jam in which the demoralized Federalists found themselves. He frankly told Washington that many leaders did not "consider Mr. Adams fit for the office he now holds." And he reminded the general that nothing less than their joint legacy of the Philadelphia convention was at stake. But Washington was dead before Morris's quixotic plea arrived. On New Year's Eve, Morris pronounced the president's funeral oration at St. Paul's Chapel in New York City. In his address, Morris quoted from memory, for the first time, his recollection of Washington's admonishing words, spoken on the eve of the Constitutional Convention to the faltering delegates who had urged cautious half-measures: "It is too probable that no plan we propose will be adopted. Perhaps another dreadful conflict is to be sustained. If to please the people, we offer what we ourselves, disapprove, how can we afterwards defend our work? Let us raise a standard to which the wise and honest can repair. The event is in the hand of God."[18]

With Washington's death and Robert Morris now in the debtor's prison in Philadelphia, two of the New Yorker's most important mentors were gone from his life. He had been well aware of the Financier's mounting troubles long before returning from Europe and had learned, in spring 1797, that the Philadelphian was finally ruined by his grandiose land speculations. Morris recorded his visit to the Philadelphia prison not long after his return. The prison was not far from where the two men had run the country's economy out of the office of the superintendent of finance in the early 1780s. In 1803, when Robert was released, a broken bankrupt, he was invited to stay at Morrisania to recover. "He came to me lean, low spirited, and as poor as a commission of bankruptcy can make a man.... I sent him home fat, sleek, in good spirits," Gouverneur reported to John Parish, "and possessed of the means of living comfortably the rest of his days."[19]

Even with all the work at Morrisania, including the supervision of the cutting of stone for the new house, Gouverneur found it difficult to come down from the elevated, racy experience of his years in Europe. Nor had he found it easy to adjust his style of living—even in small details—to more egalitarian standards. Driving into the city one day to join a friend for lunch, he was forced to fire his attendant on the way for refusing to ride behind his carriage. "Wherefore," he ruefully noted in his diary, "I am in town without a servant."[20]

By April 1800, the presidential election had kicked into high gear, and Morris listened in on all the back-room intrigue in New York. Burr had taken charge of Jefferson's campaign in the state, and particularly the wards of New York City, to elect the legislature, which in turn elected the presidential electors. The Federalists' horror of "party politics" was a reality. Morris was philosophical when the Republican candidates backing Jefferson captured the state of New York by a narrow margin. Without Burr's colossal efforts, the pivotal state would have gone to Adams, insuring Jefferson's defeat. Jefferson's thin lead was reinforced by the South's inclusion of three-fifths of its slave population. Hamilton's desperate attempt to get the governor, John Jay, to call a special session of the legislature to change the rules for the selection of electors backfired when Burr's agents got a copy of Hamilton's letter and published it. An aghast Jay refused to be a party to such an attempted coup.

With the mounting excitement of the national election shifting the attention to Congress, Morris did not resist his nomination and election to the Senate in April 1800 to fill the three remaining years of James Watson's term. When he received the support of his friend the Chancellor, a Republican, Livingston's brother was stunned. "Can you believe," Edward Livingston exclaimed, "in his [Robert's] conversion? or do you think his [Federalist] principles will make converts to republicans by their violence?" Knowing that the Federalists would send one of their own to Congress, Robert Livingston decided it might as well be an old and trusted friend.[21]

Morris could not refuse the honor. After all, he had been the strongest voice in the Philadelphia convention to insist that the Senate should be made up of the men "of *ability* and *virtue*" who "support consistency and permanency." The superior body had a moral duty to check on "the turbulency of democracy" in the House, which originated directly from the people, the fountainhead of "*precipitancy, changeability* and *excess*." It would "act as an outward conscience, and prevent the abuse of power."[22]

A month later the new senator traveled to Philadelphia for a short two-week session and enjoyed being back on the national stage. He obviously basked in the aura of respect he was given as a senator in Abigail Adams's "drawing room" but claimed that it was only a sign of deference for a, so far, presentable (and Federalist) government rather than a personal tribute. On his first day in the Senate, he heard the ominous but not surprising news that the New York election had been "carried by the democrats, and it is from thence concluded that Jefferson will be President." The Senate adjourned in the middle of May, its last session in Philadelphia. The next meeting would be in the new Federal City on the Potomac.[23]

The early end of the session in Philadelphia allowed the freshman senator to return to Morrisania to savor the "splendor" of an American summer of fishing, sailing, and a long difficult trip through the wilderness of northern New York to Montreal. He did not miss Europe's "shivering June," "wet" July, "uncertain September," "gloomy October," and "dismal November." His descriptions of the country he passed through, and where he held large real estate investment, grew lyrical in his letters. The brilliance of the atmosphere, he told John Parish, reduced Claude Lorraine's landscapes to pale copies of the real thing. His imagination soared with an imperial vision of the American continent as he contemplated the lush scenery, easily linking its promise to his confidence in the country's economic progress. On this trip his dream of a vast waterway of rivers, lakes, and canals took another leap toward more concrete form. The Erie Canal would become the centerpiece of the network he envisioned linking the country's frontier with its cities and ports. He did not, however, seem to comprehend just how this dynamic, new industrial machine would translate into political and social terms, transforming his orderly world beyond recognition. "The proudest empire in Europe is but a bubble compared to what America *will* be, *must* be, in the course of two centuries—perhaps of one.... Forty years ago all America could not, without bills of credit, raise one million of dollars to defend themselves against an enemy at their doors. Now, in profound peace, the taxes bring into the treasury, without strain or effort, above ten millions. In the year 1760 there was not perhaps a million of specie dollars in this country. At present the banks of Philadelphia alone have above ten millions to dispose of in this country *beyond* the *demand*."[24]

Returning to Congress, now meeting in the embryonic Federal City in November, where the political tide had shifted to the Jeffersonians, the New Yorker checked into the only inn in the nation's raw, forlorn capital with no hint of the grandeur welling up in L'Enfant's paper scheme of authoritarian geometry. He immediately treated his friend the princesse de La Tour et Taxis with his first impressions, telling her that his chief amusement was to watch "the petty intrigues, the insane hopes, the worthless projects [of] that weak and proud animal they call man.... We only need here houses, cellars, kitchens, scholarly men, amiable women, and a few other such trifles, to possess a perfect city."[25]

As for the occupants of the unfinished capitol building, Morris was no more impressed with them than he was of the new town. "Our Senate is made of feeble men, and indeed when we consider the manner of its composition," he told Hamilton, "we cannot expect that it should be a dignified body," as it was evenly divided between the Republicans and the Federalists. The members of the House of Representatives "have talked themselves out of Self-Respect and at Headquarters there is such abandonment of Manners & such a Pruency of Conversation as would reduce even Greatness to the Level of Vulgarity."[26]

Morris was not surprised to hear insiders affirm that Adams would be defeated in the upcoming presidential election. He had a settled opinion of Jefferson as a "theoretic man" whose ideology would inevitably take the government back to the days of the old Confederation controlled by the states. But he believed that Burr was a loose canon and urged his Eastern friends to take a more outspoken position. "It is dangerous to be impartial in politics," he redundantly reminded Hamilton who had tried to suppress Republican newspapers during the campaign. While the candidates may be "equal in worth" or "equally void of it," Morris had not the slightest doubt in the choice between "Messrs J. & B." He accurately predicted in his diary that the Federalists would dump Burr in the end, leaving him in the second slot. He was wickedly amused by the whole thing: "Indeed my dear friend," he wrote to Robert Livingston, "this Farce of life contains nothing which should put us out of humor."[27]

Hamilton, who failed to see any humor in the election, or anything else for that matter, was more scathing in the indictment of Burr he relayed to Morris: "He is sanguine enough to hope every thing—daring enough to attempt every thing—wicked enough to scruple nothing." Not long after he had arrived in Washington, Morris reported to Hamilton that some Federalists had cooked up a plan "to prevent any Election" with a prolonged deadlock in the House that would last beyond the end of Adams's term on March 4. To Morris it was "a wild measure" and would have thrown the government into the hands of the Federalist president pro tempore of the Senate until the new Senate convened. Neither Morris nor Hamilton would be a party to such a "dangerous and unbecoming" plot. Just before the showdown, Morris wrote Livingston: "Had you run with Mr. Jefferson you would beyond all question under the present circumstances have been chosen by the representatives to fill the first office of the Union. How much I lament the case," he went on, "I need not say, but I feel equal and trust that you will feel greater Regret that you shall be bound in the Chains of Opposition to your oldest and best friends." The Chancellor replied that if the Federalists were his oldest friends they were not always his best ones, Morris, of course, excepted.[28]

After thirty-six ballots through six days of voting, on February 17, 1801, the House of Representatives settled the tied election. The chief relief was that Burr had lost. To Morris, there was an obvious if painful legitimacy in the results. After all, Jefferson was the leader of his party, and it had carried the country. Not a single state had voted for Burr as a first choice. Morris, of course, found the new president's inaugural speech poorly delivered and "too long by half," but its conciliatory tone, if not its metaphysical subtleties, resonated somewhere deep in Morris's conscience.[29]

Arch Federalists were outraged by the new administration's sweeping changes of executive officeholders, but Morris did not rise to the partisan bait, considering it the normal—if unhappy—consequences of politics and an election he considered legitimate. He would have done much the same thing if he had been Jefferson. Recalling Adams's Alien and Sedition Acts, he admitted to John Parish that "we have done some foolish things as a party, over and above the many wild ones for which we are indebted to the unsteady temper of the late President." Before the election was declared, Morris spoke to Jefferson about party spoils if he won, and the Virginian assured him that changes in personnel would not extend to foreign posts. When Jefferson later changed his mind, Morris defended his right to do so; indeed Morris thought, as president he "was duty bound to change when good reason occur for the change."[30]

For all of the acrid political haze lingering in the Washington air, a few weeks after the election was settled, the two men entered into an unlikely private negotiation when Morris offered to sell the president some of his splendid French silver to brighten the bare and still unfinished presidential residence. The collection weighed in Paris before shipping to New York came to 408 pounds Troy and was valued at an impressive $6,528. The magnificent tureen and casseroles in the service were made by Catherine the Great's favorite silversmith, and she had ordered a similar service for her lover Gregory Orlov.

Jefferson was seriously tempted by the treasure, telling Morris that the larger pieces were "desirable in the first degree." At the same time, the president was drawing up new "Canons of Etiquette" in the spirit of democracy to abolish all signs of social and class distinction at his official dinners, and it was not clear just what message this noble silver would send to the multitudes. When the president could not find the funds for the entire collection but offered to take part of it, Morris replied that just as in the spirit of national unity, it ought to be kept together. Morris later sold the large tureen and other pieces to Robert Livingston, like the president, a consummate Francophile. Livingston had been named minister to France by Jefferson in fall 1801, and Morris no doubt convinced his friend that the grand silver salvaged from the ancient regime would set just the right tone at his Paris table to impress the parvenu Bonaparte crowd.[31]

The tie of "Messrs. J. & B." in the House gave Morris an opportunity to provide the history of the Constitution's provision not to designate the election of a vice president, allowing that office to go to the runner-up for the presidency. This insured that both men were voted on as being equally fit for

Silver tureen and two vegetable dishes by Jacques-Nicolas Roettiers, ca. 1775/6 purchased by Gouverneur Morris in Paris and later sold to Robert R. Livingston.
The Metropolitan Museum of Art, Gift of Mrs. Robert R. Livingston, 1973 (1983.318a–c),
Anonymous Gift, in memory of Robert Livingston Clarkson, 1976 (1976.206.a–c),
Gift of Mrs. Reginald McVitty and Estate of Janet C. Livingston, 1976 (1976.357.1a–c)

the first office and not as coattail understudies. When an amending resolution to name specifically the candidates for the second office was introduced in the Senate, Morris voted against it. First of all, he thought that amendments "lessened respect" for the Constitution. "Reverence for it," he warned, was "essential to that prompt compliance, with its injunctions, without which we cannot enjoy a mild and free government.... Secondly, it was better to bear an evil, which we know, than to chance one that is not known." Besides, the original provision was better than the one proposed. The Convention had considered the possibility of murder, artifice, fraud, and monetary corruption used throughout history to thwart the will of the people, and he remained unconvinced that tinkering with the document now would give any greater security to "the unbiased voice of the people."[32]

To Morris, the most serious threat to the Constitution and the national government by the new administration was the repeal of the Judiciary Act of 1801. Although a myth, the assumption that the defeated John Adams carried out last-minute revenge by appointing "midnight judges"—a myth perpetuated into the Jeffersonian era—has distorted the background to the fight that stirred up the New Yorker's combative juices, to lead the assault against the repeal act.

During the first decade, widespread distrust of the federal courts—all manned by Federalists—reached a peak with the prosecution under Adams's infamous Sedition Act. As Republican strength developed, alarmed Federalists decided that the original statute, which had been the subject of partisan arguments, needed to be overhauled and streamlined. In March 1801, a new judiciary statute was enacted. At the heart of the bill was the creation of twenty-nine new judicial districts to encompass the country. In a compromise, the number of districts was reduced to nineteen, but the act restated the language of the Constitution granting jurisdiction over all cases in law and equity arising under the Constitution, laws, and treaties of the United States. In its final form, the act simplified the work of the judiciary, saved the high court endless travel on the circuit, and widened the privilege to remove litigation from the state courts to the federal circuit courts.

The lame-duck Congress passed the act a week before Jefferson's inauguration. Adams filled the new judgeships, but the new administration moved to oust them by repealing the Federalist statute. The stage was now set for a full-scale battle over the meaning and power of the judiciary article of the Constitution. To Morris, the independence of the court was paramount and embedded in the spirit if not the express language of the Constitution. Because the country would not tolerate a standing army and, from experience in the Revolution, could not rely on the militia, the unarmed court remained the only instrument to settle disputes that might otherwise lead to violence and civil disorders. The New Yorker stated in melodramatic terms just how this independence was intended to be established. "A contract...is made between the Government and the Judiciary; the President appoints; the Legislature affixes his salary; he accepts the office, the Contract is complete. He is then under the protection of the Constitution which neither the President or the Congress can infringe. If you can you may throw the Constitution into the flames—it is gone—it is dead."[33]

During the debate, Morris made one of his most eloquent speeches defending the core purpose of the original article. The judicial power was the "fortress of the Constitution" and could not be fiddled with at the whim of Congress. As author of the Preamble, he had proclaimed that "to form a more perfect union" the people intended first to "establish justice." The framers "had seen much, read much, and deeply reflected" on this crucial provision. "They knew by experience the violence of popular bodies" and had anticipated "the very act you now attempt." He concluded his appeal with pure Federalist dictum. Warning that the framers "knew also the jealousy and power of the States; and they established for *your* and for *their* protection this most important department," he begged his rapt audience to remember carefully what he said: "It is this department alone, and it is the independence of this depart-

ment, which can save you from civil war." When he finished, even the "democratical paper at Washington" claimed Morris's speech "the greatest display of
eloquence ever exhibited in a deliberative body."[34]

The Federalists could not stop the repeal of their judiciary statute and the
words "disunion," "anarchy," and "civil war" were suddenly heard in Congress.
In the face of an aggressive Republican majority, James Bayard threatened
armed resistance on the floor of the House. But the Federalists' own chief justice conceded, years later, that the Republican intervention was an improvement. There was the threat that the Supreme Court might overrule the repeal,
but Marshall let it be known the he intended to avoid any judicial confrontation with Congress.[35]

With his keen instincts and experience, Morris continued to keep his
practiced eye on European affairs, undistracted by domestic politics. He was
well aware that the rise of Napoleon and his imperial ambitions needed to be
closely monitored even before the smoldering crisis triggered by Spain's
rumored transfer of Louisiana to France erupted. To the wary Morris, Napoleon
was a "varlet" who had as his "patron-saint Beelzebub." Jefferson who still
adored France, was also aware of the dangers of the high-stakes maneuverings
by its unstable neighbors to the west. In late fall of 1801, he had sent Robert
Livingston as envoy to Paris to find out just what was happening. After being
passed over for high office by Washington, the patroon of Clermont had been
easily wooed by Jefferson and Madison away from what Morris called "the
Mother Church of Federalism" into their camp. In Morris's opinion, he only
added more "discordant material" to the emerging party.[36]

The French had long made it known that they wanted to take over New
Orleans to control the Mississippi. The French acquisition of the Louisiana
Territory from the Spanish would increase the growing hostility between the
two revolutionary allies. Morris saw this as the worst possible policy for the
French. "The hauteur of a French General, and the rudeness of an american
Jockey will not comport together," he wryly told John Parish, and Louisiana
must belong to us. "The next general war," he predicted, "will be with France if
the transfer went through." To allow the French to straddle the continent and
control the central river arteries would reduce the country "to mere speculators
and philosophers," a barb directed at the rising populist mood.[37]

To Morris, France was far too dangerous a neighbor at any price. Just
before his term expired, he urged on the floor of the Senate that the territory
be taken by force. In February 1803, when James Ross introduced resolutions
to mount a military force of fifty thousand to seize New Orleans, Morris was
on his feet supporting him. The New Yorker was by then speaking as a lame
duck, which no doubt helped to sink the Ross resolutions. Contemptuously,
he dismissed any complaint of the cost of the conquest: "counting-house policy, which sees nothing but money" was from his perspective "a poor, short-

sighted, half-witted, mean, and miserable thing, as far removed from wisdom as a monkey from a man."[38]

On July 3, 1803, Jefferson learned that Livingston had signed a treaty confirming the United States' willingness to buy the entire province of Louisiana. Morris was stunned by the boldness of the move. A few months earlier he had been at his most sardonic in his attack on the spineless Jefferson. When "those discontented creatures called federalists...say that our President is not a Christian...they must acknowledge that in true Christian meekness, when smitten on one cheek he turns the other.... He believes in payment of Debts by diminution of revenue, in defense of Territory by reduction of Armies, and in vindication of rights by appointment of Ambassadors." But by more than doubling the territory of the United States without military action and at a bargain price, the "Lama of the Mountain," (Marshall's label) had confounded his loudest critics. Morris confessed that the president had done more in this one move to strengthen the executive than the Federalists "dared think of, even in Washington's day."[39]

Morris wrote Livingston that the treaty was "one of the best we have made," though most of his party opposed it for partisan reasons. When the question of the treaty's constitutionality came up, Morris wrote a frank letter to Henry Livingston, admitting that no one in 1787 had thought about limiting the territory. In retrospect, it would have been "perfectly utopian to oppose a paper restriction to the violence of popular sentiment in a popular government." But there was one thing he was confident of: "I knew as well then as I do now that all North America must at length be Annexed to us," adding the hope that it would be "happy indeed if the lust of dominion stop there." As for the treaty itself, since "the president was the organ by which the public will is pronounced in transactions with foreign nations," it was essential that he be supported "unless for reasons of the highest imports."[40]

Jefferson, himself, had constitutional hiccups over the purchase at first, but he recovered when he received word that Napoleon was also having second thoughts and might call the whole thing off. When the special session of the Congress convened, the president decided "the less that is said about my constitutional difficulty, the better," and Congress should do what was necessary "*in silence*." Morris had serious problems with the section of the treaty where Jefferson promised Napoleon to give the citizens of Louisiana the same rights and privileges as Americans. This would, of course, include the right to own slaves, the very catastrophe Morris had predicted in the Convention when he tried to stop its deadly spread into new states.[41]

In spring 1803, Morris's enemies had once again relieved him of public office. In adopting the republican form of government, he had taken it "for better or for worse," as a man takes a wife, but unlike most men, he took it knowing all of its bad qualities, adding that "neither ingratitude, therefore, nor slander can disappoint expectation, nor excite surprise." The Republicans had captured the New York Assembly and with the help of Aaron Burr, DeWitt Clinton was elected senator. Unlike Hamilton whose craving for fame was insatiable, Morris remained untempted by public life, longing to live a private life devoid of popular causes, petty politicians and irritations. But before he left Washington, Morris aimed a parting shot at slavery, voting unsuccessfully to block its expansion into the Mississippi Territory before the same question had been raised over the Louisiana Territory.

His release from the Senate allowed him to take several more extended trips into the spectacular northeastern wilderness of western New York, the lakes, and the St. Lawrence where his land holdings were measured in square miles. Eighty years later his granddaughter captured the sheer physical zest the New Yorker took in these explorations, revealing a special dimension of his personality in his passionate love of the natural world: "enjoying the dangers by water, lulled to sleep by the sighing of the wind among the trees, digesting plans for making roads through the country, seeking proper sites for towns, and inspecting his lands, taking care of his men ill with fever, and rejoicing over the settlement of the country." These trips were a microcosm of that postrevolutionary spirit of adventure, imagination, ambition, and innovation that defined Morris's still exuberant life. It was the same creative spirit that had animated his revolutionary colleagues in the War of Independence and in Philadelphia in 1787. In these explorations, the personal and economic, the commercial and the political, the measurable and the emotional were united. The emotional, sensual pleasure of nature itself was combined with the economics and profits of the sale of large tracts of land to the ambitious mass of immigrants pouring into the country. From the planning of everything from the details of the trip itself, to projecting roads and cities, "rejoicing over the settlement of the country," the calculable and the political were drawn together in his imagination.[42]

But long trips with bracing air and scenery and a busy private life managing his extended investments in lands interspersed with a steady procession of guests at Morrisania did not improve Morris's judgment of Jeffersonian democracy. At times, he would try to be philosophical, bemoaning that his lifelong friend Livingston had left the party of the "honorable, just and patriotic." He would not, however, "preach politics in the vain hope of making converts" but rather would "accept with resignation what the will of God has offered." When that offering turned out to be President Jefferson for a second term, he was despondent, if not apocalyptic. "Our democrats are split (from New England southward) under various appellations...between those who have got into power and those who are getting into power on the shoulders of the mob." And as everyone knew "a democracy" without restraint "will ever be in the hands of weak and wicked men." If anyone thought democracy "a bad species of government," they were mistaken for, in his opinion, it was not a system or form of government at all but a dangerous mirage. He continued to have nightmares of revolutions leading to despotism unless as he told Livingston, "our government is to be wound up, by constitutional means, to a tone sufficiently vigorous for the conduct of national concerns." Yet without any real political clout to alter the course of things, his dire predictions and illusions, as Henry Adams remarked, remained largely "rhetorical."[43]

Morris believed that constitutional monarchy was an unrealistic hobbyhorse a few radical Federalists had ridden far too long, with disastrous results. Hamilton and other extremists had turned against republicanism because they could not see how a system, in itself, could be good rather than merely "bad in relation to particular circumstances." Even in his darkest despair Morris believed that Hamilton's alternative of monarchy would inexorably lead to civil war and injustice. Like Jefferson on the left, Hamilton too was blindly theoretic, humorless, and, in Morris's opinion, hopelessly unrealistic in his ideology. Morris was not surprised by Hamilton's tragic end in a senseless duel at Weehawken, New Jersey.

On July 14, 1804, Morris delivered Hamilton's funeral oration in the portico of Trinity Church in New York City and acknowledged Hamilton's words that the Constitution was "a frail and worthless fabric," but Morris softened those misgivings, characterizing Hamilton's affection for monarchy as "speculative opinions" rather than "deliberate designs." Aside from the philosophical issues, the eulogy presented a number of personal difficulties, Morris privately confessed. He must pass over "handsomely" Hamilton's "illegitimacy" and deftly admit that he was "indiscreet, vain and opinionated." He had also "foolishly published the avowal of conjugal infidelity" with Mrs. Reynolds, to Morris an admission worse than the adultery itself. As he rode in the funeral procession behind Hamilton's mahogany coffin that the widow could not afford, he was still troubled by the duel and Burr's role in it. "I find no Way to get over the Difficulty which attend the Details of [Hamilton's] Death," he silently admitted to himself. "It will be impossible to command either myself or my Audience; their Indignation amounts almost to a frenzy already." In his measured, considerate, Olympian style, he managed, however, to dampen the outrage toward Burr, whom he "must consider in the same light with any other man who had killed another in a duel." It was a delicate balancing act and he believed he had succeeded "tolerably well." Before he closed and true to his humane instincts, Morris made a compassionate plea of "public pity" for Hamilton's indigent widow and the "poor orphan children."[44]

In fall 1804, a few months after the fatal confrontation on the ledge above the Hudson, Morris realized that Jefferson would be reelected for a second term. To the gloomy New Yorker, the consolidation of the president's support in the slave-holding South and the West confirmed his worst fears voiced during the Convention in Philadelphia in 1787. The European conflict between England and France had already resumed full scale in the early years of the new century, followed by naval blockades in the Atlantic and Caribbean. The Jefferson administration was caught flat-footed in the middle of its program to reduce the size of government, reduce taxes, and eliminate the national debt, which of course meant the virtual destruction of the infant navy that Morris had for so long promoted. To Morris, the Republicans' devious course was "sacrificing permanent public interest to a fleeting popularity." All this added up to a policy utterly opposed to the New Yorker's vision of an expansive commercial republic with a reasonable national debt serving as an investment in the future development of the country. Supporting both internal development and international trade was, in the judgment of Morris, the only progressive way the country was going to grow and prosper.

Jefferson's response to the blockades was the Embargo Act of 1807, closing American ports to all foreign trade. As Morris predicted, it was a disaster that wrecked the American economy, hitting the Northeast particularly hard. In one year American exports were nearly wiped out. Widespread opposition was immediate. The depression that followed stirred up public defiance of the law, leading a desperate president to call up federal troops to enforce it. "Never before or since," Leonard Levy the constitutional historian has written, "did American history exhibit such a spectacle of derangement of normal values and perspectives.... This was the only time in American history that the President was empowered to use the army for routine day-to-day execution of the law."[45]

As early as summer 1806, war seemed an inevitable consequence of the administration's foreign policy. Morris's warning of economic disaster would be regularly repeated until Madison, by then president, finally did declare war against England in 1812. Aside from the perils of war, it was very possible that in the face of the running disputes with Britain over maritime rights, foreign agents, for their own ulterior reasons, might promote internal divisions that could lead to the breakup of the republic. But complaining about drifting American politics seemed increasingly fruitless since the New Yorker had no real political standing in the face of the precipitate decline of the Federalist party. The affairs in the distant Federal City were increasingly replaced in his correspondence by the more ominous events in Europe. Following closely Napoleon's conquests and the reshaping of Europe, he wrote Germaine de Staël, her father Jacques Necker—both had invested in New York real estate on Morris's advice—and other European luminaries he had known, letters filled with solemn divinations and gratuitous opinions on the consequences. In their long-windedness, his letters often sound like those of a superannuated secretary of state longing to get back into the international fray of power politics. But to his friend Madame Damas, who Morris had protected from the revolutionary mob at Seine-Port, he confessed just how much he now enjoyed his private life at Morrisania: "With good air, a good cook, fine water and wine, a good constitution and a clear conscience I descend gradually toward the grave, full of gratitude to the Giver of all Good."[46]

Yet Morris was a man of the city as much as a man of the country. For all his rural airs and trappings of the squire, he was a cosmopolitan. He was at home not only in New York and Philadelphia but, more than any of his contemporaries, he was equally at home in Paris, London, Amsterdam, and the smaller cities of northern Europe. The contrast between the New Yorker and Jefferson, the agrarian ideologue, could not be more sharply drawn. As much as he professed to like Paris, the Virginian's letters during his years there were filled with moral alarm on what he saw as the city's corrupting atmosphere. His ideological attacks often take on theological tones. "A city life," he warned his protégé, William Short, "offers you indeed more means of dissipating time, but more frequent, also, and more painful objects of vice and wretchedness. New York, for example, seems to be a Cloacina of all the depravities of nature." For good measure, he added, "Philadelphia doubtless has its share."[47]

In 1807 Morris was named by the state of New York to head the commission to lay out a plan for New York City. No one on the commission had traveled as widely in European cities and had more exposure to their metropolitan workings. Morris the urban planner was clearly a man of the future with a vision that embraced the entire island of Manhattan, not just the small portion most people thought would be the city's future limits.

The commission was charged with laying out "the leading streets and avenues of a width not less than 60 feet, and in general to lay out said streets, roads and public squares of such ample width as they may deem to secure a free and abundant circulation of air among said streets and square." Faced with a vast, rough, irregular territory, interlaced with random winding streets in place long before Morris was born and hostile property owners waiting to ambush the surveyors, Morris and the commission were in for a tough battle. But when it made its final report in 1811, the commission ignored all obstacles, both physical and political, imposing a relentless grid of straight, north-south avenues from the base line of Houston Street in Lower Manhattan to the hills of Harlem at 155th Street. These were crossed every two hundred feet by smaller streets running between the two rivers. Slightly less than five hundred acres were set aside for open space. The results confirmed the Republican commitment to balance and order very much in the spirit of the Constitution. Manhattan's grid, anticipating the city's congenital instability, also confirmed Morris's compulsive sense of order, resisting the growing tensions of romantic disorder and unpredictability. Although the plan was uncompromising in its monotony, John W. Reps, the dean of urban planning history, considers that its great achievement was its efficiency for the buying and selling of real estate. During the four years of its existence, Morris was the most active member of

Mrs. Gouverneur Morris (Anne Cary Randolph Morris)
after James Sharples, 1810.
Collection of the New-York Historical Society.

the commission, and its final report defending its rationale of an all-encom-
passing a grid has a distinctive Morris tone, a "plain and simple" Morris logic
in the language.

If a city "was to be composed principally of the inhabitants of men living
[in] strait sided, and right angled houses," convenience, economy, and utility
dictated that the plan itself reflect these fundamental conditions. While deco-
rative "circles, ovals and stars" might look good on paper, a swipe at L'Enfant's
network plan of Washington, such supposed improvements had nothing to do
with the way cities worked and people lived. During his visit to Bath in summer 1795, he had been struck by the beauty of the city, but its appeal was in the
color of the stone used in the buildings, not in its romantic, irregular streets,
which lacked "that unity of Design which seems to me essential. Curved lines
are beautiful and should certainly be adopted when Nature is to be imitated
and concealed," the future urban planner noted, "but no one I believe ever
heard of a natural City."[48]

The report's defining strategy, to take the offensive in the debate, is also a
sure sign of Morris's hand.

Gouverneur Morris by James Sharples, 1810.
National Portrait Gallery, Smithsonian Institution. Gift of Miss Ethel Turnbull in memory of her brothers, John Turnbull and Gouverneur Morris Wilkins Turnbull.

It may, to many, be a matter of surprise, that so few vacant spaces have been left, and those so small, for the benefit of fresh air, and consequent preservation of health. Certainly, if the City of New York were destined to stand on the side of a small stream, such as the Seine or the Thames, a great number of ample spaces might be needful; but those large arms of the sea which embrace Manhattan Island, render its situation, in regard to health and pleasure, as well as to convenience of commerce, peculiarly felicitous; when therefore, from the same causes, the price of land is uncommonly great, it seemed proper to admit the principles of economy to greater influence than might, under circumstances of a different kind, have consisted with the dictates of prudence and the sense of duty.[49]

Aside from the complexities of city planning on a prodigious scale and laying out an equally monumental canal system, the plot of the last chapter of Morris's life appears simple in its structure, but its opening is abrupt, without warning or even subtle hints in the preceding narrative. Its implications were unforeseen and, at times, devastating. Now deep into his personal affairs, at the gouty age of fifty-seven, Morris was well aware that time was running out if he was to marry and perhaps produce an heir for Morrisania.

On April 23, 1809, Morris cryptically noted in his diary that he had that day "brought home Miss Randolph of Virginia." Anne Randolph was the daughter of Morris's friend Thomas Mann Randolph of Tuckahoe. Nine months later, after a family dinner at Morrisania on a cold, raw Christmas day, the aging host, showing accumulating signs of indulgence, suddenly announced to the shocked guests that they were about to witness a wedding. The sumptuous setting for the ceremony—the winter twilight falling on neo-classical tapestries, gilded chairs, the splendid clock by Lépine ticking off the tense hours—left no doubt in anyone's mind just what was at stake in the ancient words of the marriage service from the *Book of Common Prayer*. The service was read by the Reverend Isaac Watkins, Morris's brother-in-law. Some of the relatives present that evening, with their own plans for their bachelor kinsman's fortune, never recovered from the blow. Still savoring the drama, later that night, the New Yorker wrote in his diary; "I marry this day Anne Cary Randolph, to no small surprise to my guests."[50]

Anne Randolph called Nancy by her family, was thirty-five years old when she moved to Morrisania in the spring of 1809. She was born at Tuckahoe, the Randolph estate just west of Richmond, Virginia's new capital. Her grandfather, the first Thomas Mann Randolph, was a close friend of Jefferson's father, who was also his executor. When Randolph died, the Jefferson family moved to Tuckahoe from Albemarle County, and the young Jefferson studied in the little frame schoolhouse of the plantation. Anne and her brothers and sisters were also tutored there. Even with a declining fortune, enough money was scraped together to give Anne and her sister all the right "finish" demanded by their elevated rank in Virginia society. This included French, music lessons, and a fair grounding in literature.

By her generation, the Turkey Island branch of the exalted Randolph clan that had first settled in Virginia in the 1660s, claiming kinship with Pocahontas, had extended its reach into most of the established families of the Tidewater. It was a network of families linked by blood, proud and erect in their provincial self-regard. But the economy of the post-revolutionary years had taken a toll on these first families of the Old Dominion. Like Nancy's father, most were land-poor, deeply in debt, and living on the credit of their British factors. Men of this first class, the duc de Liancourt noted, not only had impeccable manners, they were also impressively well-read even though "the populace is perhaps more ignorant there than elsewhere."

In spite of declining fortunes, Anne's Tuckahoe family still had formidable connections to the power and political establishment. Her relatives, Jefferson and John Marshall, both of Piedmont frontier stock, were, in turn, famously hostile cousins, connected through their Randolph mothers. Nancy's brother, Thomas Mann Randolph Jr., had married his cousin, Jefferson's oldest daughter Martha. Nancy's sister Judith married her cousin Richard Randolph, brother of the seriously erratic John Randolph of Roanoke. As a senator, Morris had taken Randolph's measure as he served in the House at the same time. The Randolph brothers were stepsons of St. George Tucker, the distinguished Williamsburg jurist and lawyer who had married their widowed mother.

In fall 1793, Nancy, her sister Judith, and her brother-in-law Richard Randolph had been engulfed in a dark and ugly scandal. Theodorick, Richard and John's younger brother, died before he was implicated. Rumors of incest, poisonings, and murder spread throughout Virginia. Years after the sensational details had passed into riveting gossip, repeated like a gothic horror story, the charges continued to hang over Nancy, a sinister cloud following her wherever she went. Without a penny of her own when she met Morris, she nevertheless radiated a natural intelligence, a fierce courage, and a will to survive. Like Adelaide de Flahaut, she was endowed with an uncanny inner resourcefulness against all odds. Shortly after the wedding at Morrisania, she wrote a friend in Virginia: "I glory that I was married in a gown patched at the elbows, one of only two I now own."[51]

The opening scene, leading eventually to the wedding, has all the stock conventions of a period romance. A good-looking though not beautiful spinster with mischievous eyes and mouth whose well-bred manners give her away finds herself destitute and alone in a boarding house in Greenwich Village. She had been turned out of her widowed sister's house in Virginia three years earlier and was moving aimlessly from place to place when suddenly a rich, mature bachelor, ruddy and tall, appears to rescue her in a fine carriage driven by a French servant. Nancy's granddaughter and namesake, Anne Cary Morris, later gives a discreet Victorian gloss to Nancy's deliverance. "Morris, the old and trusted friend of her father and mother, hearing of her reduced pecuniary condition, and that she was teaching in New England, proposed in the most delicate terms, that she accept the shelter of his roof, and take charge of his household. This offer was accepted by Miss Randolph in the spirit in which it was made."[52]

Given his instinctively pragmatic turn of mind, the chance appearance of his old friend's daughter, in fact, offered a sudden and reasonable solution to the New Yorker's annoying problems of running the expanded house at Morrisania in the style he had perfected during his ten years in Europe. After a series of disastrous housekeepers, equipped with little more than "vulgar" pretense, here at last was a reduced gentlewoman whose assured presence and experience could "command the respect of domestics." His letter proposing the job is a masterpiece, sympathetically confronting in realistic yet "delicate terms" the humiliation that Nancy must have suffered by the offer. "Pride may exclaim, 'Miss Randolph cannot descend to the rank of a servant under whatever name, or however elevated and distinguished,'" Morris admitted to her, but she must understand and be reassured that "our real relations shall be that of friends."[53]

Sometime before they had met at Mrs. Pollok's boardinghouse, Morris had begun a correspondence with Nancy. Vaguely aware of her misfortunes, he wrote offering to help her in any way that he could. He told her that he had once heard passing gossip but had "no distinct recollection of events which brought distress" to her family. Over a period of time, and here we do not have the details or sequence, she would confide her life story to Morris, the "history of her sorrows." As a seasoned yet compassionate man of the world in every sense, he reassured her that one should not "quarrel with the order of nature" and with "the incidents of pleasure and pain" scattered equally in everyone's life. The pleasure of both the body and the mind are connected and "is generally obtained by aid of our senses." After "the cards are dealt with fairness," what remains is "patiently to play the game; and then to sleep."[54]

Nancy was not yet seventeen when she left Tuckahoe in the fall of 1790. After she had quarreled with her difficult stepmother—nearly her own age— whom her widowed father had recently married, she moved in with her sister Judith and Judith's spirited but improvident husband Richard Randolph, at Bizarre, one of the family's isolated and run-down plantations in Cumberland County. Richard's unmarried brother John, malignant and obsessed, with his strangely wrinkled beardless skin, lived nearby at Roanoke, another family plantation. Like all the Randolph plantations in the neighborhood, Bizarre was heavily "hampered" by British debt and, like many of the old Virginia establishments, appearances were barely maintained. Foreign visitors were surprised to see a well-served table covered with silver, but half the window panes in the dining room missing and replaced with rags and paper.[55]

Not long after Nancy appeared at Bizarre, Richard's nineteen-year-old brother Theodorick also turned up and became a part of the ménage. Full of animal vitality, he and Nancy began a flirting romance, although there had also been a noticeably warm relation with her brother-in-law Richard. John Randolph, in his perverse way, was also attracted to Nancy. But the relationship between Nancy and Theodorick quickly ripened into something more serious, and they had made plans to marry shortly before he died. "I was betrothed to him, and considered him as my husband," she later admitted in the famous exchange of letters with Theodorick's brother John. "He [Theodorick] was my husband in the presence of God. . . . We should have been married, if death had not snatched him away a few days after the scene which began the history of my sorrows."

Theodorick Randolph died on February 14, 1792. By the following September, some members of the family began to suspect that Anne was pregnant, although her cousin Patsy Jefferson Randolph thought it was only "hysterics." She recommended that Nancy take gum guaiacum but warned that it was dangerous and known to "produce an abortion." Toward the end of the month, Richard, Judith, Nancy, and John visited cousin Randolph Harrison at Glentivar. Exactly what happened during the house party is uncertain, but on the morning after they had arrived, following a night rent by occasional screams, Nancy apparently miscarried or delivered a stillborn baby. When what appeared to be the remains of a fetus was later discovered outside the house near a woodpile, rumors began to spread in the slave quarters that it was Nancy's child and that Richard, its father, had killed it. Incest, under Virginia law, included intercourse with a brother-in-law and was thus added to murder.

Sensational rumors of what had gone on at Glentivar continued for some months. Richard consulted St. George Tucker, who knew Nancy's secret, and he also probably spoke to the family friend John Marshall on ways to quell the gossip. He decided to publish a challenge, saying that he would appear before the Cumberland County Court as a prisoner and "answer in the due course of law, any charge or crime" that anyone might allege. The extraordinary strategy was to force the slanderers out into the open.

John Marshall and Patrick Henry were engaged to handle Richard's examination before the court although exactly what role each played in the interrogation is not clear from Marshall's informal transcript of the proceedings. Although charges were made against Richard in the day-long hearing, Nancy was never accused or asked to testify. The editors of the Marshall Papers have reasonably concluded that Marshall's notes were actually prepared to aid him in proving Nancy's innocence. If he could prove that she was not in fact pregnant, then the case against Richard would of course collapse. At the close of his notes, Marshall makes a final summation of Nancy's defense, admitting that there was "some foundation on which suspicion may build" and enemies would undoubtedly try to impute guilt to her. Then sounding like a plea to a jury, he insists, "In this Situation Candor will not condemn or exclude from society, a person who may be only unfortunate."[56]

"You have perhaps heard," Morris wrote Marshall on December 2, 1809, "that Miss R., the daughter of our old friend of Tuckahoe, is in my House and has the care of my Family." Morris did not reveal his marriage plans to the chief justice, but he did need his counsel. He was aware of "sundry reports respecting this unfortunate young Lady, founded on events when [I] was in Europe." He told the justice he needed to know if there was anything in Nancy's past that might form a "foundation of calumny against me." He did not want to be accused of violating "not only the Morals but the Decencies of Life." Marshall replied vaguely that the circumstances surrounding the case were "ambiguous" and "rumor, with her usual industry, spread a thousand [tales that] were probably invented by the malignant, or magnified by those who love to supply any defects in the story they relate." He assured Morris that, while opinion remained divided in Virginia, Judith Randolph, "who had the fairest means of judging the transaction and who was most injured if the fact was true," had continued to let Anne live with her at Bizarre long after Richard had died. He did not mention, or perhaps he did not know, that

Judith later accused Nancy of poisoning Richard. The justice's circumspect conclusion, along with whatever Nancy, who now had reverted to her Christian name Anne, had revealed at this stage, was sufficient for Morris to proceed with his wedding plans on Christmas Day. Marshall's letter arrived only a few days before the wedding.[57]

The portly bridegroom was prepared for the inevitable assaults that his family would immediately launch against the marriage. With wicked pleasure, a sign that the old Morris spirit had revived, he apologized to one impertinent niece for having committed "a folly in marrying," acting "undutifully in not consulting you," adding that "whether the liberty of a bachelor be more virtuous than the bondage of a married man" was beyond his competence to judge. He closed the letter by saying that no one would have objected if he had married a rich woman of seventy but that by his decision to "take one of half that age without a farthing" he had merely intended "to suit myself, and look rather into the head and heart than into the pocket."[58]

To the great disappointment of the Morris relatives who had already spent their inheritance at least in fantasies, the marriage was an obvious success from the beginning. Although Morris was twenty-two years older than his wife, they shared a wide taste in reading and in outdoor life. Her early French lessons allowed her to deal with Morris's imported servants. She not only understood the fine points of running a serious household, regularly filled with guests, but she was also an accomplished horsewoman, something she had first mastered at Tuckahoe.

Nor was she daunted by the rugged trips she made with her husband to western New York. These journeys to inspect his lands also to allowed him to enlarge his vision of canals as the key to the development of New York's frontier. Morris knew boats very well, had ridden on Mr. Fulton's amazing steamboat, had fished off Fisher's Island, and had bought, shortly after he was married, an elegant sailboat for travel into the city. One of his great sports was running races under sail with the new steam boats on the Hudson. Hydraulic transportation was in his blood. After seeing the amount of development along the frontier that shortly before had been a wilderness. He was gripped by a vision of a booming American empire that demanded an easy way to move: "Say what they will of republican government, and it no doubt has its dark side, none other is so favorable to the multiplication of the human race and the decoration of the earth within its limits."[59]

These ideas had percolated in Morris's mind for some time. Thirty years earlier, in 1777, when Burgoyne advanced into New York, Morris was sent by the state to meet with the retreating General Philip Schuyler at Fort Edward. In the evenings, "Mr. Morris whose temperament admitted of no alliance with despondency" lifted the sagging morale of Schuyler's officers by painting with his Technicolor words pictures of the future glories of the country. In one of his

Thomas Cole panoramas he conjured a network of watercourses of rivers and canals connecting the Hudson and "the great inland western seas" of Lake Erie and beyond. He later told Robert Fulton that his first hints of a canal system had been treated as nothing more than the sales pitch of a stock promoter.[60]

He had no doubt repeated his reverie to a receptive George Washington who was also turning over in his mind the development of waterways as a means of binding the backcountry to the union. In 1783, the Virginian toured the waterways of eastern New York and saw for himself just what Morris was talking about. But it was not until the 1790s that a tentative start on the New York canal was made and the usual partisan bickering erupted among the leaders. Wrangling over whether the proposed canal was going to favor the Federalists or the Republicans, and their respective land speculations, managed to stall things.[61]

Shortly after his return from Europe, Morris, whose chief land holdings centered on the Genessee Valley, paid a visit to the western frontier and saw the progress that had been made. In his travels, Morris had been impressed by the great canals of Scotland, which lifted water as much as one hundred and sixty feet. Seeing them immediately rekindled in his imagination the possibilities in the sprawling and by no means connected United States.

In 1801, during a trip to Canada and up the St. Lawrence to Lake Ontario, Niagara Falls, and Lake Erie, Morris's conception of waterways became more intense. In a letter to John Parish he graphically documents the epiphany he experienced on the shore of Lake Erie, another leap of his creative imagination toward the reality of the Erie Canal. "In turning a point, the Lake broke on our view. I saw riding at anchor nine vessels, the least of them above a hundred tons. Can you bring your imagination to realize the scene? Does it not seem like magic? Yet this magic is but the early effort of victorious industry. Hundreds of large ships will, at no distant period, bound on the billows of this inland sea."[62]

Nine years after reporting his dream to Parish, Morris was named chairman of the board of canal commissioners in 1810. During the six years that he served, he wrote three of the four crucial reports to the state legislature. The membership of the commission was carefully balanced with Federalists, Republicans, and the new Tammany faction of New York City. Morris and Stephen Van Rensselaer were assigned to explore the ground from Albany to Buffalo. Other commissioners examined an alternative Ontario route. By the time the board was ready to make its report, Morris was in the driver's seat, and like the committee reports in the Continental Congress, he would write it. The Erie route was picked, and in spring 1811 the first canal law was passed by the legislature. In addition to writing the report, Morris drew up the technical instructions for the engineers who were to survey the 636-mile system.

Morris then turned to the national government for badly needed capital for the venture, suggesting that federal lands be used to secure private financing for the development of a national canal network. Before going to Washington, he drafted a comprehensive bill for Congress, translating his vision into a blueprint for political action on a grand scale. This was just the kind of national "energy" he envisioned in Philadelphia in 1787. Morris and his wife arrived in Washington with DeWitt Clinton, the mayor of New York City and a fellow canal commissioner, in mid-December of 1811 to lobby their scheme. Morris's efforts to sell this legislation was a failure. Sectional jealousies managed to derail it. The language of the commission's argument at this critical juncture is pure Morris as it lays into the opposition, made up of "microcosmic minds which, habitually occupied in the consideration of what is little, are incapable of discerning what is great.... The commissioners must, nevertheless, have the hardihood to brave the sneers and sarcasm of men, who with too much pride to study, and too much wit to think, undervalue what they do not understand, and condemn what they cannot comprehend."[63]

On January 1, 1812, noting in his diary that the portentous year came in "blustering on wings of a westerly wind, of which we feel in our elevated position a full share," he then added, "Visit at the palace, and pay our respects to the President and his lady." When Morris spoke briefly to Madison about canal financing, the Virginian dodged the issue by mumbling doubts of constitutionality. With a fervent wish that did not come true, Morris predicted that Madison would not be reelected because the House had publicly insulted the president by refusing, for the first time, to adjourn for the presidential reception. Morris believed that the rejection of federal support of the canal was partisan, and the commissioners decided that New York should proceed on her own, full throttle.

Later that year Morris was at his "dear quiet, happy home," when James Madison announced, on June 18, 1812, that war had been declared against Britain. Morris had mistakenly thought that such a move would be too audacious for the "scrawny," ever-cautious little president, amounting to an act of madness. New York, he wrote friends in Baltimore, was unalterably opposed to war. The Federalists without exception were against it as were the Republicans (he called them "democrats") except for "office-holders, office-hunters, Jacobin mob, and the bankrupts in fame and fortune."[64]

When Madison announced a plan to invade and occupy the British provinces of Canada, not only Morris thought he had lost his mind. The object was to force the British to abandon the infamous Orders in Council, a sweeping system of blockades interdicting American ports, and to respect American maritime rights, which the Royal Navy regularly violated. The one thing favoring the Americans was that their adversary was also worn out with protracted wars, and the administration might, with luck, negotiate a settlement before sentiment hardened into militant policy.

Morris believed that the gale now gathering in the eastern states and in New England might well "blow our Union flag from the mast-head," portending the breakup of the republic along sectional and geographical lines. The prospect of war had once again opened the question of whether the Union was fixed forever or whether the states on their own initiative could withdraw. The question had been first raised by Jefferson's and Madison's inflammatory Kentucky Resolutions of 1798–99 that proclaimed the right of states to nullify federal laws and to secede as well. This issue of the Union's perpetuity versus state sovereignty provoked Morris and other Federalists to revisit the question of the ultimate value of the union they had created on paper in 1787.

The three-fifths clause that allowed the South to count slaves in calculating representation in Congress had given the slave states, as Morris predicted in 1787, the upper hand. The British embargo and the threatened war had seriously damaged commerce, to Morris's mind probably the most important factor in holding the Union together. By violating the Constitution and disrupting commerce particularly in the Northeast, it seemed to him that the Union could no longer survive. It was an honorable experiment that had failed. To put it plainly, as he usually did, it was all about "strangling commerce, whipping Negroes, and bawling about the inborn inalienable rights of man." In December of 1812, he reminded a New York audience that domestic slavery might well produce a monarchy and aristocracy in the South, but the Middle and New England states would remain a bastion of liberty made up of "emigrants from every nation." If Pennsylvania went with the South in the breakup of the Union, it would be sad, Morris declared in his most imaginative flight, to see the beautiful city of Philadelphia reduced to a backwater town on the frontier of the new country.[65]

In a letter to the Bostonian Harrison Gray Otis, also an opponent of slavery and Madison's war, Morris again expressed his alarm over both the vastness of the country and the divisive differences within the Union. The threat of extending slavery into the new territory of the Louisiana Purchase could be fatal to national unity, an ominous cloud that now announced a full-scale storm. To him it was a profound cultural as well as political fracture embracing "the awful secret that commerce and domestic slavery are mortal foes," and then in foreboding words ringing louder than Jefferson's "fire bell in the night," he concluded, "bound together, one must destroy the other." Two weeks after war was declared, he again nailed the issue to the South's commitment to its "peculiar institution." "If Peace be not immediately made with England, the Question on Negro votes must divide this Union."[66]

A son, Gouverneur Morris Jr., was born on February 9, 1813, eight months after the declaration of war. Morris considered the war "criminal" and challenged Congress to refuse to pay the war debt incurred by the Madison administration. A pledge of public faith "wickedly given," he told Josiah

Quincy, "is not to be redeemed." Pressing the argument of the Quakers' opposition to all wars, he declared the war, and any financial support of it by taxes, immoral. "Those who consider themselves as moral Agents, accountable to God, hold it impious to support an unjust War.... The Debt, therefore, now contracted by Messrs. Madison and Co. is void, being founded in moral Wrong of which the lenders were well apprised."[67]

By spring 1814, the antiwar movement in the Northeast had picked up steam. Otis in Boston chaired a committee calling for a convention of the New England states to meet in Hartford, Connecticut, and coordinate their opposition. Madison summoned his cabinet to an emergency meeting. To Morris, the building of the canal and the war policies had become intertwined. In his vision an interstate system of canals (like the later interstate highways) was part of the infrastructure necessary to bind the nation and its commercial interests together. He saw, in an attempted repeal of some of the canal bills in Albany, a covert retaliation by the Republican party.

At first, he was convinced that the New England convention could throw off the shackles of the partisan, "unconstitutional" government in Washington. The Hartford firebrands could take possession of New York City and the hated embargo would be lifted by the citizenry. One can feel the old Morris fire shoot up in a letter to his nephew David Ogden, which captures the energy of the young New Yorker in Philadelphia in 1778 doing verbal battle against the imperial enemy during the darkest days of the Revolution. He restated the issue by giving it a pointed, rhetorical twist: "Shall the citizens of New York be the slaves or masters of Virginia? If the Republicans ever redeem the pledge of the lives, fortune and sacred honor to defend their war game, you can have my skin to cover a drum."[68]

Madison's war party in the West had managed to combine its calculated move against the Indians in the new territories with the fight against the British. The threat posed by the Indians and the British gave the Republicans a very loud war drum to beat. The offense launched by Canada would justify taking Indian lands. All this accelerated when the British and Indians forced the surrender of the American fort at Detroit, giving a pretext to the war hawks to annihilate the Indian terrorists. With indignant irony, Morris wrote Timothy Pickering, a member of Congress, that it appeared that the Indians "belong to us, because Great Britain ceded to us the land on which they live, but whether her right was derived from Adam or St. Peter does not appear. At any rate," he continued, now with a caustic moral edge, "the Indians passed with the soil, and we acquired an incontestable right to hunt them like deer, and take what was their country, and what, according to the principles of public law, is still their country, if they be, as they pretend, human creatures." Adding to his moral outrage was the fact that taxpayers in the eastern and northern states had to pay for this slaughter of native Americans.

Morris had made his final defense of a wronged minority, adding this last example of the violation of human rights to his list of human folly, a list unique in the record of any Founding Father. He had never harbored an ounce of confidence that popular sovereignty was capable of acting in a responsible way to protect the liberties of those unable to defend themselves. "Expect heroism from a sheep, charity from a wolf, and music from a crow," he told Benjamin Walker, "but do not expect, or even hope for reason from the populace." By 1816, the Indian tribes east of the Mississippi had been reduced to a weak and helpless people only waiting until the whites demanded the surrender of their last remnant of land.[69]

But the squire of Morrisania admitted he was living comfortably in his "chimney corner" and increasingly unable to read the turbulent political signs as well as he had once done. Besides, married life had agreed with him very well. With that vivacious mixture of "virtues, defects and talents," so appealing to his friend Madame Dumas, he insisted that he still retained that boyish "gayety of inexperience and the frolic of youth." The aura of rustic freedom bred in the open society he had first experienced as a boy at Morrisania never quite deserted him.

The British forces were repulsed at Baltimore in the fall of 1814. After all the heated, apocalyptic rhetoric, some of it continuing to come from Morrisania, to form "a cordial union with the Eastern States," the Hartford meeting to dismember the Union released its report on January 12, 1815. It tamely condemned the war and recited the tired litany of the well-known grievances of embargoes, the South's slave representation in Congress, and New England's rights to a share of the national revenues. Even before the convention finally got under way, the New Yorker had accurately predicted that the Yankees who liked nothing better than to make bargains would end up doing just that. The news of peace, based on status quo antebellum, finally arrived in February 1815. When the word reached Morrisania, Morris noted in his diary, "The news of peace...may prevent a separation of the states, patch up our tattered Constitution," then with mordant resignation added, "and perpetuate the blessings of a Jacobin Administration."

There is a certain mellow quality to Morris's private correspondence of the last two years of his life even though his spleen could quickly rise over Madison's war "rashly declared, prodigally maintained, weakly conducted, and meanly concluded." Gout and other ailments took their toll, but in the summer of 1815, he and Anne made another long trip to the northern part of the state to look after his complicated land investments.

In addition to his ill health, other dark clouds cast a growing shadow over what appeared to be a calm family life. Always generous to a fault, he had compromised his finances by loans of large sums of money advanced over the years to his nephew David Bayard Ogden, son of his sister Euphemia. Ogden, an

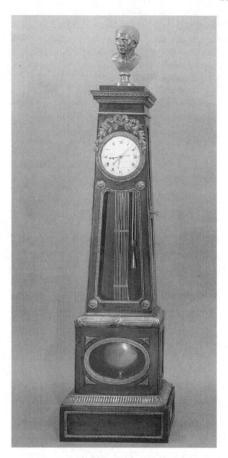

Ormolu-mounted mahogany regulateur by Jean-Antoine Lépine, ca. 1789,
purchased by Gouverneur Morris in Paris.
Photo courtesy of the Photographic Archives, National Gallery of Art, Washington, D.C.

ambitious New York lawyer and land speculator who was always pressed for
cash, deeply resented his uncle's marriage. The arrival of Gouverneur Jr. cut him
off from the inheritance with which he had planned to pay his debt to his uncle.

When Ogden met John Randolph in fall 1815 and heard the Virginian's
venomous gossip, Ogden was ready to add his own slander—that Anne had
deceived Morris about her background, making the marriage a fraud. Ogden
embellished his tale with the charge that her son "Gouverno" was in fact "the
offspring of an illicit amour" with a servant at Morrisania. He added that
Anne was planning to murder anyone who contradicted her version of the earlier events at Glentivar. Against this background, Randolph wrote a malicious
letter to Anne in November 1815 in his vendetta to make her the evil sorceress

who had brought disgrace and death to the Randolph family, the perfect denouement to the gothic romance. This served Ogden's design to destroy the marriage. The conspirators' scheme created a dark subplot to Morris's final years, but it did not faze his devotion to his wife as he gently smoothed her understandable torment.

Taking the offensive in an unprecedented public relations war, Anne sent a militant response to Randolph's "filthy accusations," a reply that is all the more remarkable for her aggressive public of the exchange. There were no surprises for her husband in her reply and, no doubt, a deep admiration for her strength in the face of adversity. In the middle of Anne's press war, Morris received a warm letter from her old mentor St. George Tucker of Williamsburg, commending him for his "unshaken tenderness and regard for her, whom you have redeem'd from Missery & Misfortune, and have found worthy of your Confidence, your Affection, & conjugal regard."[70]

On July 6, 1816, Morris wrote his last letter to John Parish in Europe, admitting that he had a fine old time living through so much incredible, improbable history, the grand adventure of his existence no one could have imagined or invented. He also confessed that, nearing the end of an extraordinary journey, for which fate had well prepared him, he now found himself happier than most of his fellow mortals and happier than he had any right to be. He closed with a moving tribute to his sensible wife: "The woman to whom I am married has much genius, has been well educated, and possesses, with an affectionate temper, industry and a love of order," personal qualities that were an important part of his own personality. Having put off marriage so long, he was grateful to have found such a "fine woman who could love an old man." In his will, Morris gave the estate to his son, while Anne held it with a life interest. He reconfirmed her antenuptial income of twenty-six hundred dollars a year for life and in a remarkable and gallant gesture gave her another six hundred dollars a year should she remarry. Not long before he died, he wrote a kinsman of Anne's in Virginia, saying that through all the tangled and bruising Randolph affair, she had never deceived him.[71]

Earlier in the spring of 1816, Joseph Story, James Madison's first appointee to the Supreme Court, handed down the landmark decision in *Martin v. Hunter's Lessee*, asserting federal supremacy over the states. For decades the Virginia courts had denied federal jurisdiction over the state's interpretation of land laws central to the case. The irony that it was a Massachusetts Republican who unequivocally pronounced Morris's nationalist doctrine no doubt amused the ailing squire of Morrisania. In his decision Story invoked Morris's language of the Preamble: "The Constitution of the United States was ordained and established not by the states in their sovereign capacities but emphatically, as the preamble of the Constitution declared, by 'the people of the United States.'... It is a mistake that the Constitution was not designed to operate upon states in their corporate capacity. It is crowded with provisions which restrain or annul the sovereignty of the states in some of the highest branches of their prerogative...the states are stripped of some of the highest attributes of sovereignty, and the same are given to the United States."[72]

Gouverneur Morris died at Morrisania on November 6, 1816. "Sixty-four years ago," he said not long before he died, "it pleased the Almighty to call me into existence—here on this spot, in this very room; and now shall I complain that he is pleased to call me hence?" Buried first in a new vault Anne built near the house, Morris was later reburied in St. Ann's Church, commissioned by his son in memory of his mother Anne Cary Randolph Morris.[73]

Notes

Introduction

1. James Madison to Jared Sparks, April 8, 1831, Sparks, 1:286.
2. AH to Robert Morris, April 30, 1781, Syrett, 11:606.
3. Farrand, *Records,* 1:529. Sparks, 1:286.
4. Renwick, 161.
5. GM, "An Oration Delivered on Wednesday, June 29, 1814...In Celebration of the Recent Deliverance of Europe from the Yoke of Military Despotism," 22.

CHAPTER 1. The Pedigree

1. GM to Robert Walsh, February 5, 1811, *The Diary and Letters of Gouverneur Morris,* ed. Anne Cary Morris, 2 vols. (New York, 1888) (hereafter cited as A. C. Morris), 2:524.
2. On Jefferson's passion to become the most complete gentleman in America, see Gordon S. Wood, "The Trials and Tribulations of Thomas Jefferson," in Onuf, ed., 402–3.
3. Smith, *History,* 1:139; Sheridan, 13; Jones, 1:140.
4. Chastellux, 294n4; Broglie, 234.
5. Bailyn, 65.
6. Bonomi, 279–86.
7. Gouverneur Morris, "Discourse, Delivered Before the New-York Historical Society.... 6th December 1812," 23; Lefferts.
8. See Warner. Warner's unpublished essay complements the work of John Strassburger, and I have used both in reconstructing this genealogy; Strassburger, 1–40.
9. Sheridan, 1–3.
10. See Beckles, 20–40, for a summary of the social and political history of the island 1644–92.
11. Kammen, *Colonial New York,* 87. The northern boundary of the estate was a diago-

nal line running from present-day 165th Street to 180th Street. On the south it bordered on the East River. The Mill Brook (now Brook Avenue) ran down the center of the property. The house stood slightly south of 132nd Street and Cypress Avenue within the shadow of the Bronx ramp onto Triborough Bridge. Warehouses now block any view to the river and sound.

12. Strassburger, 91.

13. Franklin, *Autobiography,* 212–13. Strassburger, 95–96.

14. Sheridan, 1–17.

15. Ibid., esp. 11–12.

16. Lustig, 119–20, 158–59. See also Kammen, 183–89.

17. Kline, 14. Throughout her limited study of Morris's career, Kline accepts the vague label of "aristocrat" as the defining characteristic of both his public and private life; Sheridan, 8.

18. Lewis Morris to James Alexander, London, February 25, 1736. Katz, 482; see also Bonomi, 103–39.

19. *Brief Narrative of the Case and Tryal of John Peter Zenger,* 2; See also Rutherford.

20. Memoir of John Wakefield Francis, N.Y., November 17, 1860, MSS, transcription by Henry B. Dawson, Francis Collection, New York Public Library; Levy, 204–5. Quoted in Dunlap, 1:302.

21. A frequent question has been, "How do you pronounce Gouverneur?" The late Philip Bonsal, a descendant, confirmed to the author that the tradition in the family was the Anglicized "Governor."

22. Gouverneur Morris, "Discourse," 15.

23. Ibid., 16.

24. Sparks, 1:507.

25. Ibid., 1:12.

26. Swiggett, 378.

27. Sparks, 1:10; Jones, 1:140n.

28. Franklin, *Papers,* 3:397–421.

29. Will of Lewis Morris, November 19, 1760, Liber 23, 426, Surrogate's Office, Hall of Records, New York City.

30. *Alexander Graydon's Memoirs,* 40.

31. *Spur of Fame,* eds. Schutz and Adair, 9; Bridenbaugh and Bridenbaugh, *Rebels and Gentlemen,* 42.

32. John Adams, *Diary and Autobiography,* 2:109.

33. Geradi, 166; see also Bridenbaugh, *Mitre and Scepter.*

34. Kline, 22–23.

35. Sparks, 1:5.

CHAPTER 2. A Profession

1. Hamlin, 37.

2. Will of Lewis Morris, November 19, 1760, Liber 23, Surrogate's Office, Hall of Records, New York City.

3. Van Schaack, 9.

4. See Morgan, "American Revolution Considered as an Intellectual Movement," 11–33. A. C. Morris, 2:468. Smith, *History,* 1:xxviii. Sparks, 1:19.

5. See *Historical Memoirs...of William Smith,* 1:xxviii.

6. Smith, *History,* 1:xxviii.

7. Jones, 1:1–3.

8. William Livingston, *Independent Reflector,* 15. Gouverneur Morris, *Diary of the French Revolution,* 2 vols., ed. Davenport (hereafter *Diary*), 1:3.

9. *Diary,* 1:22–3.

10. Jones, 1:19; Bridenbaugh, *Mitre and Sceptre,* 296–303.

11. Bridenbaugh, *Mitre and Sceptre,* 307.

12. Goebel, 3:3–43.

13. Root, 7–8; Swiggett, 40.

14. GM to William Smith Jr., February 20, 1772, Sparks, 1:17.

15. Ibid., 16; Namier and Brooke, 3:168. Bridenbaugh, *Cities in Revolt,* 367. See Horace Walpole's description of the duchess in a letter to John Chute, May 14, 1754, *Letters of Horace Walpole,* 2:383–84.

16. A. C. Morris, 2:385–86.

17. Sparks, 1:21.

18. Minutes of the Moot, entry "At the Moot—4th March 1774," New-York Historical Society (hereafter cited as NYHS); Monaghan, 46.

19. Van Schaack, 28.

20. Flick, *History of the State of New York* 3:224.

21. Ibid., 225.

22. Simmons and Thomas, 4:75–6.

23. *Historical Memoirs...of William Smith,* 1:186.

24. GM to Thomas Penn, May 20, 1774, Sparks, 2:23–26.

25. Pauline Maier's portrait "Isaac Sears" in *Old Revolutionaries,* 51–100, provides a succinct background on popular New York politics leading up to and during the Revolution.

26. The quote "fair or foul words" comes from another revolution in a letter Morris wrote to Madame de Lafayette, July 29, 1793, Morris Papers, Library of Congress (hereafter LC).

27. See Bonomi, 75–78. Morris briefly mentions Leisler in his summary of New York history in his "Discourse," 12. Arthur M. Schlesinger's *The Colonial Merchants and the American Revolution, 1763–1776,* remains a classic on the role of the merchants and lawyers in evolution of the colonial revolt in New York and the other colonies.

28. Van Schaack, 28.

29. Monaghan, 50.

30. Alexander C. Flick, *Loyalism* 24; Becker, 119.

31. See Mason, intro., 31–40, for a sorting out of the tensions in New York over the Continental Association; Jay's address is quoted in Monaghan, 62.

CHAPTER 3. Things Fall Apart

1. *American Archives,* 4th ser., 1:506–8.

2. Gouverneur Morris, *Observations on the American Revolution,* 3. Historians have struggled to pinpoint some profound inner explanation why men like Morris, John Jay, and Robert Livingston became patriots given their roots of privilege and position. I believe that Morris's pragmatic character shaped by the commercial, trading world that he grew up in determined his evolution.

3. Schlesinger, 541–42; Mason, 70; *American Archives,* 4th ser., 2:345–471; *Historical Memoirs . . . of William Smith,* 1:222; "Colonel Marinus Willett's Narrative," in Dawson, 53–65.

4. Hamilton's role in Cooper's escape is recalled by contemporaries Robert Troup and Hercules Mulligan in Schachner, 211–12. Thomas Jones approved of Cooper's priorities when his abandoned library was later sold at auction for 5 pounds while his wine cellar brought a handsome 150 pounds. Syrett, 1:48.

5. *Rivington's New York Newspaper,* 13–14.

6. At the opening of the First Provincial Congress, Morris seconded the resolution of Isaac Low calling for "implicit obedience . . . to every recommendation of the Continental Congress," Mason, 206.

7. GM to Charles Lee, [May] 1775, NYHS.

8. GM to Richard Henry Lee, Force, *American Archives,* 4th ser., 1:726; William Livingston, 147–48.

9. *Rivington's New York Newspaper,* 16; *American Archives,* 4th ser., 2:402.

10. Dangerfield, 60; Sparks, 1:24.

11. Launitz-Schürer, 135.

12. Address to the People of Great Britain, *Journals of the Continental Congress, 1774–1789* (hereafter *JCC*), 1:83. The full text of the association is in *American Archives,* 4th ser., 2:471.

13. *John Jay: Unpublished Papers* (hereafter *JJ:UP*), 1:148–49.

14. "Willett's Narrative," in Dawson, 59.

15. Gouverneur Morris, *Observations on the American Revolution,* 26.

16. Becker, 213; *Historical Memoirs . . . of William Smith,* 1:228.

17. Mason, 206.

18. Sparks, 1:39n–40n.

19. Morris Collection, Columbia University.

20. *JJ:UP,* 1:156–57.

21. Monaghan, 72.

22. Becker, 221.

23. Jones, 1:56–57; *Historical Memoirs . . . of William Smith,* 1:228.

24. Freeman, 3:469.

25. Mason, 136.

26. Ibid., 113; Jones, 1:64. Jones asserts that John Morin Scott, Livingston, and both brothers of William Smith Jr. were in the raiding party.

27. Ibid., 106.

28. Ibid., 132; *Historical Memoirs...of William Smith,* 1:256.

29. Van Schaack, 50; Wedgewood, 113.

30. GM to Charles Lee, n.d. [1775–76?], Morris Miscellaneous Manuscripts, NYHS.

31. GM to Lewis Morris, February 25, 1775, Emmet Collection, New York Public Library (hereafter NYPL).

32. Kline, 46; GM to RRL, February 26, and n.d. [November?], 1775, Livingston Papers, NYHS.

CHAPTER 4. "The Great Question of Independency"

1. *JCC,* 2:200–201; Alexander C. Flick, "The Provencial Congress and the Declaration of Independence," in Flick, *History of the State of New York,* 3:276.

2. Washington moved on to the Mortier house when Martha arrived a few days later. See Freeman 4:635.

3. Freeman, 4:80; Jones 1:83.

4. Bliven, 158; The best essay on Lee's military role in the Revolution is "American Strategy: Charles Lee and the Radical Alternative," in Shy, 133–62.

5. Flick, *Loyalism,* 71. *American Archives,* 4th ser., 5:1409, 1410; Flick, *Loyalism,* 60.

6. *Journals of the Provincial Congress* (hereafter *JPC*), 1:460; *JCC,* 4:358.

7. Becker, 256.

8. See Deposition of John Roome, Vincent Ashfield et al., June 28, 1776, John Jay Papers, Columbia University.

9. Becker, 139n20.

10. Paine, *Common Sense,* 42, 52.

11. *JJ:UP,* 1:254.

12. See Aston.

13. The quotations from Morris's oration are taken from the manuscript in the Morris Collection, Columbia University. See also the edited text printed in Sparks, 1:94–107. The fragmentary manuscript has been dated by an archivist as 1776. It is not evident who titled the document "Oration on necessity for declaring independence from Britain," but there is reason to believe that it was given before the New York Congress on May 24, following *American Archives,* 4th ser., 6:1332, reference to debate on independence on that date.

14. Mason, 148.

15. See Gary Wills's discussion on constitutions and the state in *A Necessary Evil,* 71–72.

16. Ibid., 68. In his unpublished dissertation, Arthur Kaufman suggests that the "bifurcation" may have been due to interruptions by members of the audience during Morris's presentation (p. 142).

17. Ellis, *Founding Brothers,* 13. On the floor of the Senate in 1802, Morris described how out of "melancholy experience," the states found they could not manage "national concerns," and while "State pride slumbered...the people of America," through the Constitution, "bound the States down by this compact."

18. *Sources and Documents Illustrating the American Revolution,* 177.

19. Edward Everett's recollections of visit with Morris in 1814, "Eighteen Hundred Fourteen" in *Old and New* 7 (January 1873).

20. GM to AH, May 16, 1777, Syrett, 1:254.

21. Flick, *Loyalism*, 74.

22. Mintz, 63. Mintz is a useful source for Morris's years in the Revolution and the Constitutional Convention, but he devotes only one chapter to the rest of Morris's life.

23. Smith, *History*, xxx.

24. *Historical Memoirs...of William Smith*, 1:277.

25. Van Schaack, 132.

26. Freeman, vol. 4, quoted in caption following p. 131.

27. Maier, *American Scripture*, 45, 157–58. See also Thomas Starr, "Separated at Birth: Text and Context of the Declaration of Independence," *Proceedings of the American Antiquarian Society* 110, pt. 1 (April 2000): 153–99.

28. John Adams copied the New York resolution of July 9, 1776, into his autobiography. *Diary and Autobiography*, 3:398.

29. *American Archives*, 5th ser., 1:1465. Only John Hancock as president of the Congress signed John Dunlap's first printed version of the Declaration "*by* Order *and in Behalf of the* Congress." The delegates signatures would be added to the calligraphic version of August 2. See Starr, 161–62.

30. Sparks, 1:230. Sparks believed that there was a party who thought the moment was premature given the political and social breakdown resulting from the war; the Chase and Carroll quotations as well as the lines from the Livingston letter to George Clinton are from Rakove, *Beginnings of National Politics*, 121–22.

CHAPTER 5. Breaking the Fetters

1. *Rebels & Redcoats*, 179.

2. *JJ:UP*, 1:315. On September 16, the Provincial Convention ordered Lewis Morris to leave the Continental Congress and return to his brigade in Westchester County.

3. GM to Sarah Morris, Fishkill, December 19, 1776, quoted in Sparks, 1:117–18.

4. *American Archives*, 5th ser., 2:123. The extract is dated New York, September 2, 1776.

5. There is no agreement as to who set the fire, but on September 5, 1776, General Greene told Washington that New York was of no strategic value and urged that the city and suburbs be burned.

6. Jones, 1:137–38.

7. Mintz, 69.

8. Dangerfield, 86.

9. Sparks, 1:119–20.

10. Lincoln, 1:726, quoting Governor Joseph C. Yates who had been a justice of the Supreme Court under the first constitution, at the close of the Convention of 1821; Monahan, 92.

11. *Historical Memoirs...of William Smith*, 2:81.

12. William Strictland, Journal, NYHS, quoted in Dangerfield, 6.

13. *JJ:UP*, 1:307.

14. Dangerfield, 87.

15. Allan Nevins called the New York provision for the election of the governor "popular" but then admitted that as late as 1790 hardly 10 percent of the male population of New York City possessed enough property to vote for governor (p. 164); see Kenyon, 153–82, for a thoughtful analysis of the problems of the use of loose and misleading labels when discussing the political issues and patterns of the revolutionary period.

16. John Adams, *Diary and Autobiography*, 3:398

17. Dangerfield, 86.

18. John Adams to TJ, September 18, 1823, *Adams-Jefferson Letters*, 2:598–99; Nevins, 161; Monaghan, 97.

19. Lincoln, 1:194.

20. *JPC*, 1:552.

21. Ibid., 590–91. Lincoln's account of the first constitution is summarized here. The estimated number of slaves is taken from *A History of Negro Slavery in New York* by Edgar J. McManus. The population in 1771 was 19,883.

22. "Liberty: several essays on the nature of liberty—natural, civil, political," Morris Collection, Columbia University, a manuscript draft [1776?], 10 pages.

23. *The Federalist*, ed. Jacob E. Cooke (Middletown, Conn., 1961), no. 10, 64–65; Morgan, *Challenge of the American Revolution*, 53–56. As Morgan points out in his response to the progressive historians, during the Revolution the cry was "Liberty and Property," not "Liberty and Democracy."

24. *JPC*, 1:96. Neither of the two surviving drafts appear to be in Jay's hand: *JPC*, pt. 2, 842, March 18, 1777.

25. Rossiter, *Seed Time of the Republic*, 144. Rossiter presents a good summary of anti-Catholic propaganda at the time of the Revolution.

26. Van Schaack, 131.

27. Mintz, 75.

28. Strassburger, 421.

29. Years later in 1785, now Chancellor Livingston fought the Council of Revision, which tried to block unconditional legislative emancipation, contrary to Morris's stirring admonition. See also McManus for a summary account of abolition in New York (pp. 161–79). McManus confirms that the delegates adopted Morris's policy statement on slavery (p. 161).

30. GM to AH, May 16, 1777, Syrett, 1:253.

31. The New Yorkers had hoped to see the controversial Pennsylvania experiment collapse and disappear. As a congressional delegate, Morris went out of his way to challenge Pennsylvania's authority, disputing conflicting jurisdictions between Congress and the state whenever he had a chance.

32. Mason, 231; Jensen, 43.

33. *JPC*, 1:866.

34. Montesquieu, bk. 2, pt. 2, p. 12. See also Kaufman, 211–36, for a balanced discussion on the balloting and representation issues.

35. Quoted in Kaufman, 452.

36. JJ to GM, September 13, 1778, *JJ:UP*, 1:496.

37. RRL to JJ, February 3, 177[9], ibid., 550.

38. The new slate included Philip Schuyler, Philip Livingston, James Duane, and William Duer.

39. Ketchum, 79. Ketchum's stirring account of Saratoga replaces all others.

40. *Historical Memoirs ... of William Smith,* 2:178.

41. AH to GM, July 6, 1777, Syrett, 1:282.

42. GM to the Council of Safety, July 16, 1777, *JPC,* 1:511. Quoted in Swiggett, 33.

43. GM to RRL, October 8, 1777, Livingston Papers, NYHS. Although Morris supported Schuyler, he realized that the New England troops would follow only Gates. See Mintz, 83n50; quoted in Nickerson, 1:282.

44. Dangerfield, 103.

45. Ibid.

46. Ibid., 105. Livingston, in fact, rebuilt Clermont, and it is now open to the public.

47. Ketchum, 444–45.

CHAPTER 6. The Continental Congress, 1778–1779

1. Robert Morris to Richard Peters, January 25, 1778, quoted in Ver Steeg, 82.

2. Laurens to Lafayette, January 28, 1778, Burnett, ed., *Letters of Members of the Continental Congress* (hereafter *LMCC*), 3:59–60; GM to Henry Laurens, January 26, 1777, *LMCC,* 3:50.

3. Henry Laurens to GW, January 5, 1778, *LMCC,* 3:13; Laurens to Jonathan Trumbull, York Town, January 5, 1778, *LMCC,* 3:14.

4. GM to RRL, February 5, 1778, Livingston Papers, NYHS.

5. Committee at Camp to Henry Laurens [draft by GM], February 11, 1778, *Letters of Delegates to Congress,* 24 vols. (Washington, D.C., 1976–200), vol. 9, ed. Paul H. Smith, 72–5.

6. GM to John Jay, February 1, 1778, John Jay Papers, Columbia University quoted in Sparks, 1:153–54. GM to George Clinton, Camp Valley Forge, February 17, 1778, Emmet Collection, NYPL.

7. Henry Laurens to John Laurens, January 8, 1778, *LMCC,* 3:21 and note 8 suggesting that Mifflin was a ringleader.

8. Washington, *Writings,* 10:192; See also Trussell.

9. Morris arrived at camp by January 26. Committee of Conference, Minutes, January 28–March 12, 1778, *LMCC,* 3:61–62, 68–69, 71, 73, 80, 83, 86, 91–92, 96–97, 101, 104, 109, and 115.

10. GM to George Clinton, March 16, 1778. Morris Papers, LC.

11. Sparks, 1:159–60.

12. Morgan, *Genius of George Washington.* Morris's youth and lack of military experience may excuse his misreading of Washington's regard as recounted in the well-known anecdote.

13. GW to Henry Laurens, Valley Forge, April 10, 1778. Washington, *Writings,* 11:237.

14. Burnett, *Continental Congress,* 311–16; Mintz, 99–101.

15. The Committee of Conference to George Washington, [March 9? 1778], 115–20.

The draft is in Morris's hand although Francis Dana has also been suggested as a contributor.

16. GM to Robert Morris, Philadelphia, August 17, 1778, *LMCC*, 3:376–77.

17. A. C. Morris, 1:12.

18. Burnett, *Continental Congress*, 322–23.

19. *JCC*, 10:374–80.

20. Ibid.

21. George Clinton to JJ, Poughkeepsie, April 29, 1778, *JJ:UP*, 1:474. On February 6, 1778, a Treaty of Amity and Commerce and a Treaty of Alliance were signed at Paris by American commissioners Benjamin Franklin, Silas Deane, and Arthur Lee and the French minister plenipotentiary, Conrad Alexandre Gérard.

22. GM to JJ, York Town, April 29, 1778, *JJ:UP*, 1:472–73; GM to RRL, May 3, 1778, NYHS.

23. JJ to GM, Albany, April 29, 1778, *JJ:UP*, 1:475.

24. *JCC*, 10:374, 377–78. *JCC*, 11:474–81.

25. Dangerfield, 112.

26. GW to Henry Laurens, November 14, 1778. Washington, *Writings*, 13:256.

27. Henry Adams, *History of the United States of America during the Administrations of James Madison*, 919.

28. For the background of the various British strategies, see John Shy's chapter "The Military Conflict Considered as a Revolutionary War" in *A Numerous People Armed*, 193–224. The royal instructions to the Peace Commission is reproduced in *Sources and Documents Illustrating the American Revolution*.

29. Burnett, *Continental Congress*, 336. See William Henry Drayton's draft letter to Lord Howe, [June 6, 1778], in *LDC*, 10:34–35.

30. Burnett, *Continental Congress*, 336–37. See also Samuel Adams to James Warren, June 13, 1778, *LMCC*, 3:291.

31. Burnett, *Continental Congress*, 352.

32. Ibid., 352–53.

33. GM to GW, May 28, [1778], *LMCC*, 3:265–67.

34. Both parties would have to agree to any treaty entered into by the other party; Burnett, *Continental Congress*, 350–55; Henry Laurens to GW, July 31, [1778], *LMCC*, 3:356.

35. Samuel Adams to James Warren, July 15, 1778, *LMCC*, 3:332; Josiah Bartlett to William Whipple, Philadelphia, July 20, 1778, *LMCC*, 3:340.

36. Elias Boudinot to his wife, [August 8, 1778], *LMCC*, 3:363.

37. Henry Laurens to John Rutledge, June 3, 1778, *LMCC*, 3:272; Burnett, *Continental Congress*, 356.

38. GM to Peter Van Schaack, September 8, 1778. Van Schaack, 131.

39. GM to JJ, Philadelphia, August 16, 1778, *LMCC*, 3:376. Morris's Instructions, *JCC*, 12:1039–42.

40. Mintz, 111.

41. Bemis, 197–99; Burnett, *Continental Congress*, 370–77; GW to Henry Laurens, November 14, 1778, Washington, *Writings*, 13:254–57.

42. Sparks, 1:193–92. *JCC*, 12:1043. In the instructions, Morris specifically refers to the

"Observations" on "the deranged state of our finances." See Ogborn, 163–70. Ogborn's discussion of the work of Charles Davenant on "the art of reasoning by figures upon things related to government," in *The Political and Commercial Works of That Celebrated Charles Davenant... Collected and Revised by Sir Charles Whitworth,* 5 vols. (London, n.d.), is relevant to Morris's political economy buttressed by contemporary writing.

43. GM to RRL, May 30, 1779, NYHS.

44. JJ to GM, Poughkeepsie, October 21, 1778, *JJ:UP,* 1:500–501.

45. GM to RRL, Philadelphia, August 17, 1778, *LMCC,* 3:376.

46. Morgan, "Puritan Ethic."

47. On January 9, 1779, an embarrassing conversation between Henry Laurens and Francis Lewis, raising "a suspicion of fraudulent proceedings" by Robert Morris's mercantile firm, Willing, Morris, & Co., was spread on the Congressional Journal. *JCC,* 13:46–47.

48. Francis Lightfoot Lee to Arthur Lee, Philadelphia, December 10, 1778, *LMCC,* 3:530–31; Charles Carroll of Carrollton to William Carmichael, May 31, 1779, *LMCC,* 9:239. See also Pauline Maier's perceptive study of both Richard Henry Lee and Charles Carroll of Carrollton in *Old Revolutionaries,* chaps. 4 and 5. See also Henderson, *Party Politics,* 218–45. Since Carroll was a successful merchant as well as landowner, "trade" was to him, as well as for others, the popular code word for speculation.

49. Henderson, *Party Politics,* 229.

50. Sparks, while partial to Morris, has a good account of the Deane affair and reproduces Morris's address in Congress, 1:200–204. Morris noted on his copy, "Taken down Afterwd from Memory to Obviate Misrepresentation." Morris Papers, LC.

51. In this brief analysis of French-American relations I have been influenced by Lawrence S. Kaplan, *Colonies into Nation,* in particular chap. 5, pp. 108–44.

52. On Gérard's meetings I have relied on Burnett, *Continental Congress,* 428–41, as well as on details in *JCC* and the *LMCC.*

53. Corwin, chap. 10, pp. 217–62.

54. Thomas McKean to John Adams, November 8, 1779, *LMCC,* 4:510. See Henderson, "Congressional Factionalism."

55. *JCC,* 14:955–66.

56. Morris's political support had slipped steadily since his election from 32 of 40 votes in 1778, to 23 of 42 in 1779, and only 3 votes out of 39 in 1780.

57. Morris would serve three lame-duck months in Congress after his defeat. The remark on Vermont's independence is in a letter from GM to RRL, January [?] 1781. Bancroft Transcript, vol. 277, 223–25, NYPL; Sparks, 1:216.

CHAPTER 7. Money Matters

1. GM to RRL, October 5, 1779, Livingston Papers, NYHS. GM to RRL, [December ?, 1780], Livingston Papers, NYHS.

2. GM to Robert Morris, February 20, 1780, Robert Morris Papers, Rutgers University.

3. Gouverneur Morris, "Political Enquiries," in Willi Paul Adams, ed., "'Spirit of Commerce,'" 329.

4. Dangerfield, 114.

5. GM to JJ, March 20, 1780. *JJ:UP,* 1:746. Morris was often singled out for his imagination by contemporaries. But the word "imagination" was somewhat ambiguous at this time, meaning both fanciful projections not based on reality and the highest form of creative faculty with the power of framing new and striking intellectual concepts.

6. *Pennsylvania Packet,* April 11, 1780. The other essays may be found in the issues of March 4, 11, and 23 of the same year.

7. RRL to GM, November 25, 1780, Livingston Papers, NYHS.

8. Sparks, 1:27, 105; E. James Ferguson, *The Power of the Purse: A History of American Public Finance, 1776–1790,* is indispensable in understanding the broader picture of finance during this critical period. It has, with authority, put the Morrises and their international business in an understandable context.

9. Dangerfield, 136.

10. Ibid., 138.

11. AH to James Duane, September 3, 1780, Syrett, 2:400–418.

12. Kline, 182–83.

13. GM to Governor Clinton, January 26, 1781, Kline, 185.

14. Sparks, 1:228–30.

15. See Gordon Wood's discussion of the reconstruction of post-Revolutionary American society in *Radicalism of the American Revolution,* 213–25.

16. Sparks, 1:228–30.

17. *JCC,* 19:290–91, 326–27, 429, 432–33, 20:455–56, 499.

18. GM to Robert Morris, July 6, 1781, Morris Collection, Columbia University.

19. Robert Morris, a self-made man and rough diamond was born into an obscure family in Liverpool, England, on January 31, 1734, and arrived in Maryland at age thirteen in 1747. Moving on to Philadelphia where he became a clerk for the merchant Charles Willing at the age of sixteen, Morris had, on the eve of the Revolution, advanced to principal partner in the firm, one of the powers in the second largest city in the empire.

20. Chastellux, 1:135–36. John Adams rightly suspected that Robert Morris's fortune was mostly on paper and heavily mortgaged.

21. Ferguson, 122–23.

22. Ibid., 135.

23. Robert Morris, *Papers,* 2:172–76.

24. *JCC,* 21:1090–91.

25. Rakove, *National Politics,* 309.

26. GM to Nathanael Greene, December 24, 1781, Nathanael Greene Papers, William L. Clements Library, University of Michigan.

27. Ver Steeg, 166–68; Rakove, *National Politics,* 298–307.

28. GM to JJ, January 1, 1783, *JJ:UP,* 2:485–86. Cipher passage indicated by parenthesis.

29. GM to General Greene, February 15, 1783, Sparks, 1:249, 250–51; GM to General Knox, February 7, 1783, *LMCC,* 7:34n.; AH to GW, February 7, 1783, *LMCC,* 7:33–34. Arthur Lee to Samuel Adams, January 29, 1783. See Ferguson, "Aristocracy Supressed," 146–76, and Ver Steeg, 166–86.

30. A schedule of federal taxes to energize the central government along the lines that

Gouverneur had proposed two years earlier, in 1778, was laid before Congress by Robert Morris with the request that the states ratify it. It was the Financier's price for continuing in office.

31. GW to AH, April 16, 1783. Washington, *Writings,* 26:323–26.

32. Kohn, "Inside History of the Newburgh Conspiracy"; Paul David Nelson, "Horatio Gates at Newburgh, 1783: A Misunderstood Role with a 'Rebuttal,' by Richard H. Kohn," *William and Mary Quarterly,* 3d ser., 29 (1972): 143–58.

33. Ferguson, 175. This brief summary of the plight of federal finances after the Morrises left is based on Ferguson's chapter "The Economics of Disunion," 220–50.

34. GM to JJ, January 10, 1784, *JJ:UP,* 2:57; Morris's optimistic words are quoted in Rakove, *National Politics,* 333.

35. Samuel Osgood to John Adams, December 7, 1780, *LMCC,* 7:379. Osgood's judgment was directed to Robert Morris, but it fits both men well.

36. A copy of the articles of Morris's partnership in the Constable firm, dated June 4, 1784, is in the NYHS.

37. A transcript of Morris's "Liberty: several essays on the nature of Liberty—natural, civil, political" is in the Morris Collection, Columbia University. It has also been included as appendix 1 in Kaufman, *Constitutional Views.* Kaufman's work has been particularly useful in the chapter on the Constitutional Convention, supra.

38. McDonald, 59.

39. GM to Richard Morris, May 12, 1784, Gouverneur Morris Collection, Columbia University.

40. GM to JJ, January 19, 1784, *JJ:UP,* 2:675.

41. Farrand, *Records* 1:29–35.

CHAPTER 8. The Convention

1. Quoted in Rakove, *Original Meanings,* 30.

2. GM to JJ, January 10, 1784, *JJ:UP,* 2:675.

3. Warren, *History of the...American Revolution,* 2:658. Warren is speaking of the Anti-Federalist suspicions during ratification, but the attitude was in place before the Convention.

4. Quoted in Rakove, *National Politics,* 328. His chapter "The Administration of Robert Morris" is a convincing analysis of the Morris regime in the Office of Finance.

5. This paragraph relies on Rakove's interpretation in chap. 15, "Toward the Philadelphia Convention," in *National Politics.* The quotes can be found on pp. 374–79.

6. Quoted in Mintz, 177.

7. For an analysis of prerevolutionary discrimination in Pennsylvania, see Casino, "Anti-Popery in Colonial Pennsylvania."

8. TJ to John Adams, August 30, 1787, Boyd, 12:69; Rakove, *National Politics,* 398. Although minutes were not kept, a journal of the proceedings was maintained throughout.

9. Mintz, 181; Farrand, *Records,* 3:236.

10. Roosevelt, 140.

11. With unwavering consistency, Morris first declared his belief in the paramount

importance of supremacy in government as a young lawyer during the Stamp Act crisis. He was firm in his belief that there must be a supreme power in all governments even in 1774 when he conceded Parliament's supremacy while groping for some kind of reconciliation for the colonies. Sparks, 1:27.

12. Farrand, *Records*, 1:33, 30.

13. Ibid., 43.

14. Ibid.

15. The Morris quote and the story of Franklin's unlikely call for divine intervention is from the account of the Convention in Max Farrand, *Framing of the Constitution*, 94–95. Farrand's classic as well as his *Records* has been relied on throughout this chapter.

16. Farrand, *Records*, 1:514.

17. Ibid., 551–52.

18. GM to Robert Walsh, February 5, 1811, Sparks, 3:260–65; Farrand, *Records*, 1:512.

19. Farrand, *Records*, 1:512.

20. See Joseph J. Ellis and his comparison of Adams with Jefferson on their differing views on the definition and role of aristocracy in America in *Passionate Sage*, 133–37.

21. There are a number of obvious similarities between Morris's and Adams's intellectual independence. This seems particularly relevant in their belief that American society could never be, in Gordon Wood's words, "truly egalitarian," which led to Adams's isolation "from the main line of American intellectual development." See Wood, *Creation of the American Republic*, 569.

22. Farrand, *Records*, 2:202–3.

23. Ibid., 2:52–54, reports Morris's extended lecture on the executive; see GM to William Carmichael, July 4, 1789, where he expands on his views on the role of the executive, Morris Papers, LC.

24. Farrand, *Records*, 2:551. Other presidential powers were recommended by Morris as a member of the Committee of Eleven, set up to resolve thorny issues surrounding the executive branch. The committee report, written by Morris, authorized the president to make treaties and nominate and appoint ambassadors and Supreme Court justices "and all other Officers of the U.S." with the advice and consent of the Senate, a two-thirds vote being required for the approval of treaties.

25. GM to Uriah Tracy, January 5, 1804, Sparks, 3:198–202.

26. Sparks, 3:322–24, 381.

27. Farrand, *Records*, 1:193, 249–80, 551–52. See also Richards, *Slave Power*. "Morris's Prophecy," 28–51, is the most persuasive analysis of Morris's antislavery position in the Convention. For a probing analysis of the Great Compromise, see Rakove, "The Great Compromise."

28. Farrand, *Records*, 1:603–04.

29. The quotations in the above paragraphs are from Morris's speech on August 8, 1787, Farrand, *Records*, 2:221–23.

30. Kaufman, 391–92.

31. Farrand, *Records*, 2:221–22. Morris's argument would be used later by Federalists during the election of 1800. The environmental condition of Jefferson's slave-owning Virginia became a political issue during the campaign. See Kerber, 23–66.

32. Farrand, *Records,* 3:534.

33. Ibid., 1:583.

34. Ibid., 1:585.

35. Ibid., 2:121–23. His amended version, voted down ten to one, would have read: "The House of Representatives shall, at its first formation, and until the number of citizens and *free* inhabitants shall be taken in the manner herein described, consist of sixty five members."

36. Ibid., 2:454–55; GM to Henry W. Livingston, December 4, 1803, Farrand, *Records,* 3:404.

37. Ibid., 2:478. Rakove makes the point that Morris's timing of his move, a week after the crucial compromise vote on equal representation in the Senate, may have contemplated calling a grand convention to attempt to amend the compromise. See Rakove, *Original Meaning,* 385n21.

38. GM to Timothy Pickering, December 22, 1814, Farrand, *Records,* 3:419; Sparks, 1:284–85.

39. Abraham Baldwin confirmed Morris's role and added the name of James Wilson, telling Ezra Stiles that both had "the chief hand in the last Arrangt & Composition." Farrand, *Records,* 3:170; Morris also confirmed his role in a letter to Timothy Pickering on December 22, 1814, saying, "That Instrument was written by the Fingers which write this Letter"; Farrand, *Records,* 2:344, 438.

40. GW to Henry Knox, August 19, 1787, Farrand, *Records,* 3:70; Levy, 395.

41. Locke, *Two Treaties of Government,* ed. Laslett, bk. 2, chap. 2, sec. 14, 317–18. Rossiter, *Convention,* 231. Rufus King had proposed that the states be restrained from meddling with any contractual arrangements. This was, of course, straight out of John Locke's *Second Treaty on Government,* but King was defeated on the floor. As a member of the Committee on Style, King persuaded his friend Morris, who had originally opposed him, to make a last attempt by incorporating such a ban in the committee's proposed version. Morris had opposed King saying that in such matters "a majority must rule," an unlikely argument by the New Yorker. The committee itself may have overruled Morris. Farrand, *Records,* 2:439.

42. Farrand, *Records,* 2:641–49; 3:104–5.

43. The letter to Congress drafted by Morris is in Farrand, *Records,* 2:666–67. From Morris's standpoint, probably the most indispensable power created by the document was the unlimited power conferred upon Congress to tax. It was the binding ingredient that would hold the disparate, indigestible parts together. As George Mason conceded, "The assumption of this power of laying direct taxes, does, of itself, entirely change the confederation of the states into one consolidated government."

44. Farrand, *Framing the Constitution,* 201; Farrand, *Records,* 2:584; Sparks, 1:291.

45. The summary in this paragraph is influenced by Cecelia M. Kenyon's paper "Men of Little Faith."

46. Colonel Randolph had thirteen children but the three mentioned here will later figure in Mrs. Gouverneur Morris's life.

47. Beveridge, 1:412–13.

48. GM to AH, June 13, 1788, Syrett, 5:7–8. The main purpose of Morris's letter was to ask Hamilton to handle some legal matters for Thomas Mann Randolph Sr.

49. When Gouverneur finally returned from Europe to Philadelphia in 1798, the wildly indebted financial empire of his friend and business partner had collapsed. The two men would meet in the Prune Street jail for debtors where Robert Morris was held until 1800 when, under the new Jefferson administration, he was released from prison, a bankrupt. Morris would support him for the remainder of his life. GM to GW, November 12, 1788, Sparks, 1:292. Morris carried nine letters of introduction from Washington.

CHAPTER 9. Paris, 1789

1. "Gallantry" was a euphemism for seduction in the late eighteenth century. In Byron's words, "what men called gallantry the gods called adultery." Quoted in the *OED*. John Adams claimed that when he arrived in Paris, at the same age as Morris, thirty-seven, he believed his own "sense, spirit, activity" were already in serious decline.

2. Hamilton reported to Madison that Morris left New York on November 23, 1788, to catch the *Henrietta* in Philadelphia for France, Hamilton to Madison, November 23, 1788, Syrett, 5:235–36. A revised version of Morris's essay, a part of his "maritime meditations," was sent to Robert Morris on May 8, 1789. Reprinted in Sparks, 3:469–78. See Boyd, 14:339 and 529. Madison's use of cipher was to hide his criticism from French eyes. Jefferson passed Morris's financial study on to Madison.

3. GM to Robert Morris, February [n.d.], 1789, *Diary*, 1:xxix. Once properly introduced, an acquaintance could drop by unannounced, as Morris did regularly, casually screened of course, by the maître d'hôtel; A. C. Morris, 1:420.

4. Mercier is quoted in William Howard Adams, *Paris Years*, 38. See also Ogborn, 22–38.

5. *Diary*, 1:45. The intimate thoughts and impressions recorded in Morris's diary begun in Paris in 1789 suddenly transform the narrative tone of the biography.

6. Ibid., 1:35. The "Circus" Morris accurately describes was a public entertainment hall built beneath the gardens. It is remarkable that Morris's widow turned the diary over to his first biographer, Jared Sparks. She attempted to censor a number of entries but without consistency, leaving plenty for later generations to ponder. The Paris portion was charmingly edited and published by Morris's great-granddaughter Beatrix Cary Davenport in 1939, but it is still largely unknown. His granddaughter, Anne Cary Morris, included portions of it in *Diary and Letters*. It was, in fact, the women in Morris's family that kept Morris's memory alive well into the twentieth century.

7. Morris's portrait from life was done in Philadelphia by the Swiss artist Pierre Eugene Du Simitière and published along with twelve other subjects first in Paris and later in London.

8. Chastellux, *Travels*, 2:301n28. The French edition of the *Travels* was published in Paris in 1786. See Howard Rice's note, "Chastellux's *Travels*: A Biblio-biography," on pages 25–29.

9. GM to the Count Moustier, Paris, February 23, 1789, Sparks, 2:59–61.

10. Ibid., 2:60.

11. GM to the marquis de La Luzerne, March 8, 1789, *Diary*, 1:xli; GM to Carmichael, February 25, [1789], *Diary*, 1:xli

12. TJ to David Humphreys, March 18, 1789, Boyd, 14:676.

13. Ibid.; GM to JJ, March 4, 1789, Sparks, 2:64–65.

14. GM to Carmichael, July 14, 1789, Sparks, 2:76; *Diary*, 1:76.

15. *Diary*, 1:13.

16. GM to JJ, July 1, 1789, Sparks, 2:70; TJ to David Humphreys, March, 18, 1789, Boyd, 14:677.

17. *Diary*, 1:100.

18. The Rush quote is from Schwartz, 18–19; *Diary*, 1:107.

19. *Diary*, 1:106–10.

20. GM to William Carmichael, July 4, 1789, ibid., 1:135.

21. William Howard Adams, *Paris Years*, chap. 7, "The Women in His Life." According to his slave Sally Hemings, Jefferson's relationship with her may be the only one in Paris that was not platonic; TJ to Angelica Schuyler Church, September 21, 1788, Angelica Schuyler Church Papers, Manuscript Collection, University of Virginia.

22. Morris does qualify this passage by concluding that women's influence has not always been "to the greatest Advantage to the Community." *Diary*, 1:38–39.

23. Ibid., 1:2–3.

24. GM to GW, April 29, 1789, Sparks, 2:68.

25. *Diary*, 1:23. Morris admired Ségur's style and his table. About the time the Convention was deciding the fate of the king, Morris dined with the count, who served him what appeared to be cheap Greek wine with the oysters. In fact, it was a rare bottle of Tokay, which the New Yorker proceeded to enjoy, to the shock of his host, until the mistake was discovered. Ibid., 2:586.

. 26. Ibid., 1:110, 27.

27. See Marie-José Fassiotto, "Le comtesse de Flahaut et son cercle: un example du salon politique sou le Révolution," *Studies on Voltaire and the Eighteenth Century*, vol. 303.

28. *Diary*, 1:xix, 22, 17. Morris does not mention her novel *Adèle de Sénage* while he is in Paris and may not have known about it. Writing on women novelists of the period, Joan Hinde Stewart in "The Novelists and Their Fiction" places Mme. de Flahaut—she was published as Mme. de Souza—in the forefront of "female fictions and discourse, . . . modifying the symbolic order of things." *French Women and the Enlightenment*, ed. Samia I. Spencer, 197–211.

29. Fiechter, 71–76, has a useful summary of the Flahaut family. The bluestocking Mme. de Genlis placed Flahaut definitely in the second rank. Adelaide de Flahaut was born May 14, 1761, and died in Paris on April 19, 1836. Her son Charles, aide-de-camp to Napoléon, became the lover of Queen Hortense of the Netherlands. Their son, in turn, became the duc de Morny, half-brother and confidant of Napoléon III.

30. *Diary*, 1:17, 362–63. The reference to the provenance of the apartment as a gift to Adèle's mother is from Cooper, 44; LeBrun, *Memoirs*, quoted in Fiechter, 73.

31. For further discussion on Condorcet and Jefferson, see William Howard Adams, *Paris Years*, 135–40. There are also extended references to Sally Hemings, pp. 135–40.

32. *Diary,* 1:25.

33. Ibid., 25, 56; a verse addressed to the duchess can be found in the *Diary,* 1:88.

34. Ibid., 1:108; GM to GW, December 27, 1791, Sparks, 2:159.

35. *Diary,* 1:53.

36. Ibid., 1:64–65.

37. Ibid., 1:67–68.

38. Ibid., 1:64, 68–70. See William Howard Adams, *Paris Years,* 273–76.

39. *Diary,* 1:119.

40. Schama, 359.

41. GM to JJ, July, 1, 1789, Sparks, 2:69–70; TJ to JJ, June 24, 1789, Boyd, 15:359.

42. GM to William Carmichael, July 4, 1789, Sparks, 2:75–76.

43. *Diary,* 1:145.

44. Ibid., 1:341.

45. Ibid., 1:249.

46. Ibid., 1:156–57.

47. Quoted in Swiggett, 172–73. A truly maddening, eccentric work of admiring journalism, bereft of sources and poorly organized but with some useful details on GM's private life.

48. *Diary,* 1:162–64.

49. GM to GW, July 31, 1789, Sparks, 2:79,

51. *Diary,* 2:62. Morris's widow for some reason overlooked the steamy encounter in the convent as well as many other revelations.

52. Ibid., 1:235.

53. Ibid., 2:235–36.

54. Ibid., 1:246–47.

55. The record of this turn of events are in *Diary,* 1:237, 238, 244–45.

56. Ibid., 1:291–92, records the details of the dinner at Necker's house.

57. Ibid., 1:252–53, 269. In a conversation on October 23, 1789, with Madame de Staël present, he admits that he would accept the job as minister, not so far-fetched since de Staël's father Jacques Necker was also a foreign national. Given the circumstances, Morris might well have restored the authority of the monarchy operating under a constitution.

CHAPTER 10. Business as Usual

1. I have been the beneficiary of the work of Melanie Randolph Miller's doctoral dissertation, "Gouverneur Morris and the French Revolution, 1789–1794." It is the first scholarly investigation of Morris's commercial and diplomatic career in France. The depth and quality of her work places me and anyone else working on French-American affairs during the French Revolution in her debt. This note is to back up any citations to Miller's work that I may have overlooked. I am in general agreement with her analysis of Morris's and Jefferson's conflicting positions on tobacco and on the American debt. The Morris quote at the end of the paragraph is from Miller, pt. 3, p. 143.

2. GM to TJ, March 7, 1793, Boyd, 25:333.

3. "Oration on the Love of Wealth," n.d. [June 1805?], Morris Collection, Columbia University.

4. "Notes respecting Tobacco," copy attached to letter to TJ, March 16, 1791, Morris Papers, LC.

5. Farrand, *Records,* 2:221–22.

6. On the farmers-general, see William Howard Adams, *Paris Years,* 41–46, 186–87.

7. TJ to James Monroe, December 10, 1784, Boyd, 7:563.

8. Ibid., 2:728–87, "The Last Years, 1783–91," provides a detailed account of the Franco-American tobacco trade and the history of the Morris contract as well as Jefferson's efforts to scuttle it; TJ to John Adams July 9, 1786, Boyd, 10:105–6.

9. *Diary,* 2:54.

10. TJ to Robert Crew, September 10, 1789, Boyd, 15:410–11.

11. Quoted in Miller, pt. 3, chap. 5, p. 133. In this brief account of the issues Gouverneur belatedly had to confront on Robert Morris's behalf, the New Yorker's role was professional and minor, but the affair provides another telling contrast between Morris and Jefferson and illuminates how Jefferson allowed both his ideological prejudices and his personal interests to "interfere," in Price's words, "with his judgment as a statesman and national representative." See Price, 2:786–87.

12. GM to GW, May 27, 1791, *Diary,* 2:193.

13. Miller, pt. 1, chap. 6, p. 145; *Diary,* 1:318.

14. GM to GW, January 24, 1790, Sparks, 2:93–94; *Diary,* 1:272–73.

15. GW to GM, October 13, 1789, Washington, *Writings,* 30:442–45; GM to GW, January 24, 1790, 1:376–77.

16. There is much more to the Dutch double-cross than can be comfortably be fitted into this biographical narrative, as there is to the question of the fairness of the U.S. government profiting from shortfalls in the exchange rate at the expense of France. Although Morris had been quite open as to his plans to make a reasonable profit by acquiring the debt, in a remarkable self-serving memorandum, the Dutch bankers paint Morris as a greedy speculator while claiming their own motives were selfless and *their* profit somehow more pure than those generated under Morris's plan. Jefferson, who professed to abhor any taint of private speculation saw nothing wrong with the sizable commissions earned by the Dutch bankers. See Miller, pt. 3, chap. 6, pp. 160–64; also see the extended note on the "The Debt to France" in Boyd, 20:175–97. The editorial note on the bankers' letter to TJ of September 24, 1789, Boyd, 15:472–73, has been useful in identifying the undercurrents surrounding Jefferson's and Morris's relationship over the debt.

17. Miller, pt. 3, chap. 5, p. 183.

CHAPTER 11. A Presidential Mission

1. GW to GM, October 13, 1789, Sparks, 2:1–5, *Diary,* 1:373–74; GM to GW, January 22, 1790, Sparks, 2:5–6, *Diary,* 2:376–77.

2. An excellent account of the background of the Morris mission can be found in Elkins and McKitrick, 212–23.

3. GM to JJ, January 10, 1784, *JJ:UP,* 1:674–75.

4. Washington, *Diaries*, 4:16.

5. GM to Robert Morris, July 31, 1790, Sparks, 3:11.

6. I have considered in this chapter the somewhat "overwrought" opinion of Hamilton's duplicity presented by Julian P. Boyd in *Number 7: Alexander Hamilton's Secret Attempt to Control American Foreign Policy*, but I do not believe that Hamilton's bad judgment to attempt to take over foreign policy had much influence on the outcome of Morris's negotiations. Nor do I agree, as Boyd and others have stated, that Hamilton first proposed Morris's name for the mission. My reading of Washington's diary suggests that he approved of the president's suggestion, an idea that had already been in Washington's mind before he mentioned it to Hamilton. Washington, *Diaries*, 4:16. For the conversation with Beckwith, see Syrett, 5:482–90. See also Combs, 52–53. Combs finds Boyd's evidence ambiguous, giving a more favorable reading in Hamilton's defense.

7. *Diary*, 1:355.

8. Ibid., 409, 410, 411, 413.

9. Ibid., 197.

10. Ibid., 460–71 provides details of his negotiations. See also Syrett, 7:70–71 for Hamilton's conversation with Beckwith. Both Boyd, *Number 7*, 69, and Roosevelt, 203, unjustly criticize him for briefing La Luzerne, a move that Washington approved of. There were no instructions for secrecy from Washington, which I believe was deliberate. Hamilton's duplicitous message to Beckwith used number 23 for Morris's name.

11. GM to GW, April 13, 1790, Sparks, 2:9–10.

12. GM to Lafayette, May 7, 1790, ibid., 114. See also GM to the cavalier Ternant, on the same day, ibid., 112–13. Morris's strategic advice went far beyond these two letters. British intelligence easily could have picked up on Morris's activities. It may well have been an aggressive if dangerous ploy to advance his negotiations with the British ministry. Morris's instinct always was to take the offensive.

13. Sparks, 2:14–15.

14. GM to GW, May 29, 1790, Sparks, 2:20–28.

15. The exchange with Pitt is taken from GM's long and animated letter to the president, GM to GW, May 29, 1790, ibid., 20–28, and from *Diary*, 1:520–21. See also Elkins and McKitrick, 219 and 794n20.

16. GM to John Parish, January 20, 1801, Sparks 3:145–46.

17. See William Howard Adams, *Paris Years*, 268–94.

18. The quotations and details of Hamilton's conduct are taken from Boyd's *Number 7*, chap. 6, "Libel on an Honorable Public Servant." But see also Combs's different interpretation, *The Jay Treaty*, 56–57 and Miller, pt. 4, chap. 7, "Morris and the British," 191–217.

19. GM to William Constable, July 4, 1790, *Diary*, 1:543–44, 487.

20. GM to GW, September 24, 1790, and GM to His Grace the Duke of Leeds, September 24, 1790, *Diary*, 1:609–12. Morris's remarks on diplomatic negotiations are in a letter to Robert Morris quoted on page 616.

21. *Diary*, 1:616.

22. TJ to GM, December 17, 1790, Boyd, 18:303–4. Contrary to the editor's note, 18:220–83, and in spite of biased criticism of Morris's diplomatic style in London particularly over the handling of impressment of American seamen, Jefferson assured Morris

that he had "met the President's entire approbation." Frank Reuter in his study of Washington's foreign policy, *Trials and Triumphs,* 80–81, 142–43, simply repeats the attacks of Morris's critics on his London mission without bothering to look at the record of Morris's correspondence and ignores both Washington's and Jefferson's approval. Reuter also follows the bias of Boyd and the editors of the Papers of Thomas Jefferson in their general criticism of Morris's ministry in Paris.

CHAPTER 12. Minister to France

1. The critic Sainte-Beuve found in Adèle's novels "that quality of freshness and delicacy, that limpidity of emotion, that sobriety of word, those soft and restful nuances" missing in turn-of-the-century work. See Steward, "The Novelists and Their Fiction," in *French Women and the Age of the Enlightenment,* ed., Spencer, 204–5.

2. *Diary,* 1:546n1.

3. Lefebvre, 1:149.

4. GM to William Short, December 12, 1790, quoted in Miller, pt. 4, chap. 8, p. 241. Once again I am indebted to Miller's research confirming and refreshing my own research in the diaries, letters, and manuscripts. She adds details from unpublished letters, linking them to obscure diary entries.

5. *Diary,* 2:55, 229, 118.

6. GM to TJ, December 24, 1790, Boyd, 18:362.

7. GM to William Constable, January 8, 1791, quoted in Miller, pt. 4, chap. 8, p. 254n86.

8. *Diary,* 1:284.

9. Joel Barlow to TJ, October 1, 1792, Boyd, 18:24.

10. GM to GW, November 22, 1790, Sparks, 2:117.

11. GM to Robert Morris, September 26, 1789, quoted in Miller, pt. 2, chap. 4, p. 105.

12. GM to GW, January 22, 1790, *Diary,* 1:376–77.

13. For a discussion on the gap between the reality of the French aristocracy and its perception, see David D. Bien, "Aristocracy" in *A Critical Dictionary of the French Revolution,* ed. Furet and Ozouf, 616–28. The French nobility's stereotype image as licentious, lazy, and useless, inspiring popular hostility toward it, was strongly shaped by the moral condemnation of the nineteenth century. Bien calls these generalizations "a thicket of truths and half-truths."

14. GM to TJ, October 3, 1791, Boyd, 22:184.

15. "Address to the Queen of France, on the Course to be pursued by the King," January 26, 1790, Sparks, 2:472–73.

16. "Speech Composed for the King of France, with some Observations on the Constitution," Sparks, 2:490–512. I am indebted to John Hardman for his succinct account of the constitution and the crisis of the monarchy laid out in *Louis XVI,* 208–22. The king's remarks to Moleville on the constitution can be found on page 209. Hardman quotes the future Louis-Philippe as saying that the king failed to put his inherited authority in support of the constitutional leadership, regaining peacefully "all his prestige" but only "a portion of his rights," the king's own words in a letter to his brothers why he had accepted

the constitution, Hardman, 204–7. But see Woloch, 24–26, who argues that the king had substantial executive powers.

17. Hardman, 207; Lefebvre, 1:153.

18. Miller, pt. 4, chap. 6, pp. 281–82.

19. King, 1:419–21.

20. GW to GM, January 28, 1792, *Diary*, 2:401–2.

21. Boyd, 23:85–86, for Washington's draft softened by Jefferson's emendations and the quoted excerpts from Morris's reply; GM to TJ, April 6, 1792, 23:382–83 and note quoting Morris's and Washington's confidential communications.

22. King, 1:419–21.

23. Lafayette to GW, March 15, 1792, *Letters of Lafayette*, 361–62.

24. Monroe to St. George Tucker, January 24, 1792, quoted in Miller, pt. 5, intro., p. 295. Morris was confirmed 16 to 11. Those who voted against Morris were Roger Sherman, Aaron Burr, James Monroe and Lee of Virginia, Few and Gunning of Georgia. Strong and Cabot of Massachusetts also voted "no" in opposition to any mission in France.

25. Jefferson's memorandum may be found in Boyd, 23:258–65; Jefferson's quotes, which cannot be glossed, are from William Howard Adams, *Paris Years*, 295–97.

26. Boyd, 23:382.

27. Quoted in Miller, pt. 5, chap. 12, pp. 403–4.

28. GM to Samuel Ogden, June 12, 1792. Quoted in Miller, pt. 6, chap. 12, pp. 404–5.

29. *Diary*, December 6, 1791, Morris Papers, LC. The document is translated in Sparks, 3:481–500.

30. Leopold had died in March so the declaration actually named his son, Francis II, king of Bohemia and Hungary. *Diary*, 2:342. Even though Morris did not personally care for the bishop, this kind of acute, sophisticated analysis drew his admiration. When Mirebeau died, leaving a huge political gap, Morris urged Talleyrand to assume leadership according to Chateaubriand, to "nationalize" the monarchy, a course that Morris believed to be the only one that might head off either civil war or a dictatorship.

31. Hardman, 211; *Diary*, 2:450.

32. Morris's house had belonged to Henry Seymour, "*grand seigneur anglais*" who was Madame Du Barry's last lover before she went to the guillotine.

33. *Diary*, 2:436–37.

34. GM to TJ, June 10, 1792, *Diary*, 2:438–44; GM to TJ, June 17, 1792, ibid., 449–50.

35. Hardman, 218–19; Miller has an inconclusive analysis of Morris's involvement in this murky business, pt. 6, chap. 12, pp. 429–40; *Diary*, 2:489.

36. *Diary*, 2:465, 472, 472–79, for memoir written by Morris from Vienna in 1796 to Madame Royale, the daughter of Louis XVI, recalling the confidence and money the king had placed in his hands in July 1792. Morris gave her a detailed accounting of the funds and returned to her what was left.

37. Roosevelt, 229–30.

38. Hardman, 221–22. I have relied extensively on Hardman's fine summary of the August days; GM to Short, August 13, 1792, *Diary*, 2:505.

39. GM to TJ, August 16, 1792, *Diary*, 2:492.

40. GM to Rufus King, October 1792, King, 1:434.

41. GM to TJ, August 22, 1792, Sparks, 2:205.

42. GM to TJ, August 22, 1792, *Diary,* 2:523. When Short expressed doubt about making payments on the American debt to "the usurpers in France," Morris quickly set him straight. "The Corner Stone of our Constitution is the Right of the People to establish such Government as they think proper." The payment should be made to the present government. GM to Short, Syrett, 12:465.

43. Ibid., GM to Hamilton, October 24, 1792, Syrett, 12:617–18.

44. GM to TJ, September 10, 1792, *Diary,* 2:540.

45. *Diary,* 2:574; GM to Thomas Pinckney, September 23, 1792, *Diary,* 2:555.

46. GM to TJ, December 21, 1792, A. C. Morris, 2:8–9; ibid., 2:23.

47. GM to TJ, January 25, 1793, Boyd, 25:95; GM to TJ, December 21, 1792, *Diary,* 2:590; TJ to Joseph Fry, March 18, 1793, 25:402; Thomas Pinckney to TJ, January 30, 1793, Boyd, 25:103. In his enthusiasm for capital punishment in the name of liberty, Jefferson surely did not believe that the mockery of the king's trial met even a minimal standard of criminal justice and due process. In his own personal tribute to the king in a letter to Washington, Morris said the he believed Louis "wished sincerely for this Nation the Enjoyment of the utmost degree of Liberty which their Situation and Circumstances will permit. He wish'd for a good Constitution, but unfortunately he had not the Means to obtain it or if he had he was thwarted by those about him."

48. GM to Joseph Fenwick, November 16, 1793, Miller, pt. 6, chap. 14, p. 526.

49. Seine-Port, or "Sain Port" as Morris sometimes spelled it, was then a three and one-half hour drive from Morris's house in Paris. See Paladile, *Seine-Port,* for details on the history of the town and Morris's retreat.

50. GM to Robert Morris, March 27, 1794, Sparks 3:49.

51. Quoted in Malone, 472.

52. Quoted in Miller, pt. 6, chap. 13, p. 500; GM to David Humphreys, June 5, 1793, Sparks, 2:323. Still the most useful account of Morris's collection is the article by Louis Schrieder III, "Gouverneur Morris: Connoisseur of French Art," *Apollo* (November 1971): 470–83. See also William Howard Adams, *Eye of Thomas Jefferson,* 215–17. On reporting the weight of the silver, see GM to James Monroe, September 21, 1794, Morris Papers, LC. A "mark" was a measure of gold and silver of roughly one-half pound. The last bottle of Tokay was served at a Morris family wedding party in New York in 1848, A. C. Morris, 2:67.

53. GM to TJ, November 16, 1793, Morris Papers, LC. See Schama, 767–80 on the Terror and dechristianization; also see Mona Ozouf's essay, "Dechristianization," in *A Critical Dictionary of the French Revolution,* ed, Furet and Ozouf, 20–32. Ozouf argues that the movement had deep roots and, as Morris detected, was well underway before it was apparent in revolutionary violence during the Great Terror.

54. Four hundred fifty people were killed and many houses burned in the Gordon Riots started in response to the act lifting civil restraints imposed on Catholics. Gordon was charged with high treason and died in Newgate Prison in 1793. For the exchange of letters and note, see *Diary,* 2:451–52; Lefebvre, 2:118–19.

55. GM to TJ, January 21, 1794, Sparks, 2:393; GM to M. Deforgues, February 14, 1794, Keane, 402–7.

56. GM to GW, April 10, 1794, Sparks, 2:419; GM to Edmund Randolph, May 6, 1794, ibid., 431–32.

57. A. C. Morris, 2:63. Morris's accurate quote presumably from memory is from act 1, scene 7. Shakespeare's tragedies were on his mind; he quoted *Julius Caesar* to Washington to illuminate Robespierre's character: "He loves no sport as thou dost Anthony."

58. Miller, pt. 7, chap. 15, p. 568.

59. GM to Robert Morris, March 10, 1794, A. C. Morris, 2:57.

60. A good background on the Jay Treaty can be found in Elkins and McKitrick, 406–31.

61. GM to Edmund Randolph, July 23, 1794, Sparks, 2:452–53; "The Recall of Edmond Charles Genet," editorial note, Boyd, 26:685–92.

62. *Diary,* 1:xxiii.

CHAPTER 13. The Long Journey Home

1. Rothschild, 7–51. I am indebted to Rothschild's elegant exposition on the economic implications of the late eighteenth century, in which Morris might serve as a case study. The Tocqueville quote is on page 25.

2. GM to Samuel Ogden, February 2, 1996, Miller, pt. 7, chap. 16, p. 606.

3. A. C. Morris, 2:73.

4. GM to GW, December 30, 1794, ibid., 77–78.

5. It is estimated that the total amount of principle and interest on Morris's advances, finally repaid after Morris's death, came to more than thirteen thousand dollars. The exchange of letters regarding Morris's assistance for the duc d'Orléans can be found in Sparks, 1: 463–74.

6. *Diary,* Morris Papers, LC.

7. GW to GM, December 22, 1795, Sparks, 3:62–68.

8. In his letter that crossed the president's of the twenty-second, Morris rebuked the troublesome Republicans as "bookish statesmen who make for themselves a world of their own in their closets, and govern it as maids do their children and bachelors their wives." GM to GW, January 5, 1796. ibid., 3:70.

9. GM to AH, March 4, 1796, Sparks, 3:78.

10. GW to GM, March 4, 1796, ibid., 3:80.

11. GM to Samuel Ogden, February 2, 1796. The two constitutions were that of the state of New York and that of the United States.

12. Swiggett, 310.

13. GM to TJ, August 22, 1792; GM to William Short, September 12, 1792, *Diary,* 2:531–33, 556–57.

14. Sparks, 1:410–11.

15. A. C. Morris, 2:371; 2:407–12; Interview with Lafayette by Jared Sparks, Sparks Papers, Houghton Library, Harvard University, in which Lafayette also accused Morris of undermining his relationship and credibility with Washington.

16. GM to John Parish, December 4, 1797, Sparks, 3:106.

CHAPTER 14. On Native Ground

1. *Diary,* December 27, 1798, Morris Papers, LC. A. C. Morris, 2:377.

2. GM to John Parish, January 27, 1799, A. C. Morris, 3:118.

3. Beveridge, 3:214–317.

4. Ibid., 168. See also Simon, 40–46.

5. Beveridge, 3:368.

6. GM to Necker, September 17, 1798, Sparks, 3:112; Elkins and McKitrick, 561–618; GM to Necker, September 17, 1798, Sparks, 3:112.

7. GM to John Parish, December 4, 1797, Sparks, 3:104.

8. GM to Germaine de Staël, October 1806, A. C. Morris, 2:489.

9. Ibid., 1:486, 493; Morris, "Discourse," 8.

10. The new house appears to have incorporated the original house. Morris told Parish that he had built on the foundations of "the house where I was born." TJ to GM, November 1, 1801, Morris Papers, LC.

11. GM to Necker, September 17, 1799.; GM to John Parish, Sparks, 3:118.

12. Marshall, *Life of George Washington,* 5:33.

13. GM to Robert Walsh, February 5, 1811, A. C. Morris, 2:524.

14. Elkins and McKitrick, 751.

15. For a perceptive analysis of the social and cultural shift in American society, see Burstein, particularly chap. 7.

16. A. C. Morris, 2:380; Tocqueville, 1:166.

17. A. C. Morris, 2:379. The most succinct account of the tangled story of the critical New York vote of 1800 is in Elkins and McKitrick, 727–43. I have relied on it and the accompanying notes extensively.

18. Gouverneur Morris, "An Oration upon the Death of General Washington."

19. A. C. Morris, 2:379.

20. A. C. Morris, 2:515.

21. Quoted in Dangerfield, 303.

22. Farrand, *Records,* 1:517; GM to Rufus King, June 4, 1800, Sparks, 3:128.

23. Sparks, 2:386.

24. GM to John Parish, January 20, 1800, Sparks, 2:390–92.

25. GM to the princesse de la Tour et Taxis, December 14, 1800, Sparks, 2:394–95.

26. GM to AH, March 11, 1802, Syrett, 25:561.

27. GM to RRL, February 20, 1801, Livingston Papers, NYHS.

28. Syrett, 25:266–69; The Morris-Livingston exchange is in the Livingston Papers, NYHS. See Dangerfield, 303–4.

29. GM to AH, January 5, 1801, Syrett, 2:398, 402; AH to GM, December 24, 1800, Syrett, 25:272.

30. GM to John Parish, November 13, 1801, A. C. Morris, 2:415; GM to Timothy Pickering, February 16, 1809, Sparks, 3:249–50.

31. Six letters in the Morris Papers in the Library of Congress, dated between April 8, 1801, and October 23, 1801, document the negotiations over the silver. Barbara Oberg,

editor of the Papers of Thomas Jefferson kindly provided a transcript of Jefferson's letters. Jefferson's initial response to Morris is dated June 6, 1801.

32. GM to the President of the Senate, and Speaker of the Assembly of New York, December 25, 1803, Sparks, 3:172; GM to Lewis Morris, December 10, 1803, 3:173–76.

33. *Annals of the Congress,* 7 Cong., 1 sess., p. 36.

34. Second Speech on the Judiciary Establishment, Delivered in the Senate of the United States, January 14, 1802, Sparks, 3:378–402; Farrand, *Records,* 3:391–93; Beveridge, 3:71. See also Levy, 75–88.

35. A. C. Morris, 2:421.

36. GM to RRL, August 21, 1802, Sparks, 3:171; GM to RRL, October 10, 1802, Livingston Papers, NYHS.

37. GM to John Parish, June, 20, 1802, A. C. Morris, 3:169.

38. Roosevelt, 294; "Letters of William T. Barry," *William and Mary Quarterly* 13, no. 2 (October 1904): 107-16.

39. GM to James Parish, January 14, 1803, A. C. Morris, 2:431; GM to Roger Griswold, November 25, 1803, Sparks, 3:184.

40. GM to Henry W. Livingston, November 25, 1803, A. C. Morris, 2:441–42; GM to Jonathan Dayton, November 1803, Sparks, 3:183.

41. Quoted in Ellis, *American Sphinx,* 210.

42. A. C. Morris, 2:440.

43. GM to RRL, 1805, A. C. Morris, 2:469–70; GM to Mountflorence Morris, June 22, 1805, ibid., 468; GM to RRL, October 10, 1802, Sparks, 2:172.

44. Syrett, 26:324–29.

45. Quoted in Wills, *James Madison,* 53–54.

46. Swiggett, 401.

47. See Morton and Lucia White's study, *The Intellectual Versus the City,* 19.

48. *Diary,* August 12, 1795, Morris Papers, LC.

49. My brief discussion on the New York commission is taken from Reps, 296–99. The reference to Paris and London in the report as well as its rationale suggests Morris's hand in the drafting. I have been unable to confirm that Morris was the chairman of the commission but given his position, experience, and his travels, it would have been infra dig for him not to be given that role.

50. A. C. Morris, 2:516.

51. Anne Cary Morris to Joseph C. Cabell, May 30 [?], Bruce-Randolph Collection, Virginia State Archives.

52. A. C. Morris, 2:515–16.

53. Swiggett, 398.

54. Ibid., 396.

55. See Henry Adams, *History of the United States During the Administrations of Thomas Jefferson,* 25.

56. There are a number of sources available on the Randolph scandal. I have consulted the published accounts in William Cabell Bruce, *John Randolph of Roanoke, 1773–1833,* 2 vols. (New York, 1922); Hugh Garland, *The Life of John Randolph of Roanoke,* 2 vols. (New York, 1859); and Alan Pell Crawford, *Unwise Passions: A True Story of a Remarkable*

Woman and the First Great Scandal of Eighteenth-Century America (New York, 2000), as well as relevant manuscript documents in the Virginia Historical Society; the Library of Virginia; the Alderman Library, University of Virginia; and the Tucker-Coleman Collection, Swem Library, College of William and Mary. I have found, however, that the notes and documents called "Commonwealth v. Randolph" in *The Papers of John Marshall*, ed. Charles T. Cullen and Herbert A. Johnson (North Carolina, 1977), 2:161–78, to be the most succinct and useful in sorting out the affair.

57. John Marshall to GM, December 12, 1809, Morris Papers, LC; letter to niece is quoted in A. C. Morris, 2:516.

58. A. C. Morris, 2:516.

59. Ibid., 2:519.

60. Sparks, 1:497. For some reason, DeWitt Clinton is usually given the credit for envisioning the canal because as governor in 1816 he secured the state backing to complete it.

61. Ibid., 1:497–98.

62. GM to John Parish, January [?] 1801, ibid., 1:498–99.

63. Quoted from N.Y. Laws I, 79, in Shaw, 49. Shaw does not attribute the language to Morris.

64. A. C. Morris, 2:543.

65. GM, "Discourse," 16, 26; see also Kenneth M. Stampp, "The Concept of a Perpetual Union," in *Imperiled Union*, ed. Stampp, 1–36.

66. GM to Harrison Gray Otis, April 29, 1813, Sparks, 2:55; GM to Charles W. Hare, June 30, 1812, Morris Papers, private correspondence, III, 123, LC.

67. GM to Harrison Gray Otis, April 29, 1813, and to Josiah Quincy, May 15, 1813, Sparks, 3:288–93; Quoted in Mintz, 239. On the Hartford Convention, see Stagg, 465, 471–72, 474, 477–80, 482–3.

68. GM to Timothy Pickering, October 17, 1814, Sparks, 2:312–13; GM to David B. Ogden, February 11, 1814, ibid., 2:557.

69. GM to Benjamin Walker, December 28, 1814, ibid., 2:325.

70. Correspondence between John Randolph of Roanoke and Anne Cary (Mrs. Gouverneur) Morris, typescript from the files of the Virginia Historical Society, Richmond, January 1919. There are numerous copies of this correspondence in the history libraries of Virginia, giving the scandal a life of its own. Apparently it was still being copied and circulated at the beginning of the twentieth century. The originals have not been located. The letter from Tucker to Morris, January 5, 1815, Morris Collection, Columbia University.

71. Gouverneur Jr.'s birth was a blow to Morris's disinherited relatives who called him "General Kutusoff" after the Russian general. During the last two years of Morris's life, Anne Morris was under increasing attack by several members of the Morris family and from John Randolph of Roanoke who had become unhinged over the old scandal. In replying to Randolph's charges that she had manipulated her ailing husband in order to inherit his fortune, Anne had her husband's letter to Parish reprinted in several newspapers. One clipping of the letter, believed to be from a New York City newspaper, is in the

Swem Library at the College of William and Mary and was kindly called to my attention by the collection's senior curator, Margaret Cook.

72. Wills, *James Madison,* 159.

73. Ibid., 2:602. Morris's final illness, probably prostate cancer blocking the urinary tract, complicated by gout, was short but painful—he attempted an appalling self-surgery with a whale bone. The ordeal allowed him to demonstrate his stoic resolve to the end.

Bibliography

Primary Sources

MANUSCRIPTS

College of William and Mary, Manuscripts and Rare Books Departments,
Earl Gregg Swen Library, Williamsburg. Va.
    Tucker Collection

Columbia University Libraries Special Collections, New York
    Gouverneur Morris Collection
    John Jay Papers

Harvard University, Houghton Library, Cambridge, Mass.
    Jared Sparks Manuscripts

Library of Congress, Washington, D.C.
    Affaires Etrangères, Mémoires et Documents, États-Unis, II
    Papers of Gouverneur Morris—correspondence, account books, diaries,
    commercial and legal papers

Museum of the City of New York, Print Department
    Mrs. Gouverneur Morris Papers

New York City Hall of Records, Surrogate's Records
    Will of Lewis Morris, Liber 23
    Will of Sarah Morris, Liber 23

New-York Historical Society, New York, N.Y.
    Gouverneur Morris Papers
    Constable Rucker & Co. Accounts, 1786–1800
    Robert R. Livingston Papers

Morris Miscellaneous Manuscripts
Smith Papers

New York Public Library, New York, N.Y.
Constable-Pierrepont Papers
Gouverneur Morris, Miscellaneous
Robert Morris Papers, 1785–95
Robert R. Livingston Papers (Bancroft Transcript)
Thomas A. Emmet Collection
William Smith Papers

New York State Court of Appeals, Albany, N.Y.
Staats Long Morris, Mary Lawrence and Richard Morris v. Sarah Morris,
December 1785, Packet 68
Morris et al. v. Morris et al., April 15, 1786, Packet 71

Parke-Bernet Galleries, Inc., New York, N.Y.
Americana: Printed Books, Manuscripts & Autograph Letters, Including
Selections from the Papers of Gouverneur Morris…, Public Auction,
Tuesday, April 7, 1970

Princeton University, Editorial Office of The Papers of Thomas Jefferson,
Princeton. N.J.
Transcripts of Jefferson Correspondence to Morris

Rutgers University Library
Robert Morris Papers, Special Collections

Stanford University, Department of Special Collections, Stanford, Calif.
Gouverneur Morris to Peter Van Schaak, Sept. 8, 1778

University of Virginia, Manuscript Collection, Alderman Library, Char-
lottesville, Va.
Angelica Schuyler Church Collection
Papers of John Randolph of Roanoke

Virginia State Historical Society, Richmond, Va.
Papers of John Randpolph of Roanoke

DIARIES, AUTOBIOGRAPHIES, AND JOURNALS

Adams, John. *The Diary and Autobiography of John Adams.* Ed. Lyman H. But-
terfield. 4 vols. Cambridge, Mass., 1961.
*Annals of the Congress of the United States: The Debates and Proceedings in the
Congress of the United States;*…Compiled from Authentic Materials by
Joseph Gales Sr. Washington, 1851.
Franklin, Benjamin. *Autobiography.* Ed. Leonard W. Larabee et al. New York,
1964.
Morris, Gouverneur. *The Diary and Letters of Gouverneur Morris.* Ed. Anne
Cary Morris. 2 vols. New York, 1888.

————. *A Diary of the French Revolution.* Ed. Beatrix C. Davenport. 2 vols. Boston, 1939.

Stiles, Ezra. *Literary Diary of Ezra Stiles.* Ed. F. B. Dexter. New York, 1966.

Washington, George. *The Diaries of George Washington: 1748–1799.* Ed. John C. Fitzpatrick. 4 vols. New York, 1925.

LETTERS

The Adams-Jefferson Letters: The Complete Correspondence between Thomas Jefferson and Abigail and John Adams. Ed. Lester J. Cappon. Chapel Hill, 1959.

Barbé-Marois, Francois, Marquis de. *Our Revolutionary Forefathers: The Letters of Francois, Marquis de Barbé-Marois during His Residence in the United States as Secretary of the French Legation, 1779–1785.* Trans. and ed. Eugene P. Chase. New York, 1929.

The Letters of Horace Walpole. Ed. Peter Cunningham. Edinburgh, 1906.

The Letters of Lafayette to Washington: 1777–1799. Ed. Louis Gottschalk. Philadelphia, 1976.

PAPERS

Adams, John. *The Works of John Adams.* Ed. C. F. Adams. 10 vols. Boston, 1851.

Franklin, Benjamin. *Papers of Benjamin Franklin.* Ed. Leonard W. Larabee et al. 18 vols. New Haven, 1959–78.

Hamilton, Alexander. *The Papers of Alexander Hamilton.* Ed. Harold Syrett et al. 27 vols. New York, 1961–87.

Jay, John. *The Correspondence and Public Papers of John Jay.* Ed. Henry P. Johnson. 4 vols. New York, 1890–93.

John Jay: The Making of a Revolutionary: Unpublished Papers 1745–1780. Ed. Richard B. Morris. 2 vols. New York, 1975.

Jefferson, Thomas. *The Papers of Thomas Jefferson.* Ed. Julian P. Boyd et al. Princeton, 1950–.

Madison, James. *The Papers of James Madison.* Ed. William T. Hutchinson et al. 17 vols. Chicago and Charlottesville, 1962–91.

Marshall, John. *The Papers of John Marshall.* Ed. Charles T. Cullen and Herbert A. Johnson. 4 vols. North Carolina, 1977.

Morris, Robert. *The Papers of Robert Morris, 1781–1784.* Ed. E. James Ferguson et al. 9 vols. Pittsburgh, 1975.

WRITINGS

Alexander Graydon's Memoirs of His Own Times. Ed. John Littell. Philadelphia, 1846.

Historical Memoirs from 16 March 1763 to 9 July 1776 of William Smith. Ed. W. H. Sabine. 2 vols. New York, 1956.

Memoir of John Wakefield Francis, N.Y., Nov. 17, 1860. MSS transcription Henry B. Dawson. Francis Collection, New York Public Library.

Morris, Gouverneur. *Observations on the American Revolution*. Published by the Continental Congress. Philadelphia, 1779.

———. "An Oration upon the Death of General Washington, Delivered in New York, December 31, 1799." In *Washington: Or Memorials of the Death of George Washington…*, ed. Franklin B. Hough. 2 vols. Roxbury, Mass., 1865. 2:136–50.

———. "Discourse Delivered Before the New-York Historical Society at Their Anniversary Meeting, 6th December 1812." New York, 1813. 40 pp.

———. "An Oration Delivered on Wednesday, June 29, 1814,…on the Recent Deliverance of Europe from the Yoke of Military Deposition." New York, 1814. 23 pp.

———. "Inaugural Discourse Delivered Before the New-York Historical Society by the Honourable Gouverneur Morris (President), 4th September 1816." New York, 1816. 24 pp.

Paine, Thomas. *Thomas Paine, Collected Writings*. Ed. Eric Foner. New York, 1995.

Washington, George. *The Writings of George Washington from the Original Manuscripts, 1746–1799*. Ed. J. C. Fitzpatrick. 39 vols. Washington, 1931–1944; repr. New York, 1962.

OTHER CONTEMPORARY SOURCES

American Archives. Ed. Peter Force. 9 vols. Washington, 1837–53.

A Brief Narrative of the Case and Tryal of John Peter Zenger. Sold at the Bible and Heart, Cornhill, Boston, 1799.

Burnett, Edmund C., ed. *Letters of Members of the Continental Congress*. 8 vols. Washington, 1921–36.

Chastellux, J. F., Marquis de. *Travels in North America in the Years 1780, 1781, and 1782*. Ed. and trans. Howard C. Rice Jr. 2 vols. Chapel Hill, 1963.

Dawson, Henry H., ed. *New York during the American Revolution, Being a Collection of Original Papers*. New York, 1861.

Jones, Thomas. *History of New York during the Revolutionary War*. Ed. Edward de Lancey. 2 vols. New York, 1879; repr. 1968.

Journals of the Continental Congress, 1774–1789. Ed. W. C. Ford et al. 24 vols. Washington, 1904–37.

Journals of the Provincial Congress, Provincial Convention, etc. of the State of New York (1775–1777). 2 vols. Albany, 1842.

Katz, Stanley, ed. "A New York Mission to England: The London Letters of Lewis Morris to James Alexander, 1735 to 1736." *William and Mary Quarterly*, 3d ser., 28 (July 1971): 439–82.

Lafayette, Marquis de. *Mémoires, Correspondence et Manuscripts du Général Lafayette*. Ed. H. Fournier Ainé. 3 vols. Leipzig, 1838.

Livingston, William. *The Independent Reflector*. Ed. Milton M. Klein. Cambridge, 1963.

Rebels & Redcoats: The American Revolution through the Eyes of Those Who Fought and Lived It. Ed. George F. Scheer and Hugh F. Rankin. New York, 1957.

The Records of the Federal Convention of 1787. Ed. Max Farrand. Rev. ed. in 4 vols. New Haven, 1966.

Rivington's New York Newspaper: Excerpts from a Loyalist Press, 1773–1783, comp. Kenneth Scott. New York, 1973.

Smith, William, *The History of the Province of New York.* Ed. Michael Kammen. 2 vols. Cambridge, 1972.

The Spur of Fame: Dialogues of John Adams and Benjamin Rush. Ed. John A. Schutz and Douglas Adair. San Marino, 1980.

Sources and Documents Illustrating the American Revolution, 1764–1788. Ed. Samuel Eliot Morrison. New York, 1965.

Secondary Sources

BOOKS

Abbot Wilbur C. *New York in the American Revolution.* Port Washington, N.Y., 1962.

Adair, Douglas, *Fame and the Founding Fathers.* Ed. Trevor Colbourn. New York, 1974.

Adams, Henry. *History of the United States during the Administrations of Thomas Jefferson 1801–1809.* New York, 1986.

———. *History of the United States of America during the Administrations of James Madison 1809–1817.* New York, 1986.

Adams, William Howard. *The Paris Years of Thomas Jefferson.* New Haven, 1997.

Adams, William Howard, ed. *The Eye of Thomas Jefferson.* Washington, D.C., 1976.

Adams, Willi Paul, *The First American Constitutions: Republican Ideology and the Making of State Constitutions in the Revolutionary Era.* Trans. Rita and Robert Kimber. Chapel Hill, 1980.

Bailyn, Bernard. *The Ideological Origins of the American Revolution.* Cambridge, 1967.

Beard, Charles A. *An Economic Interpretation of the Constitution.* New York, 1960.

Becker, Carl L. *The History of Political Parties in the Province of New York, 1760–1776.* Madison, 1960.

Beckles, Hilary McD. *A History of Barbados: From Amerindian Settlement to Nation-State.* Cambridge, 1990.

Bemis, Samuel Flagg. *The Diplomacy of the American Revolution.* Bloomington, 1957.

———. *Jay's Treaty: A Study in Commerce and Diplomacy.* New Haven, 1962.

Beveridge, Albert J. *The Life of John Marshall.* 4 vols. New York, 1916.

Bliven, Bruce, Jr. *Battle for Manhattan*. New York, 1955.

Bonomi, Patricia U. *A Factious People: Politics and Society in Colonial New York*. New York, 1971.

Boyd, Julian P. *Number 7: Alexander Hamilton's Secret Attempt to Control American Foreign Policy*. Princeton, 1964.

Bridenbaugh, Carl, and Jessica Bridenbaugh. *Rebels and Gentlemen: Philadelphia in the Age of Franklin*. New York, 1942.

Bridenbaugh, Carl. *Cities in Revolt: Urban Life in America, 1743–1776*. New York, 1955.

———. *Mitre and Scepter: Transatlantic Faiths, Ideas, Personalities and Politics, 1689–1775*. New York, 1968.

Bruce, William Cabell. *John Randolph of Roanoke, 1773–1833*. 2 vols. New York, 1922.

Burnett, Edmund C. *The Continental Congress*. New York, 1942.

Burstein, Andrew. *Sentimental Democracy: The Evolution of America's Romantic Self-Image*. New York, 1999.

Combs, Jerald A. *The Jay Treaty: Political Battlegrounds of the Founding Fathers*. California, 1970.

Cooper, Duff. *Talleyrand*. New York, 1986.

Corwin, Edward S. *French Policy and the American Alliance of 1778*. New York, 1916; repr. 1970.

Crawford, Alan Pell. *Unwise Passions: A True Story of a Remarkable Woman and the First Great Scandal of Eighteenth-Century America*. New York, 2000.

Dangerfield, George. *Chancellor Robert R. Livingston of New York, 1746–1813*. New York, 1960.

Elkins, Stanley, and Eric McKitrick. *The Age of Federalism*. New York, 1993.

Ellis, Joseph J. *Passionate Sage: The Character and Legacy of John Adams*. New York, 1993.

———. *American Sphinx: The Character of Thomas Jefferson*. New York, 1997.

———. *Founding Brothers*. New York, 2001.

Farrand, Max. *The Framing of the Constitution*. 23d printing. New Haven, 1967.

Ferguson, E. James. *The Power of the Purse: A History of American Public Finance, 1776–1790*. Chapel Hill, 1961.

Fiechter, Jean-Jacques. *Un diplomate américain sous la Terreur*. Paris, 1983.

Flick, Alexander C. *Loyalism in New York during the American Revolution*. New York, 1901–2.

Flick, Alexander C., ed. *A History of the State of New York*. 5 vols. Fort Washington, N.Y., 1962.

Freeman, Douglas Southhall. *George Washington*. 5 vols. New York, 1948–52.

Furet, François, and Mona Ozouf, eds., *A Critical Dictionary of the French Revolution*. Trans. Arthur Goldhammer. Cambridge, Mass., 1989.

Garland, Hugh. *The Life of John Randolph of Roanoke*. 2 vols. New York, 1859.

Hamlin, Paul. *Legal Education in Colonial New York*. New York, 1939.

Hardman, John. *Louis XVI.* New Haven, 1993.

Henderson, H. James. *Party Politics in the Continental Congress.* New York, 1974.

Hufeland, Otto. *Westchester County during the Revolution, 1775–1783.* White Plains, 1926.

Jay, William. *The Life of John Jay.* 2 vols. New York, 1833.

Jenkins. Stephen. *The Story of the Bronx, from the Purchase Made by the Dutch from the Indians to the Present Day.* New York, 1912.

Jensen, Merrill. *The New Nation: A History of the United States during the Confederacy, 1781–1789.* New York, 1950.

Kammen, Michael. *Colonial New York—A History.* New York, 1975.

Kaplan, Lawrence S. *Colonies into Nation: American Diplomacy, 1763–1801.* New York, 1971.

Keane, John. *Tom Paine.* New York, 1995.

Kerber, Linda K. *Federalist in Dissent: Imagery and Ideology in Jeffersonian America.* New York, 1970.

Ketchum, Richard M. *Saratoga.* New York, 1997.

King, Charles R., ed. *The Life and Correspondence of Rufus King.* 6 vols. New York, 1927.

Kline, Mary-Jo. *Gouverneur Morris,* New York, 1978.

Launitz-Schürer, Leopold S., Jr. *Loyal Whigs and Revolutionaries: The Making of the Revolution in New York, 1765–1776.* New York, 1980.

Lefebvre, Georges. *The French Revolution: From Its Origins to 1793.* 2 vols. New York, 1962.

Lefferts, E. M. W. *Descendants of Lewis Morris of Morrisania.* New York, 1907.

Levy, Leonard W. *Original Intent and the Framers of the Constitution.* Chicago, 1988,

Lincoln, Charles Z. *The Constitutional History of New York.* 2 vols. Rochester, N.Y., 1905.

Locke, John. *Two Treaties of Government.* Ed. Peter Laslett. Cambridge, 1963.

Lustig, Mary Lou. *Robert Hunter, 1666–1734: New York's Augustan Statesman.* Syracuse, 1983.

Maier, Pauline. *The Old Revolutionaries: Political Lives in the Age of Samuel Adams.* New York, 1980.

———. *American Scripture.* New York, 1997.

Malone, Dumas. *Jefferson and the Rights of Man.* Boston, 1951.

Marshall, John. *The Life of George Washington.* 5 vols. Philadelphia, 1804–7.

Mason, Bernard. *The Road to Independence: The Revolutionary Movement in New York, 1773–1777.* Lexington, Ky., 1966.

Matson, Cathy D., and Peter S. Onuf, *A Union of Interests: Political and Economic Thought in Revolutionary America.* Lawrence, Kan., 1990.

McDonald, Forrest. *We the People: The Economic Origins of the Constitution.* Chicago, 1965.

McManus, Edgar J. *A History of Negro Slavery in New York*. Syracuse, 1966.

Mintz, Max M. *Gouverneur Morris and the American Revolution*. Oklahoma City, 1970.

Monaghan, Frank. *John Jay: Defender of Liberty*. New York, 1935.

Montesquieu, Charles Louis de Secondat. *Spirit of the Laws*. Trans. Thomas Nugent. New York, 1949.

Morgan, Edmund S., *The Challenge of the American Revolution*. New York, 1976.

———. *The Genius of George Washington*. New York, 1977.

———. *Benjamin Franklin*. New Haven, 2002.

Namier, Sir Lewis, and John Brooke, eds. *The History of Parliament: The House of Commons*. 7 vols. London, 1964.

Nevins, Allan. *The American States during and after the Revolution, 1775–1789*. New York, 1924.

Nickerson, Hoffman. *The Turning Point of the Revolutions*. 2 vols. Port Washington, N.Y., 1967.

Ogborn, Miles. *Spaces of Modernity*. New York, 1998.

Onuf, Peter S., ed. *Jeffersonian Legacies*. Charlottesville, 1994.

Paladile, Dominique. *Seine-Port: Son Histoire Ses vieilles maisons*. Le Mée-sur-Seine, 1995.

Palmer, R. R. *Twelve Who Ruled: The Year of the Terror in the French Revolution*. Princeton, 1941.

Price, Jacob M. *France and the Chesapeake: A History of the French Tobacco Monopoly (1674–1791)*. 2 vols. Ann Arbor, 1973.

Rakove, Jack N. *The Beginnings of National Politics: An Interpretive History of the Continental Congress*. New York, 1979.

———. *James Madison and the Creation of the Republic*. Glenview, Ill., 1990.

———. *Original Meanings: Politics and Ideas in the Making of the Constitutrion*. New York, 1996.

Renwick, James. *Life of Dewitt Clinton*. New York, 1840.

Reps, John W. *The Making of Urban America: A History of City Planning in the United States*. Princeton, 1965.

Reuter, Frank. *Trials and Triumphs*. Fort Worth, 1983.

Richards, Leonard L. *The Slave Power: The Free North and Southern Domination, 1780–1860*. Baton Rouge, 2000.

Root, R. K., ed. *Lord Chesterfield's Letters to His Son*. New York, 1963.

Roosevelt, Theodore. *Gouverneur Morris*. New York, 1888.

Rossiter, Clinton. *Seed Time of the Republic*. New York, 1953.

———. *1787: The Grand Convention*. New York, 1966.

Rothschild, Emma. *Economic Sentiments: Adam Smith, Condorcet and the Enlightenment*. Cambridge, 2001.

Rutherford, Livingston. *John Peter Zenger, His Press, His Trial, and a Bibliography of Zenger Imprints*. New York, 1904.

Schama, Simon. *Citizens: A Chronicle of the French Revolution.* New York, 1989.

Scharf, J. T., ed. *History of Westchester County, New York,* 2 vols. Philadelphia, 1886.

Schlesinger, Arthur M. *The Colonial Merchants and the American Revolution, 1773–1776,* New York, 1917.

Schlesinger, Arthur M., Jr., and Morton White, eds. *Paths of American Thought.* Boston, 1963.

Schwartz, Barry. *The Making of an American Symbol.* Boston, 1958.

Shaw, Ronald E. *Erie Water West: History of the Erie Canal, 1792–1854.* Lexington, Ky., 1966.

Sheridan, Eugene R. *Lewis Morris, 1671–1747: A Study in Early American Politics.* Syracuse, 1981.

Shy, John. *A People Numerous and Armed: Reflections on the Military Struggle for American Independence.* New York, 1976.

Simmons, R. C., and P. D. G. Thomas, eds. *Proceedings and Debates of the British Parliament Respecting North America, 1754–1783.* 7 vols. London, 1983.

Simon, James F. *What Kind of Nation: Thomas Jefferson, John Marshall, and the Epic Struggle to Create the United States.* New York, 2002.

Sparks, Jared. *The Life of Gouverneur Morris.* 3 vols. New York, 1832.

Spencer, Samia I., ed. *French Women and the Enlightenment.* Bloomington, 1984.

Stagg, J. C. A. *Mr. Madison's War: Politics, Diplomacy, and Warfare in the Early American Republic, 1783–1830.* Princeton, 1983.

Stampp, Kenneth M., ed. *The Imperiled Union: Essays on the Background of the Civil War.* New York, 1980.

Swiggett, Howard. *The Extraordinary Mr. Morris.* New York, 1952.

Tocqueville, Alexis de. *Democracy in America.* Ed. Phillipps Bradley et al. 2 vols. New York, 1976.

Trussell, John B. B., Jr. *Birthplace of an Army: A Study of the Valley Forge Encampment.* Harrisburg, 1976.

Upton, L. F. S. *The Loyal Whig: William Smith of New York & Quebec.* Toronto, 1969.

Van Schaack, Henry C. *The Life of Peter Van Schaack.* New York, 1842.

Ver Steeg, Clarence L. *Robert Morris, Revolutionary Financier, with Analysis of His Early Career.* New York, 1954.

Walther, Daniel. *Gouverneur Morris, Témoin de Deux Revolutions.* Lausanne, 1932.

Wedgewood, C. V. *Velvet Studies.* London, 1946.

White, Morton, and Lucia White. *The Intellectual Versus the City.* Cambridge, 1962.

Whitworth, Sir Charles. *The Political and Commercial Works of That Celebrated*

Charles Davenant, as Collected and Revised by Sir Charles Whitworth. 5 vols. London, n.d.

Wills, Garry. *A Necessary Evil.* New York, 1999.

———. *James Madison.* New York, 2002.

Woloch, Isser. *Transformations of the French Civic Order, 1789–1820: The New Regime.* New York, 1994.

Wood, Gordon S. *The Creation of the American Republic: 1776–1787.* New York, 1969.

———. *The Radicalism of the American Revolution,* New York, 1992.

ARTICLES

Adams, Willi Paul, ed. "'The Spirit of Commerce, Requires that Property Be Sacred': Gouverneur Morris and the American Revolution." *Amerikastudien/American Studies* 21 (1976).

Aston, Rick J. *The Loyalist Experience: New York, 1763–1789.* Ann Arbor, Mich.: University Microfilms, 1973.

Broglie, Prince de. "Narrative of the Prince de Broglie [1782]." Trans. E. W. Balch. *Magazine of American History* 1 (March 1871).

Casino, Joseph J. "Anti-Popery in Colonial Pennsylvania." *Pennsylvania Magazine of History and Biography* 105 (July 1981): 279–309.

Champaigne, Roger J. *The Sons of Liberty and the Aristocracy in New York Politics, 1765–1790.* Ann Arbor. Mich.: University Microfilms, 1960.

Cody, William Berm. *An Analysis of the Issues of Democracy and Nationalism at the Constitutional Convention of 1787.* Ann Arbor, Mich.: University Microfilms, 1980.

Davis, William A. "William Constable, New York Merchant and Land Speculator." Ph.D. diss., Harvard University. 1955.

Everett, Edward. "Eighteen Hundred Fourteen." *Old and New* 7 (January 1873).

Gillen, Jerome J. *Political Thought in Revolutionary New York, 1763–1789.* Ann Arbor Mich.: University Microfilms, 1972.

Geradi, Donald F. M. "The King's College Controversy." *Perspectives* 11 (1977–78).

Goebel, Julius, Jr. "The Courts and the Law in Colonial New York." In Flick, ed., *The History of New York State,* 3: 3–43.

Henderson, H. James. "Congressional Factionalism and the Attempt to Recall Benjamin Franklin." *William and Mary Quarterly,* 3d ser., 27 (1970): 246–67.

Kaufman, Arthur Paul. *The Constitutional Views of Gouverneur Morris.* Ann Arbor, Mich.: University Microfilms, 1992.

Kenyon, Cecelia M. "Republican and Radicalism in the American Revolution: An Old-Fashioned Interpretation." *William and Mary Quarterly,* 3d ser., 9 (April 1962): 153–82.

———. "Men of Little Faith: The Anti-Federalists and the Nature of Representatives Government." *William and Mary Quarterly*, 3d ser., 12 (January 1955): 3–43.

Kohn, Richard H. "The Inside History of the Newburgh Conspiracy and the Coup d'État." *William and Mary Quarterly*, 3d ser., 27 (1970): 187–220.

Independent Reflector. February 22, 1753, pp. 147–48.

Miller, Melanie Randolph. *Gouverneur Morris and the French Revolution, 1789–1794.* Ann Arbor, Mich.: University Microfilms, 2000.

Morgan, Edmund S. "The American Revolution Considered as an Intellectual Movement." In Schlesinger and White, eds., *Paths of American Thought,* 11–33.

———. "The Puritan Ethic and the American Revolution." *William and Mary Quarterly*, 3d ser., 14 (October 1967): 3–27.

Pennsylvania Packet. March 4, 11, and 23; April 11, 1780.

Rakove, Jack N. "The Great Compromise: Ideas, Interests, and the Politics of Constitution Making." *William and Mary Quarterly*, 3d ser., 44, no. 3 (July 1987): 424–57.

Schachner, Nathan. "Alexander Hamilton Viewed by His Friends: The Narratives of Robert Troup and Hercules Mulligan." *William and Mary Quarterly*, 3d ser., 4 (1947): 211–12.

Strassburger, John Robert. *The Origins of the Morris Family in the Society and Politics of New York and New Jersey, 1630–1746.* Ann Arbor, Mich.: University Microfilms, 1976.

Ultan, Lloyd. "Gouverneur Morris and the Convention." *Bronx County Historical Society Journal* 24, no. 2 (fall 1987): 59–66.

Warner, William W. "Puritans and Patriots." Typescript, n.d.

Index